Companion to The Song Book of The Salvation Army

North American Edition
Companion to The Song Book of The Salvation Army

compiled by
Gordon Taylor

The Salvation Army
Atlanta, Ga.

North American Edition
Copyright © The Salvation Army
First Published 1990
ISBN 0-86544-064-6

GORDON TAYLOR

is a soldier at Croydon Citadel, British Territory. He was educated at Brancroft's School and the University of London. After serving for a number of years on the staff of the Greater London Council (1965-86), he is currently employed as a senior researcher in the Heritage Centre, International Headquarters. A member of the Hymn Society of Great Britain and Ireland and the Hymn Society of America, he published *A Short Companion to Keep Singing!* in 1976.

Cover by Jim Moss
Available through bookstores
or Salvation Army Supplies
or through the publisher
The Salvation Army Supplies and Purchasing Dept.
1424 Northeast Expressway
Atlanta, Georgia 30306 USA

Contents

Foreword vii

Compiler's Note ix

Historical introduction xiii

PART ONE

Notes on songs 1

PART TWO

Notes on authors 233

PART THREE

Notes on songs and authors
North American supplement 455

Bibliography 469

Foreword

To salvationists *The Song Book of The Salvation Army* is a liturgy for public worship, an aid to personal devotion, a means of proclaiming the gospel and a help to rekindling fires of enthusiasm and devotion.

It is also an ecumenical instrument, drawing on many religious traditions and confirming that the salvationist an heir to the riches of the whole Christian Church, whilst still reminding him of those emphases which are typical of his own part of it.

Gordon Taylor has made a devoted and detailed study of hymns and their writers and his knowledge of this vast and varied field is here offered to all who love sacred song. Here is information about the lives of the authors as well as the origin of their hymns, providing at the same time glimpses of Christian activity and fellowship in many different eras.

The results of Gordon Taylor's scholarship are always interesting, sometimes surprising (even the compilers of the 1986 Song Book did not get all the details right) and frequently inspiring.

May this book be an aid to worship and devotion, to understanding and discipleship.

David E. Guy
Lieut-Colonel
Literary Secretary

Compiler's Note

This companion to *The Song Book of The Salvation Army*, 1986, has been written to provide clear and reliable information about the songs and their authors. As I was not involved in the selection of songs for the Song Book, my task began when the work of the Song Book Council concluded.

I have tried to discover the circumstances which inspired the songs, or something about the period or context in which they were written, so that the reader can gain some understanding of the continuity and development of congregational singing through successive generations. As many people will not have had access to other sources of similar information, it is hoped that this book will serve as an introduction to the subject, and perhaps open the door to further reading.

For easy reference, the information about the songs and their authors is presented in two parts:
Part 1: notes on the songs and their sources;
Part 2: biographical notes on the authors, with a list of their contributions to the 1986 Song Book.
With the amount of information available, particularly about some of the songs, it would have been possible to write a much longer book, but I have been conscious throughout of the need to keep the size of this book within reasonable limits, and to complete my task as quickly as possible.

The starting point for my research was Julian's *Dictionary of Hymnology*, 1907, and the other hymnal handbooks and companions listed in the bibliography. Also, Dr Leonard Ellinwood and Mrs Mary L. Van Dyke have in recent years provided me with valuable information from the incomparable resources of the *Dictionary of American Hymnology* files.

For Salvation Army songs, I am especially indebted to Richard Slater's *Salvation Army Song Writers*, 1929; the series, 'The Songs of the Salvationist', by Arch R. Wiggins, in *The Bandsman and Songster* and *The Musician*, 1935-38; and Gordon Avery's *Companion to the Song Book*, 1961, as well as his extensive research, newspaper cuttings and correspondence which I inherited.

I have obtained biographical information from various

sources, including year books, newspaper reports, obituaries and biographies of individual authors, and also from the *Dictionary of National Biography*, the *Dictionary of American Biography*, *Who Was Who*, and *Who Was Who in America*. For the dates of birth and death of British hymn writers, I have relied mainly on the work of Andrew Hayden and Robert Newton, and their published 'checklist', supplemented by my own research in national and local newspapers, the registers of births, marriages and deaths, and probate records.

Living authors have responded readily to my requests for assistance. I am extremely grateful to them, and to other correspondents too numerous to name, for their prompt and helpful replies. I must also express my gratitude to the staff of the Salvation Army archives in London, New York and Toronto; other officers at territorial headquarters in Australia, Canada, Denmark, Finland, the Netherlands, and New Zealand; and librarians, particularly at the British Library, the Evangelical Library, and the Newspaper Library, at Colindale.

Tracing the authorship of a song and when it was written is not always as simple as it might appear. Some songs have at different times been attributed to more than one author, or have appeared anonymously. Also, in some instances, new verses or choruses have been added to a song, often many years after its first appearance. Although I have undertaken extensive research in a wide range of possible sources, in an attempt to establish the correct authorship, some searches were inconclusive, and it has not been possible to resolve all the uncertainties.

Authors do not always remember exactly when their songs were written, or the particular circumstances that inspired them. Where there are several accounts of the story behind a song, each giving different facts or dates, it is often difficult to decide which source is most reliable and which information is correct.

While I have tried to find confirmation of the dates and circumstances, it has sometimes been necessary to omit or abbreviate well-known stories about some of the songs, because of doubts about their authenticity, or because the facts seem to have been exaggerated. Despite the impression given by some writers, not every song was written as a result of an intense spiritual struggle, or in difficult circumstances, such as sickness or bereavement.

Often, nothing more is known about the origin of a song than the publication in which it first appeared, and in some cases, earlier sources may yet come to light. Although I have checked as many of the sources as possible, there are some which I have been unable to locate, and I have not been able to examine every American publication.

I have indicated where a song has been significantly altered since its first publication, but as the majority of songs have been altered to some extent, it is impossible to include full details of every change. My series, 'Revisions and Excisions', in *The Musician*, 24 August 1974—16 July 1983, gives further information on this subject in respect of many of the songs.

Even though every effort has been made to check the accuracy of all the information, I know that my sources were not infallible, and I may sometimes have misunderstood the historical, theological, denominational, geographical, national or cultural context of the information. However, if there are mistakes in some details, I hope that the overall picture will be reliable, and I would welcome additional information from any source, so that errors can be corrected in future editions.

Gordon Taylor
24 May 1988

Historical introduction

In the preface to *Salvation Army Songs*, 1899, William Booth wrote: 'Surely no man has ever been called upon to make, or direct the making of, so many Song Books as I have'. While there is no complete list of the song books issued under his direction, it is clear that he had a significant influence on all the principal collections used by The Christian Mission and The Salvation Army for congregational singing between 1865 and 1930. This short historical review outlines the continuity and change between successive editions of the major hymn and song books published since 1865.

Revival Hymns

The earliest hymn book known to have been compiled by William Booth was *The Revival Hymn Book*, a booklet of 112 hymns, with six additional hymns printed on the title page and covers. A fading inscription on the front cover of this book appears to be dated 4 August 1866. Thirty-four songs from this book are included in the 1986 Song Book.

This was followed within two years by *The Enlarged Revival Hymn Book*, which included 333 hymns, with five additional hymns printed on the title page and end pages. An inscription inside a copy of this book is dated 7 June 1868. An advertisement for this hymn book, on the cover of *The East London Evangelist*, November 1868, showed that it was then used by the East London Christian Mission in meetings 'at the New East London Theatre, and the other Stations connected with this Mission'.

The Christian Mission Hymn Book

About a year later, William Booth compiled *The Christian Mission Hymn Book*, a collection of 531 hymns, which was published, as he explained in the preface, because 'we have not found one containing a sufficient number of hymns suitable for the regular services of a congregation, and at the same time adapted to all the requirements of open air and revival meetings'. Unlike the earlier revival hymn books, this hymn book was arranged in sections, on various themes, with hymns for specific occasions, including the Lord's Supper, and Baptism, and the Admission of Members. Although it was not dated, this hymn book must have been published after September 1869, when the East London Christian Mission (which had established branch missions in Edinburgh and Croydon) adopted the name 'The Christian Mission'. It probably appeared early in 1870, as it was advertised as 'Just published' in *The Christian Mission Magazine*, 1 February 1870.

At about the same time, a revised edition of *The Revival Hymn Book* appeared (with 118 numbered hymns, and seven additional hymns printed on the covers), and William Booth also compiled *The Children's Mission Hymn Book* (with 120 hymns, and three additional hymns printed inside the covers). Slightly later, he published *The Hallelujah Hymn Book*, described as 'a collection of modern revival hymns and songs, adapted for Special Services and Religious Festivals'. This included 103 hymns, with three additional hymns and two other verses printed inside the covers.

Revival Music

Up to this time, all the hymn books published for The Christian Mission included the words of the hymns only. It is still the practice in Salvation Army meetings for congregations to sing from books with words only, with the music being published in separate tune books for band, organ or piano accompaniment.

William Booth's first tune book, *Revival Music*, included 494 tunes, 'for evangelistic services, open-air meetings, and the home circle'. It was published in 1876, though some of the tunes had appeared in *The Christian Mission Magazine* during 1875. Above most of the tunes there were cross-references to the numbers of the hymns in *The Christian Mission Hymn Book* and *The Hallelujah Hymn Book*.

In the preface to *Revival Music*, William Booth said: 'It contains such a collection of popular revival melodies as has never before appeared'. Responding in advance to possible objections to the use of secular tunes, he stated: 'I have sought to print just that music which has been sung amidst the most overpowering scenes of salvation in this country and America during the last 30 years, and only those who appreciate such music can be expected to favour my design'. He concluded: 'To "sing with the understanding" surely means not so much with musical correctness as with the solemn consciousness of the eternal truth of that which is sung, for we sing of salvation and aim to save souls by singing as well as by proclaiming the gospel of the Grace of God.'

1878 Song Book

When The Christian Mission adopted the name 'The Salvation Army' in 1878, there was an immediate need for new song books reflecting this change. A revised edition of *The Christian Mission Hymn Book* was published in August 1878, under the title: *Songs of The Salvation Army, known as The Christian Mission*. The songs were numbered 1-496 and 498-532, but with 14 additional songs numbered 3a, 7a, etc, and a supplement of 101 songs. Apart from the supplement, *Songs of The Salvation Army* included 89 songs not in *The Christian Mission Hymn Book*, omitting 75 hymns from the earlier hymn book. The supplement, which was a revision of the earlier *Hallelujah Hymn Book*, was also published separately as *The Hallelujah Book*, with three additional songs printed on the covers. Tune numbers from *Revival Music* were printed above many of the songs.

In the preface, William Booth said: 'This Song Book stands alone—firstly, from the violent religion it represents; secondly, from the plain, straightforward language of much of the contents; thirdly, from the fact that so many of its songs are only capable of being sung to secular tunes, for which purpose, indeed, they were in many cases composed.' Indicating that he had no static concept of congregational song, he explained: 'We have added to the bulk of the *Christian Mission* hymn book more than 100 hymns in this edition, and whenever we can find another 100 new songs of equal value to our Salvation Army we shall consider the propriety of enlarging it further still.'

Apparently before the end of 1878, a revised edition of the earlier *Revival Hymn Book* was published with the title *The Salvation Army Song Book,* including as before 118 songs, with seven additional songs on the title page and the covers. This book was advertised as being suitable for services in opening new Stations, and where 'large numbers of strangers' were unlikely to purchase the large Song Book.

New Songs, 1879-99

A small collection of 14 songs, *The Hosanna Songs of The Salvation Army,* dated 6 July 1879, was published 'when the Lord had led them to victory for 14 years, and had enabled them to establish the 102nd corps'. This collection marked the emergence of distinctive original Salvation Army songs, which continued to appear each week in *The War Cry* (first published 27 December 1879).

The first penny song book with the title *The Salvation Soldier's Song Book* appeared in 1880, and during the next 20 years there were several editions published under this title, incorporating new songs with old favourites.

In October 1880, *Holiness Hymns*, a booklet of 101 songs was published, 'Selected from the various Song Books of The Salvation Army, and specially adapted for use at Holiness Meetings and All Nights of Prayer'. Also, a revised edition of the tune book, *Revival Music*, appeared under the title *Salvation Army Music*, with supplementary tunes bringing the total to 532 tunes. (A later edition had 533 tunes.)

Salvation Solos, a collection of 323 original songs reprinted from *The War Cry*, was published in February 1883. Although it was apparently issued as a book for soloists, many of the songs later came into general use for congregational singing.

Salvation Music, Volume II, 'a collection of the favourite songs of The Salvation Army', appeared in December 1883. It included 99 songs with music, later enlarged to 102 songs in 1890. In the preface, William Booth said: 'The Salvation Army must always be singing new songs whilst it continues to win new victories. Old songs will not do where there is plenty of new life.'

As *The War Cry* continued to provide an outlet for the words of new songs, the words and music of eight songs were published in February 1885 on Salvation Army musical leaflets. These were followed, a few months later, by the first of a new series, *Favourite Songs of the Salvation Songsters*, which appeared at intervals until June 1886 when No. 8 was published, including songs from the International Congress, 29 May-4 June 1886. From July 1886, the series continued under the title *The Musical Salvationist*, published monthly until December 1941, bi-monthly 1942-1960, and quarterly from January 1961.

1899 Song Book

In November 1897, William Booth asked Richard Slater to begin collecting together songs for a new song book. From a total of over 11,000 songs, Richard Slater selected about 2,500, from which William and Bramwell Booth and a council of officers made the final selection. The new song book, *Salvation Army Songs*, published in July 1899, included 870 songs and

216 choruses. In the preface, William Booth, at the age of 70, wrote: 'It has seemed good to me at this time to attempt something like a thorough selection of those songs which we have found most helpful in all lands . . . but it is not intended in any degree to limit the flow of new songs; for wherever these songs are sung they will cause the production of others, and many here may yet be left behind should the number of our best song-makers be multiplied.'

In May 1900, a new tune book, *Salvation Army Music*, appeared, including 303 tunes. (This was enlarged to 319 tunes in 1905.) Brass band parts were published in July 1900. As this tune book was smaller than the previous edition, some of the songs in *Salvation Army Songs*, 1899, had references to tunes in the earlier publications, including *Salvation Army Music*, 1880; *Salvation Music, Volume II; The Musical Salvationist;* and the *Band Journal*.

1930 Song Book

A new song book, *Salvation Army Songs*, 1930, compiled by a Song Book Council established by General Bramwell Booth, included 1,003 songs and 730 choruses. About 170 songs from the 1899 Song Book were omitted and about 300 new songs were included.

A new *Band Tune Book*, with 541 tunes, was published in 1928, though the four-part harmony edition, *The Salvation Army Tune Book for Congregational Singing*, did not appear until 1931. As the new tune book did not include music for all the songs in *Salvation Army Songs*, 1930, some of the songs included references to tunes from other publications, including *Salvation Army Music*, 1900; *Gems for Songsters; The Musical Salvationist; The Salvation Soloist;* and the *Band Journal*. A small *Supplement to the Tune Book*, with 54 songs, was published in 1943.

1953 Song Book

The next new song book, *The Song Book of The Salvation Army*, 1953, included 983 songs and 457 choruses. Two hundred and eight songs from the 1930 Song Book were omitted, and 186 new songs were chosen by the Song Book Revision Council from 390 songs considered. To supplement the tunes already available, *The Salvation Army Tune Book Supplement*, containing tunes 542-756, was published in 1953.

In 1963, *The Young People's Song Book of The Salvation Army*, including 395 songs, was published, together with *The*

Salvation Army Tune Book Supplement, No. 2, containing tunes 757-807, to provide tunes needed for the new young people's song book, and some additional tunes for general use.

Keep Singing!

In May 1974, a Song Book Council was established to consider the need for a new song book. In a series of nine meetings, 1974-75, the Council initially prepared *Keep Singing!*, 1976, a supplement to the 1953 Song Book, including 102 songs (words and music), many of which had also been included in *Songs of Faith*, a collection of 100 songs (words and music) published in Canada, in 1971.

1986 Song Book

After the publication of *Keep Singing!*, the Song Book Council continued to meet from October 1976 to October 1982, and from February 1984 to April 1985, with a final meeting on 21 February 1986, a few months before the new song book was published. *The Song Book of The Salvation Army*, 1986, includes 962 songs and 251 choruses. Two hundred and thirty-six songs from the 1953 Song Book were omitted, and 217 new songs were added: 131 from *The Young People's Song Book*, 1963, *Songs of Faith*, and *Keep Singing!* and 86 from other sources.

Simultaneously, a new tune book was in preparation, to provide tunes for the 1986 Song Book, and for a new young people's song book, *Sing for Joy,* which was compiled by a separate Young People's Song Book Council, and was also published in 1986. *The Tune Book of The Salvation Army*, published in 1987, included 870 tunes, as well as the music for the 251 choruses in the 1986 Song Book. Band parts for the new Tune Book were published in August 1988, including an additional tune which was subsequently incorporated into the keyboard edition.

Last word

Although salvationists in every generation sing many new songs, the words of William Booth, quoted in each new edition of the Song Book since 1899, are still relevant today: 'Sing till your whole soul is lifted up to God, and then sing till you lift the eyes of those who know not God to Him who is the fountain of all our joy.'

PART ONE

Notes on songs

A boy was born in Bethlehem (855)
Catherine Baird (1895-1984)

Entitled: 'A Boy was born', the song was published in *Songs for Young People's Anniversaries and Special Occasions, No. 38*, 1975, with music by Diane Berry and with a different chorus for each verse. It was selected for *Sing for Joy*, 1986, and then for the present Song Book, omitting the choruses.

A charge to keep I have (472)
Charles Wesley (1707-88)

Published in volume 1 of the author's *Short Hymns on Select Passages of the Holy Scriptures*, 1762, under the heading: 'Keep the charge of the Lord, that ye die not' (Leviticus 8:35). Originally there were two eight-line verses. The hymn is a paraphrase of Matthew Henry's commentary on Leviticus 8:31-36: 'We have every one of us a charge to keep, an eternal God to glorify, an immortal soul to provide for, needful duty to be done, our generation to serve; and it must be our daily care to keep this charge, for it is the charge of the Lord our Master, who will shortly call us to account about it, and it is our utmost peril if we neglect it. Keep it "that ye die not"; it is death, eternal death, to betray the trust that we are charged with; by the consideration of this we must be kept in awe.'

A child this day is born (72)
Anonymous

Included in the second part of *Christmas Carols, Ancient and Modern*, 1833, compiled by William Sandys, 'containing a selection from carols still used in the West of England'. There were 21 verses and the chorus. The present version, which differs considerably from the traditional text, appeared in *The Song Book of The Salvation Army*, 1953.

A friend of Jesus! O what bliss (709)
Joseph C. Ludgate (d 1947)

Four verses and the chorus appeared in *The Young Soldier*, 2 July 1898, but in *One Hundred Favorite Songs and Music of The Salvation Army*, 1899, compiled by Commander Booth-Tucker, there were five verses, entitled: 'Friendship with Jesus'. The third verse of this version has now been omitted. It is said that the writing of this song was linked with the serious illness of one of the author's children, while he was in Toronto, but the details of the circumstances vary in different accounts and cannot now be verified.

A light came out of darkness (94)
William A. Hawley (c1870-1929)
Appeared in *The Musical Salvationist*, October 1901, under the title: 'Shall You, Shall I?'. The chorus has been slightly altered.

A mighty fortress is our God (1)
Martin Luther (1483-1546)
translated by Frederic H. Hedge (1805-90)
The German hymn 'Ein feste burg ist unser Gott', inspired by Psalm 46, was published in *Form und Ordnung Gaystlicher Gesang und Psalmen*, 1529, and probably also in Joseph Klug's *Geistliche Lieder*, 1529, though no copies of this volume have survived. The translation, written in 1852, appeared under the heading 'Luther's Psalm' in *Hymns for the Church of Christ*, 1853, edited by Frederic H. Hedge and Frederic D. Huntington.

A needy sinner at thy feet (282)
verses: Christopher Strang (1854-81)
chorus: from Emily E. S. Elliott (1836-97)
Originally beginning 'A wretched sinner . . .', the song, entitled 'The Penitent's Cry!' appeared in *The War Cry*, 31 March 1881, and again in the author's obituary in *The War Cry*, 1 September 1881. The verses were altered for *The Song Book of The Salvation Army*, 1953, when the fourth and fifth verses were omitted. The chorus is from *Sacred Songs and Solos*, 1877, compiled by Ira D. Sankey, where it is linked with the verses of Emily Elliott's 'Thou didst leave thy throne and thy kingly crown'. Sankey, who composed the music, probably also arranged the chorus.

A wonderful Saviour is Jesus, my Lord (710)
Fanny Crosby (1820-1915)
Published in *The Finest of the Wheat, No. 1*, 1890, compiled by George D. Elderkin, R. R. McCabe, John R. Sweney and William J. Kirkpatrick.

Abide with me; fast falls the eventide (670)
Henry Francis Lyte (1793-1847)
Apparently written during the author's final weeks in Devon before he left for the south of France in September 1847. He enclosed a copy of the hymn, described as 'my latest effusion', in a letter to a friend named Julia, on 25 August 1847. A few days later (probably on 4 September 1847) he gave a copy to

his daughter, Anna Maria Maxwell Hogg, who published it in *Remains of the Late Rev Henry Francis Lyte*, 1850, with the heading: 'Abide with us: for it is towards evening, and the day is far spent' (Luke 24:29). She dated the hymn 'Berryhead, September 1847', though it now seems that it was written in August. The third, fourth and fifth verses of the original have been omitted.

Above the waves of earthly strife (872)
Mary Ann Kidder (1820-1905)

Appeared in *Fresh Laurels for the Sabbath School*, 1867, compiled by William B. Bradbury, with the title 'My Home is There'. The second verse of the original has been omitted.

Above the world-wide battlefield (774)
Will J. Brand (1889-1977)

Written in April 1948, at the request of Commissioner John Bladin, Principal of the International Training College, for the flag ceremony at the close of the 'King's Messengers' Session. It was published in *The Musical Salvationist*, November-December 1948, under the title: 'Blood and Fire', but was revised for *The Song Book of The Salvation Army*, 1953, with a new chorus, to fit the tune: 'Haste away to Jesus'.

Afar from Heaven thy feet have wandered (225)
Richard Slater (1854-1939)

Written 9-10 November 1885 as a duet for the author and his wife, and apparently introduced in a meeting which they conducted at Great Western Hall, Marylebone. Entitled 'God is near thee', it later appeared in *The Musical Salvationist*, April 1887, arranged for soprano and tenor duet.

Alas! and did my Saviour bleed (105)
verses: Isaac Watts (1674-1748)
chorus: Anonymous

The verses, headed 'Godly Sorrow arising from the Sufferings of Christ', were published in the second part of the author's *Hymns and Spiritual Songs*, 1707. The second and fifth verses of the original have been omitted and several lines in the other verses have been altered. The origin of the chorus is unknown. A similar chorus was linked with verses beginning 'Lord, I despair myself to heal' in *Revival Hymns, principally selected by the Rev R. H. Neale*, 1842, but this was probably not its earliest appearance.

All creatures of our God and King (2)
Francis of Assisi (c1182-1226)
translated by William H. Draper (1855-1933)

'The Canticle of the Sun', traditionally attributed to Francis of Assisi is said to have been written during 1225 while Francis was seriously ill at San Damiano. (He later added other verses on the theme of forgiveness and on the subject of his approaching death, but these are not among the verses included in the present Song Book.) The English paraphrase was written between 1899 and 1919, and appeared in *The Public School Hymn Book*, 1919, and *School Worship*, 1926.

All glory to Jesus be given (535)
Annie Turner Wittenmyer (1827-1900)

Published in *The Voice of Praise for the Sunday School*, c1872, edited by Ebenezer T. Baird and Karl Reden, and later in *Gospel Hymns, No. 2*, 1876, compiled by P. P. Bliss and Ira D. Sankey.

All hail the power of Jesus' name (56)
Edward Perronet (c1726-92)

The first verse appeared in *The Gospel Magazine*, November 1779, and later the complete hymn, with eight verses, was in *The Gospel Magazine*, April 1780, headed 'On the Resurrection, The Lord is King'. It was extensively altered for *A Selection of Hymns*, 1787, compiled by John Rippon, and has subsequently been revised by other editors. The verses in the present Song Book are from the version in *Salvation Army Songs*, 1899.

All have need of God's salvation (824)
William J. McAlonan (1863-1925)

Appeared in *The Musical Salvationist*, October 1890, entitled 'It is written, "Whosoever"'. The original fifth verse has been omitted.

All I have, by thy blood thou dost claim (473)
verses: Richard Slater (1854-1939)
chorus: Herbert H. Booth (1862-1926)

Herbert Booth sang the chorus during holiness meetings at Great Western Hall, Marylebone, 16 June 1885, marking the 30th wedding anniversary of his parents, General and Mrs William Booth. It was printed in *The War Cry*, 26 August 1885.

Richard Slater wrote the verses on 7 November 1887 by request and the complete song was included in *Songs of Peace and War*, 1890.

All my heart this night rejoices (73)
Paulus Gerhardt (1607-76)
translated by Catherine Winkworth (1827-78)

The German hymn, 'Fröhlich soll mein Herze springen', is from Cruger's *Praxis pietatis melica*, 1656. The translation appeared in Catherine Winkworth's *Lyra Germanica*, 2nd series, 1858, and *The Chorale Book for England*, 1863.

All our hearts rejoice this morning (74)
Ernest H. Parr (*b* 1909)

Written for the tune 'Europe' (the 'Ode to Joy' from Beethoven's Ninth Symphony). The verses were printed on a card as a Christmas greeting for the author's friends, and appeared in *The War Cry*, in Canada, Christmas 1980.

All people that on earth do dwell (3)
William Kethe (*d* 1594)

This version of Psalm 100 appeared in two different editions of the 'Anglo-Genevan' Psalter of 1561. The first, *Four score and seven Psalmes of David in English mitre by Thomas Sternholde and others*, 1561, gives the author's initials 'W. Ke.' alongside the title of the psalm. It also includes a short commentary on the psalm, taken from the Geneva Bible, 1560: 'He exhorteth all to serve the Lord, who hath chosen us, and preserved us, and to entre into his assemblies to praise his Name'. The second copy is set in different type and has several printing and copying mistakes, and in this edition Psalm 100 is incorrectly attributed to Thomas Sternhold. In a third source, *Psalmes of David in Englishe Metre* (usually known as 'Day's Psalter'), Psalm 100 appears anonymously. This copy was probably also published in 1561. The present Song Book has 'Him serve with mirth' (in verse 1) as in the Scottish Psalter, 1650, and 'We are his flock' (in verse 2), which probably originated as a misprint for 'folck' (ie folk = people).

All praise to thee, for thou, O King divine (174)
F. Bland Tucker (1895-1984)

Based on Philippians 2:5-11, it was written in 1938 with the tune 'Sine Nomine' in mind, but was included in *The Hymnal 1940* linked with C. V. Stanford's tune 'Engelberg'.

All round the world the Army chariot rolls (775)
William J. Pearson (1832-92)

Originally beginning: 'All round the world our Army chariot rolls', the song appeared in *The War Cry*, 5 January 1884, entitled 'All round the world', and was then included in a small booklet, *Salvation Songster's Songs, Part 2*, 1884.

All scenes alike engaging prove (556)
Jeanne de la Mothe Guyon (1648-1717)
translated by William Cowper (1731-1800)

The original French poem, with nine verses, beginning 'Amour que mon ame est contente', was published in the author's *Poésies et Cantiques Spirituels*, 1722. The translation is from *Poems Translated from the French of Madame de la Mothe Guion*, 1801, by William Cowper. It was entitled 'The Soul that loves God finds Him every where', and began with a verse now omitted:

> Oh thou, by long experience tried,
> Near whom no grief can long abide;
> My Love! how full of sweet content
> I pass my years of banishment.

The present Song Book includes verses 2-4, 6 and 9, with some alterations, as in *The Song Book of The Salvation Army*, 1953.

All the guilty past is washed away (188)
Richard Slater (1854-1939)

Written in March 1888 for music by Staff-Captain (later Colonel) Thomas W. Emerson, and included in *The Musical Salvationist*, April 1888, with the title 'Holy Spirit, come'.

All things are possible to him (407)
Charles Wesley (1707-88)

Published in volume 2 of the author's *Hymns and Sacred Poems*, 1749, with the title 'All things are possible to him that believeth' (Mark 9:23). It was one of a group of hymns under the heading: 'Hymns for those that wait for Full Redemption'. The third and sixth verses of the original have been omitted, as in *A Collection of Hymns for the Use of the People called Methodists*, 1780, compiled by John Wesley.

All things bright and beautiful (25)
Cecil Frances Alexander (1818-95)

Published in the author's *Hymns for Little Children*, 1848, with the heading: 'Maker of Heaven and Earth'. It was one of a group of hymns (Nos. 8-20) written to explain articles of the Christian faith. There were seven verses, originally beginning:

> All things bright and beauteous,
> All creatures great and small,
> All things wise and wondrous,
> The Lord God made them all.

Later editions of *Hymns for Little Children* give the familiar version. The third and sixth verses of the original have been omitted.

All to Jesus I surrender (474)
Judson W. Van de Venter (1855-1939)

While he was conducting a meeting in East Palestine, Ohio, the author was in the home of George Sebring, and wrote this song remembering the time when, after a long struggle, he had surrendered and dedicated his life to active Christian service. It was published in *Gospel Songs of Grace and Glory*, 1896, compiled by the author, with Winfield S. Weedon and Leonard Weaver.

Almost persuaded now to believe (226)
Philip P. Bliss (1838-76)

The song, entitled 'Almost Persuaded', was published in *The Charm: A Collection of Sunday School Music*, 1871, compiled by P. P. Bliss. The inspiration apparently came from a sermon preached by the Rev Mr Brundage, which concluded with the words: 'He who is almost persuaded is almost saved, but to be almost saved is to be entirely lost'. (*P. P. Bliss: His Life and Life-Work*, by D. W. Whittle and W. Guest.)

Am I a soldier of the cross (678)
verses: Isaac Watts (1674-1748)
chorus: Anonymous

The verses were published in the author's *Sermons on Various Subjects*, Volume 3, 1729, linked with a sermon entitled 'Holy Fortitude, or Remedies against Fear', based on the text: 'Stand fast in the Faith, quit you like Men, be strong' (1 Corinthians 16:13). The fifth and sixth verses have been omitted. The chorus is from *New Hymns and Solos*, 1888, compiled by Ira D. Sankey, where the hymn is set to the tune: 'A soldier of the cross', composed by Sankey.

Amazing grace! how sweet the sound (308)
verses 1-3: John Newton (1725-1807)
verse 4: Anonymous

Verses 1-3 are from a hymn with six verses in part 1 of the *Olney Hymns*, 1779, where it was entitled 'Faith's review and expectation', with the scriptural reference: 1 Chronicles 17:16-17. The fourth verse, which has sometimes been incorrectly attributed to John P. Rees (1828-1900), appeared anonymously in *A Collection of Sacred Ballads*, 1790, compiled by Richard and Andrew Broaddus, where it was the last verse of a hymn beginning: 'Jerusalem, my happy home'.

And are we yet alive (915)
Charles Wesley (1707-88)

Published in a section headed: 'Hymns for Christian Friends' in volume 2 of the author's *Hymns and Sacred Poems*, 1749, where it was entitled 'At meeting of friends'. Since John Wesley's later years it has been the opening hymn at the annual Methodist Conference, in Britain. The fourth verse of the original has been omitted, as in *A Collection of Hymns for the Use of the People called Methodists*, 1780, compiled by John Wesley.

And can it be that I should gain (283)
Charles Wesley (1707-88)

Published by John and Charles Wesley in *Hymns and Sacred Poems*, 1739, with the title: 'Free Grace'. (Although some handbooks, following Julian's *Dictionary of Hymnology*, have said that it appeared in *A Collection of Psalms and Hymns*, 1738, this seems to be incorrect.) It has been suggested that Charles Wesley wrote this hymn at the time of his conversion, 21 May 1738, but Frank Baker (*Representative Verse of Charles Wesley*, 1962, p9) concludes that the hymn written on that occasion was probably 'Where shall my wond'ring soul begin'. Some hymnologists, including Edward Houghton (*The Hymn Society Bulletin*, September 1979, pp93-99), have argued that 'And can it be' was one of the hymns probably written by John Wesley rather than Charles. However, as John and Charles Wesley did not distinguish their individual contributions to books which they published jointly, this cannot be established with certainty.

And is it so? A gift from me (475)
Richard Slater (1854-1939)

Written on 16-17 March 1888 and included in a booklet of

Songs of Love and Service to be sung at the marriage celebrations of Miss Emma Booth and Commissioner Tucker in the St James's Hall and Clapton Congress Hall, 9-10 April 1888. There were originally seven verses, but one was omitted when the song, entitled 'I have not much to give Thee, Lord', appeared in *The Musical Salvationist*, May 1888.

And now to thee we render (950)
James F. Swift (1847-1931)

This was the fifth verse of the author's 'Evening Hymn' which began:

> When evening shadows gather,
> And twilight gently fades;
> When all is still and silent
> In midnight's darker shades,
> Then, O my God, be near me,
> Do Thou protect my bed,
> From evil and from danger
> Let angels guard my head.

It was written in 1873, first sung in public at the Wesleyan Choral Festival in St George's Hall, Liverpool, in 1874, and was then included in the first series of the author's *Hymns for Home and Sacred Festivals*, 1875, where it was headed: 'I will both lay me down in peace and sleep, for Thou, Lord, only makest me dwell in safety' (Psalm 4:8).

Angels, from the realms of Glory (75)
James Montgomery (1771-1854)

Published in the Sheffield newspaper *The Iris*, 24 December 1816, and then in *The Christian Psalmist; or Hymns, Selected and Original*, 1825, by James Montgomery, where it was headed: 'Good tidings of great joy to all people'. The third verse of the original has now been omitted.

Approach, my soul, the mercy seat (284)
John Newton (1725-1807)

Published in the third part of the *Olney Hymns*, 1779, with the title 'The effort'. (The preceding hymn had the same title, but was in 10.10.10.10. Iambic metre, beginning, 'Cheer up, my soul, there is a mercy-seat'.) The sixth verse has now been omitted.

Are you seeking joys that will not fade (227)
Sidney E. Cox (1887-1975)

Appeared in *Songs and Music*, 1922, published in New York,

and later included in *The War Cry*, 4 January 1930, and *The Musical Salvationist*, March 1932, entitled: 'Swing wide the door of your heart'.

Arise, my soul, arise (106)
Charles Wesley (1707-88)

Published by John and Charles Wesley in *Hymns and Sacred Poems*, 1742, with the title 'Behold the Man!'

Army flag! Thy threefold glory (776)
Albert Orsborn (1886-1967)

The author said that this song was inspired by the International Congress, 1914. The third verse echoes lines from a poem 'From Lands Afar' which he wrote at that time:

> We shall behold a nobler empire rising,
>   Vaster than any mortal eyes have seen;
> Throned in what state, above man's vain despising,
>   Shall we behold the lowly Nazarene!

The song, entitled 'Following the Flag', appeared in an arrangement for women's voices in *The Musical Salvationist*, June 1932, where each verse had nine lines. The present version was included in *Songs and Choruses for the British Commissioner's Officers' Councils, No. 2*, 1948, and then in *The Song Book of The Salvation Army*, 1953.

(See also: 'Yet once again, by God's abundant mercy'.)

Art thou weary, art thou languid (228)
John Mason Neale (1818-66)

Published in the first edition of *Hymns of the Eastern Church*, 1862, by J. M. Neale, as a translation of a Greek hymn by Stephen the Sabaite (725-794), copied from 'a dateless Constantinopolitan book'. However, in the third edition (1866), he said that it contained so little from the Greek that it should not have been included in the collection. In the light of this statement it is now accepted as an original hymn by J. M. Neale and not as a translation. The seventh verse of the original has now been omitted.

As I am before thy face (285)
Herbert H. Booth (1862-1926)

Apparently first used as a solo in 1891, and later included in *The War Cry*, 18 November 1893, on a page headed: 'Boundless Salvation Songs'. The second verse and the chorus have now been omitted.

As pants the hart for cooling streams (557)
Nahum Tate (1652-1715) and Nicholas Brady (1659-1726)

This paraphrase of Psalm 42 appeared in *A New Version of the Psalms of David, fitted to the Tunes used in Churches*, 1696, by N. Tate and N. Brady. The original six eight-line verses were slightly altered for *The Second Edition corrected*, 1698, and the verses in the present Song Book are from the revised edition.

As the varied way of life we journey (711)
Lily K. Sampson (b 1906)

Written for the Swedish tune 'Trust in God', for Senior-Major Olive Gatrall, later Mrs General Coutts (R), to sing at the marriage of Major Ivar Sörman and Captain Rene Nicholson, at Camberwell Citadel, 25 March 1950. Although the words seemed rather sombre for a wedding, they were particularly appropriate eight years later, when Brigadier Sörman was promoted to Glory from Östersund, Sweden, 22 October 1958.

As with gladness men of old (76)
William Chatterton Dix (1837-98)

Apparently written during an illness in about 1859. The version in the present Song Book appeared in a booklet of *Hymns* issued in 1859 as a draft of the forthcoming *Hymns Ancient and Modern* expected to be published in Advent 1860. A slightly different version was included in *Hymns for the Services of the Church, and for Private Devotion*, 1860, compiled by Arthur H. Ward for use at the Church of St Raphael, Bristol, where the author was a lay-clerk.

At even, ere the sun was set (558)
Henry Twells (1823-1900)

Written in 1868, while the author (the headmaster of the Godolphin School, Hammersmith) was supervising an examination. He wrote it at the request of Sir Henry Baker for the 1868 Appendix to *Hymns Ancient and Modern*, where it appeared with the heading 'And at even, when the sun did set, they brought unto Him all that were diseased, and all that were possessed with devils. And all the city was gathered together at the door' (Mark 1:32-33). The fourth and fifth verses have been omitted.

At harvest time our eyes behold (923)
Ruth F. Tracy (1870-1960)

Inspired by the thoughts of Commissioner Mildred Duff

speaking on the words of Jesus: 'If it die' (John 12:24). Included in 'Songs for Harvest Festivals', a special issue of *The Musical Salvationist,* August 1902, where the song was entitled: 'The Sowing and the Reaping'. The chorus has been omitted.

At peace with God! How great the blessing (536)
Richard Slater (1854-1939)

Written on 25 July 1887 to a 'Swedish tune' and included in *The Musical Salvationist,* July 1888, with the title: 'At Peace with God'. This title is inscribed on the headstone of the author's grave at Margate, Kent.

At the name of Jesus (141)
Caroline Maria Noel (1817-77)

Based on Philippians 2:5-11, it appeared under the heading 'Ascension Day' in the author's book *The Name of Jesus, and other poems, for the sick and lonely,* Enlarged edition, 1870. The second, sixth and eighth verses of the original have been omitted.

Awake, awake! Fling off the night (408)
John R. Peacey (1896-1971)

Based on Ephesians 5: 6-20, it was included in *100 Hymns for Today: a Supplement to Hymns Ancient and Modern,* 1969, with the title 'The New Life'. The *New English Bible* translation of Ephesians 5:14 seems to assume that the lines:

> 'Awake, sleeper,
> rise from the dead,
> and Christ will shine upon you'

are from an early Christian hymn.

Awake, my soul, and with the sun (665)
Thomas Ken (1637-1711)

Probably written before 1674 (with the evening hymn 'Glory to thee, my God, this night') for the scholars of Winchester College. In *A Manual of Prayers for the Use of the Scholars of Winchester College,* 1674, the author wrote: 'Be sure to sing the Morning and Evening Hymn in your chamber devoutly. . . .' In 1692, the hymns were published (apparently without the author's consent) in a pamphlet, headed 'A Morning and Evening Hymn'. They were then included, with a midnight hymn, in a pamphlet entitled *Three Hymns. By the Author of the Manual of Prayers for the Use of the Scholars of Winchester College,* 1694. The morning hymn had 12 verses in the 1692 pamphlet and 14 in 1694, and subsequently appeared in several different versions (not always with the author's approval).

Awake, our souls; away, our fears (559)
Isaac Watts (1674-1748)

Based on Isaiah 40:28-31, and published in the first part of the author's *Hymns and Spiritual Songs*, 1707, with the title: 'The Christian Race'.

Away in a manger, no crib for a bed (77)
Anonymous

Verses 1 and 2 appeared anonymously in a *Little Children's Book: for schools and families*, 1885, published by the Evangelical Lutheran Church in North America. Subsequently, they were included in *Dainty Songs for Little Lads and Lasses*, 1887, by James R. Murray, with the statement: 'Luther's Cradle Hymn. (Composed by Martin Luther for his children, and still sung by German mothers to their little ones).' Research by Richard S. Hill (published in an article, 'Not so far away in a manger, forty-one settings of an American carol', in the *Music Library Association Notes*, December 1945), concluded that the verses probably first appeared in a play or story based on the life of Martin Luther, written in about 1883 for the 400th anniversary of Luther's birth. No early German version has been discovered and there is no evidence to support any other connection with Martin Luther. The earliest known appearance of the third verse is in *Gabriel's Vineyard Songs*, 1892, compiled by Charles H. Gabriel, so it cannot have been written (as is sometimes suggested) by Dr John T. McFarland, *c*1904-08.

Be glad in the Lord and rejoice (537)
Mary E. Servoss (1849-?)

Published under the title 'Rejoice in the Lord' in *Sacred Songs and Solos No. 2*, 1881, compiled by Ira D. Sankey, where it was headed 'Let the righteous be glad! yea, let them exceedingly rejoice!' (Psalm 68:3). The second verse of the original has now been omitted.

Be strong in the grace of the Lord (679)
Walter H. Windybank (1872-1952)

Based on 2 Timothy 2:1, it was written for the *Junior's Guide, Attendance Record and Song Book*, 1944, after the author had seen a need for new songs to familiar tunes from the Band Journals.

Beautiful Jesus, bright star of the earth (175)
Elizabeth Ashby (1881-1988)

Written for the tune 'Beautiful flowers', it appeared in *The Musical Salvationist*, February 1900, under the title 'Beautiful Jesus', with the note: 'The range of the verse makes it suitable for an Alto or Bass solo'. A slightly different version (possibly written earlier) was included in *The War Cry*, 24 March 1900, entitled 'Beautiful Christ'.

Beautiful land, so bright, so fair (873)
R. Moorcock

Appeared in *The Christian Mission Hymn Book*, 1870, compiled by William Booth, with the chorus:
> Will you go? will you go?
> Go to that beautiful land with me?

Gordon Avery said that the song was attributed to Miss R. Moorcock in 'an old Gospel Tune Book', but this source has not been traced.

Before I found salvation (309)
William G. Collins (1854-1931)

Appeared in *The Musical Salvationist*, June 1887, with the title: 'Before and After', and originally beginning: 'Before I got salvation'.

Before Jehovah's aweful throne (4)
Isaac Watts (1674-1748)
altered by John Wesley (1703-91)

This paraphrase of Psalm 100 appeared with the heading 'Praise to the Lord From All Nations', in the author's *Horae Lyricae*, 1706, and then in the first edition of his *Hymns and Spiritual Songs*, 1707. There were originally five verses, beginning:
> Sing to the Lord with Joyful Voice,
> Let every Land his Name adore,
> The Brittish Isles shall send the Noise
> Across the Ocean to the Shore.

A revised version by the author appeared, with six verses, in *The Psalms of David Imitated in the Language of the New Testament, and apply'd to the Christian State and Worship*, 1719, by I. Watts. Later, the opening lines were altered by John Wesley for *A Collection of Psalms and Hymns*, Charlestown, 1737, the first hymn book which he published.

Before thy face, dear Lord (409)
Herbert H. Booth (1862-1926)

Colonel Frederick Hawkes said that the song originally had some eight or ten verses, and was first used in 'Two Days with God' meetings at the Exeter Hall, London, conducted by William Booth. The first verse and chorus appeared in *The War Cry*, 10 January 1891, in a report of a 'Great Salvation Musical Festival' held in the Exeter Hall on 29 December 1890. The complete text of the original song has not yet been discovered, though early versions include a total of ten verses. (See: *The Soldier Soloist*, New York, 1892; *The War Cry*, 26 January 1895; *All the World*, November 1896; and *Salvation Army Songs*, 1899.)

Begin, my tongue, some heavenly theme (26)
Isaac Watts (1674-1748)

Published in the second part of the author's *Hymns and Spiritual Songs*, 1707, with the heading: 'The Faithfulness of God in his Promises'. Originally there were nine verses, beginning:

> Begin my Tongue, some heav'nly theme
> And speak some boundless thing,

The present Song Book includes verses 1, 2, 6 and 9 in an altered form.

Begone, unbelief (712)
John Newton (1725-1807)

Published in part 3 of the *Olney Hymns*, 1779, under the heading 'I will trust and not be afraid'. A footnote at the end of the last verse refers to the text 'In all these things we are more than conquerors through him that loved us' (Romans 8:37). The fourth, fifth and sixth verses of the original have now been omitted.

Behold! behold the Lamb of God (107)
Richard Jukes (1804-67)

Appeared in *The Primitive Methodist Magazine*, April 1839, under the title 'The Cross of Christ', and then included, in a slightly different version, in the author's *Hymns for the Living and the Dying, Volume 1,* Fourth edition, 1852. The sixth verse has now been omitted. In a short biography of the author, in *The Primitive Methodist Magazine*, February 1868, James Pritchard wrote: 'The cross of Christ was our poet's charming and oft-recurring theme', and then quoted the fifth verse of this hymn. (It was incorrectly attributed to Joseph Hoskins in *The Song Book of The Salvation Army*, 1953.)

Behold him now on yonder tree (108)
George S. Smith (1865-1944)

Apparently written in 1887, it was included in *The Musical Salvationist*, June 1891, under the title: 'It was for me'.

Behold me standing at the door (229)
Fanny Crosby (1820-1915)

The verses and chorus as in the present Song Book appeared anonymously in *Notes of Joy, for the Sabbath School, the Social Meeting and the Hour of Prayer*, 1869, compiled by Mrs J. F. Knapp. Verses 1-3 are similar to verses 1, 3 and 5 of an earlier song with five verses in *The Revival Hymn Book*, Second Series, 1864.

Behold the throne of grace (560)
John Newton (1725-1807)

This was one of three hymns related to the text: 'Ask what I shall give thee' (1 Kings 3:5), in part 1 of the *Olney Hymns*, 1779. The second, fifth and eighth verses of the original have been omitted.

Believe him! Believe him! the holy one is waiting (410)
Albert Orsborn (1886-1967)

The author said that this song, written by request for a central holiness meeting at Clapton, was one of three songs he wrote on one occasion before breakfast. It appeared in *The War Cry*, 26 June 1915, to be sung to the tune 'The harvest is passing'.

Beneath the cross of Jesus (476)
Elizabeth C. Clephane (1830-69)

Published in the magazine *The Family Treasury*, 1872, edited by William Arnot, where it was the first of two hymns on pages 398-9 under the heading 'Breathings on the Border'. They were introduced by the editor's note:

> These lines express the experiences, the hopes and the longings of a young Christian lately released. Written on the very edge of this life, with the better land fully in the view of faith, they seem to us footsteps printed on the sands of Time, where these sands touch the ocean of Eternity. These footprints of one whom the Good Shepherd led through the wilderness into rest may, with God's blessing, contribute to comfort and direct succeeding pilgrims.

The second and third verses of the original, which reflect on Heaven and eternity have been omitted.

Beyond the farthest bounds of earth (27)
Miriam M. Richards (*b* 1911)

Written while on holiday in Devon, by request, for *The Young People's Song Book of The Salvation Army*, 1963.

Blessèd and glorious King (561)
Thomas H. Mundell (1849-1934)

This song was placed first in a Jubilee song competition and was published in a special issue of *The War Cry*, 7 July 1894, celebrating the 50th anniversary of General William Booth's conversion. The second verse originally began:

> Our General spare and bless,
> Give joy and happiness,

and the final verse concluded:

> With hearts from sin set free,
> With lips new touched by Thee,
> Make us this Jubilee
>   All flames of fire!

Blessèd are the poor in spirit (95)
Arch R. Wiggins (1893-1976)

This paraphrase of Matthew 5:3-11, originally written to the tune 'St Oswald', was published under the title 'The Beatitudes' in *The Musical Salvationist*, March-April 1947, with music by Brindley Boon.

Blessèd assurance, Jesus in mine (310)
Fanny Crosby (1820-1915)

Written in 1873, after the author had been listening to the tune, recently composed by her friend, Mrs Phoebe Knapp. The melody immediately suggested the theme, 'Blessèd assurance', and, within a short while, the words were completed. The song appeared in *Gems of Praise*, 1873, compiled by John R. Sweney.

Blessèd Lamb of Calvary, Let thy Spirit fall on me (205)
Barbara Stoddart (1865-1915)

Published in *The War Cry*, 12 August 1893, when the author was Captain Barbara Wilson.

Blessèd Lamb of Calvary, Thou hast done great things for me (538)
George S. Smith (1865-1944)

Written at home one Sunday evening when the author (the

bandmaster of Kingswood Corps, Bristol) was looking after his children, while his wife was at the meeting. The song appeared in *The Musical Salvationist,* September 1887, entitled 'Thou art a mighty Saviour'. The title is inscribed on the kerbstone at the foot of the author's grave in the burial ground, Park Road, Kingswood.

Blessèd Lord, in thee is refuge (713)
                                       Herbert H. Booth (1862-1926)
Included in a booklet of *Songs of the Nations,* for the International Congress, 1886, and later in the author's collection, *Songs of Peace and War,* 1890. The song is said to have been written either during a period of spiritual darkness when the author was tempted to leave the Army, or at a time when he was particularly concerned about the substantial cost of the training home premises at Clapton. The *Free Church Council Hymnal,* 1906, includes an additional verse which has not been found in any earlier publication:

> Faith triumphant—blessèd victory!
>   Every barrier swept away!
> Heaven descending, joy and fulness,
>   Dawn of everlasting day!
>   Jesus only—
>   Him to love and Him obey.

Blessèd Saviour, now behold me (477)
                                       William Baugh (1852-1942)
Written at Stockport in 1886 and published in *The War Cry,* 20 November 1886, under the title: 'Make me what I ought to be'. Later, when the author was stationed in Canada, it was set to a 'Secular Melody' and appeared in *The Musical Salvationist,* January 1891, entitled: 'Wholly the Lord's'.

Blest are the pure in heart (411)
                    verses 1 and 3: John Keble (1792-1866)
        verses 2 and 4: attributed to William J. Hall (1793-1861)
Verses 1 and 3 are from a poem with 17 verses written on 10 October 1819. Entitled 'The Purification', it was published in the author's *The Christian Year,* 1827, with the heading 'Blessed are the pure in heart, for they shall see God' (Matthew 5:3). Verses 2 and 4, combined with the first and last verses of John Keble's poem, appeared in *Psalms and Hymns Adapted to the Services of the Church of England,* 1836, edited by W. J. Hall.

Blest be the dear uniting love (659)
Charles Wesley (1707-88)

Published by John and Charles Wesley in *Hymns and Sacred Poems*, 1742, with the heading 'At Parting'. (The preceding hymn was headed 'At the meeting of Christian friends'.) The five verses in the present Song Book appear as in *A Collection of Hymns for the Use of the People called Methodists*, 1780, compiled by John Wesley, though the fifth, sixth and eighth verses of the original have been omitted.

Blest be the tie that binds (660)
John Fawcett (1740-1817)

Although there is no supporting evidence, it is said to have been written in 1772, when the author decided not to move to Carter Lane Chapel, London, preferring to stay with his congregation in Wainsgate, Yorkshire. It was published with the title 'Brotherly Love' in the author's *Hymns: Adapted to the Circumstances of Public Worship and Private Devotion*, 1782. The original fifth verse has been omitted.

Boundless as the mighty ocean (230)
Josiah H. Waller (1865-1938)

Appeared in *The War Cry*, 18 November 1893, on a page of 'Boundless Salvation Songs', published after 'Two Days with God', special 'Boundless Salvation' meetings conducted by William Booth in the Exeter Hall, London, 14-15 November 1893. The fourth verse was altered to its present form in *Salvation Army Songs*, 1930.

Break thou the bread of life (650)
verse 1: Mary A. Lathbury (1841-1913)
verses 2 and 3: Alexander Groves (1842-1909)

The verse by Mary Lathbury (with another verse now omitted) was written in 1877 at the request of Dr John H. Vincent for annual summer meetings arranged by the Chautauqua Literary and Scientific Circle at Lake Chautauqua, New York. These verses were included in *The Calvary Selection of Spiritual Songs*, c 1878, compiled by Charles S. Robinson and Robert S. MacArthur. Her first verse, with the second and third verses of the present version, appeared in *The Methodist Hymn Book*, 1904, where the complete hymn was ascribed to Mary Lathbury. Later, a note in *The Wesleyan Methodist Magazine*, September 1913 (based on information from Miss Mary Groves of Ipswich) indicated that, some years earlier, the hymn had been chosen for the Wesleyan Sunday-school anniversary at Henley-on-Thames. As the hymn was short, Alexander Groves, for many years the organist and superintendent of the Sunday-school there, wrote the two additional verses.

Breathe on me, Breath of God (189)
Edwin Hatch (1835-89)

First published by the author in a pamphlet, *Between Doubt and Prayer*, 1878, and then included in *The Congregational Psalmist Hymnal*, 1886, edited by Henry Allon, where it was headed: 'He breathed on them, and saith unto them, Receive ye the Holy Ghost' (John 20:22).

Brief is our journey through the years (874)
Catherine Baird (1895-1984)

Written for *The Song Book of The Salvation Army*, 1953, and later included under the title 'Brief is Our Journey' in the author's *Reflections*, 1975, where she said, 'Though we do not fear death, rarely do we long to depart from our friendly, familiar world. Jesus regarded life as the highest price one could pay to save a friend. Surely, then, the sadness of death can be changed to joy only by Him who is the "Resurrection and the Life".' Earlier, in notes for Gordon Avery, she had written, 'The last verse is, so far as I am concerned, a personal testimony.'

Brightly beams our Father's mercy (478)
Philip P. Bliss (1838-76)

Appeared under the title 'Let the Lower Lights be Burning', in *The Charm: A Collection of Sunday School Music*, 1871, by P. P. Bliss, with the following story which inspired the hymn:

> On a dark, stormy night . . . a boat . . . neared the Cleveland harbor. 'Are you sure this is Cleveland?' asked the captain, seeing only one light from the light-house. 'Quite sure, sir,' replied the pilot. 'Where are the lower lights?' 'Gone out, sir.' 'Can you make the harbor?' 'We must, or perish, sir!' And with a strong hand and a brave heart, the old pilot turned the wheel. But alas, in the darkness he missed the channel, and with a crash upon the rocks the boat was shivered, and many a life lost in a watery grave. Brethren, the Master will take care of the great light-house: let us keep the lower lights burning!—D. L. Moody.

Bring your tithes into the storehouse (920)
Barbara Stoddart (1865-1915)

Published in *The War Cry*, 28 October 1893, headed: 'Self-

Denial Song'. The fourth verse was revised for *The Song Book of The Salvation Army*, 1953.

Burning, burning, brightly burning (206)
John Gowans (*b* 1934)

From the musical *Spirit!* where it was sung when the disciples, after waiting and praying for the Holy Spirit, began to discover the presence and power of the Spirit in their lives. A pilot production of the musical was introduced at the Regent Hall, London, on 23 July 1973, and the complete version was presented in the Kelvin Hall, Glasgow, during the Scottish Congress, on 2 September 1974.

But can it be that I should prove (714)
verses: Charles Wesley (1707-88)
chorus: Anonymous

These verses are from the last of a group of hymns published under the heading 'In Temptation', in volume 1 of the author's *Hymns and Sacred Poems*, 1749. The third and fifth verses of the original have been omitted. The chorus appeared anonymously in *Salvation Army Music*, 1900, compiled by William Booth, where it was linked with the hymn 'O glorious hope of perfect love' by Charles Wesley.

By the peaceful shores of Galilee (680)
Sidney E. Cox (1887-1975)

Appeared anonymously in *The War Cry*, 8 October 1927, under the title: 'Follow thou Me', but later included in *The War Cry*, 13 April 1929, entitled 'Fishers of Men', when the author was named as 'Ensign Sidney Cox, USA'.

Children of Jerusalem (834)
John Henley (1800-42)

The original form of this song is not known. The version in the present Song Book is from *Sacred Melodies for Children*, 1843, compiled by C. H. Bateman, though verses 1 and 3 and the chorus appeared earlier in *A Selection of Hymns and Poetry*, 1838, with two other verses and a second chorus. (Another version, with five verses and the chorus, was included in *Memorials of the Rev John Henley*, 1856, edited by John G. Avery.)

Children, sing for gladness (835)
James Lainchbury (1861-?)

Appeared in *The Little Soldier*, 20 May 1886, with the title: 'Children sing for God', and signed: 'J. Lainchbury'.

Christ for the world, we sing (825)
Samuel Wolcott (1813-86)

Written on 7 February 1869 on the way home from a meeting of the Young Men's Christian Associations of Ohio. The theme was suggested by the YMCA motto over the pulpit, 'Christ for the World, and the World for Christ'. The song was apparently included in *Songs for the New Life*, 1869, compiled by Darius E. Jones, and in *Songs of Devotion*, 1870, compiled by W. H. Doane.

Christ is alive! Let Christians sing (142)
Brian Wren (*b* 1936)

Written for Easter Day, 14 April 1968, as a response to the assassination of Dr Martin Luther King a few days earlier. The author wanted to enable the congregation at Hockley, Essex (where he was the minister), to celebrate Easter with truth and integrity, in words that could be more widely applied. Verses 3 and 4 emphasise God's majestic and universal sovereignty and Christ's presence with the believer, and thus his involvement in everyday life. The hymn was published in a Lutheran collection *Sing!*, 1969, and later in *New Church Praise*, 1975. The fifth verse was rewritten in 1978, partly to remove the masculine metaphor from the last line, but more significantly to reflect the dynamism of the Holy Spirit. The revised version, entitled 'The crucified Lord', was included in the author's *Faith Looking Forward*, 1983.

Christ is our corner-stone (940)
Anonymous
translated by John Chandler (1806-76)

The Latin hymn 'Urbs beata Hierusalem' is found in manuscripts dating from the 10th and 11th centuries, though it may have originated earlier. John Chandler translated the Latin text from the *Parisian Breviary*, 1736, and his translation, in two parts, was included in *The Hymns of the Primitive Church*, 1837. The second part, beginning 'Christ is our corner-stone' was headed 'Dedication of a Church. Evensong.' The concluding verse (a doxology) has now been omitted. The last four lines of each verse were altered and re-arranged as two lines for *Salvation Army Songs*, 1930.

Christ of Glory, Prince of Peace (479)
Colin Fairclough (b 1937)

Written while the author was the corps officer at Salisbury Citadel in Rhodesia, for music composed by the corps bandmaster. The bandmaster initially asked for some verses for which he could compose his first hymn tune. After hearing the music, the author felt that his words were unworthy of the melody, and later the bandmaster's tune became the inspiration for this song, 'Christ of Glory'. It was first sung in a Sunday morning meeting at Salisbury Citadel and was printed in the second volume of a history of Salisbury Citadel. In the absence of the original melody the author said that his personal choice would be Eric Ball's tune 'Child of Mary' (*Christmas Praise* 36), or the tune 'Jesus, Saviour, pilot me'.

Christ of self-denial (921)
William J. Pearson (1832-92)

Appeared in *The War Cry*, 19 September 1891, shortly before the Self-Denial Week that year: 27 September-3 October 1891. Headed 'Self-Denial Song', it originally began: 'God of self-denial, Thou for help dost call'. Subsequently, it has been altered considerably, particularly for *The Song Book of The Salvation Army*, 1953, when the third verse was rewritten and the fourth verse and chorus were omitted.

Christ the Lord is risen today (143)
Charles Wesley (1707-88)

Published by John and Charles Wesley in *Hymns and Sacred Poems*, 1739, with the title 'Hymn for Easter Day'. The present Song Book includes verses 1-5 from the original eleven verses.

Christ, whose glory fills the skies (412)
Charles Wesley (1707-88)

Verses 1, 3 and 4, entitled 'Morning Hymn', appeared in *Hymns and Sacred Poems*, 1740, published by John and Charles Wesley. Verse 2 was the second verse of another hymn in the same book, which began:

> Lord, how long, how long shall I
> Lift my weary eyes in pain?

This hymn, based on Psalm 143:6, was headed 'My soul gaspeth for thee, as a thirsty land'. John Wesley combined the verse

'O disclose thy lovely face' with the second and third verses of the 'Morning Hymn' in *A Collection of Hymns for the Use of the People called Methodists*, 1780. The present Song Book restores the original version, 'Radiancy', in verse 4, line 3.

Christians awake, salute the happy morn (78)
John Byrom (1692-1763)

Apparently written in 1749 as a Christmas present for the author's daughter Dorothy (1730-97). The original manuscript of the poem, in 52 lines, had the note 'for Dolly' alongside the title 'Christmas Day'. A revised version, with 48 lines, was published in the *Manchester Mercury*, 19 December 1752, and was later included in *Miscellaneous Poems by John Byrom*, 1773. The verses in the present Song Book are unaltered from *The Song Book of the Salvation Army*, 1953.

Come and rejoice with me (311)
Elisabeth Charles (1828-96)

Published under the title 'Eureka', in the third part of the author's *The Three Wakings, with Hymns and Songs*, 1859. It is sometimes dated 1846. The fourth, sixth and seventh verses of the original have been omitted.

Come, comrades dear, who love the Lord (312)
Anonymous

Originally beginning 'Come, brethren dear, who know the Lord', this was the second part of a hymn 'The Lord's into his Garden come', in *A Collection of Spiritual Songs, Used in the Great Revival, at the Camp Meetings, in America*, 1806, compiled by Lorenzo Dow. The second half of verse 2 and the first half of verse 3 have now been omitted.

Come, every soul by sin oppressed (231)
John H. Stockton (1813-77)

Five verses, with the chorus 'Come to Jesus', appeared in *Notes of Joy*, 1869, compiled by Mrs J. F. Knapp, and later in the author's *Salvation Melodies No. 1*, 1874. The present form of the chorus is from *Gospel Hymns and Sacred Songs*, 1875, compiled by P. P. Bliss and Ira D. Sankey. Verses 4 and 5 of the original have been omitted from the Song Book.

Come, gracious Spirit, heavenly dove (190)
Simon Browne (1680-1732)

Appeared in the author's *Hymns and Spiritual Songs*, 1720,

in seven verses, beginning:

> Come, Holy Spirit, heav'nly Dove,
> My sinful maladies remove;
> Be Thou my light, be Thou my guide,
> O'er every thought and step preside.

Later, a revised version, with five verses, was included in the *Collection of Hymns adapted to Public Worship*, 1769, edited by John Ash and Caleb Evans, but this was altered subsequently by other editors, as indicated in Julian's *Dictionary of Hymnology*, page 246. The version in the present Song Book is from *Salvation Army Songs*, 1930.

Come, Holy Ghost, all-quickening fire (207)
Charles Wesley (1707-88)

Published by John and Charles Wesley in *Hymns and Sacred Poems*, 1739, with the title 'Hymn to the Holy Ghost'. The present Song Book omits the third verse of the original and the sixth verse, which was the same as the first.

Come, Holy Ghost, all sacred fire (208)
Francis Bottome (1823-94)

Included in *Gospel Hymns*, 1872, compiled by R. P. Smith.

Come, Holy Ghost, our hearts inspire (651)
Charles Wesley (1707-88)

Published under the heading 'Before reading the Scriptures' in John and Charles Wesley's *Hymns and Sacred Poems*, 1740. It was the third hymn in a group of three hymns addressed to the Father, the Son and the Holy Spirit.

Come, Holy Spirit, thou guest of the soul (209)
Albert E. Mingay (b 1904)

Written at the request of Brigadier Wilfred Kitching (Divisional Commander, South Yorks Division) for the tune 'Hail Calvary', which Commissioner Charles Rich brought from Sweden for use in officers' councils when he became British Commissioner in 1935. The author (who was then a corps officer in Sheffield) said that he was asked to write some words about the Holy Spirit for a holiness meeting at Sheffield Citadel. He took a long walk to memorise the melody and, thinking of Commissioner Brengle's book *The Guest of the Soul*, wrote the song, which was introduced at the holiness meeting on the following Thursday. Subsequently it was printed in a booklet of songs for officers' councils, and later appeared under the title 'Come to my heart today' in *The Officers' Review*, January-February 1936, with the footnote 'Written for and sung in the 1935 Field Councils of the British Territory'.

Come in, my Lord, come in (562)
W. Bramwell Booth (1856-1929)

Written in six minutes while the author was waiting at Aldersgate Street Station for a train home to Hadley Wood. Apparently, he missed the previous train because someone held the carriage door closed from inside. The song, entitled 'Come in, my Lord', was printed in *The War Cry*, 14 April 1881, to be sung to the tune: 'A Life on the Ocean Wave'.

Come, join our Army, to battle we go (681)
William J. Pearson (1832-92)

Entitled 'Song of the Salvation Army', in *The Salvationist*, 1 February 1879, where it was signed 'Bradford. W. J. Pearson', and then included in a booklet, *Hosanna Songs of The Salvation Army*, 6 July 1879, with the title: 'Our Marching Song'. The author is said to have written the song after hearing the town hall chimes in Bradford play the tune 'Ring the bell, watchman', but the town clerk, writing from Bradford in 1965, said that the carillon which opened in 1873 did not include this tune.

Come, let us all unite to sing (43)
Anonymous

According to the *Dictionary of American Hymnology* files, this song appeared in *Millennial Praises*, 1812, compiled by Seth Wells, published in Hancock, Massachusetts. Five verses were later included in the *Methodist Revival Hymn Book*, 1858, and *The Christian Mission Hymn Book*, 1870, compiled by William Booth. The fourth verse of this version has now been omitted from the Song Book. The words have sometimes been incorrectly attributed to Howard Kingsbury (1842-78) who arranged the music of this song in *Happy Voices*, 1865.

Come, let us join our cheerful songs (57)
verses: Isaac Watts (1674-1748)
chorus: Anonymous

The verses, headed 'Christ Jesus the Lamb of God, worshipped by all the Creation; Revelation 5:11-13', appeared in the first part of the author's *Hymns and Spiritual Songs*, 1707. The fourth verse of the original has now been omitted.

The chorus was linked with a verse of the hymn 'See Israel's gentle Shepherd stands' in *The Juvenile Harmonist, A Selection of Tunes and Pieces for Children,* 1843, arranged by Thomas Clark, of Canterbury.

Come, let us use the grace divine (784)
Charles Wesley (1707-88)

Based on the text 'Come, and let us join ourselves to the Lord' (Jeremiah 50:5), and published in the author's *Short Hymns on Select Passages of the Holy Scriptures,* 1762. Originally written in three eight-line verses, it was divided into six four-line verses, in *A Collection of Hymns for the Use of the People called Methodists,* 1780, compiled by John Wesley. The present version omits the fifth and sixth of these verses. The hymn has been associated with the annual covenant services in the Methodist Church since the days of John Wesley.

Come, my soul, thy suit prepare (563)
John Newton (1725-1807)

One of three hymns related to the text 'Ask what I shall give thee' (1 Kings 3:5) in part 1 of the *Olney Hymns,* 1779. (In the first edition the heading incorrectly refers to 2 Samuel.) The fifth and seventh verses of the original have been omitted.

Come, O come with me where love is beaming (232)
Anonymous

Published in *The Wells of Salvation,* 1881, compiled by John R. Sweney and William J. Kirkpatrick, where the words were apparently attributed to Mrs Howard Anderson.

Come, Saviour Jesus, from above (480)
Antoinette Bourignon (1616-80)
translation attributed to John Wesley (1703-91)

The French hymn 'Venez, Jesus, mon Salutaire' was written in about 1640, expressing the author's determination to dedicate her life to Christ, after refusing to marry the husband her father had chosen for her. The hymn was published in her *Works,* in 1686. The translation, entitled 'Renouncing all for Christ', appeared in *Hymns and Sacred Poems,* 1739, published by John and Charles Wesley, and was later revised in *A Collection of Hymns for the Use of the People called Methodists,* 1780, edited by John Wesley. Although the translation is usually attributed to John Wesley, it was included in *Miscellaneous Poems by John Byrom,* Volume 2, 1773, thus creating some uncertainty about its authorship.

Come, shout and sing, make Heaven ring (798)
James C. Bateman (1854-88)

The song, entitled 'White as Snow' by J. C. Bateman, Hull, appeared in *The War Cry*, 20 October 1881, to be sung to the tune: 'I traced her little footsteps in the snow'. Several lines have been altered and the original third verse has been omitted.

Come, sinners, to Jesus, no longer delay (233)
William Jefferson (1806-70)

Written for the tune of the Chartists' song 'The Lion of Freedom' in about 1842, when the author was Primitive Methodist minister in Leicester. It was apparently first printed on a circuit plan and was later included in various revival hymn books. There were six verses in *Richard Weaver's Hymn Book*, New and enlarged edition, 1861, and *The Revival Hymn Book: Second Series*, 1864, and four verses in *The Primitive Methodist Revival Hymn Book*, 1861.

Come, sinners, to the gospel feast (234)
Charles Wesley (1707-88)

Published with the title 'The Great Supper' (Luke 14:16-24) in *Hymns for those that seek and those that have Redemption in the Blood of Jesus Christ*, 1747. The present Song Book includes verses 1, 2, 20 and 21 from the 24 verses of the original.

Come, thou all-inspiring Spirit (210)
Charles Wesley (1707-88)

From a group of hymns headed 'For a Family of Believers' in the author's *Hymns for the Use of Families, and on various occasions*, 1767.

Come, thou almighty King (219)
Anonymous

Appeared anonymously on a four-page tract bound with a copy of *A Collection of Hymns for Social Worship*, Eighth edition, 1759, compiled by George Whitefield, now in the British Library. Headed 'An Hymn to the Trinity', it has sometimes been attributed to Charles Wesley because the other hymn on the tract ('Jesu, let Thy pitying Eye') was written by him. However, this hymn is not in a metre used by John or Charles Wesley and it has not been found in any of their publications. The second verse of the original has now been omitted.

Come, thou burning Spirit, come (481)
                              Charles W. Fry (1838-82)
   Published in *The War Cry*, 26 May 1881, with the heading: 'Come Thou Burning Spirit Come'. The chorus now appears as in *Salvation Army Songs*, 1899.

Come, thou everlasting Spirit (191)
                              Charles Wesley (1707-88)
   Published by John and Charles Wesley in *Hymns on the Lord's Supper*, 1745, originally in two eight-line verses.

Come, thou Fount of every blessing (313)
                        verses: Robert Robinson (1735-90)
                              chorus: Louise M. Rouse
   An entry in a Church Book kept by Robert Robinson said that this hymn was published in 1758 by Mr Wheatley of Norwich. This publication has not been traced, though subsequently the hymn, with four eight-line verses, was included in *A Collection of Hymns used by the Church of Christ in Angel-Alley, Bishopsgate*, 1759, and *A Collection of Hymns, for the Use of the Hearers of the Apostles*, 1777. Three eight-line verses were in *A Collection of Psalms and Hymns*, 1760, compiled by Martin Madan. The chorus is from the song 'Precious Saviour, thou hast saved me', by Louise M. Rouse, which appeared in *Winnowed Hymns: A Collection of Sacred Songs*, 1873, edited by C. C. McCabe and D. T. Macfarlan.

Come, thou long-expected Jesus (79)
                        verses: Charles Wesley (1707-88)
                              chorus: Anonymous
   The verses are from the author's pamphlet *Hymns for the Nativity of Our Lord*, c 1744. The chorus, linked with these verses, appeared in *The Young People's Song Book of The Salvation Army*, 1963, *Christmas Praise*, 1963, and *The Salvation Army Tune Book Supplement No. 2*, 1963, for the tune 'Sweet chiming bells'.

Come to the Saviour, make no delay (235)
                              George F. Root (1820-95)
   Published with the title 'Come to the Savior' in *The Prize: A Collection of Songs, Hymns, Chants, Anthems and Concert Pieces, for the Sunday School*, 1870, compiled by G. F. Root.

Come with happy faces (836)
                               Fanny Crosby (1820-1915)
   This song, entitled 'Come with Happy Faces', was included in *Junior Christian Endeavor Songs*, 1893, compiled by Ira D. Sankey, John Willis Baer and William Shaw, and in *The Christian Choir*, Revised and enlarged edition, 1896, compiled by Ira D. Sankey and James McGranahan.

Come, with me visit Calvary (413)
         verses and second chorus: John Lawley (1859-1922)
                 first chorus: James C. Bateman (1854-88)
   While walking from Farringdon Street station to National Headquarters at the north end of Blackfriars Bridge, the author passed a public house near Smithfield Market. Seeing drunken men and women outside, he thought of God's power to save to the uttermost. Mrs Carpenter, in her biography *Commissioner John Lawley*, said that he wrote three verses and the chorus when he arrived at the office, and added the last verse at home in the evening, as he was putting his sons to bed. He sang the song on 17 January 1893 at a meeting in Edinburgh led by the British Commissioner (Commissioner T. Henry Howard) and the chorus appeared in *The War Cry*, 28 January 1893, in a report of that meeting. The same issue of *The War Cry* also printed the complete song, with the title 'An Uttermost Salvation', but with the chorus 'To the utmost He saves'. Richard Slater said that when the song was submitted for publication objection was raised to the word 'uttermost' which had an extra syllable for which there was no note in the tune. The author said that he could sing an extra note and that he was not bound to make the words fit the tune as he found it. Later, with the chorus 'To the uttermost he saves', the song was included in *The War Cry*, 25 February 1893; *The Salvation Soldier's Song Book*, 1893; and *The Musical Salvationist*, June Supplement 1893. The alternative chorus is from a song by Captain J. C. Bateman, entitled 'Calvary's Stream', in *The Musical Salvationist*, December 1886.

Come, ye disconsolate, where'er ye languish (236)
                    verses 1 and 2: Thomas Moore (1779-1852)
                                      verse 3: Anonymous
   Verses 1 and 2 are from the second number of *A Series of Sacred Songs, Duetts and Trios*, 1824, by Thomas Moore, with music composed and selected by Sir John Stevenson and the author. The third verse appeared in *Salvation Army Songs*,

1899 (with another verse which has now been omitted). The verses were altered to their present form in *The Song Book of The Salvation Army,* 1953.

Come, ye thankful people, come (924)
Henry Alford (1810-71)

Originally appeared under the heading 'After Harvest' in *Psalms and Hymns,* 1844, selected by the author. With minor alterations it was included in *The Poetical Works of Henry Alford,* Fourth edition, 1865, but was then more extensively revised for *The Year of Praise,* 1867, edited by Henry Alford. (There were only four verses, not seven as incorrectly stated in Julian's *Dictionary of Hymnology,* 1907.) Subsequently the author's final version appeared in *The Poetical Works of Henry Alford,* Fifth edition, 1868, with a footnote referring to the unauthorised revisions made by other editors: 'This hymn having been in various collections much disfigured by alterations made without the author's consent, he gives notice that this, which is printed here, is his latest revision, and the form which he wishes to be used in future.'

Come, ye that love the Lord (314)
Isaac Watts (1674-1748)

Published in the second part of the author's *Hymns and Spiritual Songs,* 1707, with the heading 'Heavenly Joy on Earth'. Originally there were ten four-line verses, beginning:

> Come, we that love the Lord,
> And let our Joys be known;
> Join in a Song with sweet Accord,
> And thus surround the Throne.

The original second verse, now omitted, includes the memorable lines:

> Religion never was design'd
> To make our Pleasures less.

Come ye yourselves apart and rest awhile (564)
Edward H. Bickersteth (1825-1906)

Published while the author was vicar of Christ Church, Hampstead, in *Songs in the House of Pilgrimage* (a booklet of five hymns) and in *The Hymnal Companion to the Book of Common Prayer,* Revised and enlarged edition, 1877, where it was headed: 'And Jesus said unto them, Come ye yourselves apart into a desert place, and rest a while' (Mark 6:31). The fourth verse of the original has now been omitted.

Commit thou all thy griefs (715)
Paulus Gerhardt (1607-76)
translated by John Wesley (1703-91)

The German hymn 'Befiehl du deine Wege' appeared in the Frankfurt edition of Johann Crüger's *Praxis pietatis melica*, 1656. (The opening words of the 12 verses of the original hymn formed an acrostic on Luther's version of Psalm 37:5.) The translation, entitled 'Trust in providence', was published by John and Charles Wesley in *Hymns and Sacred Poems*, 1739. The verses 'Give to the winds thy fears' (721) are from the second half of the translation.

Compared with Christ, in all beside (565)
Augustus M. Toplady (1740-78)

Published in *The Gospel-Magazine, or Spiritual Library, designed to promote Scriptural Religion*, Volume 7, 1772, with the title 'Christ All in All'. Originally there were three eight-line verses, beginning:

> Compar'd with Christ, in all beside
> No comeliness I see:

The verses included in the present Song Book appeared in *Salvation Army Songs*, 1930, but have since been altered by successive song book editors.

Courage, brother, do not stumble (716)
Norman Macleod (1812-72)

Published under the heading 'Trust in God, and do the right', in *The Edinburgh Christian Magazine*, January 1857, where it was described as 'A Psalm for the New Year'. It was originally written in seven four-line verses, beginning 'Courage, brothers!' The present Song Book includes verses 1, 2 and 7 of the original, with the first verse repeated.

Crown him with many crowns (156)
verses 1, 3 and 4: Matthew Bridges (1800-94)
verse 2: Godfrey Thring (1823-1903)

The verses by Matthew Bridges are from his *Hymns of the Heart*, Second edition, 1851, part of a hymn with six verses, headed 'In Capite Ejus, Diademata Multa. Apoc. xix. 12' ['On his head were many crowns'—Revelation 19:12]. These verses have been slightly altered and rearranged. The verse by Godfrey Thring is the fourth verse of a hymn, also with six verses, headed 'Christ Ascended', in his *Hymns and Sacred Lyrics*, 1874.

Dark shadows were falling (237)
Evangeline Booth (1865-1950)

In *Songs of the Evangel*, 1927, the author wrote:

> Returning to my quarters late one November evening, after battling with cold, sleet and misery, dressed in rags that I might get nearer to the hearts and lives of the poorest of those with whom I mingled in the slums of London, I vainly struggled to banish from my mind and pitying heart the awful scenes I had looked upon. Men, women, and children with broken lives, broken hearts and broken characters; hopeless and helpless, trapped like animals at bay. One picture I could not banish: the beautiful face and golden head of the little fifteen-year-old mother, appearing in the filthy, dark, box-like room as a jewel amid ruins; the fast and bitter tears falling on the human mite dead in her arms; the despair in the frightened blue eyes as she said: 'Look, there is no place for us in life, or in death; no place for the baby, or for me. Where can I hide the baby? Where can I hide myself?' One o'clock the following morning I wrote the song which has winged its way all around the world:
>
>> The wounds of Christ are open,
>>   Sinner, they were made for thee;
>> The wounds of Christ are open,
>>   There for refuge flee.

The song, entitled 'The Wounds of Christ' was published in *The Musical Salvationist*, March 1895, and was sung at the Royal Albert Hall, London, on 11 March 1895, at the welcome meeting for William Booth, returning from his Jubilee Campaign in the United States and Canada. It was then included in *The Officer*, March 1895, with the heading 'The Albert Hall Favorite'. The third verse of the original has now been omitted.

Day by day the manna fell (566)
Josiah Conder (1789-1855)

Published in *The Congregational Hymn Book*, 1836, with the heading: 'Give us day by day our daily bread' (Luke 11:3), and then included in the author's *The Choir and the Oratory; or Praise and Prayer*, 1837, where it was the fourth part of 'The Lord's Prayer in Six Parts'. The fifth verse of the original has been omitted.

Day of judgment! Day of wonders (875)
John Newton (1725-1807)

Written in 1774 and published with the heading 'The day of judgment' in the second part of the *Olney Hymns*, 1779. There were seven verses. The author apparently said that the hymn took him 'the most of two days to finish'. In his diary for Sunday 26 June 1775 he noted: 'Spoke in the evening from a hymn on the day of judgment'. The third verse was revised for *The Song Book of The Salvation Army*, 1953, and the fourth, fifth and seventh verses of the original have been omitted.

Dear Lord and Father of mankind (567)
John Greenleaf Whittier (1807-92)

From the poem 'The Brewing of Soma' published in *The Atlantic Monthly*, April 1872. There were 17 verses, beginning:

> The fagots blazed, the caldron's smoke
> Up through the green wood curled;
> 'Bring honey from the hollow oak,
> Bring milky sap', the brewers spoke,
> In the childhood of the world.

Soma was used as an ingredient of an intoxicating drink brewed in the Indus valley about 2000 BC to stimulate ecstatic and frenzied emotions among the worshippers of the Vedic god, Indra. In the 11th verse of the poem, the author expressed his concern that similar hysterical and fanatical scenes were still occurring in Christian worship during the 19th century:

> And yet the past comes round again,
> And new doth old fulfil;
> In sensual transports wild as vain
> We brew in many a Christian fane
> The heathen Soma still!

The poem concludes with a prayer for forgiveness (verses 12-17) from which the present Song Book omits verse 15. Verses from this prayer were first used as a hymn in *Congregational Hymns*, 1884, edited by W. Garrett Horder.

Dear Lord, I do surrender (482)
William Walker (1871-99)

Appeared in *The War Cry*, 26 May 1894, where the author was described as 'Candidate W. Walker, Selkirk'. The song originally began:

> Dear Lord, I do surrender
> Myself for aye to Thee.

Dear Lord, I lift my heart to thee (717)
John C. Izzard (*b* 1924)

Referring to this song, written in the early 1950s, the author wrote:

> Arising from my own experience in comparative youth, this song is a call for help when life, for any reason, becomes difficult and

painfully bleak—beyond our own powers to redeem. Health is undermined, and we fear for our ability even to appear to cope. One has to lean fully upon facts that our feelings would deny, that God's presence and power are not conditional upon our continual awareness of them, and that although our emotional reactions fluctuate and circumstances alter, God's love and care are forever dependable.

It was published under the title 'Thy Presence and Thy Power' in the *Assurance* magazine, September 1955, and then, slightly altered, in *The Musical Salvationist*, September-October 1958. Later it was included in *Keep Singing!*, 1976, without the chorus:

> Thy will be done, whate'er it be,
> I know Thy way is best for me;
> No light I need, no other sign,
> If I may feel Thy hand in mine.

Now, the three eight-line verses have been divided into six four-line verses.

Deep were the scarlet stains of sin (176)
Olive L. Holbrook (1895-1986)

Published in *The War Cry*, 17 February 1934, with the title 'A Testimony', and later included in *Songs and Choruses for The British Commissioner's Officers' Councils (No. 2)*, 1948, and *The Song Book of The Salvation Army*, 1953. The author gave a copy of the words to the future Commissioner Dorothy Muirhead, who sang them to the tune 'Passing By' when she was on the staff of the International Training College, 1927-40. Although Mrs Holbrook said in 1952 that she had forgotten about the song until she saw it in a booklet of songs for officers' councils, she later said that she wrote it after hearing the tune 'Passing By' on the radio, when she was at home ironing clothes.

Depth of mercy! Can there be (286)
Charles Wesley (1707-88)

Published by John and Charles Wesley in *Hymns and Sacred Poems*, 1740, with the title 'After a Relapse into Sin'. From the original 13 verses the Song Book includes verses 1, 2, 8 and 9. The chorus, which appeared in its present form in *Salvation Army Songs*, 1899, has been adapted from the concluding lines of verse 9:

> God is love: I know, I feel;
> Jesus weeps! but loves me still!

Descend, O Holy Spirit, thou (211)
Arnold Brown (*b* 1913)

Written for the International Congress held in London, 30 June-9 July 1978, and printed on a leaflet *Songs for use during the International Congress*, 1978. In 1986 the author wrote:

> I felt the leadership of this great series of meetings to be an immense responsibility, and during the months of preparation preceding the Congress, I looked constantly to God for inspiration and direction. One evening, while praying for the spiritual success of the Congress, the words of the song flowed together, expressing a complete dependence upon the Holy Spirit's presence and power. Those who attended the memorable gatherings will know that the prayer was answered in remarkable ways.

Do you know the song that the angels sang (80)
A. P. Cobb

Published in *Heart Songs*, 1893, by F. A. Fillmore, and then included in *The Christian Choir*, Revised and enlarged, 1896, compiled by Ira D. Sankey and James McGranahan.

Do you sometimes feel that no one truly knows you (238)
John Gowans (*b* 1934)

From the musical *Take-Over Bid*, which was introduced on 1 October 1967 during corps officers' annual councils at Clacton-on-Sea, and was then presented at Reading Town Hall on 14 October 1967, and at Acton Town Hall, on 21 October 1967. Julie, one of the young salvationists, sings this song, entitled 'Someone Cares', when an elderly couple, Darby and Joan, say how difficult it is for them to make new friends.

Don't assume that God's dismissed you from his mind (44)
John Gowans (*b* 1934)

From the musical *Hosea*, previewed during officers' councils at Bognor Regis, in October 1969, and then presented at Lewisham Town Hall, 12 November 1969. Hosea, speaking of God's love and faithfulness, introduces this song with the words: 'Have you not known? Have you not heard? I will heal their unfaithfulness, saith the Lord' (see Isaiah 40:21 and 28, and Hosea 14:4).

Down at the cross where my Saviour died (315)
Elisha A. Hoffman (1839-1929)

Entitled 'Down at the Cross', this song appeared in *Spiritual Songs for Gospel Meetings and the Sunday School*, 1878, compiled by the author and J. H. Tenney, with the note: 'From *Dew of Hermon* by permission'.

Down in the valley with my Saviour I would go (483)
William O. Cushing (1823-1902)

The author said, 'I wrote this hymn in 1878; longing to give up all for Christ, who had given His life for me, I wanted to be willing to lay everything at His feet, with no wish but to do His will, to live henceforth only for His glory. Out of this feeling came the hymn "Follow On".' It was published in *Sacred Songs and Solos, No. 2*, 1881, compiled by Ira D. Sankey, and later appeared anonymously in *The War Cry*, 23 December 1882.

Drawn to the cross which thou hast blest (287)
Genevieve M. Irons (1855-1928)

Written in May 1880 and published in the *Sunday Magazine*, October 1880. Afterwards it was included in the author's *Corpus Christi*, 1884, a manual for Holy Communion. The verses were incorrectly attributed to Albert Orsborn in early printings of the 1986 Song Book.

Each day is a gift supernal (666)
Mads Nielsen (1879-1958)
translated by Flora Larsson (*b* 1904)

The Danish song 'Hver dag er en sjaelen gave', was translated for the present Song Book, and was accepted by the Song Book Council in March 1982.

Each little flower that opens
See: All things bright and beautiful (25)

Earnestly seeking to save and to heal (484)
Albert Orsborn (1886-1967)

Appeared in *The Officer*, May 1922, entitled: 'Earnestly, Constantly, Faithfully'. The author was then Divisional Commander, Norwich Division.

Earthly kingdoms rise and fall (799)
Will J. Brand (1889-1977)

The author said that in March 1942 Colonel Bramwell Coles wrote to him enclosing the trio of a new march 'Defenders of the Faith', and asked: 'Do you think that the title would stir your thoughts to a set of words?' Within a few days the words were written, and the song was later published in *The Musical Salvationist,* January-February 1946, under the title 'Defenders of the Faith'. The last line of each verse was altered slightly for *The Song Book of The Salvation Army,* 1953 (to fit tunes in 7.7.7.7.D. metre), and the chorus was omitted.

Emblem of a thousand battles (777)
Doris N. Rendell (*b* 1896)

This song was apparently written at the request of Colonel Bramwell Coles for a special meeting in London which had to be cancelled because of war conditions. It was published in *Special Songs for Young People's Anniversaries and Festal Occasions* No 2, New Series, 1940, under the title 'Our Glorious Flag'. Later the author wrote:

> It is a theme very near to my heart—our Army flag—that precious banner! Under the symbolic yellow, red and blue, we are called to the deep inner meaning of the precious Blood of our Lord Jesus Christ; challenged again to the necessity . . . to live holy lives; realising, too, how imperative is the empowering of the Holy Spirit. . . . Under its folds wanderers have been gathered in, 'neath its folds our children have been dedicated, our beloved dead have rested. It has led our warriors into places of danger, victory, tribulation and triumph. All these thoughts were in my mind when writing this song.

The chorus was omitted when the verses were included in *The Song Book of The Salvation Army,* 1953, and the second verse was altered by the Song Book Council in 1981 for the present Song Book.

Equip me for the war (568)
Charles Wesley (1707-88)

This was the second hymn entitled 'The Lord's Controversy' in *Hymns on God's Everlasting Love,* Second series, 1742. Originally there were 26 eight-line verses, beginning 'O all-atoning Lamb'. The present Song Book includes verses 2, 3 and 7 of the original.

Eternal Father, strong to save (569)
William Whiting (1825-78)

Written in 1860, originally beginning:

> O Thou who bidd'st the ocean deep
> Its own appointed limits keep,
> Thou Who dost bind the restless wave,
> Eternal Father, strong to save,
>   O hear us, when we cry to Thee
>   For all in peril on the sea.

The hymn was extensively revised by the compilers of *Hymns Ancient and Modern*, 1861, but was subsequently altered slightly by the author and other editors.

Eternal God, our song we raise (5)
Catherine Baird (1895-1984)

Written by request for the Salvation Army centenary celebrations in 1965, it was published that year in *Centennial Echoes, 1865-1965: A Centenary Year Souvenir*, and also in *The Musical Salvationist*, July 1965 (in a festival arrangement by Leslie Condon entitled 'A Song of Praise').

Eternal God, unchanging (6)
Albert E. Dalziel (1892-1974)

Published in Canada, in *Songs of Faith*, 1971, where it was entitled: 'A Hymn of Faith'.

Eternal Light! Eternal Light (414)
Thomas Binney (1798-1874)

Apparently written in 1826 at Newport, Isle of Wight, and later included in *The New Congregational Hymn Book*, 1859, with the heading 'God is light and in him is no darkness' (1 John 1:5). On an autograph copy of the hymn which the author transcribed from memory on 7 August 1856, he wrote: 'Composed thirty years ago while looking up at the sky, one brilliant star-light night.' Later (in notes provided for *Our Hymns: Their Authors and Origin*, 1866, by Josiah Miller) he said:

> It was written about forty years ago, and was set to music and published by Power, of the Strand, on behalf of some charitable object to which the profits went. It was some little time since set to music also by Mr Burnett, of Highgate. It has appeared, I believe, in one or two books of sacred poetry, and in a mutilated state in a hymn-book in America.

Eternal Source of every joy (925)
verses 1-4: Philip Doddridge (1702-51)
verse 5: Anonymous

The verses by Philip Doddridge, written 1 January 1736, are from a hymn 'For New-Year's Day', which was published posthumously in the author's *Hymns founded on Various Texts in the Holy Scriptures*, 1755, with the heading: 'The Year crowned with the divine Goodness. Psalm 65:11'. Verses 2, 6 and 7 of the original have now been omitted. The anonymous fifth verse in the present version appeared in *Salvation Army Songs,* 1930.

Fairest Lord Jesus (177)
Anonymous

The German hymn 'Schönster Herr Jesu' appeared anonymously in the *Münster Gesangbuch,* 1677. James Mearns, in Julian's *Dictionary of Hymnology,* page 1016, said that there is no evidence to support the statement sometimes made that it is a 12th-century crusaders' hymn. The translation of verses 1-3 is from *Church Chorals and Choir Studies,* 1850, by Richard S. Willis, and the fourth verse is apparently based on another translation, by Joseph A. Seiss, in the *Sunday School Book,* 1873, published in Philadelphia by the American Lutheran General Council.

Father, hear the prayer we offer (570)
Love M. Willis (1824-1908)

Apparently first published in *Psalms of Life,* 1857, and in *Tiffany's Monthly* in 1859, beginning: 'Father, hear the prayer I offer'. A revised version, headed 'The Prayer of Life', appeared anonymously in *Hymns of the Spirit,* 1864, compiled by Samuel Longfellow and Samuel Johnson. In this version there were four verses, but the third verse has now been omitted.

Father, I know that all my life (485)
Anna L. Waring (1823-1910)

Written at Clifton in 1846 and published in *A Selection of Scriptural Poetry,* Third edition, 1848, compiled by Lovell Squire. There were originally eight verses, headed 'My times are in Thy hand'. The present Song Book includes an altered version of verses 1, 2, 5, 8 and 4.

Father, lead me day by day (837)
John Page Hopps (1834-1911)

From the author's *Hymns, Chants and Anthems, for Public Worship,* 1877. The seventh verse of the original has been omitted.

Father, let me dedicate (916)
verses: Lawrence Tuttiett (1825-97)
chorus: Anonymous

In the author's *Germs of Thought on the Sunday Special*

Services, 1864, this was the second hymn for the Second Sunday after Christmas. It was headed 'The Circumcision. A Prayer for the New Year. Father, glorify Thy Name', and originally began:

> Father, let me dedicate
> All this year to Thee.

When set to the tune 'Love at home' in *Salvation Army Songs*, 1930, the verses were altered slightly (from 7.5.7.5.D. metre) and the chorus was added. The second verse of the original has now been omitted.

Father of love, of justice and of mercy (486)
Evangeline Booth (1865-1950)

Published under the title 'I bring Thee All' in the author's *Songs of the Evangel*, 1927, and in the new and enlarged edition, 1937, with the following notes:

> Out of the purple shadows of the Borderland God had called me back to life and service. I remember something of those days during which, semi-conscious, I hovered between two worlds. I had suffered so terribly and so long, and was broken in every fibre of my being. But as my blood quickened, as my eyes began to clear, and the fragrance of the lovely Spring breathed upon me through the open window, the precious reality of life was verified to me. Again to speak for Him, again to live for Him, again to win lost souls for Him! The pricelessness of the treasure overwhelmed me! With fingers that trembled I made my first effort upon the strings of my beloved harp, and the new consecration of my every faculty crystallized in the song: 'I Bring Thee All'.

Father, we for our children plead (791)
Thomas Hastings (1784-1872)

Included in the *Supplement to the Congregational Hymn Book*, 1873, and later in *Salvation Army Songs*, 1899.

Fight the good fight with all thy might (718)
John S. B. Monsell (1811-75)

Published as a hymn for the Nineteenth Sunday after Trinity, in the author's *Hymns of Love and Praise for the Church's Year*, 1863. It was headed 'Fight the good fight of faith, lay hold on eternal life' (1 Timothy 6:12). The third verse has been altered slightly by various editors and now appears as in *The Song Book of The Salvation Army*, 1953.

Fill thou my life, O Lord my God (7)
Horatius Bonar (1808-89)

This hymn, entitled 'Life's Praise', was printed in 12 four-line verses in the author's *Hymns of Faith and Hope*, Third series, 1866. The present Song Book includes verses 1, 2, 4, 5, 9, 10, 11 and 12, combined to form four eight-line verses.

Firm in thy strong control (571)
Anonymous

Probably printed on a song sheet for central holiness meetings at Clapton Congress Hall. The third verse is quoted in *The War Cry*, 10 May 1913, in an article, 'The Power of Congregational Singing', which describes the central holiness meetings led by Commissioner Thomas McKie. The complete song appears in *Salvation Army Songs*, 1930.

For all the saints who from their labours rest (876)
William Walsham How (1823-97)

Originally beginning 'For all Thy saints', it was published under the title 'Saints'-Day Hymn' in *Hymn for Saints' Days and Other Hymns*, 1864. There were 11 verses, headed 'A cloud of witnesses' (Hebrews 12:1). The present version includes verses 1, 2, 6, 8 and 10, as in *The Song Book of The Salvation Army*, 1953.

For ever with the Lord (877)
James Montgomery (1771-1854)

Published in *The Amethyst: or Christian's Annual for 1834*, and then included, with a few lines altered, in the author's *A Poet's Portfolio; or Minor Poems: in three books*, 1835, where it was headed: 'At Home in Heaven, 1 Thess. 4:17'. From the original 22 four-line verses, the 1986 Song Book includes verses 1-4 and 14-17, combined in pairs to form four eight-line verses.

For every rule of life required (785)
Dorothy O. Joy (1903-82)

Colonel Brindley Boon said (in 1987) that this song, based on the doctrines of The Salvation Army, was originally written in 11 verses for a special celebration of faith at a London corps. The author later reduced it to six verses when plans were being made to commemorate the centenary of the doctrines during the International Congress in 1978. Although the song was not used in the congress meetings (because a special setting of the doctrines was composed by Ray Steadman-Allen), it was accepted by the Song Book Council in 1981 for inclusion in the present Song Book.

For the beauty of the earth (28)
                              Folliott S. Pierpoint (1835-1917)
Published in *Lyra Eucharistica: Hymns and Verses on the Holy Communion, Ancient and Modern; with other poems*, Second edition, 1864, edited by Orby Shipley. It was entitled 'The Sacrifice of Praise', with the refrain (in verses 1-7) beginning 'Christ, our God, to Thee we raise'. Verses 6-8 have now been omitted, making the hymn suitable for occasions other than the Holy Communion.

For the mighty moving of thy Spirit (192)
                                           John Gowans (b 1934)
From the third section of the musical *Spirit!*, when the apostles came together for an 'Annual General Meeting' and sang this as a hymn of thanksgiving. After a pilot production of the musical at the Regent Hall, London, on 23 July 1973, the complete version was presented at the Kelvin Hall, Glasgow, on 2 September 1974, during the Scottish Congress.

For thine is the Kingdom, and thine is the power (951)
                    John Gowans (b 1934), based on Matthew 6:13
From the finale of the musical *Take-Over Bid*, which was introduced on 1 October 1967 during corps officers' councils at Clacton-on-Sea, Essex, and was then presented on 14 October 1967 at Reading Town Hall.

For those we love within the veil (878)
                                     W. Charter Piggott (1872-1943)
Apparently written in 1915 for a commemoration service at Whitefield's Tabernacle, in London. It was published in *Songs of Praise*, 1925, and *School Worship*, 1926. The third and sixth verses of the original have now been omitted.

For thy mercy and thy grace (937)
                                       Henry Downton (1818-85)
The author said that he wrote this hymn when he was an undergraduate at Trinity College, Cambridge. It was published in *The Church of England Magazine*, 7 January 1843, with the heading 'Hymn for the Commencement of the Year'. The second, fifth and seventh verses of the original have been omitted.

For thy sweet comfort in distress (719)
Doris N. Rendell (*b* 1896)
From *Songs of His Love*, a collection of the author's songs and poems published privately in about 1972.

For your holy book we thank you (856)
Ruth Carter (1900-82)
Written in about 1932 when the author (as leader of the junior department of the congregational Sunday-school at Buckhurst Hill, Essex) wanted a hymn to conclude a series of lessons on 'The Making of our Bible'. Five years later she gave it to the Graded School Adviser at the National Sunday School Union and it was published in the *Graded Schools Intermediate Quarterly*, 1937. The original version, beginning 'For Thy holy book we thank Thee', was altered for *Songs for Worship*, 1968, and the fourth verse was added, with the author's approval, for *The Australian Hymn Book*, 1977.

Forgive our sins as we forgive (572)
Rosamond E. Herklots (1905-87)
The author said: 'The idea for the hymn came to me when, digging up deeply-rooted docks in my nephew's garden, I found myself comparing them to deeply-rooted resentments in their cramping effect on the flowers near them'. She wrote the hymn on 22 June 1966 (her 61st birthday), while travelling by train from Plymouth to London. It was first published in the parish magazine of St Mary's Church, Bromley, Kent, and later, after extensive revision, was included in *100 Hymns for Today*, 1969, and *Hymns and Songs*, 1969.

Forth in thy name, O Lord, I go (667)
Charles Wesley (1707-88)
Entitled 'Before Work', in the first volume of the author's *Hymns and Sacred Poems*, 1749. It was No. 32 in a section headed 'Hymns for Believers'. The second and third verses of the original have now been omitted.

Forward! be our watchword (682)
Henry Alford (1810-71)
Written for the annual Festival of Parochial Choirs of the Canterbury Diocesan Union in Canterbury Cathedral on 6 June 1871. Apparently, the first hymn the author wrote for the occasion was considered unsuitable for a processional hymn, so he composed these verses in the cathedral as he walked

slowly along the route planned for the procession. There were originally eight verses, published in the Festival Book in 1871 and then in the *Life, Journals and Letters of Henry Alford*, 1873, with the heading 'Speak unto the children of Israel, that they go forward' (Exodus 14:15). The present Song Book includes verses 1, 3 and 4.

From every stain made clean (415)
Herbert H. Booth (1862-1926)

The author's sister, Emma Booth, sang this song at Scottish anniversary meetings in Glasgow, 28 November 1887, and it was published in *The Musical Salvationist*, March 1888.

From every stormy wind that blows (573)
Hugh Stowell (1799-1865)

Published under the title 'The Mercy Seat' in *The Winter's Wreath, a Collection of original contributions in Prose and Verse*, 1828. Slightly different versions appeared in *A Selection of Psalms and Hymns*, 1831, compiled by the author, and in his book *The Pleasure of Religion; with other poems*, 1832. The present version is derived mainly from these sources, but omits the fourth verse of the original:

> Ah! whither could we flee for aid,
> When tempted, desolate, dismay'd,
> Or how the hosts of hell defeat,
> Had suffering saints no mercy-seat?

From the heart of Jesus flowing (539)
Charles Coller (1863-1935)

Originally appeared under the title 'The Peace of God', with music by Pinsuti, in *The Musical Salvationist*, April 1914. There were three verses, beginning:

> Even as a river flowing
>   Onward to its native sea,
> Blessings from the Lord bestowing,
>   Cometh heaven's peace to me.

A revised version was included in *Salvation Army Songs*, 1930, with a chorus, which became the first half of verse 1 in *The Song Book of The Salvation Army*, 1953. The third verse was altered for the 1953 Song Book by Catherine Baird, at the request of the Song Book Revision Council.

Full salvation, full salvation (540)
Francis Bottome (1823-94)

Written in 1871. Three verses appeared in *Song Life, for*

Sunday Schools, 1872, compiled by Philip Phillips, and later the song was included in *Hymns of Consecration and Faith,* 1876, compiled by James Mountain, and *Songs of The Salvation Army,* 1878, compiled by William Booth, where there were five verses, as in the present Song Book.

Gentle arms of Jesus (792)
Flora Larsson (*b* 1904)

Written in 1973, with music by the author's son (now Colonel John Larsson), for the dedication of her grandson, Kevin Larsson, at Bromley, Kent, where it was sung by the young people's singing company. It was then published in *Songs for Young People's Anniversaries and Special Occasions,* No. 38, 1975, with the title 'The arms of Jesus'. The last two lines of each verse were omitted by the Song Book Council in 1980 so that the song could be sung to the tune 'Ruth'.

Gentle Jesus, meek and mild (793)
Charles Wesley (1707-88)

This was the first of a group of seven hymns for children in *Hymns and Sacred Poems,* 1742, by John and Charles Wesley. From the original 14 verses the present Song Book includes verses 1, 2, 13, 8, 9 and 14, slightly altered.

Give me a holy life (416)
Leslie Taylor-Hunt (1901-79)

The author said that he received the inspiration for this song while he was a cadet at Clapton, when General Bramwell Booth, speaking to the cadets about the beauty and possibility of holiness, said at the conclusion of a Spiritual Day: 'Remember, this blessing is a gift. It cannot be bought or earned or acquired in any other way. It is God's precious gift to the seeking soul.' The verses were completed a couple of years later and were first published as a poem, entitled 'Surrender', in *The Officer,* November 1924, beginning:

> God! for the Holy life,
> Radiant and free . . .

(Apparently the song was also included in a booklet of songs for use in officers' councils.) Later, a revised version (with a chorus) was published under the title 'Love's Surrender' in *The Musical Salvationist,* October 1928, with music by the author. In the same month the verses appeared in their present form in *The Officer,* October 1928, with the title 'Into Thy Hands'.

Give me a restful mind (574)
Frederick G. Hawkes (1869-1959)

Appeared in *The Musical Salvationist*, September-October 1946, under the title: 'My Petition', and then altered into regular short metre verses for *The Song Book of The Salvation Army*, 1953. The original chorus has now been omitted.

Give me the faith which can remove (720)
Charles Wesley (1707-88)

From a section headed 'Hymns for a Preacher of the Gospel' in volume 1 of the author's *Hymns and Sacred Poems*, 1749. There were eight verses, beginning:

> O that I was as heretofore
>   When first sent forth in Jesu's Name
> I rush'd thro' every open Door,
>   And cried to All, 'Behold the Lamb!'
> Seiz'd the poor trembling Slaves of Sin,
> And forc'd the Outcasts to come in.

With a few alterations, John Wesley included verses 3-7 in *A Collection of Hymns for the Use of the People called Methodists*, 1780, and the same verses are now in the present Song Book.

Give me the wings of faith to rise (879)
verses: Isaac Watts (1674-1748)
chorus: attributed to Robert Lowry (1826-99)

The verses, entitled 'The Examples of Christ and the Saints', appeared in the author's *Hymns and Spiritual Songs*, Second edition, 1709. The chorus was included in *Chapel Melodies*, 1868, edited by S. J. Vail and Robert Lowry, with verses beginning 'There is a realm where Jesus reigns', and was linked with the verses by Isaac Watts in *The Revivalist*, 1868, compiled by Joseph Hillman.

Give to Jesus glory (952)
W. H. Clark

From a song beginning 'From mountain top and dreary vale' in *The Wells of Salvation*, 1881, compiled by John R. Sweney and William J. Kirkpatrick.

Give to the winds thy fears (721)
Paulus Gerhardt (1607-76)
translated by John Wesley (1703-91)

The German hymn 'Befiehl du deine Wege' appeared in the Frankfurt edition of Johann Crüger's *Praxis pietatis melica*,

1656. The translation was entitled 'Trust in Providence' in *Hymns and Sacred Poems*, 1739, published by John and Charles Wesley. The verses 'Commit thou all thy griefs' (715) are from the first half of the translation.

Give us a day of wonders (575)
John Lawley (1859-1922)

Published in *The War Cry*, 26 November 1892, with the heading 'Special Song. Written in the train by Colonel Lawley on his way to assist in the opening of Rochdale Temple.' A fortnight earlier, *The War Cry*, 12 November 1892, had reported: 'Sunday 6th November: Still another new Citadel. Today Commissioner Howard unlocked the gate of a spacious hall for the Rochdale Corps. The opening services were very successful.' The second verse was altered by Catherine Baird for *The Song Book of The Salvation Army*, 1953, and the original third verse has been omitted.

Glorious things of thee are spoken (157)
John Newton (1725-1807)

Included in Book 1 of the *Olney Hymns*, 1779, with the heading 'Zion, or the City of God', and the scriptural reference Isaiah 33:27-28 (which apparently should have been Isaiah 33:20-21). The third and fourth verses of the original have now been omitted.

Glory to thee, my God, this night (671)
Thomas Ken (1637-1711)

Probably written before 1674 (with the morning hymn 'Awake, my soul, and with the sun') for the scholars of Winchester College. In *A Manual of Prayers for the Use of the Scholars of Winchester College*, 1674, the author wrote: 'Be sure to sing the Morning and Evening Hymn in your chamber devoutly . . .'. Apparently without his consent, the hymns were published in 1692 in a pamphlet headed 'A Morning and Evening Hymn', where the evening hymn had 13 verses. It was then included in Henry Playford's *Harmonia Sacra; or Divine Hymns and Dialogues*, The Second Book, 1693, in 11 verses, beginning 'All praise to Thee my God this night' (a variation commonly adopted in the United States). Another version, with 12 verses, appeared (with the author's morning and midnight hymns) in a pamphlet entitled *Three Hymns. By the Author of the Manual of Prayers for the Use of the Scholars of Winchester College*, 1694. Further details of these and other early versions are found in Julian's *Dictionary of Hymnology*, 1907, pp 617-622, 1537 and 1659.

Go, labour on, spend and be spent (683)
Horatius Bonar (1808-89)

Apparently written in 1836 to encourage his faithful helpers in Leith, it was published with the title 'Labour for Christ' in a small booklet *Songs for the Wilderness*, 1843. A revised version, entitled 'The Useful Life', appeared in the first series of the author's *Hymns of Faith and Hope*, 1857. The verses in the present Song Book are from this later version, omitting the fourth and eighth verses.

God be in my head (953)
Anonymous

Although a French version has been found dating from the late 15th century, the earliest known English version (with archaic spelling) is in a Book of Hours: *Hore beate marie virginis . . .*, printed in London in 1514.

God be with you till we meet again (954)
Jeremiah E. Rankin (1828-1904)

Written as 'a Christian goodbye' when the author was minister of the First Congregational Church, Washington, DC. He sent the first verse to two composers and later wrote the other verses for the tune by T. G. Tomer. The song was published in *Gospel Bells*, 1880, edited by J. W. Bischoff, Otis F. Presbrey, and the author.

God gave his Son for me (45)
Charles W. Fry (1838-82)

Included in *The Salvation Songster*, 1885 and then in the *Favourite Song Series No. 7*, 1886, where it was headed: 'God gave His Son for Me'. The second verse has been omitted.

God is keeping his soldiers fighting (800)
William J. Pearson (1832-92)

A song entitled 'When the Trumpet Sounds', with words and music by Herbert Booth, was published in *The Musical Salvationist*, August 1886. Apparently, when William Booth heard the song he commended the tune, but said to his son, Herbert, 'Why cannot we have some warlike words put to it; something about fighting and less about trumpets?' Herbert Booth could not get any inspiration, and passed the request to

William Pearson, who wrote new words for the tune. The new song was sung at Training Home anniversary meetings, 12-13 November 1887, and was later included in a booklet of *Songs of Love and Service,* 1888.

God is our light and God is our sunshine (316)
Richard Nuttall (1891-1946)

Apparently written while the author was on military service in France during the First World War. The song appeared in *The Musical Salvationist,* January 1918, where it was entitled: 'Sunshine'. The third verse has been omitted.

God is with us, God is with us (158)
Walter J. Mathams (1853-1931)

Written at the request of the National Council of Evangelical Free Churches, and apparently first sung at their congress in Nottingham, in 1896. Four verses were published in *The Christian Endeavour Hymnal,* 1896, and later a slightly different version, with six verses, appeared in *The Free Church Council Hymnal,* 1906. The present Song Book includes verses 1-3 from the earlier version, but has altered verse 1, line 5, which was originally 'Never once they feared, nor faltered.'

God loved the world of sinners lost (46)
Martha M. Stockton (1821-85)

Written in about 1871 and subsequently published in *The Voice of Praise,* 1872, edited by Ebenezer T. Baird and Karl Reden, and in *Winnowed Hymns,* 1873, edited by C. C. McCabe and D. T. Macfarlan. In *The Bandsman and Songster,* 2 November 1935, Lieut-Colonel H. Vincent Rohu said that the song was inspired by the writer's experience as a young girl, when she heard an American Indian woman describe how a missionary from Canada brought the story of God's love to her husband's village. (The source of this information is unknown.)

God make my life a little light (838)
Matilda Barbara Betham Edwards (1836-1919)

Published with the title 'Hymn for a little child' on a page headed 'Children's Hymns' in the magazine *Good Words,* June 1873, edited by Donald Macleod. The fifth verse has now been omitted.

God moves in a mysterious way (29)
William Cowper (1731-1800)

Although it is often said that William Cowper wrote this hymn in thanksgiving for God's providence when his suicide attempt was frustrated in October 1773, there is evidence that it was probably written before August 1773. Entitled 'Light shining out of Darkness', it was one of 14 hymns printed at the end of John Newton's *Twenty Six Letters on Religious Subjects. To Which are Added, Hymns, etc*, 1774. Later it was included in the third part of the *Olney Hymns*, 1779, in a section headed 'Conflict'.

God of comfort and compassion (576)
Doris N. Rendell (*b* 1896)

Two verses of this song were apparently written in the 1960s for a weekly period of intercession in the Sunday evening meetings at Thornton Heath Corps. (This had been established initially during the Second World War, when the corps prayed regularly for men and women from the corps who were away from home.) Additional verses were written later, by request. The song was included in a booklet of the author's songs and poems, *Songs of His Love*, published privately in about 1972.

God of concrete, God of steel (30)
Richard G. Jones (*b* 1926)

Written, the author said, after a discussion in the youth fellowship at Wesley Hall, Crookes, Sheffield, when the young people complained that the hymns were old-fashioned and used antiquated imagery. It was introduced at the Methodist Synod in Sheffield, in May 1964, and appeared in the *Methodist Recorder*, 14 May 1964, with the title 'A Hymn for 1964'. Omitting the third verse of the original, it was included in *Hymns and Songs*, 1969 (a supplement to the *Methodist Hymn Book*) with the heading 'The Earth is the Lord's'.

God of grace and God of glory (577)
Harry Emerson Fosdick (1878-1969)

Written during the summer of 1930 for the opening service of Riverside Church, New York (5 October 1930) and the service of dedication (8 February 1931). It was included in *The Fellowship Hymn Book*, Revised edition, 1933, and *The Methodist Hymnal*, 1935. A few lines were later revised and the fifth verse of the original has now been omitted.

God speaks to us in bird and song (31)
Joseph Johnson (1848-1926)

The first verse appeared in the author's book *Dibs: A Story* of *Young London Life,* 1887, at the beginning of Chapter 4: 'Promoted to the Choir'. Later the complete hymn was included in *School Hymns,* 1891. The fourth verse of the original has been omitted from the Song Book.

God who touchest earth with beauty (32)
Mary S. Edgar (1889-1973)

Written in 1925, it was awarded first prize in a competition organised by the American Camping Association in 1926. The version in the present Song Book is from *The Hymn Book of the Anglican Church of Canada and the United Church of Canada,* 1971, where it appeared in six four-line verses.

God's anger now is turned away (317)
Fred W. Fry (1859-1939)

The author said that the Music Department needed to obtain a certain number of songs for publication each month and on one occasion they were short of copy. He offered to fill the gap, but tried for several days without inspiration. One night he awoke singing the chorus 'My sins are under the blood', which he wrote down, quickly followed by the words and music of the verses. The song appeared in *Favourite Songs of the Salvation Songsters, Christmas Number,* December 1885. Three verses have now been omitted.

God's love is as high as the heavens (47)
Anonymous

Entitled: 'God's love', the song appeared anonymously in *The Musical Salvationist,* February 1909, arranged for female voices.

God's love to me is wonderful (48)
Sidney E. Cox (1887-1975)

Written in Atlanta, Georgia, in 1931. Lieut-Colonel Richard Fitton said that he sang this song with the author and Commissioner Alex Damon in the Sanitorium in Orlando, Florida, around the bed of Mrs Colonel Hannah Evans (who was promoted to Glory, 26 October 1931). Entitled 'God's love is wonderful', it was published in *The Musical Salvationist,* June 1932, and later in *Songs with Music,* 1939 (with the note 'Copyright Sept. 1931, The Salvation Army').

God's soldier marches as to war (801)
Harry Read (*b* 1924)

Written for the pageant *The Fulness of Time* (script by

Captain Harry Read and music by Captain John Larsson), which followed the commissioning of cadets of the 'Soldiers of Christ' Session at the Royal Albert Hall, London, on 11 May 1962. The song introduced the principal character in the pageant, the 'soldier of Christ', and originally began 'Our soldier marches as to war'. The first word was altered subsequently for wider use, and the song, entitled 'God's Soldier', appeared in *The Musical Salvationist,* January 1964.

God's trumpet is sounding: To arms! is the call (684)
verses: William J. Pearson (1832-92)
chorus: Fanny Crosby (1820-1915)

Six verses 'by Major Pearson' were published in *The War Cry,* 23 April 1887, with the title 'A Salvation Soldier I'll Be'. Later, five verses appeared anonymously in *The War Cry,* 22 April 1893, and then (with the chorus 'Stand like the brave') in *The Officer,* July 1894, edited by Commissioner Frederick Booth-Tucker. Apparently overlooking the earliest source, which indicated the authorship, Richard Slater, in his *Salvation Army Song Writers,* p 70, listed this song incorrectly among the songs of Commissioner Booth-Tucker. The second and fourth verses of the original have now been omitted. The chorus is from the song 'O soldier, awake, for the strife is at hand' (689).

Gracious Spirit, dwell with me (212)
Thomas T. Lynch (1818-71)

From the author's collection *The Rivulet: A Contribution to Sacred Song,* 1855, omitting the fourth verse of the original. The third verse was rewritten for *Salvation Army Songs,* 1930.

Great is thy faithfulness, O God my Father (33)
Thomas O. Chisholm (1866-1960)

Written in 1923, reflecting the author's experience of God's faithfulness. The first verse was based on Lamentations 3:22-23 and James 1:17. The song appeared in *Songs of Salvation and Service,* 1923, compiled by William M. Runyan, who composed the tune.

Greatest joy is found in serving Jesus (857)
Jarl Wahlström (*b* 1918)
translation versified by Brindley Boon (*b* 1913)

The Finnish song 'Parhainta on elää Jeesukselle', was published in Finland in *Nuori Sotilas* (The Young Soldier), 20 February 1954. Captain Brindley Boon, who was visiting

Sweden and Finland in 1958 to report congress meetings, obtained a free translation of the words from the author in Helsinki, and on his journey home versified the translation. Under his leadership, girls from the National School of Music (Sunbury) sang the song, entitled 'Happy Service', at Brighton Congress Hall, 6 August 1958, and it was then published in *New Songs for Young People*, September 1959.

Guide me, O thou great Jehovah (578)
William Williams (1717-91)
translated by Peter Williams (1722-96) and others

The Welsh hymn 'Arglwydd, arwain trwy'r anialwch' was published in *Alleluia*, 1745, by William Williams. The translation appeared anonymously in *The Collection of Hymns sung in the Countess of Huntingdon's Chapels in Sussex*, c1771, and was printed, with an additional verse, on an undated leaflet headed 'A Favourite Hymn, sung by Lady Huntingdon's Young Collegians', c1772. The first verse is from the translation in *Hymns on Various Subjects*, 1771, by Peter Williams, but the translator of the other verses has not been identified.

Hail, thou once despisèd Jesus (109)
attributed to John Bakewell (1721-1819) and others

This hymn appeared with two verses in *A Collection of Hymns Addressed to the Holy, Holy, Holy Triune God*, 1757, and was later expanded to four verses in *A Collection of Psalms and Hymns*, 1760, compiled by Martin Madan. (Verse 1 and the first half of verse 3 in the present Song Book are from the 1757 version. Verse 2 and the second half of verse 3 were added in 1760.) Subsequently the verses have been slightly altered by several editors, including Augustus Toplady.

Happy the home when God is there (661)
Henry Ware (1794-1843)

These verses, entitled 'The Happy Home', were signed 'Mrs W.' in *A Selection of Hymns and Poetry, for the use of Infant and Juvenile Schools and Families*, Third edition, 1846. Later the hymn was attributed to Henry Ware, though no earlier source has been identified.

Happy we who trust in Jesus (722)
Thomas Kelly (1769-1855)

This hymn, entitled 'A State of Security', was published in the author's *Hymns*, Second edition, 1806, with the heading

'He that dwelleth in the secret place of the most high, shall abide under the shadow of the Almighty' (Psalm 91:1). There were five verses, beginning:

> Happy they who trust in Jesus!
> Sweet their portion is and sure;
> When the foe on others seizes,
> God will keep his own secure:
> Happy people!
> Happy, tho' despis'd and poor.

The present version, omitting the second verse of the original, is from *The Song Book of The Salvation Army*, 1953.

Hark, hark, my soul, what warlike songs are swelling (802)
George Scott Railton (1849-1913)
based on Frederick W. Faber (1814-63)

A report in *The Salvationist*, August 1879, said that the first 'Hosanna Meeting', held soon after the London Council of War, commenced with this song. Notes from the 'Journal of the General' (30 June) also referred to the 'Hosanna Meeting', commemorating '14 years' fighting and victory'. The song was included in a booklet of 14 songs: *The Hosanna Songs of The Salvation Army, when the Lord had led them to victory for 14 years, and had enabled them to establish the 102nd corps*, 6 July 1879. It was based on a hymn by Frederick Faber, 'Hark! hark! my soul! angelic songs are swelling' from his *Oratory Hymns*, 1854.

Hark, my soul! it is the Lord (110)
William Cowper (1731-1800)

This hymn appeared in the *New Appendix* bound with *A Collection of Psalms and Hymns*, Second edition, with additions, 1768, compiled by Thomas Maxfield. It was also included in *The Gospel Magazine*, August 1771, and later in part 1 of the *Olney Hymns*, 1779, where it was headed 'Lovest thou me?' (John 21:16).

Hark the glad sound! the Saviour comes (81)
Philip Doddridge (1702-51)

The original manuscript, dated 28 December 1735, is headed 'Christ's Message', from Luke 4: 18, 19. The hymn was included in *Translations and Paraphrases of Several Passages of Sacred Scripture*, 1745, prepared for the Church of Scotland, and in *Hymns founded on Various Texts in the Holy Scriptures*, 1755, published by Job Orton from the author's manuscript. Verses 2, 4 and 6 of the original have now been omitted.

Hark! the gospel news is sounding (239)
William Sanders (1799-1882?)
and Hugh Bourne (1772-1852)

Published with the signature 'W.S. & H.B.' in the *Large Hymn Book for the Use of the Primitive Methodists*, 1824.

Hark! the herald angels sing (82)
Charles Wesley (1707-88)

Published with the title 'Hymn for Christmas Day' in John and Charles Wesley's *Hymns and Sacred Poems*, 1739. Originally there were 10 four-line verses, beginning:

> Hark how all the Welkin rings
> 'Glory to the King of kings.'

The present version consists of the first six verses of the original, altered and combined into three eight-line verses, with the revised opening couplet used as a refrain. The hymn in this form appeared in *Hymns Ancient and Modern*, 1861, though some of the revisions were made by earlier editors, including George Whitefield and Martin Madan.

Hark! the sounds of singing (803)
Charles Coller (1863-1935)

Included in *The Musical Salvationist*, March 1915, where it was entitled: 'Army of Salvation'. It originally began:

> Hark! hark! sounds of singing
> Vibrate on the breeze.

The present version is from *Salvation Army Songs*, 1930.

Hark! the voice of Jesus calling (240)
Albert Midlane (1825-1909)

Written in August 1860, and subsequently published in *The Ambassadors' Hymn Book*, 1861, and in the author's *Gospel Echoes*, 1865.

Have faith in God, my heart (723)
Bryn A. Rees (1911-83)

Published in *Congregational Praise*, 1951, having been submitted in manuscript to the compilers of that hymn book.

Have thine own way, Lord, have thine own way (487)
Adelaide A. Pollard (1862-1934)

This song is said to have been written in about 1902, after a prayer meeting where a woman prayed: 'Lord . . . have your own way with us'. The verses, based partly on Jeremiah 18:3-4, appeared in several hymn books in 1907, including the *Northfield Hymnal with Alexander's Supplement*, compiled by George C. Stebbins, and *Hallowed Hymns, New and Old*, compiled by Ira D. Sankey.

Have we not known it, have we not heard it (724)
                          Albert Orsborn (1886-1967)

Written in about 1915 for a central holiness meeting at Clapton Congress Hall, when the author was on the staff of the training college. Entitled 'He remembers Sins no more', it was published in *The Musical Salvationist*, January 1941, on the soloist's page.

Have you any room for Jesus (241)
                              Daniel W. Whittle (1840-1901)

Published in *Gospel Hymns No. 3*, 1878, compiled by Ira D. Sankey, James McGranahan and George C. Stebbins, with the heading 'Behold, I stand at the door and knock' (Revelation 3:20).

Have you been to Jesus for the cleansing power (417)
                               Elisha A. Hoffman (1839-1929)

Appeared in *Spiritual Songs for Gospel Meetings and the Sunday School*, 1878, compiled by the author and J. H. Tenney, with the title 'Are you washed in the Blood?'. The third verse of the original has been omitted.

Have you ever heard the story (96)
                         verses 1-3: Mrs S. Z. Kaufman
                          verse 4: Gordon Taylor (*b* 1946)

Verses 1-3 are from *Gospel Melodies*, 1885, compiled by Grinnel, White, Hoffman and McHose. In 1981, the Song Book Council decided to add a verse on the resurrection, to complete the gospel story, and in 1984 adopted the version submitted by Gordon Taylor, which had already been accepted by the Young People's Song Book Council for *Sing for Joy*, 1986.

Have you ever stopped to think how God loves you (49)
                                    John Gowans (*b* 1934)

From a scene in the musical *Glory!* when a meeting led by Captain Campbell begins with the singing of this song: 'As high as the sky'. Extracts from the musical were introduced at the Mermaid Theatre, London, on 7 July 1975, and the complete musical was presented at the Royal Festival Hall, on 12 July 1976, during the British Congress.

Have you heard the angels singing (242)
Cornelie Booth (1864-1920)

Published in *The War Cry*, Canada, 24 March 1894, with the title 'Jesus Lives', and then reprinted in *The Musical Salvationist*, July 1894, in a special issue headed 'Songs from many Lands'. The verses and chorus were altered for *The Song Book of The Salvation Army*, 1953, when the fifth verse of the original was omitted.

Have you on the Lord believed (418)
Philip P. Bliss (1838-76)

Written after hearing the evangelist D. L. Moody tell the following story:

> A vast fortune was left in the hands of a minister for one of his poor parishioners. Fearing that it might be squandered if suddenly bestowed upon him, the wise minister sent him a little at a time, with a note saying, 'This is thine; use it wisely; there is more to follow.'

Mr Moody concluded, 'That is just the way God deals with us'. The song appeared in *Sunshine for Sunday Schools*, 1873, compiled by P. P. Bliss.

Have you seen the crucified (243)
John Lawley (1859-1922)

According to Mrs Carpenter, in *Commissioner John Lawley*, p 145, this song was written in the train on the homeward journey after William Booth had been speaking in Holland about the needs of Java. However, the author's daughter, Florrie (in *The War Cry*, Canada, 28 May 1949), said that the song written in these circumstances was:

> Sinner, thou art speeding
> Down to death, unheeding.

She said that her father wrote 'Have you seen the crucified' on one occasion when the Founder asked for a new Easter song. The song in its present form was included in *Salvation Army Songs*, 1899. Earlier, the first three verses, with a chorus, 'Pass on His dying love', had appeared in *The Young Soldier*, 19 March 1898, with the phrase 'Please pass it on' in lines 2, 4 and 8 of each verse, instead of 'O wondrous love'.

He came to give us life in all its fulness (274)
                                      John Gowans (*b* 1934)
This song was originally written for the 'open-air meeting' scene in the musical *Hosea*, but lost its place after the first production in 1969, when the length of the musical had to be cut. It was then transferred to the musical *Jesus Folk*, to conclude the 'Lazarus sequence', after the song 'Out of my darkness' (378). An abridged version of *Jesus Folk* was introduced at the finale of the British Congress, at Wembley, on 10 July 1972, and the complete musical was presented in the Fairfield Halls, Croydon, on 25 January 1973.

He giveth more grace as our burdens grow greater (579)
                                Annie Johnson Flint (1866-1932)
Printed at Orchard Park, New York, in the 'Casterline Card' series, No. 5510, and later included in *The Officer*, May 1928, and *Annie Johnson Flint's Best-loved Poems*, 1957, where it was headed 'He Giveth More', with three scriptural references: 'He giveth more grace' (James 4:6); 'He increaseth strength' (Isaiah 40:29); and 'Mercy unto you, and peace, and love, be multiplied' (Jude 2). The present version, which is slightly altered from the original, is from *The Song Book of The Salvation Army*, 1953.

He leadeth me! O blessèd thought (725)
                                   Joseph H. Gilmore (1834-1918)
Written in the home of Deacon Wattson (a deacon of the church) after the author had spoken on the text 'He leadeth me' (Psalm 23), at a meeting in the First Baptist Church, Philadelphia, on 26 March 1862. His wife sent a copy to the Boston paper, the *Watchman and Reflector*, where it was published (4 December 1862), signed 'Contoocook'. Later it was included anonymously in *The Golden Censer*, 1864, compiled by William B. Bradbury, with the title 'He Leadeth Me'.

He walks with God who speaks to God in prayer (580)
                                   Dorothy Ann Thrupp (1779-1847)
The earliest version of this song so far discovered was published anonymously in *Hymns for the Young*, 1832, with the title 'Walking with God', and was later included in *A Selection of Hymns and Poetry*, Second edition, 1840, where it was signed 'D.A.T.' (Dorothy Ann Thrupp). The first verse has now been omitted:

> He walks with God who lives a life of faith,
> And builds his hope on what the promise saith;
> Who, letting go this world, the next secures,
> And still as seeing things unseen endures.

The verses in their present form appeared in *Salvation Army Songs*, 1930.

He who would valiant be (685)

John Bunyan (1628-88)
altered by Percy Dearmer (1867-1936)

The original version appeared in the second part of *The Pilgrim's Progress*, 1684, at the end of a conversation between Great-heart and Valiant-for-truth, after Valiant-for-truth had said: 'I believed and therefore came out, got into the Way, fought all that set themselves against me, and by believing am come to this Place'. The verses, which were a comment on the experiences and example of Valiant-for-truth, originally began:

> Who would true Valour see,
> Let him come hither;
> One here will Constant be,
> Come Wind, come Weather.

The revised version is from *The English Hymnal*, 1906.

He wills that I should holy be (419)

Charles Wesley (1707-88)

These verses are from four hymns in the author's *Short Hymns on Select Passages of the Holy Scriptures*, 1762, which John Wesley later combined to form one hymn in *A Collection of Hymns for the Use of the People called Methodists*, 1780. Verse 1 is based on the text: 'This is the will of God, even your sanctification' (1 Thessalonians 4:3). Verse 2 is based on 'The Lord thy God will circumcise thine heart' (Deuteronomy 30:6). Verses 3 and 4 are on the text: 'Let Thy loving Spirit lead me forth' (Psalm 143:10, Prayer Book version), and verses 5 and 6 are based on 'As many as touched were made perfectly whole' (Matthew 14:36).

Heavenly Father, thou hast brought us (938)

Hester P. Hawkins (1846-1928)

It was apparently written for the golden wedding of the author's parents and was published under the heading 'Golden-Wedding' in *The Home Hymn-Book*, 1885, which she compiled. The third verse, which has now been omitted, refers to these circumstances:

> Father, all Thy gifts are precious,
>   But we thank Thee most for this,
> That so many years of toiling
>   Have been soothed by wedded bliss;
> Since our hearts were first united
>   Life has not been free from care,
> But our burdens were the lighter
>   When each bore an equal share.

Help us to help each other, Lord (662)
Charles Wesley (1707-88)

From a hymn entitled 'A Prayer for Persons joined in Fellowship', in *Hymns and Sacred Poems*, 1742, by John and Charles Wesley. The Song Book includes verses 3-5 from the first part of the hymn, which originally began:

> Try us, O God, and search the ground
>   Of every sinful heart;
> Whate'er of sin in us is found,
>   O bid it all depart.

Here, Lord, assembled in thy name (581)
Edward Boaden (1827-1913)

From a section headed 'Temperance Services' in *Methodist Free Church Hymns*, 1889. Verses 5-7, the three verses of the original which were on the theme of temperance, have now been omitted.

Ho, my comrades, see the signal (804)
Philip P. Bliss (1838-76)

At a Sunday-school meeting in Rockford, Illinois, in May 1870, the evangelist, Major D. W. Whittle, described how General W. T. Sherman was advancing to relieve the fort at Altoona Pass, during the American Civil War in 1864. From the top of Kenesaw Mountain, 20 miles away, he sent the signal 'Hold the fort, for I am coming'. On hearing this story, the author was inspired to write the song, which he introduced at the YMCA in Chicago on the following day. It was published in *The Charm: A Collection of Sunday School Music*, 1871, compiled by the author.

Hold thou my hand! so weak I am, and helpless (726)
Fanny Crosby (1820-1915)

Written in about 1874. Describing the circumstances, the author said:

> For a number of days before I wrote this hymn, all had seemed

dark to me. This was quite an unusual experience, for I have always been most cheerful; and so in my human weakness I cried in prayer: 'Dear Lord, hold Thou my hand.' Almost at once, the sweet peace that comes of perfect assurance returned to my heart, and my gratitude for the evidence of answered prayer sang itself into the lines of the hymn.

It was published under the pen-name 'Grace J. Frances' in *Sacred Songs and Solos*, 1888, compiled by Ira D. Sankey.

Holy Bible, book divine (652)
John Burton (1773-1822)

Published in the author's *Youth's Monitor in Verse*, 1803; in the *Evangelical Magazine*, June 1805 (where it was signed 'Nottingham—J.B.'); and in his *Hymns for Sunday Schools*, 1806.

Holy Father, in thy mercy (582)
Isabel S. Stevenson (1843-90)

Written at Cheltenham in 1869 when the author's brother was sailing to South Africa for the sake of his health. It was printed on a leaflet which circulated widely among friends, and later the hymn was used on board HMS *Bacchante* when the future King George V and his brother were sailing round the world, 1881-82. Subsequently it was included in the *Manual of Common Prayer at Sea*, 1886, and then in *Supplemental Hymns*, the 1889 supplement to *Hymns Ancient and Modern*, where it was headed 'For Absent Friends'. The sixth verse has now been omitted.

Holy Ghost, we bid thee welcome (213)
Lelia N. Morris (1862-1929)

Published in *Songs of Redemption*, 1899, by Gill, McLaughlin, Kirkpatrick and Gilmour.

Holy, holy, holy, Lord God Almighty (220)
Reginald Heber (1783-1826)

Based partly on Revelation 4:8-11, it appeared in *A Selection of Psalms and Hymns for the Parish Church of Banbury*, Third edition, 1826, and then posthumously in the author's *Hymns Written and Adapted to the Weekly Church Service of the Year*, 1827, where it was headed 'Trinity Sunday'.

Holy Spirit, hear us (193)
William H. Parker (1845-1929)

Written in March 1880 and published in *The School Hymnal:*

A Collection of Hymns for use in Schools and Families, 1880. The fifth and sixth verses of the original have now been omitted.

Holy Spirit, truth divine (194)
Samuel Longfellow (1819-92)

Apparently written for a book of *Vespers*, 1859, and then included in *Hymns of the Spirit*, 1864, compiled by the author and Samuel Johnson. It was entitled 'Prayer for Inspiration'. The third verse of the original has been omitted.

Home is home, however lowly (663)
Arthur S. Arnott (1870-1941)

Written at the request of a home league local officer in Melbourne, who needed a suitable song for a home league demonstration. Appeared in *The War Cry*, 28 February 1925, headed 'A Home League Song'. The chorus has now been omitted.

How can I better serve thee, Lord (488)
Bramwell Coles (1887-1960)

Entitled 'Here at the Cross', the song appeared in *The War Cry*, 5 April 1947, as 'An Easter song for the "Fighting Faith" Campaign', which General Albert Orsborn had initiated for 1947 throughout the Salvation Army world. Later the song was included in *The Musical Salvationist*, November-December 1947.

How firm a foundation, ye saints of the Lord (653)
verses: Anonymous
chorus: Eliza E. Hewitt (1851-1920)

The verses, headed 'Exceeding great and precious promises' (2 Peter 1:4), appeared in *A Selection of Hymns from the Best Authors*, 1787, compiled by John Rippon. The second and sixth verses have now been omitted. The hymn, which was signed with the initial 'K—', has subsequently been attributed to Kirkham, Richard Keen or George Keith, but without any satisfactory evidence. A note in the preface stated, 'In most places, where the Names of the Authors were known, they are put at full Length, but the Hymns which are not so distinguished, or which have only a single Letter prefixed to them, were, many of them composed by a Person unknown, or else have undergone some considerable Alterations'. The chorus is from a song beginning 'Fear not, I am with Thee', in *Songs of Grace and Truth*, 1899, compiled by G. A. Collin.

How happy every child of grace (880)
                                    Charles Wesley (1707-88)
From the author's *Funeral Hymns*, 1759, where the hymn had eight verses. The Song Book includes verses 1-3 and 6, altered as in *The Song Book of The Salvation Army*, 1953.

How sweet the name of Jesus sounds (58)
                            verses: John Newton (1725-1807)
                                         chorus: Anonymous
The verses are from a hymn entitled 'The name of Jesus' in part 1 of the *Olney Hymns*, 1779. The opening line was based on the text 'Thy name is as ointment poured forth' (Song of Solomon 1:3). The fourth and fifth verses of the original have now been omitted. The chorus was linked with these verses in *Revival Music*, 1876, compiled by William Booth.

How tasteless and tedious the hours (318)
                                    John Newton (1725-1807)
Published in part 1 of the *Olney Hymns*, 1779, with the heading 'None upon earth I desire besides thee' (Psalm 73:25). Originally it began 'How tedious and tasteless the hours'.

How wonderful it is to walk with God (583)
                              Theodore H. Kitching (1866-1930)
This song was suggested by the words of Colonel Mildred Duff at a 'Day of Devotion' in the Central Hall, Westminster (18 January 1915), when she said, 'What a wonderful art it is to walk with God!'. The verses, entitled 'Wonderful', appeared in *The War Cry*, 6 February 1915, and *All the World*, March 1915; and then, with music by Bandmaster A. Bryant (Reading III), in *The Musical Salvationist*, October 1915. Later it was sung at the author's funeral at Clapton Congress Hall on 14 February 1930.

Hushed was the evening hymn (839)
                                    James D. Burns (1823-64)
Entitled 'The Child Samuel', it appeared in *The Evening Hymn*, 1857, a collection of 31 hymns and prayers (a hymn and a prayer for each day of the month).

I am amazed when I think of God's love (319)
                                    Sidney E. Cox (1887-1975)
The chorus appeared in *The Warrior*, November 1955, and

the complete song was included in *The Musical Salvationist*, January-February 1956, entitled: 'I am amazed'.

I am drinking at the fountain (320)
verses and first chorus: Anonymous
second chorus: Sidney E. Cox (1887-1975)

This song, entitled 'Is not this the Land of Beulah', appeared anonymously in *Songs of Redeeming Love*, 1882, edited by J. R. Sweney, T. C. O'Kane, C. C. McCabe and W. J. Kirkpatrick. There were five verses, beginning:

> I am dwelling on the mountain,
> Where the golden sunlight gleams.

The first and second verses have now been omitted. The *Dictionary of American Hymnology* files show that from 1890 it was occasionally attributed to William Hunter, but from 1904 it was more often attributed to Harriet Warner. The words were attributed to Harriet Warner in *The Musical Salvationist*, December 1923. The second chorus is from the song 'There's a path that's sometimes thorny' (462).

I am praying, blessèd Saviour (584)
Fanny Crosby (1820-1915)

Published in *Joyful Sound*, 1889, compiled by John R. Sweney. The second verse of the original has been omitted:

> I am praying, blessèd Saviour
> For a faith so clear and bright,
> That its eye will see Thy glory
> Through the deepest, darkest night.

I am saved, blessedly saved, by the blood (321)
Edwin Gay (1860-1952)

Apparently written when the author was a divisional officer in Boston, after a man in a railway carriage had said to him: 'I suppose you are *saved*', and he replied: 'Yes, sir—Blessedly Saved. Saved by the Blood of the Lamb.' The song, with the title: 'Blessedly Saved', appeared at the end of an anniversary report, *The Sixth Year . . . In Scotland*, November 1887, and, in a slightly different version, in *The Musical Salvationist*, November 1887.

I am saved, I am saved (322)
Annie S. Hawks (c1835-1918)

Appeared under the title 'I am saved' in *Welcome Tidings*, 1877, with the heading 'According to his mercy he saved us'

(Titus 3:5). The fifth verse has now been omitted and the other verses appear in a different order.

I am so glad that our Father in Heaven (323)
Philip P. Bliss (1838-76)

Written in about June 1870, in the home of Major D. W. Whittle, in Chicago. After hearing the chorus 'Oh how I love Jesus' repeated frequently, Philip Bliss thought, 'Have I not been singing enough about my poor love for Jesus, and should I not rather sing of His great love for me?' As a result, he wrote this song, which was included in his publications: *The Charm*, 1871; *Sunshine for Sunday Schools*, 1873; and *Gospel Songs*, 1874.

I am thine, O Lord; I have heard thy voice (585)
Fanny Crosby (1820-1915)

One evening in 1874 the author was in the home of the composer W. H. Doane, in Cincinnati, Ohio, speaking with him about the nearness of God. With this theme in mind, she apparently composed the verses before going to sleep that night and then recited them to him next morning. The song, entitled 'Draw me Nearer', was published in *Brightest and Best*, 1875, compiled by Robert Lowry and W. Howard Doane, with the heading 'Let us draw near with a true heart' (Hebrews 10:22).

I am trusting thee, Lord Jesus (727)
Frances Ridley Havergal (1836-79)

Written in September 1874 at Ormont Dessus, Vaud, Switzerland, and printed that year on a leaflet by J. & R. Parlane. Later, it was included, under the title 'Trusting Jesus', in the author's *Loyal Responses; or Daily Melodies for The King's Minstrels*, 1878. Apparently it was her favourite hymn and she is said to have kept a copy in her pocket Bible.

I believe that God the Father (324)
John Gowans (*b* 1934)

Written at the request of the British Commissioner, Albert Mingay, for corps officers' annual councils at Swanwick, Derbyshire, 11-26 October 1971, on the theme: 'I believe'. It appeared on a leaflet of songs for the councils and was later included, slightly altered, in *Keep Singing!*, 1976.

I bring my heart to Jesus, with its fears (420)
Herbert H. Booth (1862-1926)

Included in a booklet, *Songs of the Nations*, for the

International Congress, 1886, and then printed in *The War Cry*, 16 October 1886, described as 'An Old Favourite'. The fourth verse, which originally read:

> Nothing from His altar I would keep,
> To His cross of suffering I would leap,

was altered to the present version in *The Song Book of The Salvation Army*, 1953.

I bring my sins to thee (421)
Frances Ridley Havergal (1836-79)

Written in June 1870, it was printed that year on a leaflet by J. and R. Parlane, and included in *The Sunday Magazine*, 1 September 1870, edited by Dr Thomas Guthrie, where it was entitled 'To Thee'. With a few minor alterations, it later appeared in *Home Words for Heart and Hearth*, 1872, with the title 'Lord, to whom shall we go?'

I bring thee, dear Jesus, my all (422)
verses: Frederick Booth-Tucker (1853-1929)
chorus: Anonymous

The verses are from a song with three eight-line verses in *Songs of Love and Service*, a booklet prepared for the marriage celebrations of the author and Miss Emma Booth in the St James's Hall and the Congress Hall, Clapton, on 9-10 April 1888. The first and second verses of the original have been divided into four-line verses, and the third verse has now been omitted. The chorus appeared in *The War Cry*, 27 June 1885, as part of a song entitled 'Speak to Me', by Cadet George Daymond. It is not known whether he wrote the chorus, or took it from an earlier source.

I bring thee my cares and my sorrows (288)
Evangeline Booth (1865-1950)

Published under the title 'O Save Me, Dear Lord' in the author's *Songs of the Evangel*, 1927, and in the new and enlarged edition, 1937.

I bring to thee my heart to fill (489)
verses: Herbert H. Booth (1862-1926)
chorus: attributed to W. A. Williams

The verses and chorus appeared in *The Musical Salvationist*, November 1887, to be sung to the same tune as the preceding song, 'I entered once a home of care', which also used the same chorus. Although the words of the chorus are sometimes attributed to W. A. Williams, the composer of the tune 'Christ is all', there is no reliable evidence that he wrote the words, either of the chorus, or the verses 'I entered once a home of care'.

I could not do without thee (325)
Frances Ridley Havergal (1836-79)

Written at Leamington on 7 May 1873, and printed later that year on a leaflet by J. and R. Parlane. It was also included in the magazine *Home Words for Heart and Hearth,* 1873, edited by the Reverend Charles Bullock, Rector of St Nicholas', Worcester, with the heading 'I could not do without Thee'.

I do not ask thee, Lord (586)
Fanny Jolliffe (c1862-1943)

This song was published in *The War Cry,* 13 April 1895, when the author was an ensign, at Notting Hill, though it is said to have been written in 1891, apparently when she was leaving London reluctantly, to begin campaign work with cadets in the Sheffield Division. The third verse of the original has now been omitted.

I dwell within the secret place (728)
Arch R. Wiggins (1893-1976)

Inspired by an address given by General Erik Wickberg at a meeting for retired commissioners at Hildenborough Hall, Kent, on Thursday 29 April 1971. Entitled 'The guest of God', it was included in *The Musical Salvationist,* April 1974, beginning 'I dwell within His secret place', and was also printed on a leaflet *Songs for use during the International Congress,* 1978.

I feel like singing all the time (326)
Edward P. Hammond (1831-1910)

The author, writing to Ira D. Sankey, said that when he was speaking about the love of Jesus in a children's meeting in Utica, New York, he noticed a bright-looking girl bursting into tears. Afterwards she stayed for the inquiry meeting and was soon happy in the love of Christ. On the following day she handed him a letter which said: 'I think I can sing with the rest of those who have found Jesus, "Jesus is mine". The first time I came to the meeting I cried; but now I feel like singing all the time.' Later this phrase became the first line of the song, which appeared in the author's *Hymns of Salvation,* 1867. The original

fourth verse, which has been omitted, apparently referred to the girl who had inspired the song:
> O happy little singing one,
> What music is like thine?
> With Jesus as thy Life and Sun,
> Go singing all the time.

The fifth verse in the present Song Book was not in the above publication, but was included in *The Christian Mission Hymn Book*, 1870, compiled by William Booth.

I have a home that is fairer than day (881)
Ada M. Nisbett (c1866-1931)

Written in about 1884 for the tune 'A Home in the Valley,' which the author had learnt from her music teacher. It was intended as a farewell song when Hattie Yerex (later an adjutant) was leaving Lindsay (Ontario) Corps to become a cadet, but was not used at that time because the author did not have the courage to put it forward. It appeared anonymously on a leaflet, *Special Songs, for the Benefit of New York, Brooklyn and Jersey Division*, 1886, and in *The Musical Salvationist*, September 1886. Subsequently, it was printed in *The War Cry*, Toronto, 6 November 1886 (when the author was a lieutenant at Coaticook, Quebec), with a footnote: 'It was composed by the Lieut. nearly two years ago, when she was a soldier in the Lindsay corps, but the author's name has never before appeared.'

I have a song that Jesus gave me (327)
Elton M. Roth (1891-1951)

This song is usually said to have been written in 1923 in a small town in Texas where the author was conducting an evangelistic meeting. One afternoon, in a quiet church, he wrote the words and music within an hour. The song was included in *Campaign Melodies*, 1924, and *Hymns of Praise No. 2*, 1925. (Information from the *Dictionary of American Hymnology* files suggests that the song appeared in *Standard Songs of Evangelism*, 1907, compiled by George Stebbins, but this has not been confirmed.)

I have found a great salvation (328)
Thomas W. Plant (1866-1944)

Appeared in *The War Cry*, 5 November 1892, when the author was a staff-captain, and subsequently included in *Salvation Army Songs*, 1899.

I have glorious tidings of Jesus to tell (329)
Richard Slater (1854-1939)

This song, probably written in 1884 or 1885, is said to have appeared first at the end of a training home report. The earliest version found is in a booklet, *Songs of the Nations,* prepared for the International Congress, 1886. The original third verse has been omitted.

I have heard of a Saviour's love (289)
verses: Anne Shepherd (1809-57)
chorus: Anonymous

The verses, originally beginning 'I have read of the Saviour's love', appeared in the author's *Hymns, adapted to the comprehension of young minds,* Second edition, 1836, with the heading 'Say unto my soul, I am thy salvation' (Psalm 35:3). Later, the song was incorrectly attributed to Philip Phillips. The present version of the chorus appeared in *Favorite Songs of the Speaking, Praying and Singing Brigade, c*1887.

I have no claim on grace (290)
Albert Orsborn (1886-1967)

Written in 1916 or 1917, when the author had attended a meeting at Custom House in East London. After hearing several encouraging testimonies, he came away with joy in his heart. Despite an air-raid, with Zeppelins overhead, the verses formed in his mind during his journey home, and on arrival, he wrote them down before taking off his coat. Later the song was included in *The Beauty of Jesus,* 1947 (a collection of the author's songs and poems), and in *The Song Book of The Salvation Army,* 1953.

I have read of men of faith (686)
Mark W. Sanders (1862-1943)

Written in 1886 at the suggestion of Richard Slater for the tune 'The Battle Cry of Freedom', it appeared in a booklet of *Songs of the Nations,* for the International Congress, 1886. Several lines were altered for *The Song Book of The Salvation Army,* 1953.

I have seen his face in blessing (330)
William J. McAlonan (1863-1925)

The author's wife said that the song was written when she had been in hospital for nine weeks and was unable to walk for some months afterwards. Although she later improved, the doctor had told her husband that she would not recover. The song apparently reflected his feelings at that time. The verses, entitled 'An Experience', appeared in *All the World*, July 1894, and were then included (with the chorus) in *The Musical Salvationist*, October 1897, under the title 'An Abiding Salvation'. The second verse of the original has now been omitted.

I hear thy welcome voice (423)
Lewis Hartsough (1828-1919)

Written in 1872, while the author was conducting a revival meeting in Epworth, Iowa. The song was published in *The Revivalist*, Revised and enlarged edition, 1872, compiled by Joseph Hillman; in a monthly magazine, *Guide to Holiness*, and later in *Gospel Hymns No. 2*, 1876, compiled by Ira D. Sankey and P. P. Bliss.

I heard a voice so gently calling (490)
Agnes P. Heathcote (1862-?)

Entitled: 'I'll follow thee', the song appeared in *The Musical Salvationist*, January 1890, beginning: 'I heard a voice so softly calling'. There were originally six verses.

I heard of a Saviour whose love was so great (331)
Mrs Eliza(?) Read

Mrs Commissioner Richard Wilson (formerly Annie E. Lockwood) said that while she was a captain at Shankill Road (2nd Belfast) Corps, 1880-81, one of the soldiers there, Mrs Read, wrote some verses but could not put them into proper order. The captain helped her with the sequence and rhyme and later introduced the song at one of the meetings connected with the marriage of Bramwell Booth and Miss Florence Soper at the Congress Hall, Clapton (12 October 1882). The song, entitled 'He pardoned a rebel like me', appeared anonymously in *The War Cry*, 23 December 1882, with the note 'Sung by Captain Lockwood'. Subsequently it was included in *Salvation Music, Volume 2*, December 1883.

I heard the voice of Jesus say (332)
Horatius Bonar (1808-89)

Published in the author's *Hymns Original and Selected*, 1846, and later in the first series of his *Hymns of Faith and Hope*, 1857. It was headed 'The Voice from Galilee', with the text 'Of His fulness have all we received, and grace for grace (John 1:16).

I kneel beside thy sacred cross (729)
W. Elwin Oliphant (1860-1941)

First published in *The War Cry*, 25 June 1887, at the end of an article 'What is Christism?', signed 'W. Elwin Oliphant, Major'. The article, on the subject of sacrifice and self-denial, was written when the author was too ill to attend the all-night prayer meeting led by William Booth in the Training Home Lecture Hall at Clapton, 1-2 June 1887. Richard Slater said that Major Oliphant, who was seriously ill in a bedroom at Clapton Congress Hall, gave the verses to him early in 1887. After meditating 'for days, even weeks', Slater composed the music on 8 June 1887 and the song, entitled 'Thou art enough for me', was included in *The Musical Salvationist*, November 1887. The words were extensively altered after appearing in *The War Cry*, and the second verse was revised again for *Salvation Army Songs*, 1899.

I know not why God's wondrous grace (730)
Daniel W. Whittle (1840-1901)

Entitled 'I know whom I have believed' in *Gospel Hymns No. 4*, 1883, compiled by Ira D. Sankey, James McGranahan and George C. Stebbins. The chorus is from 2 Timothy 1:12 (*AV*). The fifth verse of the original has now been omitted.

I know that my redeemer lives (144)
Samuel Medley (1738-99)

The verses are from a hymn in the appendix to *A Collection of Hymns for Social Worship*, 23rd edition, 1777, compiled by George Whitefield. There were originally nine verses. The chorus is from the final couplet of another of the author's hymns, 'Now in a Song of grateful praise', in the same publication.

I know thee who thou art (59)
Albert Orsborn (1886-1967)

The author said that the song was written at his home in South London in 1942, while he was British Commissioner, after he had suffered a severe bereavement. He wrote: 'I have been permitted to endure extremely heavy and bitter sorrows.' 'The song grew out of my soul under the plowshare of suffering. Once the theme got started, it bore me along, excited and full of praise! I could not stop it flowing, though the third verse was one "born out of due time", for it came after the verse numbered four!' Verse 4, the author's favourite, originally concluded 'And find I am expected there', but he said: 'Finally, I preferred the words in the song book'. Verses 1, 2 and 4 were sung to the tune 'St John' at the 'Day of Renewal' meetings led by General Orsborn at the Central Hall, Westminster, 19 October 1949, and were printed in *The War Cry,* 5 November 1949. The complete song, with the author's tune 'Brantwood', was included in *The Musical Salvationist,* May-June 1950.

I left it all with Jesus long ago (333)

Ellen H. Willis

Published in *Philip Phillips's Singing Annual for Sabbath Schools,* 1871, and later in the author's anthology *'I left It All With Jesus' and other Poems,* 1875.

I love to hear the story (840)

Emily H. Miller (1833-1913)

While recovering from a serious illness in 1867, the author was concerned that she had not prepared her usual contribution for the magazine *The Little Corporal.* One afternoon, feeling a little stronger, she wrote this song quickly, in less than 15 minutes, and sent it for publication in the magazine. It was later included in *Chapel Gems for Sunday Schools,* Enlarged edition, 1868, edited by George F. Root.

I love to sing of the Saviour (178)

Gösta Blomberg (1905-81)

The chorus was written at Camp Wonderland, in the USA Central Territory, when the author was a guest speaker at a young people's camp. Around the camp fire, the young people, raising their right hands as a greeting, used the American-Indian expression 'How!' to show their appreciation. During the evening, or later that night, the author wrote the words and music of the chorus. Subsequently he added the verses, and the song was published in *Special Songs for Young People's Anniversaries and Festal Occasions* No. 18, New Series, 1956.

I met the good shepherd (111)

Edward Caswall (1814-78)

Published with the title 'The Good Shepherd' in the author's *The Masque of Mary, and other poems,* 1858, in a section headed 'Hymns and Meditative Pieces'. The third verse of the original has been omitted, and the last verse, which has been altered, now appears as in *The Young People's Song Book of The Salvation Army,* 1963.

I must have the Saviour with me (731)
                          Fanny Crosby (1820-1915)

This song, beginning 'I would have the Saviour with me', appeared under the pen-name 'L. Edwards' in *The Christian Choir*, Revised and enlarged, 1896, compiled by Ira D. Sankey and James McGranahan. The fourth verse of the original has now been omitted.

I need thee every hour (587)
                 verses: Annie S. Hawks (c1835-1918)
                 chorus: Robert Lowry (1826-99)

The author said that one morning she was filled with a sense of the nearness of God, and wondered how anyone could live without him. The line 'I need thee every hour' came into her mind, and, seated by the open window, she wrote the verses, almost as they are sung today. The song was published in a small booklet for the National Baptist Sunday School Association Convention in Cincinnati in November 1872, and was then included in *Royal Diadem*, 1873, compiled by Robert Lowry and W. Howard Doane, with the chorus and tune by Robert Lowry.

I often say my prayers (588)
                                    John Burton (1803-77)

It was apparently published in the 1840 edition of *The Union Hymn Book, for Scholars*, and was later included in *A Book of Praise for Home and School*, 1869, selected and arranged by S. D. Major, where it was signed 'John Burton, 1840'.

I serve a risen Saviour (334)
                              Alfred H. Ackley (1887-1960)

Written to give a positive response to a young man who asked the author: 'Why should I worship a dead Jew?' The song was published in *Triumphant Service Songs*, 1933.

I shall not fear though darkened clouds may gather round me (732)
                              Stanley E. Ditmer (b 1924)

In April 1956, while the author was on the staff of the training college in New York, his brother was seriously ill, and a month later he also was unwell and had to wait six weeks for the diagnosis of his illness. During this time of uncertainty, the chorus was born. He said that it 'evolved' at the piano keyboard and the first verse was written that same afternoon. Six months later, after he had taken up a corps appointment at Newburgh,

New York, he added what is now the third verse, when he was asked to sing a duet with his wife at an officers' retreat. Afterwards, when asked for copies, he wrote another verse and the duet arrangement of the song was published in *The War Cry*, New York, 13 April 1957. Later it was arranged by Erik Leidzén for music leaders' councils in the USA Eastern Territory and was included in *The Musical Salvationist*, July-August 1960. The author said, 'I have often heard the song used tearfully and with stressed solemnity, particularly in relation to sickness and death. Although it was born at such a time, it was not conceived by me in that manner, but rather as an expression of virile faith and forthright courage. I always use it at a quicker tempo.'

I sought for love and strength and light (541)
                    Alfred Humphrey (1864-1933)

Appeared in *The Musical Salvationist*, March 1914, under the title: 'King of my Heart'. The fourth verse of the original has now been omitted and the original chorus has become the fourth verse.

I stand all bewildered with wonder (542)
                    attributed to Wilbur F. Crafts (1850-1922)

In *Winnowed Hymns*, 1873, edited by C. C. McCabe and D. T. Macfarlan, this song was attributed to Callene Fisk, about whom nothing is known. Later, in other collections, it was sometimes attributed to W. F. Crafts, as in *Songs of Joy and Gladness*, 1885, compiled by W. McDonald, Joshua Gill, John R. Sweney and W. J. Kirkpatrick.

I stand amazed in the presence (179)
                    Charles H. Gabriel (1856-1932)

Published in *Praises*, 1905, compiled by Edwin O. Excell.

I think, when I read that sweet story of old (794)
                    Jemima Luke (1813-1906)

In 1841, the author visited the Normal Infant School in Gray's Inn Road, London, and there learnt one of the marching tunes, 'a Greek air'. Later, while travelling by stage coach to Wellington, Somerset, she wrote the first two verses in pencil on the back of an envelope, in order to teach the tune at a village school. These two verses, entitled 'The Child's Desire', appeared with the music in *The Sunday School Teachers' Magazine, and Journal of Education*, 1841. She subsequently added a third verse to make it a missionary hymn, which was then published in *The Juvenile Missionary Magazine*, June 1846.

I thirst, thou wounded Lamb of God (424)
verses 1 and 2: Nicolaus L. von Zinzendorf (1700-60)
verse 3: Johann Nitschmann (1712-83)
verse 4: Anna Nitschmann (1715-60)
translated by John Wesley (1703-91)

The German hymns: 'Ach! mein verwundter Fürste', by Zinzendorf; 'Du blutiger Versöhner' by Johann Nitschmann; and 'Mein König, deine Liebe', by Anna Nitschmann, were included in an Appendix to the *Herrnhut Gesang-Buch*, 1735. John Wesley translated verses from these hymns and another hymn by Zinzendorf, combining them to form a new hymn, with eight verses, in *Hymns and Sacred Poems*, 1740. The present Song Book includes verses 1-3 and 8 from this translation, altered as in *Salvation Army Songs*, 1899.

I want a principle within (425)
Charles Wesley (1707-88)

Published in volume 2 of the author's *Hymns and Sacred Poems*, 1749, with the title 'For a Tender Conscience'. Originally there were five eight-line verses, beginning:

Almighty God of truth and love,
In me Thy power exert.

The 1986 Song Book includes the whole of verse 2 (divided into four-line verses), the second half of verse 3 and the first half of verse 5.

I want, dear Lord, a heart that's true and clean (426)
George G. Jackson (1866-93)

Printed at the end of the author's obituary in *The War Cry*, Christchurch, New Zealand, 18 November 1893, with the note: 'The following song was composed by the ensign some months before his death'. It is said that, after the author's funeral, his unconverted brother Jack discovered the uncompleted lines of this song (ending with the first couplet of the third verse) when he was going through his brother's papers. He apparently claimed salvation, and to mark the dedication of his life to Christ added the last three lines to complete the composition. (The origin of this story is unknown.) The song was included in *The Salvation Soldiers' Song Book*, Melbourne, 1897, compiled by Herbert H. Booth.

I want that adorning divine (589)
 verses: Charlotte Elliott (1789-1871)
 chorus: Anonymous

The verses, headed: 'Thou knowest my desire', appeared in *A Christian Remembrancer*, No. 28, 1848, an annual pocketbook. From the original nine verses, the present Song Book includes verses 1-4 and 9, extensively altered, as in *The Song Book of The Salvation Army*, 1953. The chorus is from a song entitled 'Speak to Me', by Cadet George Daymond, in *The War Cry*, 27 June 1885. It is not known whether he wrote the chorus, or took it from an earlier source.

I want the faith of God (733)
 William J. Pearson (1832-92)

Appeared under the heading: 'Holiness', in *The War Cry*, 24 October 1891.

I want the gift of power within (214)
 Charles Wesley (1707-88)

Published under the title 'Groaning for the Spirit of Adoption' in John and Charles Wesley's *Hymns and Sacred Poems*, 1740. Originally there were six verses. When John Wesley compiled *A Collection of Hymns for the Use of the People called Methodists*, 1780, he omitted the first verse:

> Father, if Thou my Father art,
> Send forth the Spirit of Thy Son,
> Breathe Him into my panting heart,
> And make me know as I am known:
> Make me Thy conscious child, that I
> May, 'Father, Abba, Father', cry.

Now the fifth verse of the original has also been omitted.

I want to tell what God has done (335)
 Sidney E. Cox (1887-1975)

The author said: 'Written in Detroit for the men of the Detroit Men's Social Department'. It appeared in *The Musical Salvationist*, January 1964, under the title: 'This is what the Lord has done'.

I was sinking deep in sin (336)
 James Rowe (1865-1933)

Written in about 1912 and later published by Robert H. Coleman in *The Herald*, 1915.

I will sing of my redeemer (180)
Philip P. Bliss (1838-76)

The words were said to have been found in the author's baggage after the train crash in which he died (29 December 1876). Subsequently the music was written by James McGranahan, and the song, entitled 'My Redeemer', was published in *Welcome Tidings*, 1877, compiled by Robert Lowry, W. H. Doane and Ira D. Sankey. (The *Dictionary of American Hymnology* files suggest that the song appeared earlier, in *Precious Hymns*, c1870, printed for the Bethany Sabbath School, Philadelphia, but the precise date of this publication is not known.)

I will sing the wondrous story (337)
Francis H. Rowley (1854-1952)

Written during 1886, while the author was pastor at the First Baptist Church, North Adams, Massachusetts. He was assisted by a young musician, Peter Bilhorn, who asked for some words to set to music. On the following evening, the inspiration came to him without any particular effort. Later, Ira D. Sankey altered the verses, which originally began 'Can't you sing the wondrous story'. The song was published in *Gospel Hymns No. 5*, 1887, compiled by Ira D. Sankey, James McGranahan and George C. Stebbins, and in Sankey's *Sacred Songs and Solos*, 1888, where the author was named incorrectly as 'F. H. Rawley'.

I would be thy holy temple (786)
Brindley Boon (*b* 1913)

Written when the author was a cadet in the 'Standard Bearers' Session, for the dedication service of the cadets in the Royal Albert Hall, London, 12 May 1950. The words (originally two eight-line verses and a chorus) were printed in the commissioning programme and in *The Musician*, 13 May 1950. The song, entitled 'I Dedicate Myself to Thee', was published in *The Musical Salvationist*, November-December 1950. Subsequently, it was included in *The Song Book of The Salvation Army*, 1953, in four-line verses with a new chorus, written for the tune 'Showers of blessing'. The second chorus was added in the present Song Book, for the tune 'Jesus is looking for thee'.

I would be true, for there are those who trust me (491)
  verses: Howard A. Walter (1883-1918)
  chorus: Anonymous

The verses were apparently written in 1906 or 1907 when the author was teaching English at Waseda University, Tokyo. He sent them home to his mother in the United States, where they were published in *Harper's Bazaar*, May 1907. The chorus appeared anonymously, with these verses, in the *Junior's Guide, Attendance Record and Song Book*, 1933.

If human hearts are often tender (50)

John Gowans (*b* 1934)

From the musical *Hosea*, previewed during officers' councils at Bognor Regis in October 1969, and first presented in public at Lewisham Town Hall, 12 November 1969. The script and score of the musical were published early in 1970 and this song, entitled 'How much more', was also included in *The Musical Salvationist*, April 1970. In comparing our human capacity to love and forgive with God's infinite love and forgiveness (exemplified in the story of Hosea), the verses echo themes from the teaching of Jesus, especially Matthew 7:11.

If so poor a soul as I (492)

Charles Wesley (1707-88)

Published in John and Charles Wesley's *Hymns on the Lord's Supper*, 1745, with the heading: 'Concerning the sacrifice of our persons'. There were six verses, beginning:

> Father, Son and Holy Ghost,
>   One in Three, and Three in One,
> As by the celestial Host
>   Let thy Will on Earth be done;
> Praise by All to Thee be given,
> Glorious Lord of Earth and Heaven!

The present Song Book includes verses 3-5, with minor alterations. Verse 3 originally began 'If so poor a Worm as I'.

If you want pardon, if you want peace (427)

George P. R. Ewens (1841-1926)

Entitled: 'Beneath the Cross', the song appeared in *The War Cry*, 16 June 1881, and again 15 September 1881, when it was 'reprinted by request'. It is said to have been written one night in 1880 when the author received the inspiration for the song and awoke one of his sons at 2 am to write down the verses at his dictation. The fifth verse has now been omitted.

I'll go in the strength of the Lord (734)
Edward Turney (1816-72)

Published under the title: 'Going in the strength of the Lord', in *The Church Missionary Gleaner,* January 1861. It was headed: 'I will go in the strength of the Lord God' (Psalm 71:16) and was signed 'The Macedonian'. The verses, which originally began 'I will go', appeared with several alterations in *Salvation Army Songs,* 1930. The chorus was arranged for the tune 'In the strength of the Lord' by Ivor Bosanko, in *The Musical Salvationist,* July 1983.

I'm a soldier bound for Glory (338)
Richard Jukes (1804-67)

Included in the author's *Hymns for the Living and the Dying, Volume 1,* Fourth edition, 1852, with the title: 'The Heaven-Bound Traveller'. The verses, which began: 'I'm a pilgrim, bound for Glory', have been altered by various salvationist editors, and the fourth verse of the original (part of the author's personal testimony) has been omitted:

> Twenty years have now elapsed
> Since I first began to pray,—
> I have been in many conflicts,
> But I'm here alive today.

I'm but a stranger here (882)
Thomas Rawson Taylor (1807-35)

Apparently written for the tune 'Robin Adair', during the author's last illness. It was published with the title 'Heaven is my Home' in *Memoirs and Select Remains of the Rev Thomas Rawson Taylor,* 1836, by W. S. Matthews. The fourth verse of the original has been omitted.

I'm going to make my life into a melody (858)
Flora Larsson (b 1904)

The author said that this song was inspired by the words of Thomas R. Kelly (1893-1941) quoted in the introduction to his book *A Testament of Devotion,* 1943. Deeply moved by the events of his first day at Haverford College in 1913, he suddenly said: 'I am just going to make my life a miracle!' The chorus concludes with the lines:

> He's going to make my life into a miracle,
> A mighty miracle of grace.

The song, entitled 'A Miracle of Grace', was published in *New Songs for Young People,* May 1968.

I'm not ashamed to own my Lord (735)
Isaac Watts (1674-1748)

Published in part 1 of the author's *Hymns and Spiritual Songs*, Second edition, 1709, with the heading: 'Not ashamed of the Gospel (2 Tim. 1:12)'.

I'm set apart for Jesus (495)
William J. Pearson (1832-92)

Published in *The War Cry*, 6 November 1886, in four eight-line verses, with the title: 'Set apart for Jesus'. A revised version, with three verses (as in the present Song Book), was included in *The War Cry*, 7 April 1894.

Immortal, invisible, God only wise (8)
Walter C. Smith (1824-1908)

Published originally in the author's *Hymns of Christ and the Christian Life*, 1867, under the heading: 'Now unto the King eternal, immortal, invisible, the only wise God' (1 Timothy 1:17). The verses were then revised for *Congregational Hymns*, 1884, compiled by W. Garrett Horder. The present version omits the fourth verse and combines the opening couplets of the fifth and sixth verses, to form a new fourth verse, as in *The English Hymnal*, 1906.

Immortal love, for ever full (496)
John Greenleaf Whittier (1807-92)

From the poem 'Our Master', which the author sent to a friend in 1866 with the note: 'The poem presents my view of Christ as the special manifestation of the love of God to humanity'. It was published in the author's *The Tent on the Beach and Other Poems*, 1867, with 38 verses. The present version includes verses 1, 2, 5, 11 and 13.

In Christ there is no east or west (826)
William A. Dunkerley (1852-1941)

Written for 'The Pageant of Darkness and Light' at the London Missionary Society's exhibition 'The Orient in London' in the Agricultural Hall, London, in 1908. The pageant was in four parts: North America, Africa, the South Seas, and India, and these verses are from the last part. Entitled 'No East or West', they were published in the author's *Bees in Amber*, 1913, under his pen-name, John Oxenham.

In days long past the mercy seat (590)
Doris N. Rendell (*b* 1896)

It appeared in *The War Cry*, 25 October 1952, and later in a revised version, with a chorus, in *The Musical Salvationist*, September-October 1957. Subsequently, it was included in *Songs of His Love*, *c*1972, a collection of the author's songs and poems published privately. The chorus has now been omitted.

In heavenly love abiding (736)
Anna L. Waring (1823-1910)

Published in the author's *Hymns and Meditations*, 1850, with the heading: 'I will fear no evil, for Thou art with me' (Psalm 23:4).

In loving kindness Jesus came (339)
Charles H. Gabriel (1856-1932)

Published by the Moody Bible Institute Colportage Association, Chicago, in *Revival Hymns*, 1905, compiled by D. B. Towner and Charles M. Alexander. (The words often appear under the author's pseudonym, 'Charlotte G. Homer'.)

In my heart there's a gladsome melody (340)
Sidney E. Cox (1887-1975)

Written in Atlanta, Georgia. The author said: 'It is just one of those songs that seemed to suddenly appear from nowhere. I was amusing myself at the piano and suddenly found myself singing the chorus.' The chorus apparently became popular in the United States and Canada and was then introduced during the 'Day of Fire' meetings at the Royal Albert Hall, London (31 October 1929) when General Edward J. Higgins returned from a campaign in Canada. The complete song, entitled 'A melody in my heart today', was included in *The Musical Salvationist*, December 1929.

In the Army of Jesus we've taken our stand (687)
Fred W. Fry (1859-1939)

Entitled: 'I'll stand for Christ alone', the song appeared in *The Musical Salvationist*, July 1887, beginning: 'In the Army of Jesus I've taken my stand'. It has since been extensively altered and now appears in the version revised for *The Song Book of The Salvation Army*, 1953.

In the cross of Christ I glory (112)
John Bowring (1792-1872)

These verses, based on Galatians 6:14, appeared in the author's *Hymns*, 1825, with the title: 'The Cross of Christ'. Although the hymn is said to have been inspired by seeing a cross standing above the ruins of a church on the island of Macao, near Hong Kong, it is not certain that the author would have visited this area before 1825.

In the depths of my soul's greatest longing (493)
Margaret Lodge MacMillan (b 1923)

The author said that the song was written early in 1946. Shortly after the death of her mother, she graduated as a registered nurse from the Grace General Hospital in St John's, Newfoundland, and went home to her father in Montreal. Describing the circumstances, she wrote: 'I felt a vast emptiness on arrival home, due to the loss, a large new city and hospital environments to become accustomed to. I consequently reached further to fill the void. My words were penned at that time.' About six months afterwards, the author with her brother and sister first sang the song in three-part harmony over the radio at a youth rally in Montreal. Later, with a tune by Brindley Boon, composed in 1963 during his return journey to England from Canada, the song was published in *The Musical Salvationist*, April 1967, under the title: 'In Deeper Consecration'.

In the fight, say, does your heart grow weary (805)
Richard Slater (1854-1939)

Included in *The Musical Salvationist*, December 1886, under the title: 'Never mind: go on!'

In the love of Jesus I have found a refuge (341)
Sidney E. Cox (1887-1975)

Entitled: 'A Sure Hiding Place', the song appeared in *The Musical Salvationist*, November 1931.

In the secret of thy presence (591)
Albert Orsborn (1886-1967)

The author said that in 1920, when he was in his first year as a divisional commander, he was asked to write a song for corps officers' councils to be conducted by Mrs General Bramwell Booth at Clapton. The inspiration came after the introductory meeting, when he was staying overnight with friends at Leyton. He said: 'About 5.30 am, I awoke, with a very real sense of a Presence quite near me. Then slowly, but easily, these verses and the chorus came into my mind. All I had to do was to catch the inspiration and write down the words, which, of course, I did—by candlelight.' The song was introduced that evening at the councils. It was included in *Songs for Use during Special Campaigns in the United Kingdom,* 1923, and also in *The Musical Salvationist,* November 1923, where a note stated that it had already appeared in several Army periodicals.

In the shadow of the cross (145)
Albert Orsborn (1886-1967)

Based on the text 'In the place where he was crucified, there was a garden' (John 19:41). The author said, 'There is something beautiful in the thought that when our Lord's labour and sorrow were over, His body was taken from the cross and laid in the security and peace of a garden, from which He rose again to prove to us that there is always the promise of fulfilment and of life eternal even at the very mouth of the dark tomb.' The song, entitled 'There was a Garden', was included in *The Musical Salvationist,* April 1926, with music by Bandmaster George Marshall. The chorus has now been omitted.

In their appointed days (494)
Albert Orsborn (1886-1967)

These verses are from a song written for a central holiness meeting at Clapton in 1916 or 1917. The chorus, which began 'Let the beauty of Jesus be seen in me', has now been omitted, but is No. 77 in the chorus section of the Song Book. It was inspired by a sermon on the text: 'And let the beauty of the Lord our God be upon us' (Psalm 90:17), which the author heard at Norwich Citadel in about 1907. The verses and chorus were included in *The Beauty of Jesus,* 1947, a collection of the author's songs and poems.

In this hour of dedication (787)
Doris N. Rendell (*b* 1896)

Originally written in three eight-line verses and a chorus for the dedication and commissioning of cadets from the 'Challengers' Session, 1945-46, in the Congress Hall, Clapton, on Monday 20 May 1946. It was published in the souvenir programme under the heading: 'The Song of Dedication'. The verses were rearranged by the author, with a new chorus, for *The Song Book of The Salvation Army*, 1953.

In your heart of hearts are you a trifle weary (244)
John Gowans (*b* 1934)

From the musical *Glory!*, where Captain Campbell welcomes the congregation to a meeting in the Salvation Army hall at Folkestone, and introduces the song with these words: 'You could go out of this building a changed person, transformed by the power of Christ. Salvation is yours for the asking.' Extracts from the musical were introduced at the Mermaid Theatre, London, on 7 July 1975, and the complete musical was presented at the Royal Festival Hall on 12 July 1976, during the British Congress.

Is it nothing to you that one day Jesus came (245)
Albert E. Mingay (*b* 1904)

The author said: 'I was travelling one morning in a crowded compartment on the Piccadilly Underground railway line into the City of London. . . . I began to occupy myself by wondering about some of the people seen from my vantage point. . . . The thought which slipped into my mind became a question. What meaning, if any, had the Christian gospel for these people? How remote they seemed to be from thoughts of Calvary! The morning train lumbered inexorably on and began to form a rhythmic pattern in my subconscious mind. . . . My query about the impact of the Christian message upon these people became somehow merged with the rhythm, and into that pattern came the words: "Is it nothing to you, all ye that pass by?" (Lamentations 1:12). So the theme developed.' The song, entitled 'Is it nothing to you?' was published in *The Musical Salvationist*, May-June 1956.

Is there a heart o'erbound by sorrow (246)
Edward H. Joy (1871-1949)

The author said that the idea came to him one Saturday after reading the revised marginal version of 1 Peter 5:7—'Casting all your anxieties upon Him'. He introduced the song that evening and on the following day at Thornton Heath Corps, and later used it widely in Canada. It was included in *The Musical Salvationist*, December 1929, under the title: 'All your anxiety'.

Is there a heart that is waiting (247)
verses: Annie L. James
chorus: May Agnew Stephens (1865-1935)

The verses appeared in *Bright Gems*, 1887, compiled by Philip Phillips, with the chorus 'Jesus is passing this way'. The chorus in the present Song Book is from a song beginning 'Many a year thou hast wander'd' in *The Musical Salvationist*, December 1890.

It came upon the midnight clear (83)
Edmund H. Sears (1810-76)

Written in 1849, and published in the *Christian Register*, 29 December 1849. The present Song Book omits the second and fourth verses of the original.

It is the blood that washes white (113)
William J. Pearson (1832-92)

Published under the title: "'Tis the Blood!' in *The War Cry*, 23 February 1882, when the author was a staff-captain. Three verses and the chorus have been omitted.

It was love reached me when far away (342)
Sidney E. Cox (1887-1975)

The song was widely used by cadets in Atlanta, Georgia, when the author was training principal, and then appeared in *The Musical Salvationist*, April 1941, under the title: 'When His loved reached me'.

I've a friend, of friends the fairest (343)
Ruth F. Tracy (1870-1960)

Written for the tune 'Silver Threads', c1896-97, when the author was on the staff of *The War Cry*, editing a page of original songs and writing 'Boomers' Notes' under the name of 'Deborah Do-Better'. This song was the expression of her joy in the friendship of Jesus. It was included in *The Musical Salvationist*, December 1899, under the title 'Take the World but give me Jesus', and was later revised by the compilers of *Salvation Army Songs*, 1930.

I've felt a new and loving touch (215)
Iva Lou Samples (*b* 1946)

In January 1971, a revival occurred at the School for Officers'

Training in Atlanta, Georgia, where the author was field training officer for single women. She later said: 'It was during this revival spirit that I wrote "His Loving Touch", which was a reflection of my own personal feelings, and the joint feelings of cadets and staff as we experienced an overwhelming sense of God's love and power, and a special oneness with each other.' Written initially for guitar accompaniment and first sung by the author 'in a devotional style', the song subsequently appeared in *The Musical Salvationist*, April 1974.

I've found a friend in Jesus, he's everything to me (344)
Charles W. Fry (1838-82)

According to a note attached to the author's manuscript, the song was written in Lincoln (June 1881) in the home of a Mr Wilkinson. It was sung at an all-day holiness convention at City Road Chapel, London, on 20 December 1881 and appeared in *The War Cry*, 29 December 1881, under the title 'I've found a friend in Jesus'.

I've found a friend, O such a friend (345)
James G. Small (1817-88)

Published in *The Revival Hymn Book*, Second series, 1864, and apparently also in the author's *Psalms and Sacred Songs*, 1866.

I've found the pearl of greatest price (346)
John Mason (c1640-94)

Published in the author's *Spiritual Songs, or Songs of Praise to Almighty God upon several occasions*, 1683, with the title: 'A Song of Praise for Christ'. There were originally four eight-line verses and one four-line verse. The present version appears as in *The Song Book of The Salvation Army*, 1953.

I've found the secret of success (806)
Ruth F. Tracy (1870-1960)

Written apparently at the request of Miriam Booth (1889-1917) who was beginning to sing solos in meetings led by her father, Bramwell Booth. The author said that before writing the song she had been overwhelmed by the unhappiness of some loved and trusted by her 'who had turned back'. She also had in mind words which William Booth often said to officers: 'Hold on in the dark, in the very face of death. Have courage. Hold on!' Included in *The Young Soldier*, 13 April 1901. The chorus has now been omitted.

Jehovah is our strength (9)
Samuel Barnard (*d* 1807)

Published anonymously in *Spiritual Songs for Zion's Travellers, being a collection of Hymns from different authors; together with many original pieces*, 1799, compiled by Samuel Barnard. (Although the authors of the hymns in this collection were not identified, this hymn was later attributed to Samuel Barnard in Julian's *Dictionary of Hymnology*, 1907.) These verses, entitled 'Confidence in God', originally began: 'Jehovah is my strength', and were written in the first person singular throughout. The present version, omitting the third verse of the original, appeared in *Salvation Army Songs*, 1930.

Jesus, all-atoning Lamb (497)
Charles Wesley (1707-88)

Published in volume 1 of the author's *Hymns and Sacred Poems*, 1749, in a section headed: 'Hymns for Believers'. There were seven verses, originally beginning: 'Gentle Jesu, lovely Lamb'. The first line was altered in *A Collection of Hymns for the Use of the People called Methodists*, 1780, compiled by John Wesley. The fourth, sixth and seventh verses of the original have now been omitted.

Jesus, and shall it ever be (592)
Joseph Grigg (*c*1720-68)

First published in the author's *Four Hymns on Divine Subjects wherein the Patience and Love of our Divine Saviour is displayed*, 1765. There were seven verses, beginning:

> Jesus! and shall it ever be!
> A mortal man ashamed of Thee?
> Scorn'd be the thought by rich and poor;
> O may I scorn it more and more!

A revised version, altered by B. Francis, appeared in *A Selection of Hymns from the Best Authors*, 1787, compiled by John Rippon. The present Song Book includes verses 1, 4, 5 and 6 from this version, with a few later alterations, as in *Salvation Army Songs*, 1899.

Jesus bids us shine with a clear, pure light (841)
Susan B. Warner (1819-85)

Published anonymously in the magazine *The Little Corporal*, July 1868, and in *The American Sacred Songster*, 1868, compiled by Philip Phillips.

Jesus calls us; o'er the tumult (428)
                              Cecil Frances Alexander (1818-95)
Based on Matthew 4:18-20. Published in *Hymns for Public Worship*, 1853, under the heading 'St Andrew's Day'. Originally the second verse began 'As, of old, St Andrew heard it'.

Jesus came down my ransom to be (114)
                              Emmanuel Rolfe (1853-1914)
Appeared in *The Musical Salvationist*, July 1894, a special issue including 'Songs from many Lands'. This song, entitled 'Jesus came my Ransom to be' was headed 'Jamaica', where the author was then stationed.

Jesus came to save me (347)
                              Sidney E. Cox (1887-1975)
Written in Atlanta, Georgia, and first used in the United States, it then appeared in *The Musical Salvationist*, March 1939, entitled: 'This one thing I know'.

Jesus comes! Let all adore him (159)
                              Thomas Kelly (1769-1855)
Published in the author's *Hymns*, Third edition, 1809, with the heading: 'Prepare ye, the way of the Lord' (Isaiah 40:3). The verses, which have been extensively altered, originally began:

> Lo he comes! Let all adore him:
> 'Tis the God of Grace and Truth:
> Go, prepare the way before him:
> Make the rugged places smooth:
> Lo! he comes, the mighty Lord:
> Great his work, and his reward.

The revised version was included in *Supplementary Songs for the General's Officers' Councils*, c1946, and *The Song Book of The Salvation Army*, 1953.

Jesus, friend of little children (842)
                              Walter J. Mathams (1853-1931)
Written in May 1882, in Edinburgh, at the request of the Psalms and Hymns Committee of the Baptist Union. It was published in *Psalms and Hymns for School and Home*, 1882, with the heading 'I have called you friends' (John 15:15). The fourth and sixth verses of the original have been omitted.

Jesus, give thy blood-washed Army (593)
William J. Pearson (1832-92)

Published under the title: 'We shall have the victory', in *The War Cry*, 5 June 1886, at the time of the first International Congress of The Salvation Army, 28 May-4 June 1886. The fourth verse of the original has now been omitted.

Jesus, good above all other (97)
Percy Dearmer (1867-1936)

Written for *The English Hymnal*, 1906, beginning 'Jesu, good above all other', and later revised for *Songs of Praise*, Enlarged edition, 1931. The opening lines were based on a verse by J. M. Neale, beginning 'Jesus, kind above all other', in his *Medieval Hymns*, Second edition, 1863.

Jesus, I fain would find (594)
Charles Wesley (1707-88)

From the author's *Short Hymns on Select Passages of the Holy Scriptures*, 1762, based on the text: 'Be zealous' (Revelation 3:19). The original eight-line verse was divided into two four-line verses in *A Collection of Hymns for the Use of the People called Methodists*, 1780, compiled by John Wesley.

Jesus, I my cross have taken (498)
verses: Henry Francis Lyte (1793-1847)
chorus: attributed to Jas. L. Elginburg

The verses are from a poem with six eight-line verses, signed 'G' in *Sacred Poetry*, Third edition, 1824, published in Edinburgh, and *The Christian Psalmist*, 1825, compiled by James Montgomery. Subsequently it also appeared anonymously in other publications and was later included, in a slightly different form, in *Poems chiefly Religious*, 1833, by Henry Francis Lyte. The chorus is from a song beginning 'I will follow Thee, my Saviour', in *The Revivalist*, 1872, edited by Joseph Hillman, where the words and music were said to be by 'Jas. L., Elginburg, C. W.' The *Dictionary of American Hymnology* files indicate that the author of this song is identified as James Lawson in some hymn books.

Jesus is glorified (195)
Charles Wesley (1707-88)

Published in *Hymns of Petition and Thanksgiving for the*

Promise of the Father, 1746, a collection of 32 hymns for Whit Sunday. There were six verses, beginning:

> Sinners, lift up your hearts,
> The Promise to receive!
> Jesus Himself imparts,
> He comes in man to live;
> The Holy Ghost to man is given;
> Rejoice in God sent down from heaven.

The first and last verses of the original have now been omitted.

Jesus is my Saviour, this I know (348)
Richard Slater (1854-1939)

Written early in December 1889 to assist Herbert Booth who had promised to provide a song for the Christmas issue of *The Young Soldier*, but had only been able to compose a tune. Entitled: 'Tarry at the Cross of Jesus', the song appeared in *The Young Soldier*, 25 December 1889 and was then included in Herbert Booth's collection *Songs of Peace and War*, 1890.

Jesus is tenderly calling thee home (248)
Fanny Crosby (1820-1915)

Headed 'Arise, he calleth thee' (John 11:28) in *Gospel Hymns No. 4*, 1883, compiled by Ira D. Sankey, James McGranahan and George C. Stebbins.

Jesus, keep me near the cross (115)
Fanny Crosby (1820-1915)

Entitled 'Near the Cross', with music by W. H. Doane, in *Bright Jewels for the Sunday School*, 1869, edited by Robert Lowry, assisted by William F. Sherwin and Chester G. Allen.

Jesus, lead me up the mountain (429)
verses 1-2 and chorus: William J. Pearson (1832-92)
verse 3: Catherine Baird (1895-1984)

This song 'by Major Pearson' appeared originally in *The War Cry*, 13 December 1884, entitled: 'Higher Up'. There were five verses and the chorus. A revised version, omitting two verses, was included anonymously in *The Musical Salvationist*, February 1910. Subsequently, the third verse of the present version was written by Catherine Baird for *The Song Book of The Salvation Army*, 1953.

Jesus, Lord, we come to hail thee (595)
Catherine Baird (1895-1984)

Entitled 'Communion through Christ', the verses appeared

in *The Musical Salvationist*, July 1964, with music by Retired Bandmaster Bert T. Langworthy, of Birmingham Citadel.

Jesus, lover of my soul (737)
Charles Wesley (1707-88)

Published with the title 'In Temptation', in *Hymns and Sacred Poems*, 1740, by John and Charles Wesley. Originally there were five verses, beginning 'Jesu, Lover of my Soul', but John Wesley omitted the third verse of the original when he compiled *Hymns and Spiritual Songs, intended for the use of real Christians of all denominations*, 1753.

Jesus loves me! This I know (843)
Anna B. Warner (1827-1915)

The verses appeared on page 243 of the novel *Say and Seal*, 1860, by Anna and Susan Warner, where a sick boy, Johnny Fax, is visited by John Linden, his Sunday-school teacher. The chorus was added in *The Golden Shower*, 1862, compiled by William Bradbury, where the fourth verse was slightly altered. The third verse of the original has now been omitted:

> Jesus loves me! loves me still,
> Though I'm very weak and ill;
> From His shining throne on high,
> Comes to watch me where I lie.

Jesus, my Lord, through thy triumph I claim (543)
William Booth (1829-1912)

Entitled: 'Victory for Me', this song appeared in *The War Cry*, 22 September 1900, with the note: 'Sung for the first time at the National Staff Council at Clapton, August 30th, 1900.' The original second verse has been omitted.

Jesus, my Lord, to thee I cry (291)
Eliza H. Hamilton

Published in *The Garner*, 1878, compiled by J. R. Sweney, and *Spiritual Songs for Gospel Meetings and the Sunday School*, 1878, compiled by Elisha A. Hoffman and J. H. Tenney. Later, it was included in *Sacred Songs and Solos*, 1881, compiled by Ira D. Sankey, who found the verses in a Christian newspaper and set them to music. He said that the hymn was written when the author heard about a young girl in Scotland who was converted after attending a revival meeting. Wanting to be sure of salvation, she spoke to her minister, who advised her to read the Bible and pray, but she exclaimed, 'I canna read, I canna pray! Lord Jesus, take me as I am'.

Jesus my Lord will love me for ever (349)
Norman J. Clayton (b 1903)

Published in the author's *Word of Life Melodies, No. 1*, 1943, a collection of songs from *The Word of Life Hour*, directed by Jack Wyrtzen, which was broadcast by radio on Saturday evenings from New York.

Jesus, my strength, my hope (596)
Charles Wesley (1707-88)

Published with the title 'A Poor Sinner' in *Hymns and Sacred Poems*, 1742, by John and Charles Wesley. Originally there were seven verses, beginning 'Jesu, my strength, my hope'. The present Song Book includes verses 1, 3, 4 and 2, omitting verses 5-7.

Jesus, my truth, my way (597)
Charles Wesley (1707-88)

Published in Volume 1 of the author's *Hymns and Sacred Poems*, 1749, in a section headed 'Hymns for Believers'. There were originally seven eight-line verses, beginning 'Jesu, my truth, my way'. The present Song Book includes verse 1 of the original (divided into two four-line verses), with the first half of verse 5 and the second half of verse 7.

Jesus, precious Saviour, thou hast saved my soul (499)
William H. Davis (1854-1918)

The author's first song, it was written, he said, 'while riding on the top of an omnibus'. It appeared under the title: 'A Volunteer', in *The War Cry*, 10 January 1880, and was reprinted by request, 6 March 1880. The fifth verse has now been omitted.

Jesus, save me through and through (430)
William J. Pearson (1832-92)

This song 'by Staff-Captain Pearson' was published in *The War Cry*, 4 August 1881, with the title: 'Through and through'. Later it appeared in *The War Cry*, 13 May 1885, where it was said to be 'by W. Hildreth, Keighley Corps'. The fifth and sixth verses have been omitted.

Jesus saved me! O the rapture (350)
Sidney R. Hubbard (1898-1984)

Apparently written in Spring 1956 for a special meeting at Welling Corps in aid of the self-denial appeal. Although the author received a letter from the Head of the Music Editorial Department in 1960 saying that the song had been accepted for publication, it does not seem to have been published until it appeared in the present Song Book.

Jesus, Saviour, pilot me (598)
Edward Hopper (c1816-88)

Written while the author was pastor of the Church of the Sea and Land, in New York City. It appeared anonymously in *The Sailor's Magazine*, 3 March 1871, and then in *The Baptist Praise Book*, 1871. Originally there were six verses.

Jesus, see me at thy feet (292)
Richard Slater (1854-1939)

Written, the author said, at the Congress Hall, Clapton, in a few moments on 9 September 1887. He had been thinking about the use made by the Army of Robert Lowry's song: 'What can wash away my sin, Nothing but the blood of Jesus', and tried in the same way to explain simply and clearly that salvation comes through the blood of Jesus. It was published in *The Musical Salvationist*, November 1887, under the title: 'Nothing but thy blood can save me'.

Jesus shall reign where'er the sun (160)
Isaac Watts (1674-1748)

From the second part of the author's version of Psalm 72, entitled: 'Christ's Kingdom among the Gentiles', published in *The Psalms of David Imitated in the Language of the New Testament, and apply'd to the Christian State and Worship*, 1719. The second, third and fourth verses of the original have been omitted.

Jesus, so dear to us (955)
V. Hill

From *The Fellowship Hymn Book*, Revised edition, 1933, where it appeared 'by permission of Hills & Co, Ltd'.

Jesus, stand among us (599)
William Pennefather (1816-73)

Possibly written for the Mildmay Conferences which the author commenced at Barnet and continued for several years in London. It was published posthumously in his *Original Hymns and Thoughts in Verse*, 1875, with the heading: 'Then said Jesus to them again, Peace be unto you: as my Father hath sent me, even so send I you' (John 20:21).

Jesus, tender lover of my soul (600)
verses: Edward H. Joy (1871-1949)
chorus: Arthur S. Arnott (1870-1941)

The chorus was written for a melody which Arthur Arnott adapted from a tune he heard at a Sunday-school anniversary. Edward Joy heard the chorus at congress meetings in Melbourne when he was travelling with Commissioner T. Henry Howard, and later wrote the verses during a spiritual day for cadets at Clapton, where General Bramwell Booth spoke of Christ as the 'Gardener of the Soul'. The song was published in *The Musical Salvationist*, August 1920, a special issue entitled 'International Gleanings', which included songs collected during Commissioner Howard's world tour in 1919.

Jesus, the gift divine I know (601)
Charles Wesley (1707-88)

These verses are from the author's *Short Hymns on Select Passages of the Holy Scriptures*, 1762. Verses 1 and 2 were based on the text 'If thou knewest the gift of God, etc' (John 4:10). Verse 3 was the first verse of a hymn with three verses, based on the text 'Pure religion and undefiled before God, etc' (James 1:27).

Jesus, the name high over all (60)
verses: Charles Wesley (1707-88)
chorus: Anonymous

Published in Volume 1 of the author's *Hymns and Sacred Poems*, 1749, with the title 'After preaching (in a Church)'. There were 22 verses, beginning:

> Jesu, accept the grateful song,
> My Wisdom and my Might,
> 'Tis Thou hast loosed the stammering tongue,
> And taught my hands to fight.

The present Song Book includes verses 9, 10, 12, 13, 18 and 22. The chorus was linked with these verses in *Revival Music*, 1876, compiled by William Booth.

Jesus, the very thought of thee (61)
attributed to Bernard of Clairvaux (c1091-1153)
translated by Edward Caswall (1814-78)

The Latin hymn 'Dulcis Jesu memoria' is found in manuscripts dating from the 12th and 13th centuries, though the attribution to Bernard of Clairvaux is uncertain. The translation is from Caswall's *Lyra Catholica*, 1849. ('Jesus, thou joy of loving hearts', by Ray Palmer, was translated from another version of the same Latin hymn.)

Jesus, thou hast won us (788)
Will J. Brand (1889-1977)

Written to the tune 'Anything for Jesus', for *The Song Book of The Salvation Army*, 1953.

Jesus, thou joy of loving hearts (602)
attributed to Bernard of Clairvaux (c1091-1153)
translated by Ray Palmer (1808-87)

The Latin hymn 'Jesu, dulcis memoria' was included in Hermann A. Daniel's *Thesaurus Hymnologicus*, Vol 1, 1841. The translation appeared in the *Sabbath Hymn Book*, 1858, edited by E. A. Park, Austin Phelps, and Lowell Mason, and was later included in *The Poetical Works of Ray Palmer*, 1876, under the title 'Jesus the Beloved'. The third verse of the translation has now been omitted. ('Jesus, the very thought of thee' was translated from another version of the same Latin hymn.)

Jesus, thy blood and righteousness (116)
Nicolaus L. von Zinzendorf (1700-60)
translated by John Wesley (1703-91)

James Mearns, in Julian's *Dictionary of Hymnology*, p 230, said that the German hymn 'Christi Blut und Gerechtigkeit' was written during the author's return journey from the West Indies in 1739, either on the island of St Eustatius, in the Dutch West Indies, or on St Eustachius's Day (29 March 1739). It was published in 1739 in an Appendix to the *Herrnhut Gesang-Buch*, 1735. The translation, entitled 'The Believer's Triumph', appeared in *Hymns and Sacred Poems*, 1740, by John and Charles Wesley, in 24 verses, beginning 'Jesu, Thy Blood . . .'. Later, 11 verses, slightly altered, were included in *A Collection of Hymns for the Use of the People called Methodists*, 1780, compiled by John Wesley, from which the verses in the present Song Book were selected.

Jesus, thy fulness give (431)
William J. Pearson (1832-92)

The verses are from a song published in *The War Cry*, 6

February 1892, which originally had three eight-line verses. The chorus is from another song by the same author, which appeared in *The War Cry*, 6 October 1881, beginning:

> I'm walking with the Lord;
> I'm walking in the light;
> I'm wearing clean Salvation robes,
> To walk with Him in white.

Jesus, thy purity bestow (432)

William J. Pearson (1832-92)

Appeared under the heading: 'Holiness' on a page of songs in *The War Cry*, 7 November 1891. The fourth verse has been omitted.

Jesus wants me for a sunbeam (844)

Nellie Talbot

This song is said to have been written when the author came to a meeting in London as a delegate from her Sunday-school. It was published in *Make His Praise Glorious*, 1900, compiled by Edwin O. Excell.

Jesus, we look to thee (603)

Charles Wesley (1707-88)

Published in Volume 2 of the author's *Hymns and Sacred Poems*, 1749, in a section headed 'Hymns for Christian Friends'. Originally there were four eight-line verses, beginning 'Jesu, we look to thee'. Now, the first half of verse 2 and the last verse of the original have been omitted from the Song Book.

Jesus, where'er thy people meet (604)

William Cowper (1731-1800)

This hymn, and 'O Lord, our languid frames inspire', by John Newton, were apparently written in 1769 for the opening of a new prayer room at Olney, and appeared together in Book 2 of the *Olney Hymns*, 1779, under the heading 'On opening a Place for Social Prayer'. The third and fifth verses, which referred to this occasion, have now been omitted:

> Dear Shepherd of thy chosen few,
> Thy former mercies here renew;
> Here to our waiting hearts proclaim
> The sweetness of thy saving name.
>
> Behold! at thy commanding word
> We stretch the curtain and the cord,
> Come thou, and fill this wider space,
> And help us with a large encrease.

In a letter to Mr Clunie (April 1769), John Newton said:
> We are going to remove our prayer-meeting to the great room in the Great House. It is a noble place, with a parlour behind it, and holds 130 people conveniently. Pray for us, that the Lord may be in the midst of us there, and that as He has now given us a Rehoboth [Genesis 26:22], and has made room for us, so that He may be pleased to add to our numbers, and make us fruitful in the land.' (*John Newton*, 1868, compiled by Josiah Bull, pages 165-6.)

Jesus, with what gladness I can truly sing (859)
Gladys M. Taylor (*b* 1905)

Written in November 1927 at the Highbury Nursing Home, London, when a cycle accident, at Springbourne, Bournemouth, prevented the author from taking part in 'The Great Salvation Siege' campaign. Later, when asked at short notice for a young people's song for *Salvation Army Songs*, 1930, she wrote this song out from memory, omitting one of the original verses.

Joy! joy! joy! there is joy in The Salvation Army (807)
William J. Pearson (1832-92)

Beginning 'Joy! joy! joy! there's joy in The Salvation Army', the song was published in *The War Cry*, 13 July 1882, with the title 'Joy in the Army'.

Joy to the world! the Lord is come (84)
Isaac Watts (1674-1748)

A paraphrase of the second part of Psalm 98, entitled 'The Messiah's Coming and Kingdom', in the author's *The Psalms of David Imitated in the Language of the New Testament*, 1719. The third verse of the original has now been omitted.

Joyful, joyful, we adore thee (10)
Henry Van Dyke (1852-1933)

Apparently written c1908 when the author was visiting Williams College, Massachusetts. Inspired by the beauty of the Berkshire Mountains, he wrote the verses to be sung to the tune of the 'Ode to Joy' from Beethoven's Ninth Symphony. With the title 'Hymn of Joy' it appeared in *The Poems of Henry Van Dyke*, 1911, in a section headed 'Songs of Hearth and Altar'.

Joyful news to all mankind (249)
Charles Coller (1863-1935)

Published in *The Musical Salvationist*, February 1920, under the title: 'Mighty to save!' (a phrase derived from Isaiah 63:1).

In his introductory notes, Brigadier Arthur Goldsmith said: 'The chorus has already proved to be a great success'.

Just as I am, thine own to be (860)
Mary Anne Hearn (1834-1909)

Published under the author's pen-name 'Marianne Farningham' in *The Voice of Praise: for Sunday School and Home*, 1886, with the heading: 'Early will I seek Thee' (Psalm 63:1). The third verse of the original has now been omitted.

Just as I am, without one plea (293)
Charlotte Elliott (1789-1871)

Written in about 1834, at Westfield Lodge, Brighton, when the author was unwell and other members of her family were at a bazaar in aid of St Mary's Hall, Brighton, a school for the daughters of clergymen. While she was alone and unable to help, she wrote the verses, based on the advice given to her in 1822 by Dr César Malan: 'You must come to Christ just as you are.' The verses appeared in the 1836 edition of *The Invalid's Hymn Book*, under the heading 'Him that cometh unto Me, I will in no wise cast out' (John 6:37).

Just outside the land of promise (433)
Walter H. Windybank (1872-1952)

Written, the author said, after he had listened to an address by Major (later Brigadier) Albert Bartlett, on the wanderings of the Israelites in the wilderness. The song appeared in *The Musical Salvationist*, January-February 1949, under the title 'On the Threshold', and was then included, slightly altered, in *The Song Book of The Salvation Army*, 1953.

King of love so condescending (500)
William D. Pennick (1884-1944)

The author said that in southern India there is a vast network of waterways, some of which are extremely narrow and even go tunnelling through the hills. He wrote this prayer of adoration and consecration in Ceylon, in circumstances which reminded him of these 'narrowed waters', when his heart cried out for some new blessing in song—'something beautiful that would help and inspire the souls of men'. The song, entitled: 'Every hour and power for Jesus!' was published in *The Musical Salvationist*, December 1919. The chorus has now been omitted.

King of my life, I crown thee now (117)
Jennie E. Hussey (1874-1958)

Published in *New Songs of Praise and Power, No. 3*, 1921, and later in *The Musical Salvationist*, March-April 1946.

Kneeling before thee, Lord, I am praying (501)
Jessie Mountain (1895-1981)

Entitled: 'Into Thy Hands', the song appeared in *The Musical Salvationist*, September-October 1951, with music by the author's husband, Bandmaster Herbert A. Mountain.

Kneeling in penitence I make my prayer (605)
John Gowans (b 1934)

From the musical *Take-Over Bid*, introduced on 1 October 1967 during corps officers' councils at Clacton-on-Sea, Essex, and then presented at Reading Town Hall, 14 October 1967, and Acton Town Hall, 21 October 1967. This song, entitled 'A Prayer', is sung by the young salvationists while John, their leader, kneels in penitence to acknowledge his past failure to rely on God's strength. The third verse originally began: 'Though I am young in years, youth Thou canst use', but was altered to the present version in *Songs of Faith*, 1971, and *Keep Singing!*, 1976.

Knowing my failings, knowing my fears (294)
John Gowans (b 1934)

From the musical *Jesus Folk* when, after the resurrection of Jesus, Peter reaffirms his love for Christ three times, as in John 21:15-17. An abridged version of the musical was presented at the finale of the British Congress at Wembley, on 10 July 1972, and the first full-length presentation was in the Fairfield Halls, Croydon, on 25 January 1973.

Lamp of our feet, whereby we trace (654)
Bernard Barton (1784-1849)

Apparently written in 1826 or 1827, based on Psalm 119:105. It was published in 11 verses, entitled 'The Bible', in *The Reliquary*, 1836, by Bernard and Lucy Barton. The present Song Book includes verses 1-3, 9 and 11.

Lead, kindly Light, amid the encircling gloom (606)
John H. Newman (1801-90)

Written on 16 June 1833, while the author was becalmed for a week in the Straits of Bonifacio, on a boat bound for

Marseilles. Since December 1832 he had been travelling through southern Europe, often thinking about his future work and the state of the Church in England. The poetry which he wrote at this time reflected his personal feelings and the circumstances surrounding him. These verses were published in the *British Magazine*, March 1834, with the title 'Faith—Heavenly Leadings'; in the author's *Lyra Apostolica*, 1836, with the heading 'Unto the godly there ariseth up light in the darkness' (Psalm 112:4); and later in his *Occasional Verses*, 1868, with the title 'The Pillar of the Cloud'.

Lead us, heavenly Father, lead us (607)
James Edmeston (1791-1867)

Published in the author's *Sacred Lyrics*, Second set, 1821, with the heading 'Hymn, Written for the Children of the London Orphan Asylum'. (When the verses appeared in *The War Cry*, 9 February 1884, they were said to be original for *The War Cry*, by Sister M. Sloman, Exeter 2 Corps.)

Leave God to order all thy ways (738)
Georg Neumark (1621-81)
translated by Catherine Winkworth (1827-78)

The German hymn 'Wer nur den lieben Gott lässt walten' was written in December 1641 or January 1642, at Kiel after the author had unexpectedly secured employment, as a tutor in the family of a judge, Stephan Henning. In thanksgiving to God he wrote these verses, which were later published in his *Fortgepflantzter Musikalisch-Poetischer Lustwald*, 1657, with the title 'A hymn of consolation'. The translation, headed 'Thirteenth Sunday after Trinity', appeared in Catherine Winkworth's *Lyra Germanica: Hymns for the Sundays and Chief Festivals of the Christian Year*, 1855. The present Song Book includes verses 1, 3 and 7 of the translation.

Let all the world in every corner sing (11)
George Herbert (1593-1633)

Entitled 'Antiphon' in *The Temple*, 1633, a collection of the author's poems published shortly after his death.

Let earth and Heaven agree (62)
Charles Wesley (1707-88)

Published in a pamphlet *Hymns on God's Everlasting Love*, 1741-2, and later reprinted in *The Arminian Magazine*, in 1778, with the title 'The Universal Love of Christ'. Originally there were 10 verses. The present Song Book includes verses 1, 2, 4, 7 and 9.

Let me hear thy voice now speaking (502)
Herbert H. Booth (1862-1926)

Written early in 1884, the song appeared in *Salvation Songster's Songs, Part 2*, 1884, compiled by the author, and was introduced by the singing brigade from the National Training Barracks, Clapton, when the brigade began its third campaign on 25 February 1884, at Bath.

Let me love thee, thou art claiming (503)
Herbert H. Booth (1862-1926)

Apparently introduced at the author's marriage to Cornelie Schoch at the Congress Hall, Clapton, on 18 September 1890, and published in their collection, *Songs of Peace and War*, 1890, under the title: 'Let me love Thee'. It has been reduced to three verses by omitting the second half of the third verse and the first half of the fourth verse.

Let nothing disturb thee (956)
Teresa of Avila (1515-82)
translated by Henry Wadsworth Longfellow (1807-82)

The translation appears in *The Poetical Works of Henry Wadsworth Longfellow*, 1914, with the heading: 'Santa Teresa's Book-Mark. From the Spanish of Santa Teresa.'

Let thy heart be at rest (739)
Catherine Baird (1895-1984)

The author said: 'Shortly after I came to England, Colonel Coles sent me his arrangement of Brahms' Lullaby and asked me to give it words. I felt that no one should really write words for the classics which are complete as they stand. But I thought it would not be out of place to adapt the words of John 14 to the Colonel's arrangement. This chapter is a favourite of mine.' The song, entitled 'A Benediction', was published in *The Musical Salvationist*, June 1939, and was later included in *The Song Book of The Salvation Army*, 1953.

Let us rejoice, the fight is won (146)
Percy Dearmer (1867-1936)

Written for the tune 'Easter Alleluya' (St Francis) in *Songs of Praise*, Enlarged edition, 1931, to provide words that could be sung at Easter or other times of the year. A footnote suggested that in Eastertide the first line of the refrain could be changed to: 'Christ is risen! Alleluya'. The author also provided a doxology 'Through north and south and east and west', which could be added when required or sung separately.

Let us sing of his love once again (808)
Francis Bottome (1823-94)

The verses, with the chorus 'In the sweet by-and-by' (from the song 'There's a land that is fairer than day'), were published in *Hymns of Consecration and Faith, and Sacred Songs for Missions, Prayer and Praise Meetings*, 1876, compiled by James Mountain. The present chorus appeared in *The Hallelujah Book*, 1878, and the verses were altered in *Salvation Army Songs*, 1899.

Let us with a gladsome mind (34)
John Milton (1608-74)

This paraphrase of Psalm 136 was written in 1623, when the author was attending St Paul's School, London. It was published in *Poems of Mr John Milton, both English and Latin,* 1645, in 24 couplets, with the refrain:

> For his mercies ay endure,
> Ever faithfull, ever sure.

Life is a journey; long is the road (351)
Albert Orsborn (1886-1967)

Written for the tune: 'The voice in the old village choir', the words, based partly on the story of Jesus and the Samaritan woman at Jacob's Well, near Sychar (John 4:7-15), appeared in *The Beauty of Jesus*, 1947, a collection of the author's songs and poems. The song was later included in *The Musical Salvationist*, April 1981, entitled: 'The well is deep'.

Life is great! So sing about it (544)
Brian Wren (*b* 1936)

Written in March 1970 for a youth service at Hockley, Essex, where it was sung to the tune 'Regent Square', although no young people came. With the tune 'Litherop' by Peter Cutts, it was entered for a Southern Television hymn competition, but was not sung. It was published in *New Church Praise,* 1975, and then in the author's *Faith Looking Forward,* 1983, with the title 'A song of love and living'. The author said: 'Love and life can be—and are—celebrated by many in a completely secular way. Though all levels of loving have their source in God, that source is not intrusive and is only accepted in faith.

Hence God's love in Christ is anonymous (though by no means absent) in stanzas 1-4. Note however that stanza 1, line 2, echoes the "it is meet, right, and our bounden duty" of the eucharistic prayer, and that stanza 4 paraphrases 1 Corinthians 13.'

Like to a lamb who from the fold has strayed (740)
Ivy Mawby (1903-83)

This song, entitled 'In the Love of Jesus', was first published as a solo in *The Musical Salvationist*, April 1961, and *Vocal Solos No. 2*, 1964. The words were written for a tune by William Hammond which was composed in about 1946 for Albert Orsborn's song: 'Once, on a day, was Christ led forth to die' (129).

Living in the fountain (352)
W. Bramwell Booth (1856-1929)

On his 21st birthday (8 March 1877) the author woke early to pray, and wrote this song while kneeling at his bedside. It appeared in *The Christian Mission Magazine*, February 1878, with the title: 'A Good Soldier's Life'. Originally there were five four-line verses. The chorus and the first four lines of the present third verse were added for *Salvation Army Songs*, 1930, so that the song could be sung to an eight-line tune.

Lo! He comes with clouds descending (161)
Charles Wesley (1707-88)

Published with the title 'Thy Kingdom come!' in *Hymns of Intercession for all Mankind*, 1758. (Although this hymn is sometimes said to have been based on an earlier hymn, 'Lo! He cometh, countless trumpets', by John Cennick, the version in the present Song Book is Wesley's original, with only four words altered, as in *Salvation Army Songs*, 1930.)

Look, ye saints! The sight is glorious (147)
Thomas Kelly (1769-1855)

Published in the author's *Hymns*, Third edition, 1809, with the heading: 'And he shall reign for ever and ever' (Revelation 11:15).

Lord, as we take our chosen way (688)
Will J. Brand (1889-1977)

Written in 1961, by request, for *The Young People's Song Book of The Salvation Army*, 1963, as a song for young people leaving school and starting employment. It originally began: 'Lord, as we make our youthful way', but was altered for the present Song Book which has omitted the original third verse.

Lord, for a mighty revival we plead (608)
William H. Davis (1854-1918)

Entitled: 'Lord, Give us Souls!', the song appeared in *The War Cry*, 18 March 1893, described as 'Suitable for holiness or salvation meetings'.

Lord, give me more soul-saving love (609)
William J. Pearson (1832-92)

Appeared in *The War Cry*, 9 April 1892, headed: 'Special Holy Fire Song'. The second and fourth verses of the original have been omitted.

Lord God, the Holy Ghost (196)
James Montgomery (1771-1854)

Originally written in three eight-line verses, it appeared under the heading 'Whit Sunday' in *A Selection of Psalms and Hymns for Public and Private Use*, Eighth edition, 1819, compiled by Thomas Cotterill. Later, with a few words altered, it was included in the author's *The Christian Psalmist; or Hymns, Selected and Original*, 1825, where it was headed: 'The Descent of the Spirit—Acts 2:1-4'.

Lord, here today my great need I am feeling (610)
William H. Woulds (1874-1940)

Written when the author was the commanding officer at Bedford Congress Hall. After visiting the deputy bandmaster of the corps, who was seriously ill in hospital, the chorus came to his mind as he cycled home, thinking of Jesus, the great physician. The verses were written shortly afterwards. Later, the song entitled 'Wonderful Healer—Touch me again' was published in *The Musical Salvationist*, January 1928, with the heading: 'Jesus put forth His hand, and touched him, saying, I will; be thou clean' (Matthew 8:3).

Lord, I care not for riches, neither silver nor gold (883)
Mary Ann Kidder (1820-1905)

Published in *Joy Bells*, 1878, compiled by W. Ogden and in *Sacred Songs and Solos, No. 2*, 1881, compiled by Ira D. Sankey.

Lord, I come to thee beseeching (434)
                              Ruth F. Tracy (1870-1960)

Written at the request of Bramwell Booth, then Chief of the Staff, who wanted verses for the tune 'Oh, the bitter shame and sorrow', ('None of self'), which would be practical and definite, leading the singer step by step to full consecration. The author said: 'I left his office wanting most intensely to make a worthy song. It meant half a night of prayer, and some very deep heart-searchings.' Four verses were included in a booklet of *Songs for Field Officers' Councils,* 1899, and the complete song was in *Salvation Army Songs,* 1899.

Lord, I hear of showers of blessings (295)
                              Elizabeth Codner (1823-1919)

Written at Weston-super-Mare in about 1860, after receiving news of a spiritual revival in Ireland. The author was interested in a group of young people who had heard about the revival, and she urged them to share in the spiritual blessings. On the following Sunday, while still thinking about the young people, she wrote the verses, which were later published by the Dublin Tract Repository on a leaflet headed 'Revival Hymn'. (A copy of this leaflet in the British Library is dated '12 MA 60'). Verses 3, 5 and 7 of the original have now been omitted from the Song Book.

Lord, I make a full surrender (504)
                              attributed to Lowell Mason (1792-1872)

Appeared anonymously, with the title 'Consecration', in *The Christian Mission Magazine,* March 1875, for the tune: 'Little thought Samaria's Daughter' ('Full Surrender'). In the series 'The Songs of the Salvationist' in *The Bandsman and Songster,* 1 August 1936, it was attributed to Dr L. Mason, though there is no supporting evidence.

Lord, I pray that I may know thee (435)
                              Ruth F. Tracy (1870-1960)

The author said that she was asked to write a song about 'knowing the Lord' after Commissioner Adelaide Cox (Leader of the Women's Social Work) had spoken to officers on that theme. She felt that her initial effort was unsuccessful, but later, when asked for some verses to the tune 'I surrender all', for *Salvation Army Songs,* 1930, she quickly wrote this song, embodying more happily the ideas she had earlier tried to express.

Lord, I was blind! I could not see (353)
William Tidd Matson (1833-99)

This was Part 17 of the author's poem *The Inner Life*, published in 1866 and later included in *The Poetical Works of William Tidd Matson*, 1894.

Lord, in the strength of grace (505)
Charles Wesley (1707-88)

From the author's *Short Hymns on Select Passages of the Holy Scriptures*, 1762. The original eight-line verse, based on the text: 'Who then is willing to consecrate his service this day unto the Lord?' (1 Chronicles 29:5), has been divided into two four-line verses, as in *A Collection of Hymns for the Use of the People called Methodists*, 1780, compiled by John Wesley.

Lord Jesus, I long to be perfectly whole (436)
James L. Nicholson (c1828-76)

This song, beginning 'Dear Jesus, I long to be perfectly whole', appeared in a pamphlet, *Joyful Songs No. 4*, 1872. The chorus is based on the text 'Wash me, and I shall be whiter than snow' (Psalm 51:7). The first line was altered to 'Lord Jesus . . .' in the Biglow and Main edition of *Gospel Songs No. 2*, 1876, compiled by P. P. Bliss and Ira D. Sankey. The third and fourth verses of the original have now been omitted from the Song Book.

Lord Jesus, thou dost keep thy child (741)
Jean Sophia Pigott (1845-82)

Published in *Hymns of Consecration and Faith, and Sacred Songs for Missions, Prayer and Praise Meetings'*, 1876, compiled by James Mountain.

Lord of all glory and of grace (957)
Harry Read (b 1924)

Written when the author was training principal at the International Training College, for the dedication and commissioning of cadets of the 'God's Soldiers' Session, at the Royal Albert Hall, London, on 22 May 1981. The meeting commenced with the doxology: 'Praise God from whom all blessings flow', and concluded with this new benediction, sung to the same tune, ('Old Hundredth').

Lord of all hopefulness, Lord of all joy (611)
                              Jan Struther (1901-53)
Written for the Irish tune 'Slane', and included in *Songs of Praise*, Enlarged edition, 1931, with the title: 'All-Day Hymn'.

Lord of creation, to you be all praise (506)
                              John C. Winslow (1882-1974)
Published in the author's *A Garland of Verse*, 1961, and in *Hymns for Church and School*, 1964, beginning 'Lord of creation, to thee be all praise!' Subsequently the verses have been altered, mainly to change 'thee' and 'thy' to 'you' and 'your'. Verse 1 now appears as in *The Australian Hymn Book*, 1977, and verses 2-5 as in *100 Hymns for Today*, 1969.

Lord of Heaven and earth and sea (941)
                              Frank S. Turney (1863-1932)
Written for the University Baptist Church, Baltimore, Maryland, as an 'Ode for Dedication Day' (27 March 1927). The original eight verses were printed on a leaflet with the note:

> This Song of Prayer and Thanksgiving, specially written for the occasion, dedicates our beautiful Church to its high and holy purpose of Divine Worship, with a prayer for personal dedication as 'living stones' in a spiritual house. A note of praise for the spared lives of honored and beloved brethren, and a tribute to the revered memory of Dr A. C. Dixon, precedes a prayer for the years which are yet to be.

The present Song Book includes verses 1, 5 and 8 as in *The Song Book of The Salvation Army*, 1953.

Lord of life and love and power (789)
                              Doris N. Rendell (*b* 1896)
Originally written in three eight-line verses, with a chorus, as a 'Song of Dedication' for the cadets of the 'Fearless' Session, at their dedication service in the Congress Hall, Clapton, on 28 May 1945. It was published in *The Musical Salvationist*, May-June 1950, under the title: 'Lord of life and power', and was then included in *The Song Book of The Salvation Army*, 1953, omitting the chorus.

Lord of my youth, teach me thy ways (861)
                              Brindley Boon (*b* 1913)
The author said that the song was inspired by his contact with the young people attending the early music schools at Sunbury Court, though it was written for the National Life-Saving Guard

Display at Clapton Congress Hall, 2 April 1955, where it was 'sung by East London girls' (*The War Cry*, 16 April 1955). It was included in *New Songs for Young People*, January 1957, and then in *The Young People's Song Book of The Salvation Army*, 1963.

Lord, speak to me, that I may speak (612)
Frances Ridley Havergal (1836-79)

Written on 28 April 1872, at Winterdyne, Bewdley. Six verses, entitled 'A Worker's Prayer', appeared in the magazine *Woman's Work in the Great Harvest Field*, August 1872, under the heading 'None of us liveth to himself' (Romans 14:7). Later, a revised version, with seven verses, was included in the author's anthology *Under the Surface*, 1874.

Lord, thou art questioning: Lovest thou me (507)
Ruth F. Tracy (1870-1960)

This song, based on Christ's question to Peter, 'Lovest thou me?' (John 21:15), was apparently written at the request of Commissioner Thomas Coombs, during one of his self-denial campaigns. The author said that, except for part of the chorus, the words came with freedom. Eventually she completed the chorus with the help of Captain Wilhelmina Schoch (later Mrs Lieut-Colonel F. Malan): 'We hummed the tune "Moment by moment", in trying to catch *the* line which hovered somewhere just out of reach. . . . The line that finally came, "Ask what Thou wilt my devotion to test", was more hers than mine, and we agreed that it was the only right and possible one.' Three verses and the chorus were printed in *The War Cry*, 27 March 1897, with the title 'Thou knowest that I love Thee', and then four verses and the chorus were included in *The War Cry*, 10 April 1897, with the additional note: 'Soloed by Commissioner Coombs during his self-denial tour.' The chorus was altered slightly for *The Song Book of The Salvation Army*, 1953, when the song was set to the tune 'O for a heart whiter than snow'. The third verse of the original has been omitted.

Lord, through the blood of the Lamb that was slain (437)
Herbert H. Booth (1862-1926)

Written for the tune: 'Long, long ago', the song appeared in *The War Cry*, 27 March 1886, under the title: 'Cleansing for Me', and was then included in a booklet, *Songs of the Nations*, for the International Congress, 1886.

Lord, thy word abideth (655)
Henry W. Baker (1821-77)

Written for the first edition of *Hymns Ancient and Modern*, 1861, where it was headed 'Thy Word is a lantern unto my feet, and a light unto my paths' (Psalm 119:105).

Lord, we believe to us and ours (216)
Charles Wesley (1707-88)

Published by John and Charles Wesley in *Hymns and Sacred Poems*, 1742, where it was entitled 'Hymn for the Day of Pentecost'. There were 12 verses, beginning:

> Rejoice, rejoice, ye fallen race,
> The day of Pentecost is come;
> Expect the sure descending grace,
> Open your hearts to make Him room.

The present Song Book includes verses 5, 7, 8 and 9, altered as in *The Song Book of The Salvation Army*, 1953.

Lord, with joyful hearts we worship (795)
Marjorie B. Davies (*b* 1920)

Written when the author was travelling by car with her husband to see their first grandchild, Gareth John Chaffey, in August 1980. The song was first sung to the tune 'South Shields' at his dedication service in Swansea Citadel, and was accepted by the Song Book Council in 1981 for inclusion in the 1986 Song Book.

Love divine, all loves excelling (438)
Charles Wesley (1707-88)

Published in *Hymns for those that seek and those that have Redemption in the Blood of Jesus Christ*, 1747, in four verses, and in *Hymns for those to whom Christ is all in all*, 1761, omitting the second verse, which expressed a controversial view of Christian perfection. Commenting on the line 'Take away our Power of sinning', the Reverend John Fletcher (1729-85), of Madeley, said, 'Can God take away from us our power of sinning without taking away our power of free obedience?' In *Select Hymns: with Tunes annext*, 1761, this hymn was set to an adaptation of Purcell's 'Fairest Isle, all isles excelling', from Dryden's *King Arthur*, 1691, which may have inspired the opening line of Charles Wesley's hymn.

Love divine, from Jesus flowing (439)
Elizabeth A. Mackenzie (1853-1943)

Written when the author was a captain, at Hendon, before

her marriage in May 1887. About 50 years later, writing from Canada, she recalled that the divisional commander had spoken to her about 'the wonderful, unsearchable love of our glorious Lord'. Either then or later, her future husband, Staff-Captain George Mackenzie (aide-de-camp to the divisional commander) asked her to write a song on this theme. It was published in *The War Cry*, 26 November 1887 and in *The Musical Salvationist*, May 1897. An article in *The War Cry*, Toronto, 23 October 1971, quoted an additional verse that was not in the earlier publications:

> Love that widens, lengthens, deepens,
> Ever on its onward flow,
> Make of me a mighty channel,
> I would all its fulness know,
> And self-spending,
> Live alone that love to show.

Love has a language, all its own making (51)
Joseph Buck (1889-1945)

Entitled 'Love stands the test', the song was published in *The Musical Salvationist*, March 1929, on the Bandsmen's Page (arranged for male voices) and later appeared in a new arrangement for mixed voices, in *The Musical Salvationist*, November-December 1952.

Love of love so wondrous (250)
Herbert H. Booth (1862-1926)

Appeared in *Salvation Music, Volume 2*, December 1883, under the title: 'He is waiting, pleading, knocking', and then included in *The Salvation Songster*, 1885, and other song books. The fifth verse was revised by Catherine Baird for *The Song Book of The Salvation Army*, 1953.

Loved with everlasting love (545)
George Wade Robinson (1838-77)

Published in *Hymns of Consecration and Faith, and Sacred Songs for Missions, Prayer and Praise Meetings*, 1876, compiled by James Mountain. The third verse of the original has been omitted.

Low in the grave he lay (148)
Robert Lowry (1826-99)

Written in 1874, based on the text 'He is not here, but is risen' (Luke 24:6). It was published in *Brightest and Best*, 1875, edited by W. Howard Doane and Robert Lowry.

Make me a captive, Lord (508)
George Matheson (1842-1906)

Written at Row, Dunbartonshire, in 1890, and published under the title: 'Christian Freedom' in the author's *Sacred Songs*, 1890. The verses were headed: 'Paul, the prisoner of Jesus Christ' (Ephesians 3:1). The third verse of the original has been omitted.

Make me aware of thee, O Lord (613)
Victor Ottaway (1892-1968)

This song, entitled 'Divine Awareness', was awarded first prize in a song-writing competition in Canada in 1966, and was published with other prize-winning entries in *The War Cry*, Toronto, 2 July 1966, when the results were announced. Subsequently it was included in *Canadian Songs of Devotion* (a booklet of the author's songs) and *Songs of Faith*, 1971.

Make the world with music ring (809)
Charles Coller (1863-1935)

This song appeared in a small booklet of songs for *British Field Officers' Councils*, 1913, where it was attributed to Commissioner Lawley. Subsequently it was attributed to Colonel Pearson in *The Musical Salvationist*, June 1918, where Major Arthur Goldsmith said, in his introductory notes: 'Many readers will recognise in this piece an old favourite which was at one time often used.' Later Charles Coller said that he wrote the song and submitted it, with several others, to Commissioner Lawley, in response to a request for songs for the International Congress, 1914.

Man of sorrows! what a name (118)
Philip P. Bliss (1838-76)

Published in *The International Lessons Monthly*, 1875, and in *Gospel Hymns, No. 2*, 1876, compiled by the author and Ira D. Sankey. Philip Bliss apparently sang this song at the last meeting he conducted in the Michigan State Prison on 19 November 1876.

Many are the things I cannot understand (52)
Howard Davies (*b* 1940)

Written in the county town of Broadford, Victoria, on 11 April 1967. The author said in 1986: 'The inspiration for the song came through seeing the beauty of the Australian night sky with the stars so clear—the thought from Psalm 8 coming to mind:

"When I consider your heavens, the work of your fingers, the moon and the stars, which you have set in place, what is man that you are mindful of him, the son of man that you care for him?' ". The song, entitled 'The wonder of his grace' was published in *The Musical Salvationist*, January 1969.

Many thoughts stir my heart as I ponder alone (119)
Albert Orsborn (1886-1967)

Written for the tune: 'Mother Machree'. The chorus appeared in *The War Cry*, 9 December 1916, and, later, the first and second verses and the chorus were printed in *The Officer*, October 1919, under the title: 'The Charm of the Cross'. The complete song was included in a collection of the author's songs and poems, *The Beauty of Jesus*, 1947, and in *The Musical Salvationist*, January 1982.

March on, salvation soldiers (810)
James C. Bateman (1854-88)

This song, entitled 'The Day of Victory's coming', was published in *The Musical Salvationist*, March 1892, an issue headed 'Old Favourites'. The words and music were said to be 'by the late Capt. J. C. Bateman'. (Later, in *The Bandsman and Songster*, 3 July 1937, the song was attributed to Mark Sanders.) The third and fifth verses of this version have now been omitted. Earlier, the chorus appeared anonymously in *Salvation Songster's Songs, Part 2*, 1884, with other verses beginning: 'A War is fiercely raging'.

Marching on in the light of God (811)
Robert Johnson

This song, with five verses and a chorus, was included in the Scottish Anniversary Report for the year August 1882 to August 1883 and then in *Salvation Music, Volume 2*, December 1883. Verses 1, 2 and 4 in the present Song Book are from this version, but verse 3 is from *Salvation Army Songs*, 1899 (which included two verses that were not in the earlier version).

Master, I own thy lawful claim (509)
Charles Wesley (1707-88)

In Volume 2 of the author's *Hymns and Sacred Poems*, 1749, this was the second hymn with the title 'The Inward Cross'. There were 11 verses, headed 'And He said to them all, If any man will come after Me, let him deny himself, and take up his cross daily, and follow Me' (Luke 9:23). The present Song Book includes verses 1, 3 and 11.

Master, speak: thy servant heareth (614)
Frances Ridley Havergal (1836-79)

Written on Sunday evening 19 May 1867, at Weston-super-Mare, based on the text 'Speak, Lord; for thy servant heareth' (1 Samuel 3:9). In the author's *The Ministry of Song*, 1869, there were nine verses, with the title 'Master, Say On'. The present Song Book includes verses 1, 6, 8 and 9.

'Mid all the traffic of the ways (615)
William A. Dunkerley (1852-1941)

Written in 1916, in a small chapel on Dartmoor, which the author described as 'an abode of peace, a veritable House of God'. In *The Vision Splendid*, 1917, published under the author's pen-name 'John Oxenham', there were seven verses, entitled 'Sanctuary'. Verses 3-5 of the original have been omitted.

Mine eyes have seen the glory of the coming of the Lord (162)
Julia Ward Howe (1819-1910)

After attending a review of troops in Virginia on 20 November 1861, the author was travelling to Washington, with her husband and the Reverend James Freeman Clarke, when they heard soldiers singing the song 'John Brown's body'. Mr Clarke suggested that she should write new words to the tune, and that night she wrote the verses in her room at the Willard Hotel, Washington. The poem was published in the *New York Daily Tribune*, 14 January 1862, in six verses, and then in the *Atlantic Monthly*, February 1862, omitting one verse of the original.

Mine to rise when thou dost call me (510)
Susie F. Swift (1862-1916)

The author, telling the story of her conversion, in *The War Cry*, San Francisco, 18 March 1893, said that after attending her second Salvation Army meeting in Glasgow with her friend Ella Leonard, they went home and talked together the whole of the night. At daybreak she concluded: 'I believe there is something to be got at in Christianity, and I mean to look for it all my life long.' These verses, which also speak of discipleship as a life-long journey, appeared in *All the World*, April 1887, with the title 'Mine and Thine'. The third verse of the original has now been omitted:

> Mine to toil, when Thou dost bid me,
> At the task beyond my strength;
> Thine to weigh my every weakness,
> Portioning out my labour's length.

On 8 January 1929, members of the first High Council, meeting at Sunbury, sang this song after Commissioner Edward Higgins had directed the preliminary proceedings.

Morning has broken (35)
Eleanor Farjeon (1881-1965)

Written for the Gaelic tune 'Morning has broken' (usually known as 'Bunessan') and included in *Songs of Praise*, Enlarged edition, 1931, with the heading 'Thanks for a Day'.

My body, soul and spirit (511)
Mary D. James (1810-83)

Entitled 'Consecration', this song appeared in *Notes of Joy, for the Sabbath School, the Social Meeting and the Hour of Prayer*, 1869, compiled by Mrs Joseph F. Knapp, with the note: 'Written at the National Camp Meeting, Round Lake, July 10th, 1869.'

My faith looks up to thee, My faith so small, so slow (742)
W. Bramwell Booth (1856-1929)

First published as a poem, entitled 'Faith', in *The Salvationist*, 1 February 1879. Originally there were three verses in short metre alternating with three verses in 4.4.4.4.6. metre. It was then included in *The Musical Salvationist*, December 1889, under the title 'Faith's Victory', with a chorus not written by Bramwell Booth. The present version in double short metre appeared in *Salvation Army Songs*, 1930.

My faith looks up to thee, Thou Lamb of Calvary (743)
Ray Palmer (1808-87)

After graduating at Yale College in September 1830, the author went to New York to teach for a year at a school for young ladies. While living with the family of the lady who kept the school, he wrote the verses at a time 'when Christ, in the riches of His grace and love, was so vividly apprehended as to fill the soul with deep emotion' (*The Poetical Works of Ray Palmer*, 1876, pages 347-355). Later, in Boston, he gave a copy to Lowell Mason for a hymn book he was preparing with

Thomas Hastings. The verses, as in the present Song Book, appeared in *Spiritual Songs, for Social Worship*, 1832, compiled by Thomas Hastings and Lowell Mason.

My Father is rich in houses and lands (354)
Harriet E. P. Buell (1834-1910)

The theme came to the author during a Sunday morning service at Thousand Island Park, New York, and she began to compose the verses as she was walking home after the service. The hymn was published in the *Northern Christian Advocate*, 1 February 1877, under the heading 'Child of a King'. Two verses of the original have now been omitted.

My God, how endless is thy love (672)
Isaac Watts (1674-1748)

Published in the first part of the author's *Hymns and Spiritual Songs*, Second edition, 1709, with the title 'A Song for Morning or Evening' and the scriptural references Lamentations 3:23 and Isaiah 45:7.

My God, I am thine (355)
verses: Charles Wesley (1707-88)
chorus: Anonymous

The verses appeared in the author's *Hymns and Sacred Poems*, 1749, in a section headed 'Hymns for Believers'. The chorus was linked with these verses in *The Revival Hymn Book*, 1866, compiled by William Booth.

My God, my Father, make me strong (744)
Frederick Mann (1846-1928)

Published in *The People's Hymn Book*, 1924, edited by the Hymns Committee of the Church of St Martin-in-the-Fields, London. The author said that, without aiming at parody, he had adopted the general form of Charlotte Elliott's hymn 'My God and Father, while I stray', but had tried to present 'truer views of the will of God as the direct source of the best and most joyous things of life'. This hymn was sung at the author's funeral at Limpsfield, Surrey, in 1928.

My heart is fixed, eternal God (356)
Richard Jukes (1804-67)

This song appeared with four verses in *The Revival Hymn*

Book, for All Churches, No. 1, 1856, and *The Primitive Methodist Revival Hymn Book*, 1861; with eight verses in *Richard Weaver's Hymn Book*, 1861, and with five verses in *The Revival Hymn Book*, 1866, compiled by William Booth. The present Song Book includes verses 1-4 from the 1866 version, altered as in *The Song Book of The Salvation Army*, 1953.

My hope is built on nothing less (745)
Edward Mote (1797-1874)

The author said that the words of the chorus came to him one morning as he was on his way to work. Later that day he wrote four verses and on the following Sunday, after the evening service, he added the last two verses. He sent a copy of the hymn to *The Spiritual Magazine*, where it was published anonymously. Four verses and the chorus appeared in *An Appendix to the Second Edition of a Collection of Psalms and Hymns*, 1826, compiled by John Rees. Subsequently the complete hymn, beginning 'Nor earth, nor hell, my soul can move', was included in *Hymns of Praise. A New Selection of Gospel Hymns*, 1836, compiled by the author.

My Jesus, I love thee, I know thou art mine (357)
attributed to William Ralph Featherston (1846-73)

The opening lines of this song are based on an earlier hymn, 'O Jesus, my Saviour, I know thou art mine', published in *Hymns for Revival Prayer Meetings*, 1838, and *A Collection of Revival Hymns*, 1844. The version in the present Song Book appeared anonymously in the *Primitive Methodist Magazine*, October 1862, p 640, and in *A Selection of Revival Hymns*, c 1865. The verses have also been found in America, in a letter dated 26 January 1865, written by William Anderson, from a hospital in Beverly, New Jersey, to his wife in Flemington, New Jersey. Ira D. Sankey, in *My Life and Sacred Songs*, said that William Ralph Featherston wrote the words in 1858 when he was about 16 years of age. (Later information indicates that he would have been 16 in 1862, not in 1858.) His aunt, Mrs E. Featherston Wilson, apparently suggested that the verses should be published. (Sankey stated that the song was included in *The London Hymn Book*, 1862, and Julian's *Dictionary of Hymnology* said that it was in the 1864 edition of *The London Hymn Book*, but copies of these editions have not been located.) Later, in *The Musical Salvationist*, December 1938, the words were attributed to 'Jas. Duffill'. In 1939, in a letter to the Reverend E. C. Barton (the Methodist Book Steward), Mr

Samuel Newby of West Bromwich, Staffordshire, claimed that the words were written by J. H. Duffell under trying circumstances, and were used for the first time at a class meeting at Spon Lane, West Bromwich Circuit, early in the 1860s.

My life flows on in endless song (358)

Anonymous

Appeared anonymously, with music by Robert Lowry, in *Bright Jewels for the Sunday School*, 1869, edited by Robert Lowry, assisted by Wm F. Sherwin and Chester G. Allen. Later, in *Hymns of Consecration and Faith*, 1876, compiled by James Mountain, the author was named as 'Hartley', and in the British Library copy of *Song Life*, 1872, compiled by Philip Phillips, the name 'Fountain J. Hartly' [sic] was written in pencil at the top of the song. Fountain J. Hartley was sometime Hon. Secretary of the Sunday School Union, but his authorship of this song has not yet been confirmed.

My life must be Christ's broken bread (512)

Albert Orsborn (1886-1967)

In 1947, the author was in Berlin on Maundy Thursday and Good Friday (3,4 April) and then in Holland for Easter Day and Easter Monday (6,7 April). He later wrote:

> During my first visit to Berlin, when I met our dear officers in council in the war-damaged temple, I was burdened with a sense of my own inadequacy to match the occasion. . . . I cried to God to help me, in my own spirit, and to let His Spirit work within us all, to bring us together, to bridge what seemed to be, in all reason, an impassable gulf between our respective conditions of living. . . . God revealed to me that not only that day, but always, we have no hope of being a blessing to other souls unless our lives become a part of the Saviour's sacramental consecration. . . . Before I left Berlin, this song had begun to form itself in my mind. As I travelled toward Holland, along the straight but monotonous Autobahn, line by line the song was given to me, the last verse coming in the early morning following my return home.

The verses were published in *The War Cry*, 3 May 1947, with the title, 'Christ's Broken Bread'.

My Maker and my King (616)

Anne Steele (1717-78)

Published in six verses, in the author's *Poems on Subjects chiefly Devotional*, 1760, with the title 'God my Creator and Benefactor'. The present Song Book includes verses 1, 3, and 6 altered as in *Salvation Army Songs*, 1899.

My mind upon thee, Lord, is stayed (513)
Herbert H. Booth (1862-1926)

The words appeared in a booklet, *Songs of the Nations*, for the International Congress in London, 28 May-4 June 1886 (with the music in an appendix) and the song was then included in *The Musical Salvationist*, August 1886, under the title: 'Saviour, Dear Saviour, draw Nearer'.

My robes were once all stained with sin (359)
Edwin O. Excell (1851-1921)

Published in the author's *The Gospel in Song*, 1882, and later included in *The Musical Salvationist*, June 1890.

My Saviour suffered on the tree (360)
attributed to Hodgson Casson (1788-1851)

This song appeared anonymously in *A Selection of Revival Hymns*, c1865, and on the front cover of *The Revival Hymn Book*, 1866, compiled by William Booth. In *The Bandsman and Songster*, 25 January 1936, Arch Wiggins attributed the song to Hodgson Casson, who was said to have written the words to a dance tune. Later, in his *Companion to the Song Book*, 1961, Gordon Avery said that Hodgson Casson wrote the words one night in a tavern, when he was unable to sleep because of the noise from a dance in another part of the building. However, as the source of this information is unknown, further evidence is needed to confirm the authorship.

My soul, be on thy guard (812)
George Heath (c1750-1822)

From the author's *Hymns and Poetic Essays Sacred to the Public and Private Worship of the Deity*, 1781. The fourth verse, included in *The Song Book of the Salvation Army*, 1953, has now been omitted.

My soul is now united to Christ, the living vine (361)
Hugh Bourne (1772-1852) and
William Sanders (1799-1882?)

This was the first part of a hymn with six verses, divided into two parts, in *A Collection of Hymns for Camp Meetings, Revivals, etc*, 1824, compiled by Hugh Bourne. The second and third verses have been rearranged and altered, as in *The Revival Hymn Book*, 1866, compiled by William Booth.

My times are in thy hand (917)
William F. Lloyd (1791-1853)

Headed 'My times are in thy hand' (Psalm 31:15) in *The Tract Magazine; or, Christian Miscellany*, March 1824, where it was signed 'SPES'. The fifth verse of the original has now been omitted.

Near thy cross assembled, Master (197)
John Lawley (1859-1922)

Apparently written after hearing William Booth speaking about the 'baptism of the Holy Ghost'. During his early ministry, William Booth had been dissatisfied with his preaching and the lack of visible results, but he was greatly encouraged when he heard a visiting minister, the Reverend Richard Poole, speak from the text, 'Said I not unto thee, that, if thou wouldest believe, thou shouldest see the glory of God?' (John 11:40). It seems that William Booth's recollection of the effect this message had on his life inspired Lawley's composition. The song appeared under the heading 'Special' in *The War Cry*, 23 April 1892, and was then included in *The Musical Salvationist*, June 1895, with the title 'Sanctifying Fire'. The third verse and chorus of the original have now been omitted.

Nearer, my God, to thee (617)
Sarah F. Adams (1805-48)

Apparently written in November 1840 at Loughton, Essex, based partly on Genesis 28:10-22. It was published in *Hymns and Anthems*, 1841, compiled by William J. Fox, the minister of the unitarian church at South Place, Finsbury, where the author attended meetings.

'Neath our standard, we're engaging (778)
Gustave A. Grozinsky (c1870-1936)

The song, originally beginning ' 'Neath the standard proudly waving', appeared in *The Musical Salvationist*, February 1893, with the title 'The Standard Bearer'. Several lines were altered for *The Song Book of The Salvation Army*, 1953. Lieut-Colonel William Starling, who was stationed as a captain at Thurso in north Scotland, with Lieutenant Grozinsky, said that during the severe winter there (1893-4) he became so discouraged that he intended to resign and go home when the snow cleared. However, when everything was at its worst, the lieutenant sang the chorus of this song, 'I'll be true', and as a result the captain tore up his letter of resignation.

Never fades the name of Jesus (63)
David Welander (1896-1967)
versified by Catherine Baird (1895-1984)

Originally written in Norwegian for a Zulu melody introduced by missionary officers at congress meetings in Oslo in 1922. The Norwegian words were inspired the following year at the Salvation Army's 35th anniversary celebrations in Oslo, when Lieut-Colonel (later Commissioner) Joakim Myklebust spoke on the text: 'His name shall endure for ever: his name shall be continued as long as the sun: and men shall be blessed in him: all nations shall call him blessed' (Psalm 72:17). After the meeting, Captain Welander started to write the verses on the train going home and completed the song at home that night. It was used in officers' meetings and was then published in *Krigsropet* in Norway. The English version, entitled 'The Name of Jesus', appeared in *The War Cry*, 18 May 1940, with the note: 'From the Norwegian by Major David Welander, Divisional Commander, Trondheim. (English verse by Major Catherine Baird)'. Subsequently, it was included in *New Songs for Male Voices No. 26*, January 1961, and *The Musical Salvationist*, January 1972.

New every morning is the love (668)
John Keble (1792-1866)

Written on 20 September 1822, based on the text 'His compassions fail not. They are new every morning' (Lamentations 3:22, 23). Headed 'Morning', it was published in the author's *The Christian Year*, 1827, with 16 verses, beginning:

> Hues of the rich unfolding morn,
> That, ere the glorious sun be born,
> By some soft touch invisible
> Around his path are taught to swell;

The present Song Book includes verses 6, 8, 9, 14 and 16.

No home on earth have I (362)
George Scott Railton (1849-1913)

Written early in 1881, apparently when the author was crossing the Mississippi on his way back to London from St Louis. It was published in *The War Cry*, 31 March 1881 and 7 April 1881, headed: 'A Life on the Ocean Wave'. Bernard Watson, in *Soldier Saint*, said: 'No Salvation Army verses epitomize more closely the life of their writer.' Sometimes described as a translation from Madame Guyon, it undoubtedly expresses similar thoughts to William Cowper's translation of her verses: 'All scenes alike engaging prove'.

No, not despairingly (296)
Horatius Bonar (1808-89)

Entitled 'Confession and Peace', in the author's *Hymns of Faith and Hope*, Third series, 1866. An extra line was added to each verse in *The Musical Salvationist*, November 1911, and later the verses were altered again for *The Song Book of The Salvation Army*, 1953, omitting the fifth verse of the original.

None the love of Christ can measure (363)
Richard Slater (1854-1939)

Written on 12 July 1887 and published in *The Musical Salvationist*, October 1887, under the title: 'What a Saviour!' The original fifth verse has been omitted.

Not all the blood of beasts (120)
Isaac Watts (1674-1748)

Published in the second edition of the author's *Hymns and Spiritual Songs*, 1709, with the title 'Faith in Christ our Sacrifice'. The verses have been altered slightly as in *The Song Book of The Salvation Army*, 1953.

Not my own, but saved by Jesus (514)
Daniel W. Whittle (1840-1901)

Headed 'Ye are not your own, for ye are bought with a price' (1 Corinthians 6:19, 20) in *The Gospel Choir*, 1884, compiled by Ira D. Sankey and James McGranahan.

Not only, Lord, on that great day (618)
Miriam M. Richards (b 1911)

Published in *The Musical Salvationist*, May-June 1958, under the title 'Christ, my Judge', and then included in *Keep Singing!*, 1976.

Not unto us, O Lord (163)
Albert Orsborn (1886-1967)

Written for the Salvation Army centenary celebrations in 1965, and published that year in *Centennial Echoes, 1865-1965: A Centenary Year Souvenir*, as well as on programmes for various centenary meetings. (A festival arrangement by Charles Skinner, introduced at 'A Century of Salvation Song' festival in the Royal Albert Hall on 1 July 1965, was published in *The*

Musical Salvationist, October 1965.) The author explained that the phrase 'that foolish thing' (in verse 2) reflects Paul's words in 1 Corinthians 1:27, and 'Not yet' (in verse 4) echoes Hebrews 2:8-9. Earlier, in his autobiography *The House of my Pilgrimage,* 1958 (p 141), he said that, when seeing crowds of salvationists from different nations welcoming their General, his first response was to exclaim: 'Not unto us, O Lord, not unto us, but unto thy name give glory' (Psalm 115:1). Clearly, this text was again in his mind when he wrote this song for the centenary year.

Not what these hands have done (297)
Horatius Bonar (1808-89)

Published in the author's *Hymns of Faith and Hope,* Second series, 1861, with the heading 'Not what these hands have done'. The present Song Book includes verses 1-5 and 8 from the original 12 verses.

Now I feel the sacred fire (546)
Anonymous

Appeared anonymously in *Spiritual Songs and Hymns for Pilgrims,* 1879, compiled by B. T. Roberts.

Now I have found the ground wherein (746)
Johann A. Rothe (1688-1758)
translated by John Wesley (1703-91)

The German hymn 'Ich habe nun den Grund gefunden' is said to have been written for the birthday of Count Nicolaus von Zinzendorf, 26 May 1728, but it must have been written earlier as it appeared in Zinzendorf's *Christ-Catholisches Singe-und Bet-Büchlein,* 1727. Subsequently it was included in the Herrnhut *Gesangbuch,* 1735. The translation was published in *Hymns and Sacred Poems,* 1740, with the title 'Redemption Found'.

Now thank we all our God (12)
Martin Rinkart (1586-1649)
translated by Catherine Winkworth (1827-78)

The German hymn 'Nun danket alle Gott' appeared in Crüger's *Praxis pietatis melica,* 1648, and later in the author's *Jesu Hertz-Büchlein,* 1663, with the title *'Tisch-Gebetlein'* (ie a short prayer or grace before meals). It may have appeared in earlier editions of these publications, but copies have not been traced. Verses 1 and 2 are a paraphrase of Ecclesiasticus

50:22-24, and verse 3 is a version of the doxology 'Gloria Patri' ('Glory be to the Father, and to the Son, and to the Holy Spirit,' etc). The translation is from Catherine Winkworth's *Lyra Germanica*, Second series, 1858.

Now the day is over (673)
Sabine Baring-Gould (1834-1924)

Written in 1865 for the children of Horbury Bridge, where the author was curate. It was published in the *Church Times*, 16 February 1867, and then in the 1868 Appendix to *Hymns Ancient and Modern*, where it was headed: 'When thou liest down, thou shalt not be afraid: yea, thou shalt lie down, and thy sleep shall be sweet' (Proverbs 3:24). Verses 4-6 and 8 have now been omitted.

O blessèd Saviour, is thy love (515)
Joseph Stennett (1663-1713)

From the author's *Hymns in Commemoration of the Sufferings of Our Blessed Saviour Jesus Christ, Compos'd for the Celebration of his Holy Supper*, 1697. Originally there were 10 verses, beginning 'My Blessed Saviour, is thy Love'. The present Song Book includes verses 1-3 and 6, altered as in *Salvation Army Songs*, 1930.

O bliss of the purified, bliss of the free (364)
Francis Bottome (1823-94)

Written in 1869 and subsequently published in *Philip Phillips' Singing Annual for Sabbath Schools*, Volume 3, 1872, and *Winnowed Hymns*, 1873, edited by C. C. McCabe and D. T. Macfarlan. The verses have been altered slightly, as in *The Song Book of The Salvation Army*, 1953.

O boundless salvation! deep ocean of love (298)
William Booth (1829-1912)

Commissioner Theodore H. Kitching said that one morning, arriving at the Founder's home at 6 am, he found William Booth in his study, completing the verses of this song which he had written during the night. It was apparently first sung at 'Boundless Salvation' meetings in the Exeter Hall, London, on 14 and 15 November 1893. The verses, with a chorus 'The Heavenly gales are blowing', were published under the title: 'Boundless Salvation' in *The War Cry*, 23 December 1893. William Booth announced this song when he appeared in public for the last time at his 83rd birthday celebrations in the Royal Albert Hall, London, on 9 May 1912.

O bright eternal One (36)
Catherine Baird (1895-1984)

Published in *The Musical Salvationist*, January 1962, under the title 'God Speaks', and then included in *Keep Singing!*, 1976.

O Christ, in thee my soul hath found (547)
B.E.

Published in *Sacred Songs and Solos, No. 2*, 1881, compiled by Ira D. Sankey, with the heading 'We also joy in God through our Lord Jesus Christ, by whom we have now received the atonement' (Romans 5:11). The initials 'B.E. (arr.)' appeared above the song instead of the author's name.

O Christ of pure and perfect love (440)
William Booth (1829-1912)

Headed: 'The General's New Song', it appeared in *The War Cry*, 18 May 1895, which also included a holiness reading, 'Sanctify Me Now', based on this song. The second and sixth verses have been omitted.

O Christ, who came to share our human life (181)
Catherine Bonnell Arnott (*b* 1927)

Written in 1964. The author said:

> As a child with a gift for writing poetry, I was troubled by the mismatch between words and music in some of the hymns sung in our church. The beauty of words and meanings were sometimes lost. I thought that one day I might write a hymn that was a harmony of poetry and music. As an adult, I mentioned this to the organist of my church. In 1964 he brought me the music of an Easter anthem; he wanted fresh words for it. I played the music over and over for several days until the theme, Christ's life as a model for our own, suggested itself to me. And then I began to write the words. My strongest feeling as I did so was of deep appreciation of the generous Gift that was Christ. The hymn was sung a few weeks later in the First Baptist Church, Los Angeles, California.

It was published in *The Hymn Book of the Anglican Church of Canada and the United Church of Canada*, 1971.

O come, all ye faithful (85)
attributed to John Francis Wade (*c*1710-86)
translated by Frederick Oakeley (1802-80) and others

The Latin hymn 'Adeste fideles' was attributed to J. F. Wade in *The 'Adeste Fideles': A Study on Its Origin & Development*, 1947, by Dom John Stéphan, who compared the earliest manuscript sources, dating from *c*1743-60. The translation appeared in *Hymns Ancient and Modern*, 1860, based on an earlier version, beginning 'Ye faithful, approach ye', which Frederick Oakeley wrote for the congregation at Margaret Chapel, London, in 1841. The second verse ('God of God, Light of Light') has been omitted.

O come and dwell in me (441)
verses: Charles Wesley (1707-88)
chorus: Anonymous

These verses are from two hymns in the author's *Short Hymns on Select Passages of the Holy Scriptures*, 1762, altered as in *The Song Book of The Salvation Army*, 1953. Verses 1 and 2 were based on the text 'Where the Spirit of the Lord is, there is liberty' (2 Corinthians 3:17) and verses 3 and 4 were based on another text 'Before his translation he had this testimony, that he pleased God' (Hebrews 11:5). The chorus appeared with these verses in *Salvation Army Songs*, 1899.

O come and look awhile on him (121)
Frederick W. Faber (1814-63)

The original hymn, entitled 'Jesus Crucified', appeared in the author's *Jesus and Mary: or Catholic Hymns*, 1849, and then in his *Hymns*, 1862. Originally there were 12 verses, beginning:

> O come and mourn with me awhile;
> See, Mary calls us to her side;
> O come and let us mourn with her,—
> Jesus, our Love, is crucified!

Five verses, freely adapted, were included in *Salvation Army Songs*, 1899, while the present version (based on verses 1, 3, 2, 10, 12 and 11 of the original) is from *The Song Book of The Salvation Army*, 1953.

O do not let thy Lord depart (251)
Elizabeth Reed (1794-1867)

Headed 'The accepted time' in *The Hymn Book*, 1842, compiled by Andrew Reed, the author's husband. There were five verses, beginning 'O do not let the word depart'. The fourth verse of the original has now been omitted.

O Father and Creator (221)
Albert E. Chesham (1886-1971)

Written when the author was travelling by train between Chicago and Indianapolis. He had often felt that there were too few songs about the Trinity. It appeared in *The Musical*

Salvationist, January-February 1953, under the title: 'O Father and Creator', and was then included in *The Song Book of The Salvation Army*, 1953.

O Father, friend of all mankind (796)
Catherine Baird (1895-1984)

Written, the author said, 'with a view to avoiding anything merely sentimental, adhering only to the Army's ideals concerning this lovely ceremony of dedication'. It appeared in *The Musical Salvationist*, November-December 1949, entitled: 'Dedication', and was then included in *The Song Book of The Salvation Army*, 1953.

O Father, let thy love remain (958)
Hendrik Ghysen (1660-93)
translated by William F. Palstra (1904-73)

This benediction, published in *The Musical Salvationist*, March-April 1949, is a translation of the concluding verse of a Dutch hymn from *Den Hoonig-raat der Psalm-dichten ofte Davids Psalmen*, 1686, compiled by Hendrik Ghysen. The hymn: 'O groote Christus, eeuwig licht', was a version of the Latin hymn: 'Christe, qui lux es et dies'.

O for a closer walk with God (442)
William Cowper (1731-1800)

Written on 9 December 1769 during the serious illness of the author's friend, Mrs Unwin. On the following day, in a letter to his aunt, he referred to the writing of these verses: 'I began to compose them yesterday morning, before daybreak, but fell asleep at the end of the first two lines: when I awaked again, the third and fourth were whispered to my heart in a way which I have often experienced.' The hymn was published in *A Collection of Psalms and Hymns, from Various Authors*, 1772, compiled by Richard Conyers, and was later included in Book 1 of the *Olney Hymns*, 1779, where it was headed 'Walking with God', with a reference to the text 'And Enoch walked with God' (Genesis 5:24).

O for a heart that is whiter than snow (443)
Eliza E. Hewitt (1851-1920)

From *Junior Songs: A Collection of Sacred Hymns and Songs*, 1892, edited by John R. Sweney and William J. Kirkpatrick.

O for a heart to praise my God (444)
verses: Charles Wesley (1707-88)
chorus: Emily E. S. Elliott (1836-97)

Published in *Hymns and Sacred Poems*, 1742, by John and Charles Wesley, with the heading 'Psalm 51:10—Make me a clean heart, O God'. Originally there were eight verses, beginning 'O for an Heart to praise my God'. Verses 5-7 have now been omitted. The chorus is from 'Thou didst leave thy throne and thy kingly crown' (101).

O for a humbler walk with God (445)
Edward Harland (1810-90)

From *A Church Psalter and Hymnal*, 1855, edited by the author.

O for a thousand tongues to sing (64)
Charles Wesley (1707-88)

Published in *Hymns and Sacred Poems*, 1740, by John and Charles Wesley, with the title 'For the anniversary day of one's conversion'. (The hymn may have been written on 21 May 1739, the anniversary of Charles Wesley's conversion). The phrase 'a thousand tongues' echoes the words of Peter Böhler, a Moravian, who said to Charles Wesley, 'Had I a thousand tongues, I would praise him with them all'. Originally there were 18 verses, beginning:

> Glory to God, and Praise, and Love
> Be ever, ever given;
> By Saints below, and Saints above,
> The Church in Earth and Heaven.

The present Song Book includes verses 7-10 of the original.

O God, if still the holy place (619)
Albert Orsborn (1886-1967)

This song, described by the author as 'a natural outpouring of the soul', was written during his private devotions, when he was a captain in his first corps at Chelmsford. Later he said that he wrote it in a home of rest while recovering from sickness. It appeared anonymously with five verses in *The Local Officer*, October 1907, but subsequently a revised version, omitting the second verse of the original, was included in *Salvation Army Songs*, 1930.

O God, in whom alone is found (942)
Henry Ware (1794-1843)

Published in *Lyra Sacra Americana: or Gems from American Sacred Poetry*, 1868, compiled by Charles D. Cleveland, with the heading 'On laying a corner stone of a church'. The first verse began 'O Thou, in whom alone is found'.

O God of Bethel, by whose hand (918)
Philip Doddridge (1702-51)

On the author's manuscript, dated 16 January 1737, the verses were headed 'Jacob's Vow. From Genesis 28:20,22'. The hymn was published in *Translations and Paraphrases of Several Passages of Sacred Scripture*, 1745, and then in the author's *Hymns founded on Various Texts in the Holy Scriptures*, 1755, edited by Job Orton. Later, a revised version (as in the present Song Book) appeared in the 1781 edition of *Translations and Paraphrases*, prepared by a Committee of the General Assembly of the Church of Scotland.

O God of light, O God of love (446)
Arthur S. Booth-Clibborn (1855-1939)

The author said that he wrote the song on the continent in times of persecution and imprisonment. Described as a 'Special Holiness Song by Commissioner Booth-Clibborn', it was published in *The War Cry*, 13 April 1895, with five verses entitled 'God of light'. A revised version, headed 'A Song for Those Seeking Holiness', omitting the third verse of the original, appeared in *All the World*, September 1896, where it was attributed to the Maréchale (Catherine Booth-Clibborn). Later it was included in *The War Cry*, Christmas Number, 19 December 1896, with the heading 'A Song for Sunday Morning, 27th December 1896', attributed to Commissioner Booth-Clibborn.

O God of love eternal (943)
Maureen E. Jarvis (*b* 1928)

The author said:

In 1981 I was invited to write a song for the opening and dedication of the Wellington South Citadel. The first thoughts for writing this song came from the opening words of Psalm 127. The late Commissioner Dean Goffin, also a soldier at Wellington South, graciously agreed to adapt his arrangement of 'Aurelia' from the Band Selection 'The Light of the World' for congregation, band and songsters and the song 'O God of love eternal' was first sung on 30

May 1981. It has subsequently been used at the opening of a number of Citadels in New Zealand.

O God of love, to thee we bow (947)
W. Vaughan Jenkins (1868-1920)

Written for the author's wedding, in 1900, and published in *The Fellowship Hymn Book*, 1909. The fifth verse has now been omitted.

O God, our help in ages past (13)
Isaac Watts (1674-1748)

Based on Psalm 90:1-5, from the first part of the common metre version of this psalm, beginning 'Our God, our help in ages past', in *The Psalms of David Imitated in the Language of the New Testament*, 1719, by Isaac Watts. The first line was altered by John Wesley in his *Collection of Psalms and Hymns*, 1737. Originally there were nine verses, but verses 4, 6 and 8 have now been omitted.

O God, what offering shall I give (516)
Joachim Lange (1670-1744)
translated by John Wesley (1703-91)

The German hymn 'O Jesu, süsses Licht, appeared in the *Geistreiches Gesangbuch*, 1697, and in Freylinghausen's *Gesangbuch*, 1704. The translation was published in *Hymns and Sacred Poems*, 1739, with the title 'A morning dedication of ourselves to Christ'. Originally there were seven verses, beginning:

> Jesu, Thy light again I view,
> Again Thy mercy's beams I see,
> And all within me wakes, anew
> To pant for Thy immensity:
> Again my thoughts to Thee aspire
> In fervent flames of strong desire.

Later, John Wesley omitted the first verse and altered the opening line of verse 2 ('But O! what offering shall I give') to the present version, in *A Collection of Hymns for the Use of the People called Methodists*, 1780.

O happy day that fixed my choice (365)
verses: Philip Doddridge (1702-51)
chorus: Anonymous

The verses, entitle 'Rejoicing in our Covenant Engagements to God', with the scriptural reference 2 Chronicles 15:15, appeared in *Hymns founded on Various Texts in the Holy*

Scriptures, 1755, published from the author's manuscript by Job Orton. The fourth and fifth verses of the original have now been omitted. The chorus appeared in *The Wesleyan Sacred Harp*, 1854, compiled by W. McDonald and S. Hubbard, with the verses of this hymn and also 'Jesus, my all to heav'n is gone', by John Cennick.

O happy, happy day (366)
John Lawley (1859-1922)

Published in *Salvation Army Songs*, 1899. Although Mrs Carpenter, in her biography of the author, *Commissioner John Lawley*, 1924 (p 147), said that the song was written on the Trans-Siberian Railway, there now seems to be some uncertainty about the circumstances. Gordon Avery was aware of the above information, but in his *Companion to the Song Book*, 1961, he said only that the song was thought to have been written when the author was travelling with William Booth on one of the European railways.

O have you not heard of the beautiful stream (252)
Richard T. Torrey, jun.

Appeared in *The Sabbath School Gem*, 1863, compiled by Asa Hull.

O Holy Ghost, on thee we wait (198)
Will J. Brand (1889-1977)

Written for Whitsuntide, with the title: 'A Prayer for the Holy Spirit'. Originally there were three verses and a chorus, but when the song was included in *The Song Book of The Salvation Army*, 1953, the author added the second and fourth verses, and the chorus was omitted.

O how happy are they who the Saviour obey (367)
verses: Charles Wesley (1707-88)
chorus: Anonymous

Published in the author's *Hymns and Sacred Poems*, 1749, in a section headed 'For one fallen from grace'. Originally there were 16 verses, beginning:

> How happy are they,
> Who the Saviour obey,
> And have laid up their treasure above,
>   Tongue cannot express
>   The sweet comfort and peace
> Of a soul in its earliest love.

The first seven verses described the joy of salvation, while the second part of the hymn reflected the desolation of losing this experience, and concluded:
>I never shall rise
>To my first paradise,
>Or come my Redeemer to see:
>But I feel a faint hope,
>That at last He will stoop,
>And His pity shall bring Him to me.

The revised form of the verses, with the chorus added, appeared in *The Christian Mission Hymn Book*, 1870, compiled by William Booth.

O how I'd like to see his face (884)
Arthur S. Arnott (1870-1941)

One night, when speaking about Jesus to another officer, the author said, 'Wouldn't it be lovely to see His face?' Subsequently, he developed this thought at the organ and composed the song, which was later sung by 500 children in the town hall at Wellington, New Zealand. The chorus appeared in *The Officer*, June 1920, and the complete song, entitled 'Some glad, sweet day', was included in *The Musical Salvationist*, August 1920, a special issue headed 'International Gleanings', a collection of songs gathered during Commissioner T. H. Howard's world tour in 1919.

O Jesus, I have promised (862)
John E. Bode (1816-74)

Apparently written in about 1866, with the first line 'O Jesus, we have promised', for the confirmation of the author's daughter and two sons. With the present first line, it was printed by the Society for Promoting Christian Knowledge in 1868, on a leaflet, headed 'Hymn for the newly confirmed'. It was then included in a *New Appendix to the New and Enlarged Edition of Hymns for Public Worship*, 1869, with the heading 'Lord, I will follow Thee whithersoever Thou goest' (Luke 9:57). The fourth and sixth verses of the original have been omitted.

O Jesus, O Jesus, how vast thy love to me (368)
Anonymous

Appeared with five verses in *The Enlarged Revival Hymn Book*, 1868, compiled by William Booth. The third verse has been omitted and several lines have been altered, as in *Salvation Army Songs*, 1899.

O Jesus, Saviour, Christ divine (447)
William Booth (1829-1912)

Appeared in *The War Cry*, 23 May 1896, entitled: 'Pentecostal Salvation', and then included in *The Officer*, June 1896, headed: 'The General's Latest Song'.

O Jesus, Saviour, hear my cry (620)
Thomas C. Marshall (1854-1942)

The author, who described this as his 'blazing fire' song, said: 'It was written to the tune "Stella" . . . after I had lifted my heart to God in prayer for his assistance.' It appeared in *The War Cry*, 8 October 1887, when he was a staff-captain, on the training home staff.

O Jesus, thou art standing (299)
William Walsham How (1823-97)

The author said:

> I composed the hymn early in 1867, after I had been reading a very beautiful poem entitled 'Brothers and a Sermon'. The pathos of the verses impressed me very forcibly at the time. I read them over and over again, and finally, closing the book, I scribbled on an odd scrap of paper my first idea of the verses.

The poem, by Jean Ingelow, described how two brothers, in a village church, listened to a sermon on the text 'Behold, I stand at the door, and knock' (Revelation 3:20). The hymn, beginning 'O Jesu, thou art standing', was published in *A Supplement to Psalms and Hymns*, 1867, compiled by T. B. Morrell and W. Walsham How.

O joyful sound! O glorious hour (149)
verses: Thomas Kelly (1769-1855)
chorus: Anonymous

The verses, in their original form, appeared in the author's *Hymns on Various Passages of Scripture*, 1804, with the heading 'He is not here: for he is risen, as he said' (Matthew 28:6). Originally there were six verses, beginning:

> He's gone! see where his body lay,
> A pris'ner till th' appointed day:
>   Released from prison then,
> 'Why seek the living with the dead?'
> Remember what the Saviour said:
>   That he shou'd rise again.

The present version, based on verses 2, 3 and 5 of the original, is derived from *Hymns and Psalms adapted to the Services of the Church of England*, 1836, edited by William J. Hall. The chorus, based on the text 'I know that my redeemer liveth' (Job 19:25), was linked with verses by Charles Wesley ('O glorious hope of perfect love') in *Salvation Army Songs*, 1899, and with this song in *Salvation Army Songs*, 1930.

O Lamb of God, thou wonderful sin-bearer (448)
Catherine Booth-Clibborn (1858-1955)

A report in *The War Cry*, 28 May 1884, describing a meeting in Paris led by the Maréchale, said that the opening hymn was sung from *En Avant*. The report then quoted the third verse and chorus of this song. (It was somewhat different from the version of the present Song Book, and was probably translated from French.) About a year later, the author sang the song at the opening of the Great Western Hall, Marylebone, on 2 May 1885. Part of the first verse and chorus were printed in *The War Cry*, 9 May 1885. The complete song appeared in *Songs of Love and Service*, a booklet prepared for the 'Marriage Festivities' of Miss Emma Booth and Commissioner Frederick Tucker, 9,10 April 1888. It was then included in *The Musical Salvationist*, June 1888, with the title 'At Thy feet I fall'.

O little town of Bethlehem (86)
Phillips Brooks (1835-93)

Written for the Sunday-school at Holy Trinity Church, Philadelphia, Christmas 1868, probably inspired by the author's visit to Bethlehem in December 1865. Originally there were five verses, but when the hymn was included in *The Church Porch, a Service Book and Hymnal for Sunday Schools*, 1874, edited by William R. Huntington, the fourth verse of the original, 'Where children pure and happy', was omitted.

O Lord, how often should we be (747)
Albert Orsborn (1886-1967)

The author said that the song came to him as the result of a spiritual crisis when he was 'sick and wounded' in the home of rest at Gore Road, Hackney. He said, 'It is a heart-cry, written, I confess, with tears, at my bedside, when in prayer.' It appeared anonymously in *The Local Officer*, June 1908, under the heading 'Holiness Song'. Later, a revised version was included in *Songs for Use during Special Campaigns in the United Kingdom*, 1923, while the present version is from *Salvation Army Songs*, 1930.

O Lord, I will delight in thee (14)
John Ryland (1753-1825)

Written on 3 December 1777, and published in *A Selection of Hymns from the Best Authors*, 1787, compiled by John Rippon. Later it was included in the author's *Hymns and Verses on Sacred Subjects*, 1862. (The author noted on the manuscript, 'I recollect deeper feelings of mind in composing this hymn, than perhaps I ever felt in making any other.') Originally there were seven verses, beginning 'O Lord, I would delight in thee'. Verses 3, 5 and 6 have been omitted from the Song Book.

O Lord my God, when I in awesome wonder (37)
Carl G. Boberg (1859-1940)
English version by Stuart K. Hine (b 1899)

The Swedish hymn 'O store Gud' was written in 1885 and was published in *Mönsterås Tidningen*, 13 March 1886. (Further details of Carl Boberg's hymn are included with the notes on the translation 'O mighty God!' by Walter M. Powell.) Not knowing that it was originally Swedish, Stuart Hine initially learnt the hymn in Russian, when it appeared in a Russian hymn book, *Kimvali*, 1927. The first three verses of his English version reflected his experiences in the Carpathian mountains: the thunder echoing through the mountains, the birds singing in the forest glades, and the people seeing for the first time the revelation of God's love at Calvary. Later, in 1948, when refugees in England were asking 'When are we going home?' he wrote the fourth verse, thinking of the place prepared for all who would come to God through Christ. He published the English and Russian words in his Russian gospel magazine *Grace and Peace*, in 1949, and subsequently reprinted the hymn, distributing thousands of copies freely around the world.

O Lord of every shining constellation (38)
Albert F. Bayly (1901-84)

Written in 1946-7, to express a Christian response to life in the 20th century which has been influenced so greatly by science and technology. It first appeared in the author's collection *Rejoice, O People*, 1951. Later, a revised version was included in *100 Hymns for Today*, 1969 and in Part 2 of the author's *Rejoice Together: Hymns and Verse*, 1982, where it was entitled 'God's Age-long Plan'.

O Lord of Heaven and earth and sea (15)
Christopher Wordsworth (1807-85)

Appeared under the heading 'Charitable Collections' in the

author's *The Holy Year; or Hymns for Sundays and Holydays throughout the year, And for other Occasions*, Third edition, 1863. From the original nine verses, the present Song Book includes verses 1 and 3-6, altered as in *The Song Book of The Salvation Army*, 1953.

O Lord, regard thy people (944)
Albert Orsborn (1886-1967)

Written at the request of General Bramwell Booth, for the stone-laying ceremony of the William Booth Memorial Training College at Denmark Hill, London, on Thursday 10 May 1928. It was sung on that occasion by the recently commissioned officers, who as cadets of the 1927-28 Session had been commissioned at Clapton on the preceding Monday. The song was then included in *Salvation Army Songs*, 1930.

O Lord, thy heavenly grace impart (517)
John F. Oberlin (1740-1826)
translated by Lucy S. Wilson (1802-63)

The translation was published in the *Memoirs of John Frederic Oberlin*, 1829, by Lucy Wilson, as part of a description of a service conducted by Oberlin in the church at Waldbach, on 11 June 1820. During this service, the hymn would probably have been sung in French, but no original has been found in Oberlin's hymn book or elsewhere, either in French or in German.

O Lord, we long to see your face (748)
John R. Peacey (1896-1971)

Published in *100 Hymns for Today: a Supplement to Hymns Ancient and Modern*, 1969, with the title 'Walking by Faith'.

O Lord, whose human hands were quick (518)
Malcolm J. Bale (*b* 1934)

The author felt that, for a movement whose ministry expressed such a strong social conscience, The Salvation Army had very few songs which dealt with social issues, and he therefore submitted these verses which were accepted for inclusion in the Song Book. A revised version of the song appeared in *The Musical Salvationist*, January 1985, entitled 'Through Jesus' grace'.

O Love, revealed on earth in Christ (449)
Catherine Baird (1895-1984)

In some undated notes supplied to Gordon Avery (probably in the 1950s) the author said:

> This song has a long history. I began to write it in my mind eighteen years ago. But, during the war which I had never believed could occur, it was nearly completed through my personal reflections on the incompatibility of war with the teachings of Jesus. I did not finish it until Colonel Coles asked for some words and supplied the music.

The original version, entitled 'O Light of Heaven', appeared in *The Musical Salvationist,* March-April 1950, but it was subsequently rewritten in its present form for *The Song Book of The Salvation Army,* 1953.

O Love that wilt not let me go (621)
George Matheson (1842-1906)

The author said:

> My hymn was composed in the manse of Innellan on the evening of 6th June 1882. I was at that time alone. It was the day of my sister's marriage, and the rest of the family were staying over night in Glasgow. Something had happened to me, which was known only to myself, and which caused me the most severe mental suffering. The hymn was the fruit of that suffering. It was the quickest bit of work I ever did in my life. I had the impression rather of having it dictated to me by some inward voice than of working it out myself. I am quite sure that the whole work was completed in five minutes. (*The Life of George Matheson,* 1907, by D. MacMillan, page 181).

It seems that he must have been mistaken about the date, because the verses, headed 'If any man be in Christ, he is a new creature' (2 Corinthians 5:17), appeared in *Life and Work: A Parish Magazine,* January 1882. Later, the hymn was included in *The Scottish Hymnal,* 1884, with one line altered at the request of the hymnal committee.

O Love upon a cross impaled (122)
Albert Orsborn (1886-1967)

The author said that it was written for Easter meetings at Boscombe. It was printed on a leaflet headed *Easter Songs by General Albert Orsborn,* which Gordon Avery dated 'Boscombe, Easter 1961'. However, it also appeared on the Order of Service for 'A Day at the Cross' at Camberwell Citadel, on Good Friday, 15 April 1960, described as 'A new Easter song by General Albert Orsborn (R)'.

O Master, let me walk with thee (519)
Washington Gladden (1836-1918)

Published as a poem with three eight-line verses in the magazine *Sunday Afternoon*, March 1879, and then included in *Songs of Christian Praise*, 1880, compiled by Charles H. Richards, who omitted the second verse of the original poem.

O mighty God! When I thy works consider (39)
Carl G. Boberg (1859-1940)
translated by Walter M. Powell (1867-1956)

In the summer of 1885, the author returned home from a meeting at Kronobäck during a thunderstorm. Afterwards, a rainbow appeared and, from his home, he could see the stillness of the Mönsterås Inlet. He listened to the song of a thrush in nearby woods and, in the evening, heard the tolling of a church bell. Surrounded by the beauty of nature, he was inspired to write the poem 'O store Gud', which originally had nine verses. It was published in *Mönsterås Tidningen*, 13 March 1886, and was later set to music in *Sanningsvittnet*, 16 April 1891, which Carl Boberg edited. The translation, entitled 'O Mighty God', appeared in *The Musical Salvationist*, July 1937, in an arrangement for male voices.

O my heart is full of music and of gladness (369)
Emma Booth-Tucker (1860-1903)

Commissioner Booth-Tucker said that his wife wrote the words specially for a tune which he had composed as he was going up the steps of an omnibus on his way home from International Headquarters. The song was sung at a 'Battle of Song' at Alexandra Palace on 5 August 1895 and was printed in *The War Cry*, 10 August 1895, with the heading 'Our special presentation song'. Subsequently it was included in *The Officer*, September 1895 and *The Musical Salvationist*, October 1896.

O perfect Love, all human thought transcending (948)
Dorothy F. Gurney (1858-1932)

Written at Pull Wyke, Ambleside, in about 1883. One Sunday evening, when the author was singing hymns with other members of her family, her sister asked her to write new words for her favourite tune, 'Strength and Stay' by J. B. Dykes, for her forthcoming marriage to Mr Hugh Redmayne, of Brathay Hall. She went into the library and wrote the verses in a quarter of an hour, based on the two-fold aspect of perfect union, love and life. The hymn was sung subsequently at several weddings in London, and was published in *Hymns Ancient and Modern . . . Supplemental Hymns*, 1889. It was also set to music by Joseph Barnby for the marriage of Princess Louise and the Duke of Fife, 27 July 1889.

O sacred head once wounded (123)
Paulus Gerhardt (1607-76)
translated by James W. Alexander (1804-59)

The German hymn, 'O Haupt voll Blut und Wunden', from the 1656 edition of Cruger's *Praxis pietatis melica*, was based on part of the Latin hymn 'Salve mundi salutare', sometimes attributed to Bernard of Clairvaux. The English translation appeared in *The Christian Lyre*, 1830, edited by Joshua Leavitt, with eight verses, beginning 'O Sacred Head, now wounded'. Later, a revised version of this translation, with 10 verses, was published in Schaff's *Deutsche Kirchenfreund*, 1849, and *The Breaking Crucible*, 1861, a collection of translations by J. W. Alexander.

O Saviour, now to thee we raise (919)
Anonymous

Appeared in *Salvation Army Songs*, 1899, in the 'New Buildings' section. The last line of each verse, 'We dedicate this house to Thee', was altered by the Song Book Council in 1982, for the present Song Book.

O soldier, awake, for the strife is at hand (689)
Fanny Crosby (1820-1915)

This song, beginning 'O Christian, awake', appeared in *The Singing Pilgrim, or Pilgrim's Progress Illustrated in Song*, 1866, compiled by Philip Phillips. These verses were linked with an incident in *The Pilgrim's Progress*, where Christian, in the Valley of Humiliation, was protected by 'the whole armour of God'. The third verse of the original has now been omitted.

O soul, consider and be wise (885)
Will J. Brand (1889-1977)

Written for *The Song Book of The Salvation Army*, 1953, because of the shortage of suitable songs on the subject of 'Heaven and Hell'. The author said: 'Whilst avoiding the lurid literalism of the last century, it endeavours to utter a grave warning note, but ends with hope and invitation.'

O spotless Lamb, I come to thee (450)
Catherine Booth-Clibborn (1858-1955)

Entitled: 'Take all my sins away', the song appeared in *The War Cry*, 28 October 1882, with music by the author, and the words were again included in *The War Cry*, 23 December 1882.

O that in me the mind of Christ (451)
Edward H. Joy (1871-1949)

First published in *The War Cry*, Canada West, 28 April 1928, as a poem with six verses, entitled 'The Mind of Christ', based on Philippians 2:5-12. Omitting the second verse, but adding the chorus, it was then set to Richard Slater's tune 'Thou art enough for me' in *The War Cry*, Canada West, 11 August 1928. Later it appeared in *The Musical Salvationist*, December 1935, with a melody composed by the author. Subsequently the verses were revised by Catherine Baird for *The Song Book of The Salvation Army*, 1953.

O the bitter shame and sorrow (548)
Theodore Monod (1836-1921)

Written in July 1874, during a series of consecration meetings at Broadlands, Hampshire, and then printed on the back of a programme card for another series of meetings held in Oxford in October 1874. With the title 'The Altered Motto' it was also printed inside the front cover of the 1874 volume of the magazine *Woman's Work in the Great Harvest Field*. Subsequently it was included in *Revival Music*, 1876, compiled by William Booth, and *Hymns of Consecration and Faith, and Sacred Songs for Missions, Prayer and Praise Meetings*, 1876, compiled by James Mountain.

O the deep, deep love of Jesus (182)
S. Trevor Francis (1834-1925)

Appeared as a poem, with eight verses, entitled 'Love of Jesus' in the author's *Whence-Whither, and other Poems*, 1898. The present version, with three verses, is from *The Song Companion to the Scriptures*, 1911, compiled by G. Campbell Morgan.

O there's joy in every heart (664)
Anonymous

Apparently included in Robert Bird's *300 Best Hymns* (a source that has not been located), and then in *Salvation Army Songs*, 1930.

O think of the home over there (886)
De Witt Clinton Huntington (1830-1912)

Appeared with music by Tullius Clinton O'Kane in *Additional Fresh Leaves, a Supplement to Fresh Leaves*, 1868, compiled by T. C. O'Kane.

O thou God of every nation (622)
William J. Pearson (1832-92)

Written for the opening of the Congress Hall, Clapton, it was sung at the dedicatory service on Saturday 13 May 1882, having appeared in *The War Cry*, 11 May 1882, under the title: 'Bless our Army'. The fifth verse, particularly appropriate for that occasion, has now been omitted:

> Lord, we give to thee this building;
> Let thy light within it shine;
> Let thy glory be its gilding;
> Seal it now, for ever thine!
>   Now and ever,
> Praise and glory shall be thine.

O thou God of full salvation (452)
William J. Pearson (1832-92)

Appeared in *The War Cry*, 11 June 1887, on a page of 'Original Salvation Songs composed for *The War Cry*.' Headed 'Make us Holy', it was said to be 'by Major Pearson', who at that time contributed a new song almost every week. The original fifth verse has now been omitted and the third and fourth verses have been transposed. (The song was later attributed to Mrs Major Lilian B. Watkins (1879-1964) but this must have been a mistake as she was only seven years old when the song first appeared.)

O thou God of my salvation (370)
attributed to Thomas Olivers (1725-99)

Verses 1-3 in the present Song Book are from one version of this hymn (with five verses), published in 1775 at the end of *A Short Account of the Death of Mary Langson, of Taxall, in Cheshire; who died January the 29th, 1769*. Verse 4 is based on the last verse of a different version (also with five verses) which was included in *A Pocket Hymn Book, Designed as a Constant Companion for the Pious*, 1783. (These four verses appeared together in *Salvation Army Songs*, 1899, but were probably taken from another source that has not yet been identified.) The hymn has been attributed to Thomas Olivers, who was apparently the author of *A Short Account of the Death of Mary Langson*. He was superintendent of the methodist circuit including Taxall, in 1769-71.

O thou to whose all-searching sight (453)
Nicolaus L. von Zinzendorf (1700-60)
translated by John Wesley (1703-91)

The German hymn, 'Seelen-Brautigam, O du Gottes-Lamm', was written in September 1721 and appeared in the *Sammlung geistlicher und lieblicher Lieder*, 1725, and the Herrnhut *Gesangbuch*, 1735. The translation was published in *A Collection of Psalms and Hymns*, 1738, and then in *Hymns and Sacred Poems*, 1739, where it was entitled 'The Believer's Support'.

O thou who camest from above (199)
Charles Wesley (1707-88)

Based on the text 'The fire shall ever be burning upon the altar; it shall never go out' (Leviticus 6:13). The hymn was published in the author's *Short Hymns on Select Passages of the Holy Scriptures*, 1762, in two eight-line verses, and then in *A Collection of Hymns for the Use of the People called Methodists*, 1780, compiled by John Wesley, in four four-line verses.

O to be like thee! blessèd Redeemer (623)
Thomas O. Chisholm (1866-1960)

Published in the *Young People's Hymnal*, 1897, compiled by W. D. Kirkland, James Atkins, and William J. Kirkpatrick.

O wanderer, knowing not the smile (253)
Herbert H. Booth (1862-1926)

Written for the tune 'Footsteps on the stairs', the song appeared in *The War Cry*, 23 December 1882, entitled: 'Transformation Scenes'. It was then included in *Salvation Music, Volume 2*, December 1883, under the title: 'There's mercy still for thee'. The second verse has been omitted.

O what a wonderful, wonderful day (371)
John W. Peterson (*b* 1921)

Written in August 1961, and published in *Miracle Melodies, No. 4*, 1961. In the morning service at the Montrose Bible Conference in Pennsylvania, an elderly man gave his personal testimony. Describing how he came to Christ, he said, with his face glowing, 'Heaven came down and glory filled my soul'. Thinking this was a good theme for a song, the author made a note of the phrase and, later that week, completed the words and music.

O what amazing words of grace (254)
Samuel Medley (1738-99)

This hymn, with six verses, appeared in the author's *Hymns*, Second edition, 1789, under the heading 'I am Alpha and Omega, the Beginning and the End. I will give unto him that is athirst of the fountain of the water of life freely' (Revelation 21:6). The second verse in the present Song Book was not in the 1789 version, but was included in *Hymns for Divine Worship*, 1863, compiled for the Methodist New Connexion, where the hymn was dated 'Medley, 1800'. The source of this version has not yet been found.

O what shall I do my Saviour to praise (372)
Charles Wesley (1707-88)

Entitled 'A Thanksgiving' in *Hymns and Sacred Poems*, 1742, by John and Charles Wesley. The fourth and fifth verses of the original have been omitted.

O when shall my soul find her rest (454)
W. Bramwell Booth (1856-1929)

Entitled: 'My Soul and my Saviour', the song appeared in *The War Cry*, 15 May 1880, dated '11th May'. It is said to have been written late at night when the author was waiting at a railway station.

O worship the King, all glorious above (16)
Robert Grant (1779-1838)

This paraphrase of Psalm 104 was published in *Christian Psalmody*, 1833, compiled by Edward Bickersteth, and also in *Psalms and Hymns, for Public, Private and Social Worship*, 1835, selected by Henry Venn Elliott, and the author's *Sacred Poems*, 1839, compiled by his brother, Lord Glenelg.

O worship the Lord in the beauty of holiness (183)
John S. B. Monsell (1811-75)

Published as a hymn for the fourth Sunday after Easter, in the author's *Hymns of Love and Praise*, 1863, where it was headed 'Worship the Lord in the beauty of holiness' (1 Chronicles 16:29).

Of all in earth or Heaven (65)
Nathan A. Aldersley (1826-99)

Appeared in *The War Cry*, New Zealand, 1 April 1893, and *The Young Soldier*, 15 April 1893, and then included in *The Musical Salvationist*, October 1897, with the title: 'The Christ of Calvary'. The original third verse has been omitted.

Oft have I heard thy tender voice (749)
W. Bramwell Booth (1856-1929)

These verses are from a song entitled 'I bring my all to thee, dear Lord', in *The Musical Salvationist*, July 1889. There were two choruses, which have now been omitted. The words were said to be 'by W. Bramwell Booth', although later, in *The War Cry* (Bombay), 11 May 1895, the song was attributed to Commissioner Raheeman [Mrs Emma Booth-Tucker]. Later, the verses were altered slightly for *Salvation Army Songs*, 1930, and *The Song Book of The Salvation Army*, 1953.

Oft our trust has known betrayal (750)
verses: Richard Slater (1854-1939)
chorus: Albert B. Simpson (1843-1919)

The chorus is from a song by A. B. Simpson beginning 'O, how sweet the glorious message', in *Hymns of the Christian Life*, 1891, edited by R. Kelso Carter and A. B. Simpson. Later, the chorus appeared in *The War Cry*, 15 August 1896, as one of the popular choruses from the Salvation Army exhibition at the Agricultural Hall, London, 1-10 August 1896. With six verses by Richard Slater, it was included in *The Musical Salvationist*, October 1896, a special issue headed 'World-wide favourites'. The present Song Book includes verses 1, 2 and 4, altered as in *Salvation Army Songs*, 1930, and *The Song Book of The Salvation Army*, 1953.

On a hill far away stood an old rugged cross (124)
George Bennard (1873-1958)

Written in 1913. The author said that the theme, 'The old rugged cross', and the melody, came to him while he was leading evangelistic meetings in Michigan, but he was unable to complete the poem until he returned to Michigan, after a series of meetings in New York State. He sang the song to his friends, the Reverend and Mrs L. O. Bostwick, at their home in Pokagon, Michigan, and they offered to pay for copies to be printed. It was sung at an interdenominational convention at the Chicago Evangelistic Institute, and was later included in *Heart and Life Songs*, 1915, edited by Iva D. Vennard, Joseph H. Smith and George Bennard. The third verse of the original has been omitted from the present Song Book.

On Calvary's brow my Saviour died (125)
verses and second chorus: William M'K. Darwood (c1835-1914)
first chorus: attributed to John Fairhurst

The verses, with the second chorus, appeared in *Sacred Melodies Nos. 1 and 2 combined*, 1886, compiled by Avis and Gill, and in *Sacred Songs and Solos: With Standard Hymns, Combined*, 1888, compiled by Ira D. Sankey. The first chorus is from a song beginning 'Once I was deep-down sunk in sin', attributed to 'Sergeant Fairhurst' in *Salvation Songster's Songs, Part 2*, 1884, compiled by Herbert H. Booth. During the second campaign by the Salvation Singing Battalion, from the training barracks, this song was sung by 'Sister Fairhurst' at Stockport (*The War Cry*, 24 November 1883) and by 'Cadet Fairhurst' at Rochdale (*The War Cry*, 1 December 1883).

On Calvary's tree the King of Glory languished (126)
F. Lilian Pollock (1899-1981)

Published under the title: 'From that sacred hill' in *The Musical Salvationist*, January-February 1951, with music originally composed by Douglas Rolls for Albert Orsborn's song: 'When shall I come unto the healing waters?'

On every hill our Saviour dies (127)
Albert Orsborn (1886-1967)

In his autobiography *The House of my Pilgrimage* (p 105) the author said that this song was written at the request of General Evangeline Booth for the campaign 'The World for God' [1935-36], but 'it did not please her'. It was published in *The Beauty of Jesus*, 1947, a collection of songs and poems by General Albert Orsborn. The chorus in the present Song Book was originally the fifth verse.

On God's word relying (222)
Arnold Brown (*b* 1913)

The chorus, written for the 'I Believe' campaign in Canada in 1951, was published in *The War Cry*, Toronto, 10 February 1951. Later the complete song, entitled 'I Believe!' appeared in *The Musical Salvationist*, September-October 1955. In his autobiography, *The Gate and the Light* (p 41), the author said:

In accepting the song for publication, the head of the Music Editorial Department wrote: 'Few songs have so encapsulated in a single chorus our Articles of Doctrine.'

On Jordan's stormy banks I stand (887)
verses 1-4: Samuel Stennett (1727-95)
verse 5 and chorus: Anonymous

Verses 1-4 are from *A Selection of Hymns from the Best Authors*, 1787, compiled by John Rippon, where there were seven verses, headed 'The promised land'. The chorus appeared with the first verse of the hymn in *The Southern Harmony, and Musical Companion*, 1835, compiled by William Walker. The fifth verse in the present Song Book was not in the original version, but was included in *Songs of Faith*, 1971, edited by Norman Bearcroft, and in a festival arrangement by Norman Bearcroft in *The Musical Salvationist*, October 1981.

On the cross of Calvary (128)
Sarah J. Graham (c1854-c1889)

This song, entitled 'On the Cross of Calvary', appeared anonymously in the first issue of *The Musical Salvationist*, July 1886, which was advertised in *The War Cry*, 24 July 1886, as 'The Music of the Songs of the International Congress'. Later, in an article published in *The War Cry* (San Francisco) in 1931, Colonel Thomas W. Scott (R) said that the song was written by Sarah Graham, of Lindsay Corps in Ontario, Canada.

On to the conflict, soldiers, for the right (813)
attributed to W. Howard Doane (1832-1915)

Entitled 'Sunday-School War-Cry', this song appeared in *Royal Diadem for the Sunday School*, 1873, compiled by Robert Lowry and W. Howard Doane. The words were by W. Bennett, with music by W. H. Doane. Later, in *The Musical Salvationist*, October 1918, the words and music were attributed to W. H. Doane. (Nothing is known about W. Bennett who was originally named as the author.) Several lines have been altered, as in *Salvation Army Songs*, 1930.

Once I heard a sound at my heart's dark door (373)
verses: Sylvanus D. Phelps (1816-95)
chorus: Robert Lowry (1826-99)

Henry S. Burrage, in *Baptist Hymn Writers and their Hymns*, 1888, said that the verses were written in 1860 and that Dr Lowry, who composed the music, added the refrain. The song, entitled 'Let the Master in', was published in *Pure Gold for the Sunday School*, 1871, compiled by Robert Lowry and W. Howard Doane. It was headed: 'Behold, I stand at the door, and knock: if any man hear my voice, and open the door, I will come in to him' (Revelation 3:20).

Once I thought I walked with Jesus (549)
Francis A. Blackmer (1855-1930)

Published by the author in the *Gospel in Song*, 1884. Later, a Canadian officer introduced the song at meetings conducted by William Booth in the Rotunda, Liverpool (*The War Cry*, 10 November 1888) and it was included in *The Musical Salvationist*, April 1890.

Once I was far in sin (374)
verses: James C. Bateman (1854-88)
chorus: attributed to R. Kelso Carter (1849-1926)

The verses and chorus, signed 'Capt J. C. Bateman', appeared in the anniversary report of Salvation Army work in Scotland, August 1882-August 1883. Later, in *Glad Hallelujahs*, 1887, compiled by J. R. Sweney and W. J. Kirkpatrick, the chorus was linked with verses by R. Kelso Carter, beginning 'Rest to the weary soul'. In his *Companion to the Song Book*, 1961, Gordon Avery gave the source of James Bateman's song as *The Musical Salvationist*, March 1892, and attributed the chorus to R. Kelso Carter. He was probably not aware of the earlier Scottish anniversary report.

Once I was lost, on the breakers tossed (375)
William G. Collins (1854-1931)

Appeared in *The Musical Salvationist*, August 1887, with the title: 'Bound for Canaan's Shore'. The third verse was rewritten for *The Song Book of The Salvation Army*, 1953.

Once in misery I walked alone (376)
John Gowans (b 1934)

From the mini-musical *White Rose* by John Gowans and John Larsson, which was presented at the Royal Albert Hall, 27 June 1977, during the 70th anniversary of the Home League. The musical is set in France, where *La Rose Blanche* (The White Rose) is an emblem of the Home League and the title of the Home League magazine. In the context of the musical, this song, entitled 'When I came to him', was intended to create the impression of an exhilarating testimony period in a Salvation Army meeting in Paris.

Once, in royal David's city (87)
Cecil Frances Alexander (1818-95)

Published in the author's *Hymns for Little Children*, 1848, with the heading: 'Who was Conceived by the Holy Ghost, Born of the Virgin Mary'. It was one of a group of hymns (Nos. 8-20) written to explain articles of the Christian faith. The sixth verse has now been omitted.

Once, on a day, was Christ led forth to die (129)
Albert Orsborn (1886-1967)

This song, written for the tune 'Love's old sweet song', was introduced by cadets during a holiness meeting conducted by General Edward Higgins at Camberwell on Thursday 20 October 1932. The chorus was included in a report of the meeting in *The War Cry*, 29 October 1932, and the complete song, entitled 'Sacred Hands of Jesus', appeared in *The War Cry*, New York, 30 December 1933.

One golden dawning, one glorious morning (888)
Sidney E. Cox (1887-1975)

Written at the territorial headquarters in Atlanta, Georgia, it was published in *The Musical Salvationist*, September 1936, under the title: 'In God's Tomorrow', and later in *The War Cry*, 23 October 1937.

One there is above all others (377)
verses 1 and 4: Mary Ann Nunn (1778-1847)
verses 2 and 3: Anonymous

Verses 1 and 4 have been adapted from verses in *Psalms and Hymns*, 1817, compiled by the author's brother, John Nunn. Verse 2 was the second verse of a hymn beginning 'Sinners fly and come to Jesus', in *A Collection of Revival Hymns*, 1844. Verse 3 was added in *The Song Book of The Salvation Army*, 1953, when this song first appeared in its present form.

Only a step to Jesus (255)
Fanny Crosby (1820-1915)

Published in *Royal Diadem for the Sunday School*, 1873, compiled by Robert Lowry and W. Howard Doane, with the heading 'Then come thou, for there is peace to thee' (1 Samuel 20:21).

Onward, Christian soldiers (690)
Sabine Baring-Gould (1834-1924)

Written in 1864, apparently for the children of Horbury Bridge and a neighbouring village to sing during a procession 'with cross and banners'. The hymn was published in the *Church Times*, 15 October 1864, with six verses, and then in *A Supplement to Psalms and Hymns*, 1867, compiled by Thomas B. Morrell and W. Walsham How, omitting the fourth verse of the original.

Others he saved, himself he cannot save (130)
Albert Orsborn (1886-1967)

Printed on an undated leaflet, *Easter Songs by General Albert Orsborn*, which was apparently used during meetings led by the author at Boscombe, Easter 1961.

Our blest redeemer, ere he breathed (200)
Henriette Auber (1773-1862)

This was the first of two hymns headed 'Whitsunday' in the author's *The Spirit of the Psalms*, 1829. Part of the hymn was apparently written at some time on a window pane at the author's home in Hoddesdon, but the glass has now disappeared, so the story cannot be authenticated.

Our Father, who in Heaven art (624)
Charles Coller (1863-1935)

This version of the Lord's Prayer appeared on 'The Young People's Page' in *The Musical Salvationist*, February 1917, with the title: 'The Children's Prayer'. The chorus has now been omitted, as in *The Young People's Song Book of The Salvation Army*, 1963.

Our thankful hearts need joyful songs (926)
Richard Slater (1854-1939)

Written in August 1898, and included in *Salvation Army Songs*, 1899. The second verse was altered for *The Song Book of The Salvation Army*, 1953.

Out of my bondage, sorrow and night (300)
William T. Sleeper (1819-1904)

Published in *Gospel Hymns No. 5*, 1887, compiled by Ira D. Sankey, James McGranahan and George C. Stebbins.

Out of my darkness God called me (378)
John Gowans (*b* 1934)

From the musical *Jesus Folk*, which was presented in an abridged version at the finale of the British Congress at Wembley, 10 July 1972, followed by the first complete production at the Fairfield Halls, Croydon, 25 January 1973. This song, beginning 'Out of my darkness He called me', is sung when Lazarus emerges from the grave, after the singing of the words of Jesus, 'I am the resurrection, and the life: he that believeth in me, though he were dead, yet shall he live: and whosoever liveth and believeth in me shall never die' (John 11:25,26).

Pass me not, O loving Saviour (301)
Fanny Crosby (1820-1915)

The composer, W. H. Doane, asked Fanny Crosby to write verses on the theme 'Pass me not, O gentle Saviour'. Several weeks later, in early Spring 1868, when she was speaking at services in a Manhattan prison, one of the men called out, 'Good Lord! Do not pass me by'. This gave her the inspiration for the song, which she wrote that evening. It was published in *Songs of Devotion*, 1870, compiled by W. Howard Doane.

Peace in our time, O Lord (827)
William A. Dunkerley (1852-1941)

At the end of 1934, the author sent a typewritten copy of the hymn to Arch Wiggins, thinking that it might be useful to The Salvation Army. Entitled: 'Peace', it was published under the heading 'November 11th', in *The Bandsman and Songster*, 9 November 1935, with the note 'These verses may be sung to the tune "Diademata".' Shortly afterwards it was included in *The Musical Salvationist*, June 1936, set to Eric Ball's tune 'Peace'.

Peace, perfect peace, far beyond all understanding (751)
Erik Leidzén (1894-1962)

Entitled: 'Perfect peace', the song appeared on 'The Bandsman's Page' of *The Musical Salvationist*, November 1930, in an arrangement for male voices.

Peace, perfect peace, in this dark world of sin (752)
Edward H. Bickersteth (1825-1906)

The author's son said that the hymn was written one Sunday afternoon in August 1875, when his father was on holiday in Harrogate, Yorkshire. In the morning, he heard the Vicar of

Harrogate preach on the text 'Thou wilt keep him in perfect peace, whose mind is stayed on thee' (Isaiah 26:3), and, during the afternoon, he wrote the verses while he was visiting an 'aged and dying relative' (Archdeacon Hill of Liverpool). The hymn was published by the author in *Songs in the House of Pilgrimage* (a booklet of five hymns), and in *The Hymnal Companion to the Book of Common Prayer*, Revised and enlarged edition, 1877.

Plan our life, O gracious Saviour (863)
Wilfrid Bayliss (1882-1952)

Entitled 'The Youth Movement Hymn', it was published by the author in *Cotons selection of Community Hymns*, Fourth edition, with the heading 'And they shall build the old wastes, they shall raise up the former desolations, and they shall repair the waste Cities, the desolations of many generations' (Isaiah 61:4). The verses have been slightly altered, as in *The Song Book of The Salvation Army*, 1953, and the fifth verse of the original has been omitted.

Pleasures sought, dearly bought (379)
Agnes P. Heathcote (1862-?)

Appeared in *The Musical Salvationist*, January 1887, under the title: 'Jesus came with Peace to Me'.

Praise and thanksgiving (927)
Albert F. Bayly (1901-84)

Written in June 1961, first printed in *The Rodborough Hymnal*, 1964, published by Rodborough Tabernacle Congregational Church, and later included in the author's collection: *Again I Say Rejoice: Hymns and Verse*, 1967.

Praise God for what he's done for me (380)
Anonymous

The origin of this song is unknown. The first verse (with another verse not in the present Song Book, and a different chorus) appeared in *A Collection of Revival Hymns, Adapted to Popular Airs*, 1844. Later the song was included in *A Selection of Revival Hymns*, c1865, with five verses, and in *The Revival Hymn Book*, 1866, compiled by William Booth, with four verses and the present chorus.

Praise God, from whom all blessings flow (959)
Thomas Ken (1637-1711)

The concluding verse of the author's morning and evening

hymns: 'Awake, my soul, and with the sun' (665) and 'Glory to thee, my God, this night' (671).

Praise God, I'm saved (960)
attributed to Thomas H. C. Leighton (c1858-?)

This doxology is the chorus of a song entitled 'Praise God, I'm saved', which appeared anonymously in *The Musical Salvationist*, May 1887. The first verse began:

> A voice fell softly from on high,
> When I, for sin, was weeping sore;
> 'Lord, save me,' was my heart-felt cry,
> As loud I knock'd at mercy's door.

There seems to be no reason for attributing this song to Thomas Leighton, except that a 'Song of Farewell for Foreign Service' which appeared on the same page, set to the same tune, was by 'Staff-Capt. T. Leighton'.

Praise him! Praise him! Jesus our blessèd redeemer (184)
Fanny Crosby (1820-1915)

Published in *Bright Jewels for the Sunday School*, 1869, edited by Robert Lowry, assisted by William F. Sherwin and Chester G. Allen. Originally there were three eight-line verses, entitled 'Praise! Give Praise!'. The present version, with three six-line verses and a chorus, is from *Sacred Songs and Solos: With Standard Hymns, Combined*, 1888, compiled by Ira D. Sankey.

Praise, my soul, the King of Heaven (17)
Henry Francis Lyte (1793-1847)

This was the second of three versions of Psalm 103 in the author's *The Spirit of the Psalms, or The Psalms of David, Adapted to Christian Worship*, 1834. It was sung at the wedding of the future Queen Elizabeth II at Westminster Abbey on 20 November 1947, the 100th anniversary of the author's death. The fourth verse of the original has now been omitted.

Praise to the holiest in the height (18)
John H. Newman (1801-90)

From the author's poem 'The Dream of Gerontius', first published in *The Month: An Illustrated Magazine of Literature, Science and Art*, May and June 1865. In the poem, which traces the journey of the soul of Gerontius beyond death, this hymn, with six verses, is sung by the 'fifth choir of angelicals'. With the first verse repeated as the last, it was included in the 1868

Appendix to *Hymns Ancient and Modern*. Verses 4-6 of the original hymn have now been omitted.

Praise to the Lord, the Almighty (19)
verses 1, 2 and 5: Joachim Neander (1650-80)
translated by Catherine Winkworth (1827-78)
verses 3 and 4: Percy Dearmer (1867-1936)

The German hymn 'Lobe den Herren', based on Psalm 103:1-6 and Psalm 150, appeared in the author's *Glaub- und Liebesübung*, 1680. Catherine Winkworth's translation was published in *The Chorale Book for England*, 1863, but the third and fourth verses in the present Song Book were added by Percy Dearmer in *The English Hymnal*, 1906.

Prayer is the soul's sincere desire (625)
James Montgomery (1771-1854)

Written in 1818 for *A Treatise on Prayer*, 1818, by Edward Bickersteth, and also printed that year on a leaflet for use in Sheffield Sunday-schools. Subsequently it was included in *A Selection of Psalms and Hymns*, Eighth edition, 1819, compiled by Thomas Cotterill, and *The Christian Psalmist*, 1825, compiled by the author. These early versions were all slightly different, but the present Song Book includes verses 1-5 and 8 from the author's final version, in his *Original Hymns*, 1853.

Precious Jesus, O to love thee (520)
verses: Francis Bottome (1823-94)
chorus: Louise M. Rouse

The verses appeared with a different chorus in *Winnowed Hymns: A Collection of Sacred Songs*, 1873, edited by C. C. McCabe and D. T. Macfarlan. (There were four eight-line verses, but the present Song Book has omitted verse 2 and the second half of verse 3.) The chorus is from the song 'Precious Saviour, thou hast saved me', by Louise M. Rouse, which was also included in *Winnowed Hymns*, 1873.

Precious promise God hath given (753)
Nathaniel Niles (1835-1917)

The author apparently wrote the verses on the margin of a newspaper as he was travelling to work. The song was published in *Precious Hymns*, c1870, and in *Sunshine for Sunday Schools*, 1873, compiled by P. P. Bliss, where the words were said to be 'by N. N. in the "Episcopalian" '.

Precious Saviour, we are coming (201)
verses: Thomas McKie (1860-1937)
chorus: Anonymous

The author said that the song was written just before the Great Northern March and was printed in the song book used in that campaign. (This is probably a reference to the Northern Expedition of the 'Life Guards', August-October 1886 led by Commandant Herbert Booth, supported by Major McKie and the staff of the Men's Training Home.) However, the song appeared earlier, in a booklet, *Songs of the Nations*, prepared for the International Congress in London, 28 May-4 June 1886. The chorus was linked with the song 'Saviour, visit Thy plantation', in *The Christian Mission Hymn Book*, 1870.

Rejoice, the Lord is King (164)
Charles Wesley (1707-88)

Published in the author's *Hymns for our Lord's Resurrection*, 1746, with the title 'Rejoice evermore'. The first refrain (verses 1-5) echoes the text: 'Rejoice in the Lord alway: and again I say, Rejoice' (Philippians 4:4).

Rescue the perishing, care for the dying (691)
Fanny Crosby (1820-1915)

Written in 1869 on a theme suggested by the composer W. H. Doane. Speaking to a group of men at a mission meeting in Cincinnati, Fanny Crosby said that if there was a boy there who had wandered from his mother's teaching, she would be pleased to speak to him. After the meeting she prayed with a young man who responded and he was converted. Later that evening, before going to bed, she composed the words of the song. It was published in *Songs of Devotion*, 1870, compiled by W. H. Doane.

Return, O wanderer, return (256)
verses: William B. Collyer (1782-1854)
chorus: Anonymous

The verses, originally written in long metre, were published in *The Evangelical Magazine*, May 1806, under the heading 'Is Ephraim my dear son? &c' (Jeremiah 31:20) and then in the author's *Hymns, Partly Collected, and Partly Original*, 1812, with the title 'The Backslider'. Later, five verses, rewritten in common metre, appeared with the chorus in *The Revivalist: A Collection of Choice Revival Hymns and Tunes*, 1868, compiled by Joseph Hillman. In *Heavenly Echoes,* 1867, compiled by Horace Waters, the chorus was linked with the verses 'Am I a soldier of the cross', by Isaac Watts, and 'Am I a lover of the Lord', by Mary Ann Kidder.

Revive thy work, O Lord (626)
Albert Midlane (1825-1909)

This song, based on Habakkuk 3:2, was published in *The British Messenger,* October 1858, and subsequently in *The Evangelist's Hymn Book,* 1860, and *The Ambassadors' Hymn Book,* 1861. Originally there were six four-line verses. The second verse of the original has now been replaced by four lines which appeared as a chorus in *Sacred Songs and Solos,* 1881, compiled by Ira D. Sankey, where the words of this song were arranged by Fanny Crosby.

Ride on, ride on in majesty (150)
Henry H. Milman (1791-1868)

This was the first of two hymns for the 'Sixth Sunday in Lent' (Palm Sunday), in *Hymns Written and Adapted to the Weekly Church Service of the Year,* 1827, compiled by Reginald Heber.

Ring the bells of Heaven, there is joy today (550)
William O. Cushing (1823-1902)

The author said that, after receiving the tune 'The Little Octoroon' from the composer George F. Root, the melody ran through his mind all day. He hoped to be able to use the tune for Sunday-schools or other Christian work, and later, while he was thinking of the joy in Heaven over one sinner that repented (Luke 15:10), he wrote the words. The song, entitled 'The Prodigal Son', was included in *The Red Bird . . . the Summer Number of 'Our Song Birds', A Juvenile Musical Quarterly,* 1866, by George F. Root and B. R. Hanby.

Rise up, O youth! for mighty winds are stirring (864)
Will J. Brand (1889-1977)

Written in 1938, originally in three eight-line verses, and published in *The Musical Salvationist* supplement, August 1940, under the title: 'Battle-Song of Youth'. The author added a chorus for *The Song Book of The Salvation Army,* 1953, which omitted the second half of the second and third verses, to form four four-line verses as in the present version.

Rock of ages, cleft for me (302)
Augustus M. Toplady (1740-78)

Four lines of this hymn (the first couplet of verse 1 and the last couplet of verse 3) appeared in *The Gospel Magazine, or Treasury of Divine Knowledge,* October 1775, in an article, 'Life a Journey', signed 'Minimus', one of the author's pen-names. The complete hymn, headed 'A living and dying Prayer for the Holiest Believer in the World', was printed in *The Gospel Magazine,* March 1776, at the end of an article which drew a parallel between the National Debt and our spiritual indebtedness. This led to the conclusion expressed in the hymn: 'Thou must save, and Thou alone'. The hymn was also included in the author's *Psalms and Hymns for Public and Private Worship,* 1776, with the title: 'A Prayer, living and dying.' Local tradition maintains that the hymn was written when the author was curate of Blagdon, Somerset, 1762-64, while he was sheltering from a thunderstorm in Burrington Combe, but there is no reliable evidence to support this.

Safe in the arms of Jesus (889)
Fanny Crosby (1820-1915)

The composer, Dr W. H. Doane, is said to have gone to Fanny Crosby's home in New York, on 30 April 1868, only 40 minutes before he had to catch a train to Cincinnati. He hummed a tune to her, asking if she could write some words for it. She went into an adjoining room and within half an hour returned and dictated the verses and chorus to Dr Doane. He introduced it a few days later at a Sunday-school convention in Cincinnati. It was published in *Songs of Devotion,* 1870, compiled by W. Howard Doane, and in *Pure Gold for the Sunday School,* 1871, compiled by Robert Lowry and W. H. Doane.

Saints of God, lift up your voices (381)
Anonymous

Published in *The Revival Hymn Book, for All Churches, No. 1,* 1856, with five verses, headed 'Praise ye the Lord'. The present Song Book includes verses 1-3, altered as in *The Song Book of The Salvation Army,* 1953.

Salvation is our motto (814)
James Slack

In 1950, Commissioner J. Allister Smith said that the song was written when the author was on tour in the Cape Western Division, South Africa, while he was the guest of the Reverend

Andrew Murray, a preacher and writer on holiness. It appeared in *The Musical Salvationist*, January 1888, with the title 'Salvation is our motto', and was later altered to its present form for *Salvation Army Songs*, 1930.

Salvation! O the joyful sound (382)
verses 1 and 2: Isaac Watts (1674-1748)
verse 3: W. Walter Shirley (1725-86)
chorus: William T. Giffe (1848-1926)

Verses 1 and 2 are from a hymn entitled 'Salvation' in *Hymns and Spiritual Songs*, 1707, by Isaac Watts. (The second verse of the original has been omitted.) Verse 3 appeared in *The Collection of Hymns, Sung in the Countess of Huntingdon's Chapels*, c1773, and has been attributed to Walter Shirley, who apparently assisted with the preparation of this hymn book. The chorus was slightly altered from a song beginning 'We'll gather from the east and from the west' written by W. T. Giffe for *New Silver Song*, 1872, compiled by W. A. Ogden.

Salvation! Shout salvation (828)
Charles Coller (1863-1935)

Entitled 'Shout Salvation!', the song appeared in *The Musical Salvationist*, February 1928, and then, slightly altered, in *Salvation Army Songs*, 1930.

Saviour, again to thy dear name we raise (674)
John Ellerton (1826-93)

Written for the 1866 festival of the Malpas, Middlewich and Nantwich Choral Association, and later revised for the 1868 Appendix to *Hymns Ancient and Modern*. In the author's *Hymns Original and Translated*, 1888, there were two versions: the first, revised 1868, in four verses, and the other, described as the original form, in six verses, dated 'Nantwich Church, 1886'. [This date should presumably be 1866.] The present Song Book includes verses 1, 3, and 2 from the original, and the fourth verse from the revised version.

Saviour and Lord, we pray to Thee (692)
attributed to Thomas H. Mundell (1849-1934)

This song, beginning 'Saviour, in song we pray to Thee', appeared anonymously in the *Official Programme . . . with Selected and Original Songs* for a series of welcome meetings, 12-27 February 1892, when William Booth returned home from a tour of South Africa, Australia, New Zealand, Ceylon and

India. Later, in *Salvation Army Songs,* 1899, the first line was the same as in the present Song Book. The fourth verse of the original has now been omitted. In his series, 'The Songs of the Salvationist', Arch Wiggins said: 'It would seem that this may be another song by Private Mundell . . . the "Salvationist-solicitor",' (*The Bandsman and Songster,* 27 March 1937). The evidence for this statement is not known.

Saviour, hear me while before thy feet (303)
Herbert H. Booth (1862-1926)

Written in November 1889 for the Christmas issue of *All the World,* 1889. Herbert Booth had composed a tune about 18 months earlier, and had some ideas for the verses, but at the last moment he was having difficulty completing the chorus. Slowly he wrote three lines, but still needed words for the last four notes. Eventually, Richard Slater, who was playing the music over on the piano, suggested the final line, 'For me, for me!' Subsequently the song, entitled 'The Penitent's Plea', was included in *The Musical Salvationist,* June supplement, 1890 (reprinted from *All the World*) and in *Songs of Peace and War,* 1890. Richard Slater described the chorus as 'an epitome of theology': 'Grace—to deal with the past; Blood—to make clean the present; Power—to make the saintly life possible for the future.'

Saviour, I long to be (521)
Anonymous

This was one of three songs under the heading: 'Holiness', in *The War Cry,* 30 May 1891. It was signed: 'A.E.H., Bramley'. With minor alterations in the third verse, it was included in *Salvation Army Songs,* 1899.

Saviour, I want thy love to know (455)
Harry Anderson

Appeared in *The Musical Salvationist,* April 1887, under the title: 'Oh, live Thy life in me'. In the index to Volume 1 of *The Musical Salvationist,* the author is named as 'Auxiliary H. Anderson'.

Saviour, if my feet have faltered (522)
Albert Orsborn (1886-1967)

The author was appointed divisional commander in South London in 1922. A year later, when he heard that the division was to be subdivided, he was resentful and rebellious. Without intending to do so, he protested about the proposal and, although he continued with his work, he felt that he had lost his experience of the Holy Spirit's presence and power. One day, when he was running for a bus, he slipped and injured his knee. While recovering in the Highbury Nursing Home for Officers, he heard some officers in another room singing during their prayers:

> Nothing from His altar I would keep,
> To His Cross of suffering I would leap.
>
> (*Salvation Army Songs*, 1899, No. 372, verse 4)

He said: 'As I yielded, and quietly joined in the song, the tautness of my will relaxed, and I began to be pliant and submissive to the Holy Spirit. Quite frankly, I wept.' In these circumstances, this song was born. It was first used at officers' meetings held at West Croydon Corps, and was then published, under the title 'The Day that tries by Fire', in *The Officer*, December 1923, with the note: 'Written for the British Field Councils.'

Saviour, lead me, lest I stray (627)
Frank M. Davis (1839-96)

Written in August 1880 on a steamer in Chesapeake Bay, bound for Baltimore. It was published in *Bright Gems*, 1881, compiled by S. B. Ellenberger.

Saviour, like a shepherd lead us (845)
attributed to Dorothy Ann Thrupp (1779-1847)

Appeared anonymously in *Hymns for the Young*, 1832, with the title 'Seeking the Saviour's guidance'. It has been attributed to Dorothy Ann Thrupp, editor of *Hymns for the Young*, though in *The Children's Friend*, June 1838, edited by W. Carus Wilson, it was signed 'Lyte'.

Saviour, my all I'm bringing to thee (523)
Alice G. Edwards (1878-1958)

The author said that she had chosen her career and was making plans for the future, when God called her to consecrate her life to his service. At first she was unwilling to submit to his will, but later, after a struggle, she surrendered and felt a sense of rest, peace and assurance. Afterwards she put into verse the words which marked her dedication: 'Lord, with my all I part'. Her song was published in *The Musical Salvationist*, July 1893, with a title suggested by Richard Slater: 'The desires of a surrendered soul.'

Saviour of light, I look just now to thee (628)
                                    Robert Hoggard (1861-1935)

Written in September 1929 at the Grace Hospital, Winnipeg, when the author was Territorial Commander for Canada West. After returning from welcome meetings for General and Mrs Edward Higgins at Fort William and Port Arthur, 17-18 September 1929, he had to enter hospital for rest and treatment. He said:

> It was when meditating in the hospital that the thoughts concerning the song suggested themselves to me. For some time the words 'O Man of Galilee!' had been passing though my mind, and they eventually culminated in the song. It was on the day that my sufferings were the keenest that verse two was born. Then later, when I wanted to leave the hospital before the doctors were prepared to release me, came verse three; and, later still, I was able to complete the song.

It was sung by the Training Garrison Trio at the first Cadets' Spiritual Day of the 'Ambassadors' Session in Winnipeg, in October 1929, and afterwards appeared in *The War Cry*, Canada West, 16 November 1929.

Saviour, teach me day by day (846)
                                    Jane E. Leeson (1808-81)

Published in the author's *Hymns and Scenes of Childhood; or A Sponsor's Gift*, 1842, with the heading: 'We love Him, because He first loved us' (1 John 4:19)—'This is the love of God, that we keep His commandments' (1 John 5:3). Originally there were four eight-line verses, beginning:

>   Saviour, teach me day by day,
>   Love's sweet lesson, 'to obey;'

The verses in the present Song Book have been rearranged and altered as in *Salvation Army Songs*, 1930.

Saviour, thy dying love (524)
                                    Sylvanus D. Phelps (1816-95)

Originally written in 1862, and published in the *Watchman and Reflector*, 17 March 1864, in three verses, beginning:

>   Something, my God, for Thee,
>   Something for Thee.

Later it was apparently rewritten by the author, in four verses, at the request of Robert Lowry, for *Pure Gold for the Sunday School*, 1871, compiled by Robert Lowry and W. H. Doane.

Saviour, we know thou art (629)
Charles Wesley (1707-88)

From the author's manuscript *Hymns on the Acts of the Apostles*, based on the text 'And the Lord added to the church daily such as should be saved' (Acts 2:47). Originally there were five verses, beginning:

> The church in ancient days
> Was sinners saved from sin,
> And souls through Jesus' grace
> Were daily taken in;
> Pardon and faith together given
> Threw open wide the gates of heaven.

The complete hymn was included in *The Poetical Works of John and Charles Wesley*, Volume 12, 1871, though the three verses in the present Song Book (verses 2-4 of the original) had appeared earlier in *A Supplement to the Collection of Hymns for the Use of the People called Methodists*, 1830.

Saviour, while my heart is tender (865)
John Burton (1803-77)

Included in the author's *One Hundred Original Hymns, for the Young, and for use in Sunday Schools*, c1850, with the title: 'Youthful Consecration'. The third verse has been altered and now appears as in *Salvation Army Songs*, 1930.

Say, are you weary? Are you heavy laden (257)
Oliver M. Cooke (1873-1945)

Describing how this song came to be written, the author said that, one day, as he was closing his accounts, he found a mistake which he could not correct. To clear his thoughts, he went for a short bus ride, and had not gone far when the chorus 'I know a fount' started to form in his mind. Before his journey ended, the first two verses and the chorus were almost finished. When he arrived home, he wrote the music and two other verses, and immediately sent the song to the Music Editorial Department. It appeared shortly afterwards in *The Musical Salvationist*, April 1923, entitled 'I know a Fount'.

Say but the word, thy servant shall be healèd (456)
Albert Orsborn (1886-1967)

Written while the author was travelling by car between his home and his office at Denmark Hill (c1948-52) after he had been trying to show an unhappy, frustrated young man how Christ could help him to become a fully integrated person. The opening line echoes the words of the centurion who said to Jesus, 'But say the word, and my servant shall be healed' (Luke 7:7, Revised Version, 1881). The song was printed on a leaflet of *Songs for meetings conducted by General Albert Orsborn* (which Gordon Avery dated 'Royal Festival Hall, Thursday 21 February 1952'), and was then included in *The Song Book of The Salvation Army*, 1953.

Say, is there a name to live by
See: There's no other name but this name (71)

See amid the winter's snow (88)
                              Edward Caswall (1814-78)
Published in *Easy Hymn Tunes . . . Adapted for Catholic Schools, etc*, 1851, and later in the author's *The Masque of Mary, and other poems*, 1858, where it was headed 'Hymn for Christmas'. The present Song Book omits verses 2 and 7 of the original.

See how great a flame aspires (165)
                              Charles Wesley (1707-88)
Published in the author's *Hymns and Sacred Poems*, 1749, the last of four hymns with the title 'After Preaching to the Newcastle Colliers'. It is not known whether this refers to Newcastle-upon-Tyne, or to Newcastle-under-Lyme, Staffordshire. (Other hymns in this volume were headed 'After Preaching to the Staffordshire Colliers' and 'Before Preaching to the Colliers in Leicestershire'.) In *Representative Verse of Charles Wesley* (page 110), Frank Baker concluded that this hymn was probably written for the miners in Staffordshire in 1743 or 1744, and that it may have been suggested by the glow of the colliery fires, lighting up the night skies.

Seeds now we are sowing, and fruit they must bear (928)
                              Richard Slater (1854-1939)
Written on 12 February 1891, the song appeared in *The Musical Salvationist*, July 1891, under the title: 'Wheat or Tares?' It originally began 'Seeds we are sowing . . .', but was altered to the present version in *Salvation Army Songs*, 1930. The third verse and chorus of the original have been omitted.

Send out thy light and thy truth, Lord (457)
                              Ruth F. Tracy (1870-1960)
This song, written at the request of Commissioner James Hay,

was inspired by an address given by Commissioner Thomas B. Coombs, who subsequently used the song as a solo. It was published in *The Deliverer*, November 1905, with the title 'Bringing My All', and was then included in *The Musical Salvationist*, September 1906, where it was entitled 'Saviour, my all I am bringing'. This was also the opening line of the chorus, which was later altered for *Salvation Army Songs*, 1930, to fit the tune 'Jesus is looking for thee'. The second and fifth verses of the original have been omitted.

Servant of God, well done (890)
James Montgomery (1771-1854)

Published in the author's *Greenland, and other poems*, 1819, with the title 'The Christian Soldier', and the explanatory note, 'Occasioned by the sudden death of the Reverend Thomas Taylor; after having declared, in his last Sermon, on a preceding evening, that he hoped to die as an old soldier of Jesus Christ, with his sword in his hand.' (Thomas Taylor, a methodist minister, apparently died during the night, 14/15 October 1816.) From the original six eight-lines verses, the present Song Book includes verse 1, the second half of verse 5, and verse 6, altered slightly, as in *The Song Book of The Salvation Army*, 1953.

Set forth within the sacred word (656)
Will J. Brand (1889-1977)

Written in 1948 at the request of Commissioner William R. Dalziel, the British Commissioner, for field officers' councils on the theme of 'adorning the doctrine'. The author said that he wrote two songs in the same metre and the commissioner chose two verses from each. The song was included in *Songs and Choruses for the British Commissioner's Officers' Councils (No. 2)*, 1948, and then in *The Song Book of The Salvation Army*, 1953. It was sung during the Salvation Army centenary service of thanksgiving in Westminster Abbey on 2 July 1965. Afterwards the author said that to hear the congregation sing this song on such an occasion moved him profoundly.

Shall we gather at the river (891)
Robert Lowry (1826-99)

Written one afternoon in July 1864 when the author was pastor of Hanson Place Baptist Church, Brooklyn. He wondered why hymn-writers had said so much about 'the river of death' and so little about 'the pure water of life', described in Revelation 22:1. In one account of the circumstances, he said:

As I mused, the words began to construct themselves. They came first as a question of Christian inquiry, 'Shall we gather?' Then they broke out in a chorus, as an answer of Christian faith, 'Yes, we'll gather.' On this question and answer the hymn developed itself.

The song, entitled 'Beautiful River', appeared with five verses and the chorus in *Happy Voices*, 1865, compiled by W. W. Rand. Later, with an additional verse, it was included in *Bright Jewels for the Sunday School*, 1869, edited by Robert Lowry. The present Song Book omits the third and sixth verses of the later version.

She only touched the hem of his garment (304)
George F. Root (1820-95)

Based on Matthew 9:20-22. The song was included in *Sacred Songs and Solos, No. 2*, 1881, compiled by Ira D. Sankey.

Shout aloud salvation, and we'll have another song (815)
George Scott Railton (1849-1913)

Entitled: 'Our Grand March', the song appeared in *The War Cry*, 26 May 1881, where it began: 'Shout aloud, salvation boys, we'll have another song'. The original third and fourth verses have been omitted.

Show me thy face, one transient gleam (551)
Anonymous

Appeared anonymously in *Bright Gems*, 1881, compiled by S. B. Ellenberger, and later in *The Christian Choir*, Enlarged edition, 1896, compiled by Ira D. Sankey and James McGranahan, where it was said to be from *Stockwell Gems* (a source which has not been traced).

Silent and still I stand (131)
Albert Orsborn (1886-1967)

These verses were apparently sung during the author's tour of the Ireland Command in March 1964, when he led meetings at Ballymacarrett Mountpottinger, Belfast Citadel, and Dublin Rathmines Corps. The song, entitled 'That Weeping Tree', appeared in *The Musical Salvationist*, January 1967, with music by Howard J. Burrell, who heard the words during the General's campaign in Ireland. Subsequently the verses were included in a booklet, *Unpublished Songs of General Albert Orsborn, CBE*, issued by Boscombe Corps 'in memory of a good soldier'.

Silent night! Holy night (89)
Joseph Mohr (1792-1848)
The German carol, 'Stille nacht, heilige nacht', was set to music by Franz Gruber for a Christmas Eve service at St Nicholas Church, Oberndorf, in 1818. It was arranged for two soloists and choir, with guitar accompaniment, apparently because the organ was awaiting repair. Subsequently it became widely known through the Strasser family of Zillerthal and other folk singers. The English version in the present Song Book seems to be based on a free translation included in *Lyric Religion*, 1931, by H. Augustine Smith, the first verse of which was from an earlier version in *The Sunday School Service and Tune Book*, 1863, compiled by John C. Hollister.

Simply trusting every day (754)
Edgar Page Stites (1836-1921)
In 1876 the words were given to D. L. Moody in Chicago, on a newspaper cutting, and later that year appeared anonymously, with music by Ira D. Sankey, in *Gospel Hymns No. 2*, compiled by P. P. Bliss and Sankey.

Since the Lord redeemed us from the power of sin (755)
Albert Orsborn (1886-1967)
Appeared in *The Officer*, May 1919, with the title: 'God's promises are sure'. The author said that the chorus was based on William Booth's words to his son Bramwell: 'The promises—of God—are sure ... if you will only believe.' (*Life of William Booth*, 1920, by Harold Begbie, Volume 2, page 472).

Sing the wondrous love of Jesus (892)
Eliza E. Hewitt (1851-1920)
Published in *Pentecostal Praises*, 1898, compiled by William J. Kirkpatrick and Henry L. Gilmour, and in *Songs of Grace and Truth*, 1899, compiled by Gustav Collin.

Sing them over again to me (258)
Philip P. Bliss (1838-76)
Written at the request of the publisher, Fleming H. Revell, for the first issue of the Sunday-school magazine *Words of Life*, 1874, and later included in *Gospel Hymns No. 3*, 1878, compiled by Ira D. Sankey, James McGranahan and George C. Stebbins.

Sing to the Lord of harvest (929)
John S. B. Monsell (1811-75)
Published in the author's *Hymns of Love and Praise for the*

Church's Year, Second edition, 1866, with the heading: 'He reserveth unto us the appointed weeks of the harvest' (Jeremiah 5:24). The fourth verse of the original has been omitted.

Sing we many years of blessing (939)
Will J. Brand (1889-1977)

Written for the jubilee celebrations of the Dartford Corps in Kent, 3-23 October 1936. It originally began: 'Sing we fifty years of blessing', but was altered to the present version for *The Song Book of the Salvation Army,* 1953.

Sing we the King who is coming to reign (166)
Charles Silvester Horne (1865-1914)

Written for the tune 'The Glory Song', when the author wanted more suitable words than the original ones for the congregation at Whitefield's Tabernacle, London, where he was the minister. It was published in *The Fellowship Hymn-Book,* 1909, with the title 'The New "Glory Song" '.

Sinner, how thy heart is troubled (259)
Fanny Crosby (1820-1915)

Published in *Good News,* 1876, compiled by R. M. McIntosh.

Sinner, see yon light (260)
James C. Bateman (1854-88)

Written to the tune 'Lottie Lane', it appeared in *The Musical Salvationist,* November 1886, with the title: 'Sinner, see yon Light'. The original second verse has been omitted.

Sinner, whereso'er thou art (261)
Fanny Crosby (1820-1915)

Written 3 October 1871 and published in *Royal Diadem for the Sunday School,* 1873, compiled by Robert Lowry and W. Howard Doane. The song, beginning 'Mourner, whereso'er thou art', was headed 'And yet there is room' (Luke 14:22).

Sinners Jesus will receive (262)
verses: Erdmann Neumeister (1671-1756)
translated by Emma F. Bevan (1827-1909)
chorus: Anonymous

The German hymn 'Jesus nimmt die Sünder an!' based on

Luke 15:1-7, appeared in the author's *Evangelischer Nachklang*, 1718. The translation, entitled 'Song of Welcome', was published in *Songs of Eternal Life*, 1858, in eight six-line verses, beginning:

> Sinners Jesus will receive,—
> Say this word of grace to all,
> Who the heavenly pathway leave,
> All who linger, all who fall!—
> This can bring them back again,—
> Christ receiveth sinful men.

An adaptation of the verses, with the chorus added, appeared with music by James McGranahan in *The Gospel Male Choir, No. 2*, 1883, and *The Gospel Choir*, 1884, compiled by James McGranahan and Ira D. Sankey.

Sins of years are all numbered (893)
Lucy M. Booth-Hellberg (1868-1953)

In *The Bandsman and Songster*, 31 August 1935, Lieut-Colonel H. Vincent Rohu said that this song was written when the author was returning to London by train after visiting her mother, Catherine Booth, at Clacton-on-Sea. During the previous night, Mrs Booth, who was dying, said to her, 'I want you to love the backsliders. Tell them that when they come to where I am, with their feet in the River Jordan, when they are about to appear before the Great White Throne, nothing will avail them but the Blood of Jesus.' The song, entitled 'In the Light of the Throne', appeared in *The Musical Salvationist*, November 1890. The third verse of the original has been omitted.

So near to the Kingdom! yet what dost thou lack (263)
verses: Fanny Crosby (1820-1915)
chorus: Anonymous

The verses appeared in *Sacred Songs and Solos*, 1888, compiled by Ira D. Sankey, with the chorus:

> Pleading with thee!
> The Saviour is pleading, is pleading with thee!

An adaptation of this song was published in *The War Cry*, 2 June 1881, as an original composition 'by H.P., Cardiff', with the chorus:

> Calling for thee, sinner, calling for thee;
> Our Saviour is calling, is calling for thee.

Later, the chorus was altered to its present form in *Salvation Army Songs*, 1930.

Softly and tenderly Jesus is calling (264)
Will L. Thompson (1847-1909)

Published in *Sparkling Gems, Nos. 1 and 2 combined*, 1880, compiled by J. Calvin Bushey. The third verse of the original has now been omitted.

Softly the shadows fall o'er land and sea (675)
Ivy Mawby (1903-83)

Written by request for the tune 'Marshall' which Bandmaster George Marshall had composed earlier for other verses. The author said: 'When I played the music over I felt at once that it called for words suggesting an evening benediction'. The song, entitled 'Grant us Thy Peace', appeared in *The Musical Salvationist*, March-April 1948.

Soldier, rouse thee! War is raging (693)
attributed to George Scott Railton (1849-1913)

Appeared anonymously in *The Christian Mission Magazine*, February 1874, with the title: 'A Christian War Song'. It originally began: 'Christian, rouse thee!' Robert Sandall, in Volume 1 of *The History of The Salvation Army*, page 149, said that the song was written or adapted by Railton.

Soldiers fighting round the cross (694)
Anonymous

The earliest known version of this song appeared in the *Large Hymn Book, for the Use of the Primitive Methodists*, 1824, compiled by Hugh Bourne. It was signed 'ORIGI' (ie an original hymn 'by several hands'). There were six four-line verses, beginning:

> O ye heralds of the Lord,
> Preachers of his blessed word,
> Like a trumpet, loud and strong,
> Cry aloud and march along.

Eight couplets, with the alternate line 'Fight for your Lord' and the present chorus, were included in *The Christian Mission Hymn Book*, 1870, compiled by William Booth. The second, sixth and eighth verses of this version have been omitted.

Soldiers of Christ, arise (695)
verses: Charles Wesley (1707-88)
chorus: Anonymous

This hymn, based on Ephesians 6: 10-18, was published on

an undated broadsheet, entitled 'The Whole Armour of God', and at the end of John Wesley's pamphlet, *The Character of a Methodist*, 1742. The verses in the Song Book have been selected and rearranged from the 16 eight-line verses of the original. The chorus appeared with the tune 'Falcon Street' (originally 'Silver Street') in *A Collection of Psalm Tunes*, c1780, by Isaac Smith.

Soldiers of King Jesus (866)

Doris N. Rendell (b 1896)

Writing about this song, the author said: 'It is a call to "put on the whole armour", to carry the light of the gospel into dark places; to use the inspiration and enthusiasm and eagerness of youth in the service of the King of kings, catching too a sense of our glorious heritage, the present opportunity made possible by the faithful devotion and fearless courage of the saints of the past.' Entitled 'Soldiers of the King', the song appeared in *The War Cry*, 21 September 1935, as the first in a weekly series of songs for 'The World for God' campaign. There were six verses, beginning 'Knights in shining armour', with a four-line chorus to fit the tune 'Onward, Christian Soldiers'. A revised version of verses 1, 2 and 5 was included in *The Musical Salvationist* Supplement, February 1937, with music by Bramwell Coles, which required a different chorus. Later, the author altered the first line of the song and wrote the present chorus for *The Song Book of The Salvation Army*, 1953.

Soldiers of our God, arise (696)

Robert Johnson

Originally beginning 'Sleeping saints of God, arise', this song was published in *Salvation Songster's Songs, Part 2*, February 1884, compiled by Herbert Booth. In *The War Cry*, 8 March 1884, a report of the evening meeting led by the Salvation Songsters at Bristol Circus on 26 February 1884 said, 'Captain Johnson sang his new song—Storm the forts of darkness'. Later, it appeared with its present first line in the Scottish anniversary report, *The Fourth Year of the Advance... August 1884-5*.

Soldiers of the cross, arise (697)

William Walsham How (1823-97)

This hymn appeared in *Psalms and Hymns*, Enlarged edition, 1864, compiled by Thomas B. Morrell and W. W. How, and later in *Church Hymns*, 1871, published by SPCK, where it was headed 'Take the sword of the Spirit, which is the word of God' (Ephesians 6:17). The sixth verse of the original has now been omitted.

Son of God! Thy cross beholding (185)
Albert Orsborn (1886-1967)

Appeared in *The War Cry*, 10 July 1915, and later in *The Beauty of Jesus*, 1947, a collection of the author's songs and poems.

Songs of salvation are sounding (383)
G. Kaleb Johnson (1888-1965)

Entitled: 'Glory! Glory!', the song appeared in *The Musical Salvationist*, June 1934, with the author's melody arranged by Bandmaster Erik Leidzén.

Souls of men! why will ye scatter (265)
Frederick W. Faber (1814-63)

Published in the author's *Hymns*, 1862, with 13 verses, entitled 'Come to Jesus'. (A shorter version, with eight verses, had appeared earlier in *Oratory Hymns*, 1854.) The present Song Book includes verses 1, 2, 4, 6, 9 and 8 from the 1862 edition, but has altered the third and fourth lines of verse 9 which were originally:

> And we magnify His strictness
> With a zeal He will not own.

Sound the battle cry (698)
William F. Sherwin (1826-88)

Entitled 'Sound the Battle Cry!' in *Bright Jewels for the Sunday School*, 1869, edited by Robert Lowry, assisted by Wm. F. Sherwin and Chester G. Allen.

Sowing in the morning, sowing seeds of kindness (930)
Knowles Shaw (1834-78)

This song appeared anonymously in *The Golden Gate for the Sunday School*, 1874, compiled by Knowles Shaw, and it was later attributed to him in *The Morning Star, a New Collection of Sunday School Music*, 1877, which he also compiled.

Sowing the seed by the dawn-light fair (931)
Emily S. Oakey (1829-83)

Four verses, beginning 'They are sowing their seed in the daylight fair', appeared anonymously under the title 'The World

Harvest' in *The Family Treasury of Sabbath Reading,* February 1861, edited by Andrew Cameron. Later, an altered version, beginning 'Sowing the seed by the daylight fair', was included in *Gospel Songs,* 1874, by P. P. Bliss, and *Gospel Hymns No. 2,* 1876, compiled by P. P. Bliss and Ira D. Sankey, where it was headed 'Mrs Emily S. Oakey, 1850. Alt'. The third verse of this version has now been omitted from the Song Book.

Spirit divine, attend our prayers (217)
Andrew Reed (1787-1862)

Published under the heading 'Hymn to the Spirit' in *The Evangelical Magazine and Missionary Chronicle,* June 1829, with the note 'Sung on the late Day appointed for solemn Prayer and Humiliation in the Eastern District of the Metropolis'. (As a practical demonstration of their concern for spiritual revival, the Board of Congregational Ministers living in or near London had recommended that Good Friday, 17 April 1829, should be regarded as a special 'Day of Humiliation and Prayer'.) Later, entitled 'Prayer to the Spirit', it was included in *The Hymn Book,* 1842, compiled by Andrew Reed. The sixth and seventh verses of the original have been omitted.

Spirit divine, come as of old (218)
Brindley Boon (*b* 1913)

Written on Whit Sunday morning, 24 May 1942, when the author, serving in the Royal Air Force, was on duty in an isolated radar cabin in the New Forest. In *The Musician,* 9 June 1984, he wrote:

> I thought of my salvationist comrades gathered at Boscombe enjoying the holiness meeting, and felt a sense of loneliness as my one-man vigil continued. Words came easily to me as I imagined the congregation a few miles away. . . . A melody came with the words and the verses were merely an amplification of the refrain. The song was complete—in my mind—before one o'clock came and I went off duty.

It was published in *The Musical Salvationist,* July-August 1944, with the title: 'Spirit Divine'.

Spirit of eternal love (630)
Albert Orsborn (1886-1967)

Written for the tune 'Sweet Belle Mahone' at the request of Commissioner Thomas McKie, for a holiness meeting at Clapton in about 1917. The author said:

> The emphasis is on constancy in our spiritual life. Most of us can

believe it is possible occasionally to enjoy fellowship with the Lord, but here is a yearning prayer for that abiding sense of His Presence which is the privilege of the sanctified heart.

In *The Officer*, July 1921, the chorus was linked with verses by Captain Miriam Sheaff, South India. Later, Albert Orsborn's verses with several differences from the present version, appeared anonymously (without the chorus) in *Songs for Use during Special Campaigns in the United Kingdom*, 1923. The complete song, entitled 'Fellowship with Thee', was included in *The Musical Salvationist*, December 1923.

Spirit of faith, come down (756)
Charles Wesley (1707-88)

Published in *Hymns of Petition and Thanksgiving for the Promise of the Father*, 1746, a collection of 'Hymns for Whit Sunday'. Originally there were five eight-line verses. The present Song Book omits the third and fourth verses of the original, as well as the first half of the original second verse:

> No man can truly say
> That Jesus is the Lord,
> Unless Thou take the veil away,
> And breathe the living word.

Spirit of God, that moved of old (202)
Cecil Frances Alexander (1818-95)

Published in SPCK *Hymns for Public Worship*, 1853, with four verses, and later, in the author's *Hymns Descriptive and Devotional*, 1858, with an additional verse: 'Unseal the well within our hearts', which is not included in the Song Book.

Spirit of God, thou art the bread of Heaven (631)
Catherine Baird (1895-1984)

Written for officers' meetings conducted by Commissioner Edgar Grinsted, when he was British Commissioner. The song, entitled 'The Bread of Heaven', was published in *The Musical Salvationist*, October 1966, with music by Edgar Grinsted. The verses later appeared under the title 'Bread of Life' in the author's anthology *Reflections*, 1975.

Stand up and bless the Lord (20)
verses: James Montgomery (1771-1854)
chorus: Anonymous

The verses were printed on a leaflet of hymns headed *Sheffield Methodist Sunday-School Sermons. The Annual*

Sermons, in behalf of the three Methodist Sunday-Schools, at Red-Hill, Bridgehouses, and in the Park, will be preached on the 14th and 15th of March, 1824, etc. Originally there were seven verses, beginning:

> Stand up and bless the Lord,
> Ye children of his choice;

The author altered the second line and omitted the fourth verse when he compiled *The Christian Psalmist; or Hymns, Selected and Original*, 1825. The fifth verse of the original has now also been omitted. The chorus appeared with the tune 'Falcon Street' (originally 'Silver Street') in *A Collection of Psalm Tunes*, c1780, by Isaac Smith.

Stand up, stand up for Jesus (699)

George Duffield (1818-88)

During a period of spiritual revival in Philadelphia, Dudley A. Tyng preached to 5,000 people at a meeting in Jayne's Hall on 30 March 1858 on the text 'Go now ye that are men, and serve the Lord' (Exodus 10:11). Two weeks later, he was seriously injured in an accident at his home, and died on Monday 19 April as a result of his injuries. Shortly before he died he sent a message to those he had worked with, 'Let us all stand up for Jesus.' After the funeral, his friend George Duffield wrote this hymn and, on the following Sunday, when he preached from the text, 'Stand therefore, having your loins girt about with truth, and having on the breastplate of righteousness' (Ephesians 6:14), he recited the verses of the hymn as a closing exhortation. It was printed on a leaflet for children, and was then included in the *Church Psalmist*, 1859, and *Lyra Sacra Americana*, 1868, compiled by Charles D. Cleveland. The second and fifth verses of the original have been omitted from the Song Book.

Standing by a purpose true (847)

Philip P. Bliss (1838-76)

This song, entitled 'Daniel's Band' was published in *Sunshine for Sunday-Schools*, 1873, compiled by P. P. Bliss, with the note 'Dedicated to "Daniel's Band" of the First Congregational Church, Chicago'.

Standing on the promises of Christ my King (757)

R. Kelso Carter (1849-1926)

Published in *Songs of Perfect Love*, 1886, compiled by John R. Sweney and the author.

Still, still with thee, when purple morning breaketh (632)
Harriet Beecher Stowe (1811-96)

Written in the summer of 1853, apparently while the author was visiting a friend. It is said that she was often awake at 4.30 am to enjoy the dawn and the singing of the birds. Based on the text 'When I awake, I am still with thee' (Psalm 139:18), the verses were published in the *Plymouth Collection of Hymns and Tunes; for the Use of Christian Congregations*, 1855, compiled by Henry Ward Beecher (the author's brother). The second and third verses of the original have been omitted.

Strive, when thou art called of God (816)
Johann J. Winckler (1670-1722)
translated by Catherine Winkworth (1827-78)

The German hymn 'Ringe recht, wenn Gottes Gnade', was apparently based on three favourite Scripture passages of Ursula Zorn of Berlin (Luke 13:24; Philippians 2:12; and Genesis 19:15-22). It was published at the end of her funeral sermon, and then in *Neues Geist-reiches Gesang-Buch*, 1714, compiled by J. A. Freylinghausen. Originally there were 23 verses. The translation, with 10 verses, appeared in Catherine Winkworth's *Lyra Germanica*, 1855, under the heading 'Septuagesima Sunday'. The present Song Book includes verses 1, 2, 8 and 10.

Summer suns are glowing (40)
William Walsham How (1823-97)

Headed 'Summer', it was published in *Church Hymns*, 1871, under the text 'Truly the light is sweet, and a pleasant thing it is for the eyes to behold the sun' (Ecclesiastes 11:7).

Summoned home! the call has sounded (894)
Herbert H. Booth (1862-1926)

Herbert Booth apparently wrote this song a few weeks before his mother was promoted to Glory (4 October 1890) when he was arranging music for her funeral. It was published in *Songs of Peace and War*, 1890, with the title 'A Soldier's Reward—A Funeral March'.

Sun of my soul, thou Saviour dear (676)
John Keble (1792-1866)

Written on 25 November 1820. It was published in the author's *The Christian Year*, 1827, under the heading 'Evening', with the text 'Abide with us: for it is toward evening, and the day is far spent' (Luke 24:29). There were 14 verses, beginning:

> 'Tis gone, that bright and orbèd blaze,
> Fast fading from our wistful gaze;
> Yon mantling cloud has hid from sight
> The last faint pulse of quivering light.

The present Song Book includes verses 3, 7, 8, 12, 13 and 14.

Sweet hour of prayer, sweet hour of prayer (633)
W. W. Walford

Published in *The New York Observer*, 13 September 1845, with a note from the Reverend Thomas Salmon explaining that while he was living in Coleshill, Warwickshire, he met a blind preacher, W. W. Walford, who occasionally composed poetry. During one visit, Walford dictated these verses, which Thomas Salmon wrote down and later submitted for publication. Subsequently the song was included in *Bradbury's Golden Chain of Sabbath School Melodies*, 1861.

Sweet the moments, rich in blessing (634)
verses: W. Walter Shirley (1725-86)
chorus: Hugh Sladen (1878-1962)

The original, in six eight-line verses, beginning 'While my Jesus I'm possessing', appeared in *A Collection of Hymns, For the use of those that seek, and those that have Redemption in the Blood of Christ*, 1757, by James Allen, Christopher Batty and others. It was rewritten in three eight-line verses, apparently by Walter Shirley, for *The Collection of Hymns, Sung in the Countess of Huntingdon's Chapel*, 1770. From this later version, the present Song Book includes the first half of verse 1, the second half of verse 2, and the third verse (divided into two four-line verses). The chorus is from the song 'Touch me with thy healing hand, Lord' (531).

Take my life, and let it be (525)
Frances Ridley Havergal (1836-79)

Apparently written at Areley House, near Stourport, Worcestershire, in February 1874. The author said: 'I went for a little visit of five days. There were ten persons in the house, some unconverted and long prayed for, some converted, but not rejoicing Christians.' Before she left the house, her prayer: 'Lord, give me *all* in this house' was answered, and everyone had received a blessing. She wrote: 'It was nearly midnight. I was too happy to sleep, and passed most of the night in praise and renewal of my own consecration; and these little couplets formed themselves, and chimed in my heart one after another till they finished with "Ever, Only, All for Thee!" ' The hymn was published in the 1874 Appendix to *Songs of Grace and Glory*, compiled by Charles B. Snepp, and was later included in the author's *Loyal Responses; or Daily Melodies for the King's Minstrels*, 1878, under the title: 'Consecration Hymn'.

Take the name of Jesus with you (66)
Lydia Baxter (1809-74)

Written in about 1870 and published in *Pure Gold for the Sunday School*, 1871, compiled by Robert Lowry and W. Howard Doane.

Take thou my hand and guide me (635)
Julie K. von Hausmann (c1825-1901)
translated by F. S. Cooper

The German hymn 'So nimm denn meine Hände' appeared in *Maiblumen*, Vol 1, 1862. The translation was published in *Consecrated Melodies. Being Favourite Secular Tunes with Sacred Words*, 1897, compiled by J. Wakefield MacGill, Caroline Wichern and Ella MacGill.

Take time to be holy, speak oft with thy Lord (458)
William D. Longstaff (1822-94)

The words were apparently written in about 1882 after the author heard a sermon on the text 'Be ye holy; for I am holy' (1 Peter 1:16). Later, with music by George C. Stebbins, the song was included in *New Hymns and Solos*, 1888, compiled by Ira D. Sankey.

Talk with me, Lord, thyself reveal (636)
Charles Wesley (1707-88)

Published in *Hymns and Sacred Poems*, 1740, by John and Charles Wesley, with the title 'On a Journey'. The first verse of the original has been omitted:

> Saviour, who ready art to hear,
> (Readier than I to pray,)
> Answer my scarcely utter'd prayer,
> And meet me on the way.

Tell me the old, old story (98)
Arabella Catherine Hankey (1834-1911)

From the author's poem 'The Old, Old Story'. Part 1, entitled

'The Story Wanted', was written on 29 January 1866, apparently when the author was recovering from a serious illness. (The second part, 'The Story Told', was completed in November 1866.) The verses of Part 1, with the chorus added, appeared with music by W. Howard Doane, in *The Silver Spray*, 1868, compiled by the composer.

Tell me the stories of Jesus (848)
William H. Parker (1845-1929)

The author apparently said that he wrote the first draft of the hymn at home one afternoon, after Sunday-school, when he remembered how the children often said, 'Teacher, tell us another story'. The hymn, signed 'W. H. Parker, 1904', was published in *The Sunday School Hymnary*, 1905, edited by Carey Bonner. The fifth verse of the original has now been omitted.

Tell me the story of Jesus (99)
Fanny Crosby (1820-1915)

Published in *The Quiver of Sacred Song*, 1880, compiled by William J. Kirkpatrick and John R. Sweney.

Tell me what to do to be pure (459)
verses 1 and 2: George Scott Railton (1849-1913)
verse 3: Anonymous
chorus: Eden R. Latta (1839-?)

Two verses and the chorus of this song, attributed to Railton, appeared in a booklet, *Songs of the Nations*, published for the 1886 International Congress in London. Later, the song was included anonymously in *The War Cry*, 23 January 1892, with a third verse added. (In *The Bandsman and Songster*, 25 July 1936, Major Samson Hodges, of USA, said that his father, Samuel Horatio Hodges, was the author of the song, but this seems to have been a mistake, unless S. H. Hodges wrote the additional third verse.) The chorus is from a song beginning 'Blessed be the fountain of blood', which was published in *The River of Life*, 1873, compiled by H. S. Perkins and W. W. Bentley.

Tell out the wonderful story (384)
Sidney E. Cox (1887-1975)

Written in 1914 and published in *The Musical Salvationist*, June 1915, with the title 'You can tell out the story'. The author once said that the song was written on a Saturday evening before an open-air meeting, as he thought about the privilege of 'telling out the story'. Later, he said that he wrote the chorus for a Saturday night testimony meeting, when he was thinking of those Christians who hesitated to speak, or who claimed to have nothing to say. After the meeting, he went home and wrote the verses. It was his first published song.

Tell them in the east and in the west (829)
Arthur S. Arnott (1870-1941)

The music of the chorus was composed on board ship when Arthur Arnott was returning to Australia from the 1914 International Congress held in London. Later, thinking that it might be useful for a young people's demonstration at congress meetings in Australia, he added some music for the verses, and wrote the words as a missionary song. It was published in *The Musical Salvationist*, October 1920, with the title 'Christ for the Whole Wide World'. The second verse was revised for *The Song Book of The Salvation Army*, 1953.

Ten thousand thousand souls there are (266)
verses: Daniel Herbert (1751-1833)
chorus: Anonymous

The verses are from the author's *Hymns and Poems*, 1809. Originally there were 16 verses, headed 'Yet there is Room' (Luke 14:22). The present Song Book includes verses 1, 2, 9 and 16, altered as in *The Song Book of The Salvation Army*, 1953. The chorus was linked with five verses of this song in *Revival Music*, 1876, compiled by William Booth, but was later revised for *The Song Book of The Salvation Army*, 1953.

Ten thousand times ten thousand (167)
Henry Alford (1810-71)

Verses 1 and 2 (with a third verse now omitted) appeared in *Good Words: An Illustrated Monthly Magazine*, 1 March 1867, and in *The Year of Praise*, 1867, edited by Henry Alford. The concluding verse was added in *The Lord's Prayer*, 1870, a series of illustrations by F. R. Pickersgill, with poetry by Henry Alford. These verses were headed 'Song of the Angels'. The hymn was sung at the author's funeral, 17 January 1871.

Thank you, Lord, for all your goodness (552)
August L. Storm (1862-1914)
translated by Flora Larsson (*b* 1904)

The Swedish song was published in *Stridsropet*, 5 December

1891, and later in Salvation Army song books in Sweden. It is sung at anniversaries, birthdays, congresses and family gatherings in Scandinavia, and was translated by Flora Larsson for the 1986 Song Book to provide an equivalent song of thanksgiving in English. Other translations appeared in *The Deliverer*, October 1910, and *The Officer*, December 1964.

The cross that he gave may be heavy (758)
Ballington Booth (1857-1940)

Published in *The Soldier Soloist*, 1892, a collection of songs sung in meetings conducted by Commander Ballington Booth, and in *The Officer*, January 1893, where it was entitled 'The Cross is not Greater'. The fifth verse of the original has been omitted.

The day thou gavest, Lord, is ended (677)
John Ellerton (1826-93)

Written in 1870 for *A Liturgy for Missionary Meetings*, and apparently revised for *Church Hymns*, 1871. The version in the present Song Book is from the author's *Hymns Original and Translated*, 1888.

The first Nowell the angel did say (90)
Anonymous

This carol first appeared in *Some Ancient Christmas Carols*, Second edition, 1823, collected by Davies Gilbert. Later, a different version, headed 'For Christmas Day in the Morning', was included in *Christmas Carols, Ancient and Modern*, 1833, compiled by William Sandys. There were nine verses, but the fifth, seventh and ninth verses have now been omitted.

The flag is yours, the flag is mine (779)
Arch R. Wiggins (1893-1976)

Written in 1917 at the request of Commissioner A. G. Cunningham when the author was stationed at Kingswood, Bristol. The song, entitled 'Yellow Star and Red and Blue', was published in *The Musical Salvationist*, July 1922, on 'The Soloist's Page'. Later, a third verse was added at the request of Bandmaster George Marshall, but this has not been included in the Song Book.

The glorious gospel word declares (385)
Thomas Bowman Stephenson (1839-1912)

This song was 'called forth by a religious Convention at

Brighton' (Julian's *Dictionary of Hymnology*, page 1093). It was published in *Gospel Hymns and Songs*, 1875, with seven verses, beginning:

> This is the glorious Gospel word—
> Our God His heavens doth bow,
> And cry to each believing heart,
> Jesus saves thee now!

This verse was altered for *The Song Book of The Salvation Army*, 1953. Verses 3, 6 and 7 of the original have now been omitted.

The God of Abraham praise (223)
Thomas Olivers (1725-99)

Based on the 'Yigdal', a metrical version of the Jewish creed, which was paraphrased by Thomas Olivers to give the verses a Christian character. He is said to have written the hymn in 1770 in the home of John Bakewell, in Westminster, for a melody sung by Meyer Lyon (Leoni) at the synagogue in Duke's Place, Aldgate. It was published as 'A Hymn to the God of Abraham' (various editions, 1772-3), with 12 verses, divided into three parts. The present Song Book includes verses 1, 2, 11, 4 and 12.

The great physician now is near (67)
William Hunter (1811-77)

According to Julian's *Dictionary of Hymnology*, page 543, this song was from the author's *Songs of Devotion*, 1859, but it is not in the copy of *Hunter's Songs of Devotion* in the British Library. In *Hymns of our Faith*, 1964, William Reynolds said that it was included with the tune by John H. Stockton in *Joyful Songs, Nos. 1, 2 and 3 combined*, 1869. With minor alterations, the present Song Book includes verses 1-4 and the chorus from the version with seven verses in *Revival Music*, 1876, compiled by William Booth.

The head that once was crowned with thorns (168)
Thomas Kelly (1769-1855)

Published in the author's *Hymns on Various Passages of Scripture*, Fifth edition, 1820, under the heading: 'Perfect through sufferings' (Hebrews 2:10).

The heart that once has Jesus known (267)
Mildred B. Duff (1860-1932)

Published in *The War Cry*, 28 September 1889, and later

included in *The Musical Salvationist*, January 1898, in a revised version, with the title: 'Backslider, turn again'. The present version, omitting the second verse of the original, is from *Salvation Army Songs*, 1930.

The homeland! the homeland (895)
Hugh R. Haweis (1838-1901)

Entitled 'A Hymn of the Home-land', it was published in *Good Words: An Illustrated Monthly Magazine*, 1 March 1867, edited by Norman Macleod. There were six four-line verses, signed 'H. R. Haweis'. (Julian's *Dictionary of Hymnology*, page 1711, noted that in some hymn books it was attributed to William Lindsay Alexander.)

The King of love my shepherd is (53)
Henry W. Baker (1821-77)

Based on Psalm 23. This paraphrase was published in the 1868 Appendix to *Hymns Ancient and Modern*. The fifth verse of the original has now been omitted. John Ellerton said that the third verse was the last audible sentence spoken by the author before he died, 12 February 1877.

The little cares which fretted me (41)
attributed to Elizabeth Barrett Browning (1806-61)

The verses appeared anonymously in *The Officer*, September 1926, under the title 'Out in the Fields with God'. The poem has been attributed to Elizabeth Barrett Browning and to the American poet Louise Imogen Guiney (1861-1920), but it has not been found in their publications. *The Home Book of Quotations*, Tenth edition, 1967, selected and arranged by Burton Stevenson, said that the verses were published in the Boston *Sunday Globe*, 30 April 1899, credited to *St Paul's Magazine*, but its appearance in the magazine has not been traced.

The Lord bless thee, and keep thee (961)
Numbers 6:24-26

Translation from the Authorised Version, 1611.

The Lord is King! I own his power (867)
Darley Terry (1847-1933)

Published in *The Methodist School Hymnal*, 1911, and then in the author's *Poems and Hymns*, 1914, where it was entitled 'The Lord is King'.

The Lord's command to go into the world (700)
Charles Mehling (1889-1969)

Published in *The Musical Salvationist*, July-August 1946, with the title: 'On we march with the Blood and the Fire'.

The Lord's my shepherd, I'll not want (54)
Anonymous

Paraphrase of Psalm 23, from *The Psalms of David in Meeter*, 1650, prepared by a committee for the General Assembly of the Church of Scotland. Julian's *Dictionary of Hymnology*, p1154, indicates that several lines in this version are based on earlier paraphrases.

The love of Christ doth me constrain (526)
Johann J. Winckler (1670-1722)
translated by John Wesley (1703-91)

The German hymn, 'Sollt ich aus Furcht vor Menschenkindern', was in Porst's *Gesangbuch*, 1708, and Freylinghausen's *Gesangbuch*, 1714, in 17 verses. The translation appeared in *A Collection of Psalms and Hymns*, 1738, and then in *Hymns and Sacred Poems*, 1739, where it was entitled 'Boldness in the Gospel'. There were 10 verses, beginning:

> Shall I for fear of feeble man,
> Thy Spirit's course in me restrain?
> Or, undismay'd, in deed and word
> Be a true witness to my Lord.

The present Song Book includes verses 7-10, as in *Salvation Army Songs*, 1899.

The name of Jesus is so sweet (68)
W. C. Martin

Published in *Joyful Praise*, 1902, compiled by Charles H. Gabriel, and later included in *The Musical Salvationist*, November 1938, with the title 'The Name of Jesus'.

The sands of time are sinking (896)
Anne R. Cousin (1824-1906)

Written as a poem with 19 verses, incorporating phrases from the letters of the Scottish minister Samuel Rutherford (c1600-61). The poem, headed 'The Last Words of Samuel Rutherford', was published in *The Christian Treasury*, 1 December 1857, edited by Andrew Cameron. It was later included in the author's *Immanuel's Land, and Other Pieces*,

1876. The present Song Book includes verses 1, 5 and 13 of the original.

The Saviour of men came to seek and to save (527)
Albert Orsborn (1886-1967)

Commissioner James Hay asked the author to write some verses for the tune 'The old rustic bridge'. Some time later, when he became the Divisional Commander for South London in 1922, he was thinking about the number of derelict churches and the thousands of Londoners living in the area: 'Crowds of the very people for whom the Army was born.' In *The Officer*, January-February 1957, he said:

> They were an immense challenge to my spirit; what were we doing to reach and save them? Did we care enough? I thought of the One who 'wept over Jerusalem'. Thus came this song.

In comments for *The Musician*, 2 July 1938, he wrote:

> The simple chorus took a lot of time and trouble. I turned phrases again and again, trying and discarding words until, at last, I was satisfied. The song was first used at Swanwick Councils for Corps Officers.'

The verses, entitled 'Thy Spirit in Me', appeared in *The War Cry*, 9 December 1922, and the complete song, with the chorus, was included in *The Deliverer*, April 1923, under the title 'Moved with Compassion'.

The Saviour sought and found me (386)
Sidney E. Cox (1887-1975)

Apparently written in 1934, at the territorial headquarters in Atlanta, Georgia, the song was widely used during meetings led by General Evangeline Booth and was then published in *The Musical Salvationist*, December 1935, under the title: 'Oh, what a wonderful day'.

The Son of God goes forth to war (701)
verses: Reginald Heber (1783-1826)
chorus: Catherine Baird (1895-1984)

Headed 'St Stephen's Day', the verses appeared in the author's *Hymns Written and Adapted to the Weekly Church Service of the Year*, 1827. The original four-line verses have been combined to form four eight-line verses. The chorus is from the song: 'We're in God's Army' (705).

The Spirit breathes upon the word (657)
William Cowper (1731-1800)

Published in the second part of the *Olney Hymns*, 1779, with the title 'The light and glory of the word'. The third verse of the original has been omitted.

The strife is o'er, the battle done (151)
Anonymous
translated by Francis Pott (1832-1909)

The Latin hymn, 'Finita jam sunt praelia', appeared anonymously in *Symphonia Sirenum Selectarum,* 1695, published in Cologne. The translation, made in about 1859, was published in *Hymns Fitted to the Order of Common Prayer,* 1861, where it began:

> Alleluia! Alleluia! Alleluia!
> The strife is o'er, the battle done!
> The victory of life is won!
> The song of triumph has begun!
> Alleluia!

This verse has now been altered as in *Keep Singing!,* 1976.

The voice that breathed o'er Eden (949)
John Keble (1792-1866)

Written on 12 July 1857, apparently prompted by legislation that year permitting divorce. The hymn, in eight verses, was published in *The Salisbury Hymn Book,* 1857, under the heading 'Holy Matrimony', with the text 'A threefold cord is not quickly broken' (Ecclesiastes 4:12). The present Song Book includes verses 1, 5, 7 and 8, altered as in *The Song Book of The Salvation Army,* 1953.

The wise may bring their learning (849)
Anonymous

Published anonymously in *The Book of Praise for Children,* 1881, edited by George S. Barrett, for the Congregational Union of England and Wales.

The world for God! The world for God (830)
Evangeline Booth (1865-1950)

Written shortly after the author was elected General in September 1934. She said: 'I wrote it at three o'clock in the morning, bowed under the immeasurable burden of the stupendous responsibilities of the call that had come to me.' It was introduced at her farewell meetings in Chicago (25 October 1934) and New York (1 November 1934), and at her welcome meeting in the Royal Albert Hall, London (6 December 1934). Subsequently, it was printed in *The War Cry,* 15

December 1934; in *The Musical Salvationist*, January 1935; and again in *The War Cry*, 31 August 1935, as a song for 'The World for God' campaign.

There are hundreds of sparrows, thousands, millions (850)
John Gowans (b 1934)

From the musical *Take-Over Bid*, which was introduced during corps officers' annual councils at Clacton-on-Sea, on 1 October 1967, and was then presented at Reading Town Hall on 14 October 1967 and Acton Town Hall on 21 October 1967. In the musical, Ethel's three children sing this song which they had learnt at The Salvation Army.

There are wants my heart is telling (460)
Herbert H. Booth (1862-1926)

The chorus was quoted in *The War Cry*, 7 December 1889 and the first verse appeared in *All the World*, January 1890, in reports of 'Two Days with God' meetings on the theme 'Victorious Religion' conducted by William Booth in the Exeter Hall, London, 25-26 November 1889. The song was apparently printed at that time on a song sheet containing eight new songs by Herbert Booth, and was then included in *Songs of Peace and War*, 1890, a collection of songs by Herbert and Cornelie Booth.

There is a better world, they say (268)
John Lyth (1821-86)

Written on 30 April 1845 at Stroud, Gloucestershire, for the anniversary of an infant-school at Randwick. The author thought that the song first appeared in the *Home and School Hymnbook* (but this source has not been traced). The song was included in *The Methodist Revival Hymn Book No. 1*, 1858, under the title 'O! So Bright'. The fifth and sixth verses of the original have now been omitted.

There is a fountain filled with blood (132)
verses: William Cowper (1731-1800)
chorus: Anonymous

The verses, written in about 1771, were published in *A Collection of Psalms and Hymns, from Various Authors*, 1772, compiled by Richard Conyers, and later in *Olney Hymns*, 1779, with the title 'Praise for the fountain opened', and the reference, Zechariah 13:1. The last two verses of the original have now been omitted. The chorus, in its present form, appeared in *Salvation Army Songs*, 1930, though a similar chorus was linked with these verses in *The Golden Censer*, 1864, compiled by William B. Bradbury, and may have originated earlier.

There is a green hill far away (133)
Cecil Frances Alexander (1818-95)

Published in the author's *Hymns for Little Children*, 1848, with the heading: 'Suffered under Pontius Pilate, was Crucified, Dead and Buried'. One of a group of hymns (Nos. 8-20) written to explain articles of the Christian faith, it originally began:

> There is a green hill far away,
> Beside a ruined city wall,

but later editions of *Hymns for Little Children* give the present version.

There is a happy land (897)
Andrew Young (1807-89)

Written in 1838 for a tune called 'Happy Land', often described as an Indian air. The author heard the tune played on the piano, either in the home of Mrs Marshall (the mother of some of his pupils), or in the drawing room of a friend, while he was on holiday in Rothesay. The song was sung in his classes at Niddry Street School, Edinburgh, and was published in *Sacred Melodies for Children*, 1843, compiled by C. H. Bateman. Later it was included in the author's *The Scottish Highlands and other poems*, 1876.

There is a holy hill of God (461)
William D. Pennick (1884-1944)

This song, based on Psalm 24:3-4, appeared in *The War Cry*, 10 November 1928, under the title 'The Hill of the Lord'. After revision, it was included in *Salvation Army Songs*, 1930. The author said:

> The story which lies behind the writing of this song is just one of a seeking after Holiness. Strange to tell, although the song speaks so clearly of faith as the ground of reward in this seeking, the writer was still only a Seeker.

However, soon after writing the song he was reading the book *The Model Preacher* by William Meadows Taylor, and realised that he had been foolishly putting his own good resolutions in the place of faith. There, on his knees, he prayed, 'Lord, I believe', and received the blessing which he was seeking.

There is a land of pure delight (898)
Isaac Watts (1674-1748)
From the second part of the author's *Hymns and Spiritual Songs*, 1707, where it was headed: 'A prospect of Heaven makes Death easy'. Originally written in six four-line verses, it is sometimes said to have been inspired by views across Southampton Water, or the Solent, towards the Isle of Wight, but these claims cannot be substantiated.

There is a mercy seat revealed (269)
Arthur R. Gibby (c1862-1932)
Awarded first prize in a competition for 'an original Salvation Song suitable for congregational singing', and published in *The War Cry*, 23 April 1921. It was a revised version of an earlier song by the same author (written in common metre), which appeared in *The Young Soldier*, 23 August 1902, beginning:

> There is a mercy-seat revealed,
> A throne of Sovereign grace,
> Where broken hearts may all be healed,
> And feel Love's warm embrace.

The second verse of the prize-winning song was subsequently altered for *Salvation Army Songs*, 1930, and again for *The Song Book of The Salvation Army*, 1953.

There is a message, a simple message (270)
John Gowans (b 1934)
In the musical *Glory!* Captain Archibald Campbell sings this introductory song soon after his arrival in Folkestone. Extracts from the musical were presented at the Mermaid Theatre, London, on 7 July 1975, and the first complete presentation was at the Royal Festival Hall on 12 July 1976 during the British Congress.

There is a name I love to hear (69)
verses: Frederick Whitfield (1829-1904)
chorus: Anonymous
Published on a leaflet in 1855 and then in the author's *Sacred Poems and Prose*, 1859. There were nine verses, entitled 'Jesus'. The present Song Book includes verses 1, 2, 7 and 9, altered as in *Salvation Army Songs*, 1930. The chorus was added in *The Musical Salvationist*, March-April 1946, for the tune 'The Saviour's Name'.

There is beauty in the name of Jesus (70)
Will J. Brand (1889-1977)

Written at the request of Colonel Bramwell Coles who composed the tune and sent it to Will Brand in August 1944, with some words suggested for the first line of the chorus. Three days later the song was completed. It was published in *The Musical Salvationist*, January-February 1945, under the title 'Dearest Name of Names'.

There is coming on a great day of rejoicing (169)
Richard Slater (1854-1939)

Written, the author said, in July 1887 for the special song book used in connection with the Army's anniversary meetings that month at Alexandra Palace. It was included in *The Musical Salvationist*, August 1887, under the title: 'Oh, the Crowning Day is Coming!' The original third and fourth verses have been omitted.

There is life for a look at the crucified one (271)
Anna Matilda Hull (c1812-82)

Entitled 'The Life Look', in *Heart Melodies and Life Lights*, 1864, by A. M. H. (In the copy of this book in the British Library, the name 'Amelia Matilda Hull' has been written on the title page. However, subsequent research has indicated that the author's name was probably Anna, not Amelia.) From the eight verses of the original, the present Song Book includes verses 1, 2, 3 and 7.

There is never a day so dreary (186)
Anna B. Russell (1862-1954)

Published in *Hosanna in the Highest*, [1921?] compiled by Gipsy Smith and William McEwen, and in *Wonderful Jesus, and Thirty other solos*, 1924, sung by Gipsy Smith.

There is strength in knowing Jesus (759)
Ivy Mawby (1903-83)

This song, entitled 'Casting all your care on Him', based on 1 Peter 5:7, was published in *The Musical Salvationist*, January-February 1948.

There is sunshine in my soul today (387)
Eliza E. Hewitt (1851-1920)

After recovering from a serious injury, the author was able to take a short walk in Fairmount Park, Philadelphia. In gratitude for her recovery, she wrote this song when she returned home. Originally beginning 'There's sunshine', it was published in *Glad Hallelujahs*, 1887, edited by William J. Kirkpatrick and John R. Sweney.

There shall be showers of blessing (637)
Daniel W. Whittle (1840-1901)

Published in *Gospel Hymns No. 4*, 1883, compiled by Ira D. Sankey, James McGranahan and George C. Stebbins, and in *The Gospel Choir*, 1884, compiled by Ira D. Sankey and James McGranahan, with the heading 'There shall be Showers of Blessing' (Ezekiel 34:26).

There was a Saviour came seeking his sheep (388)
Edward H. Joy (1871-1949)

The author described this song as 'a pot-boiler, put together in a few lunch-time moments at Headquarters'. He introduced it in public for the first time at Folkestone, but then put it away, thinking: 'That will never go!' Later, it appeared in *The Musical Salvationist*, December 1922, under the title: 'He is Mine'.

There's a crown laid up in Glory (899)
Arthur W. Bovan (c1869-1903)

The song appeared originally in *The War Cry*, 15 April 1893, but was later linked with the tune 'Heavenly Mansions', introduced by members of the German Staff Band during the International Congress, 1914. The chorus was adapted to fit this tune in *The Musical Salvationist*, September 1914, and the third verse was revised for *The Song Book of The Salvation Army*, 1953.

There's a land that is fairer than day (900)
Sanford F. Bennett (1836-98)

One day, while the author was at work, Joseph P. Webster, a music teacher, came in looking rather despondent. When asked what was the matter, he replied, 'It will be all right by and by'. Prompted by this thought, the author quickly wrote the words of the song and handed them to Mr Webster, who immediately composed the melody. Within half-an-hour they sang the completed song with two friends who had arrived while they were working on the song. It was published in *The Signet Ring*, 1868, compiled by J. P. Webster, and later in *Winnowed Hymns*, 1873, compiled by C. C. McCabe and D. T. Macfarlan.

There's a path that's sometimes thorny (462)
Sidney E. Cox (1887-1975)

This song, entitled 'The Path of Duty' (dedicated to Commissioner T. Henry Howard), was published in *The Musical Salvationist*, August 1920, a special issue headed 'International Gleanings'—songs collected during Commissioner Howard's world tour, 1919. It was based on the commissioner's words, 'Alongside the pathway of duty there ever flows the River of God's Grace'. Later, remembering how he had heard Commissioner Howard speak at officers' councils in Canada, the author said:

> The Commissioner was speaking about duty and drew a picture of God's grace on one side, and the reality of our duty on the other. He reminded us that sometimes our duty becomes so real we are apt to forget the river of grace. . . . He was trying to tell us that there is never a duty without a corresponding grace. It is one of the things I've never forgotten.

There's a road of high adventure (868)
verses: Will J. Brand (1889-1977)
chorus: Sidney E. Cox (1887-1975)

The verses are from a song entitled 'Call to Adventure', in *The Musical Salvationist*, May 1939. The original chorus has been replaced by the chorus of the song: 'There's a path that's sometimes thorny'.

There's a song that's ringing in my heart today (389)
Sidney E. Cox (1887-1975)

Appeared in *The Musical Salvationist*, May 1917, with the title: 'The Song in my Heart'.

There's no other name but this name (71)
John Gowans (*b* 1934)

From a scene in the musical *Jesus Folk*, based on Acts 3:1-10, where Peter says to the lame man at the gate of the temple, 'I have no silver or gold, but what I have I'll give you. . . . In the name of JESUS!—get up and walk!' An abridged version of the musical was presented at the Empire Pool, Wembley, on 10 July 1972, followed by the first full-length presentation in the Fairfield Halls, Croydon, on 25 January 1973. The second and third verses of this song have been added since the vocal score of the musical was published in 1973.

There's within my heart a melody (390)
Luther B. Bridgers (1884-1948)

Published in *The Revival No 6*, 1910, compiled by Charlie D. Tillman, and later included in *The Musical Salvationist*, May 1915, one of the songs introduced by the American contingent at the International Congress, 1914.

They all were looking for a king (91)
George MacDonald (1824-1905)

Published with the title 'That Holy Thing' in *A Threefold Cord: Poems by Three Friends*, 1883, edited by George MacDonald, and then, with the third verse revised, in *The Poetical Works of George MacDonald*, 1893.

They bid me choose an easier path (780)
Frederick Booth-Tucker (1853-1929)

Appeared in *The War Cry*, 14 August 1897, when the author was Commander of The Salvation Army in the United States, following the secession of Ballington Booth. Subsequently it was included in *One Hundred Favorite Songs and Music of The Salvation Army*, New York, 1899, compiled by the author, and in *Salvation Army Songs*, 1899. The second verse was altered for *The Song Book of The Salvation Army*, 1953.

They shall come from the east (170)
John Gowans (*b* 1934)

Based on the text: 'And they shall come from the east, and from the west, and from the north, and from the south, and shall sit down in the kingdom of God' (Luke 13:29). From the musical *The Blood of the Lamb*, previewed at the Mermaid Theatre, London, in July 1977, and later presented at the Wembley Conference Centre during the International Congress, on 7 and 8 July 1978.

Thine is the glory, Risen, conquering Son (152)
Edmond L. Budry (1854-1932)
translated by Richard B. Hoyle (1875-1939)

The French hymn 'A toi la gloire' is said to have appeared in *Chants Evangéliques*, 1885, and later in the *YMCA Hymn Book*, 1904. The translation, made in 1923, was published in *Cantate Domino*, 1925, the hymn book of the World Student Christian Federation.

Thine is the Kingdom, Lord (171)
Arch R. Wiggins (1893-1976)

The author wrote a song on every phrase of the Lord's Prayer. These verses, written to the tune: 'For ever with the Lord', have not previously been published.

This is my Father's world (42)
Maltbie D. Babcock (1858-1901)

Apparently written in Lockport, New York, during the author's first pastorate. As he left home for an early morning walk, he would often say, 'I am going out to see my Father's world'. His poem based on these words was published in 16 four-line verses in *Thoughts for Everyday Living*, 1901. Later, six verses (combined to form three eight-line verses) were included in a Sunday-school song book, *Alleluia*, 1915, compiled by Franklin L. Sheppard.

This is the day of light (669)
John Ellerton (1826-93)

Written in 1867 and published in *Hymns for Special Services and Festivals*, 1867, compiled by the Dean of Chester, John S. Howson. In the author's *Hymns Original and Translated*, 1888, there is an additional fifth verse, 'This is the day of Bread'.

This is the field, the world below (932)
Joseph Hinchsliffe (1760-1807)

From a tract, *Favourite Hymns, Odes, and Anthems, as Sung at the Methodist Chapels in Sheffield, Rotherham, Doncaster and Nottingham Circuits*, Fifth edition, 1797.

This joyful Eastertide (153)
George R. Woodward (1848-1934)

Written for the Dutch carol melody 'Hoe groot de vrugten zijn' in *Carols for Easter and Ascensiontide*, 1894, compiled by G. R. Woodward.

This, our time of self-denial (922)
Will J. Brand (1889-1977)

Written for the 'Self-Denial' section of *The Song Book of The Salvation Army*, 1953, where it was published for the first time. It originally began: 'This, our week of Self-Denial'.

This stone to thee in faith we lay (945)
James Montgomery (1771-1854)

Written in 1822 for the laying of the foundation stone of Christ Church, Attercliffe, Sheffield, 30 October 1822. It was printed with an account of the ceremony in the Sheffield newspaper *The Iris*, 5 November 1822, and was then included in *The Christian Psalmist*, 1825. The first verse has been altered, as in a *A Collection of Hymns for the Use of the People called Methodists . . . With a New Supplement*, 1876, and the fourth and fifth verses of the original have been omitted.

This, this is the God we adore (962)
Joseph Hart (c1712-68)

Beginning 'This God is the God we adore', this was the last verse of a seven-verse hymn, 'No prophet, nor dreamer of dreams' (based on Deuteronomy 13:1, etc), from the author's *Hymns composed on Various Subjects*, 1759.

Those first disciples of the Lord (760)
John Hunt (1897-1982)

This song was included in *Keep Singing!*, 1976, with a chorus which has now been omitted. Earlier, the song appeared on an undated, duplicated leaflet of songs for officers' councils at Swanwick, Derbyshire, to be sung to the tune 'Maryland'. Also, three verses and the chorus were printed on a leaflet of songs for corps officers' annual councils, 11-26 October 1971, on the theme 'I believe'.

Thou art holy, Lord of Glory (528)
Brindley Boon (b 1913)

Inspired by a service of thanksgiving held in Croydon Parish Church on 29 September 1968, to commemorate the 90th anniversary of Salvation Army bands. The author, who was National Secretary for Bands and Songster Brigades in the British Territory, said:

> It was, for me, a moving moment as we approached the high altar before taking up our allotted places. In that moment, I saw again the incident of Isaiah's calling, so vividly described in the sixth chapter of his prophecy. In that 'vision' the inspiration for this song was born.

It was written shortly afterwards for corps officers' councils at Bognor Regis, Sussex, in October 1969. Later it was printed on a leaflet of songs for Christian Stewardship Renewal, 1972, at Croydon Citadel, and was included in *Keep Singing!*, 1976.

Thou art the way, none other dare I follow (529)
                              Arch R. Wiggins (1893-1976)
After Tunstall Band played the selection 'Scandinavian Songs' at a congress festival in the City Hall, Birmingham, 25 October 1937, the British Commissioner, Charles Rich, asked the author to write some words for the tune 'Finlandia'. While travelling by train from London to Leeds, he sketched out the words of the first verse, which he completed during another congress festival, in the Drill Hall, Leeds, 1 November 1937. He said, 'About this time I was worried because even some Christians were beginning to question the very existence of God, and I thought it good to make a reaffirmation of my Creed.' The first verse was printed as a chorus on a sheet of Congress Choruses (December 1937), and also appeared in *The Bandsman and Songster*, 4 December 1937. Later he added the second and third verses when he was asked to write a dedication song for cadets of the 'Peacemakers' Session in Melbourne, 1949-50. The song was published in *The Warrior*, August 1950, with the title 'Christ is the Way', and was then included in *The Song Book of The Salvation Army*, 1953.

Thou art the way: to thee alone (100)
                              George W. Doane (1799-1859)
Published under the heading 'I am the Way, and the Truth, and the Life' (John 14:6), in the author's *Songs by the Way; chiefly Devotional; with Translations and Imitations*, 1824.

Thou Christ of burning, cleansing flame (203)
                              William Booth (1829-1912)
Entitled 'The Fire', it appeared in *The War Cry*, 14 April 1894, with the note: 'Another song by the General to be sung at the Jubilee campaigns in this and other countries'. Jubilee celebrations in 1894, marking the 50th anniversary of William Booth's conversion, were combined with an international congress in London, 2-6 July 1894, celebrating the 29th anniversary of The Salvation Army.

Thou didst leave thy throne and thy kingly crown (101)
                              Emily E. S. Elliott (1836-97)
Printed privately in 1864 for the choir and the schools of St Mark's Church, Brighton, and subsequently published in *The Service of Praise*, 1870, edited by James H. Wilson; *The Church Missionary Juvenile Instructor*, December 1870; and the author's *Chimes for Daily Service: being Hymn-thoughts*

chiefly for the Sick or Sorrowing, 1881. The third verse of the original has now been omitted.

Thou hast called me from the byway (463)
Brindley Boon (*b* 1913)

Written for the tune 'South Shields' when the author was National Secretary for Bands and Songster Brigades in the British Territory. The British Commissioner, William Cooper, asked him for a song on the theme 'Our Mission—Today and Tomorrow', for corps officers' councils at Clacton-on-Sea, Essex, 30 September-3 October 1967. He wrote this song in the form of a 'mid-career challenge' as a companion to his song of dedication 'I would be thy holy temple' which was written at the beginning of his officership.

Thou Lamb of God, whose precious blood (638)
William H. Davis (1854-1918)

Appeared in *The War Cry,* 16 June 1888, and then later included in *Salvation Army Songs,* 1899, omitting the original fourth verse.

Thou Shepherd of Israel, and mine (639)
Charles Wesley (1707-88)

From the author's *Short Hymns on Select Passages of the Holy Scriptures,* 1762, based on the text 'Tell me, O thou whom my soul loveth, where thou feedest, where thou makest thy flock to rest at noon' (Song of Solomon 1:7).

Thou, whose almighty word (224)
John Marriott (1780-1825)

Written in about 1813, but apparently not published during the author's lifetime. The Reverend Thomas Mortimer, Lecturer of St Olave's, Southwark, read the hymn at the Annual Meeting of the London Missionary Society in Great Queen Street Chapel on Thursday 12 May 1825, and it was printed in *The Evangelical Magazine and Missionary Chronicle,* June 1825, in a report of the meeting. A slightly different version appeared in the magazine *The Friendly Visitor,* July 1825, headed 'Missionary Hymn'.

Though I wandered far from Jesus (391)
James C. Bateman (1854-88)

Apparently the author's last completed song, it was published in *The Musical Salvationist,* April 1888, with the title: 'Joy without alloy'. Several lines were revised by Catherine Baird for *The Song Book of The Salvation Army,* 1953.

Though in declaring Christ to the sinner (530)
Arch R. Wiggins (1893-1976)

This paraphrase of 1 Corinthians 13 was written at the author's home in High Barnet for music by George Marshall. It was published in *The Musical Salvationist,* August 1930, under the title 'The Greatest of these'. (The music was originally composed for other words by Arch Wiggins, which were published with music by Arthur Bristow in *The Musical Salvationist,* May 1930, under the title 'The Wanderer's Prayer'.)

Though thunders roll and darkened be the sky (761)
John Lawley (1859-1922)

Written at Watford during the author's last illness, it was sung at his funeral service in the Congress Hall, Clapton, 14 September 1922 and was published in *The Officer,* September 1922 and *The Musical Salvationist,* April 1923, with the title: 'I'll trust in Thee'.

Though thy waves and billows are gone o'er me (762)
Albert Orsborn (1886-1967)

The author, who described this as a meditation on Psalm 42, said: 'Of course, one's own sorrows and struggles come through the years into a song of this character'. It was written while he was travelling by train to Scotland, 6 October 1951, for congress meetings in Glasgow, and was then printed on a leaflet *Songs for Meetings conducted by General Albert Orsborn,* and in *The Song Book of The Salvation Army,* 1953.

Though troubles assail (763)
John Newton (1725-1807)

Written in February 1775 for a Sunday evening service at the Great House, Olney. It was published in *The Gospel Magazine,* January 1777, under the title 'Jehovah-Jireh' (Genesis 22:14), and then appeared, slightly altered, in the *Olney Hymns,* 1779, headed 'The Lord will provide'. Verses 3, 5 and 6 have been omitted.

Though your sins be as scarlet (272)
Fanny Crosby (1820-1915)

This song, based on Isaiah 1:18 and other texts, appeared in

Gospel Music, 1876, compiled by Robert Lowry and W. Howard Doane, who composed the tune. It was later rearranged for a duet and quartet in *Gospel Hymns No. 5,* 1887, compiled by Ira D. Sankey, James McGranahan and George C. Stebbins.

Through all the changing scenes of life (21)
Nahum Tate (1652-1715)
and Nicholas Brady (1659-1726)

These verses, based on Psalm 34:1-10, are from the first part of the paraphrase of this psalm which appeared in *A New Version of the Psalms of David, fitted to the Tunes used in Churches,* 1696, by N. Tate and N. Brady. A few lines were altered for *The Second Edition corrected,* 1698, and the verses in the present Song Book are from the revised version.

Through the love of God our Saviour (764)
Mary Peters (1813-56)

From the author's *Hymns Intended to help the Communion of Saints,* 1847.

Through the night of doubt and sorrow (765)
Bernhardt S. Ingemann (1789-1862)
translated by Sabine Baring-Gould (1834-1924)

The Danish hymn 'Igjennem Nat og Traengsel' is from *Nyt Tillaeg til Evangelisk-christelig Psalmebog,* 1859. The translation, in four eight-line verses, appeared in *The People's Hymnal,* 1867, and then in a revised version, in *Church Hymns,* 1871. The present Song Book includes verses 1-3 from the revised version, now divided into six four-line verses.

Thy Kingdom come, O God (172)
Lewis Hensley (1824-1905)

Written in 1867, and published in the author's *Hymns for the Minor Sundays, From Advent to Whitsuntide,* 1867, as a hymn for the fourth Sunday in Advent.

Thy presence and thy glories, Lord (946)
Samuel Medley (1738-99)

Published in the author's *Hymns,* 1800, with the heading: 'On opening a new Place of Worship'. There were nine verses, beginning:

> Great God! thy glory and thy love
> Our humble songs employ;
> Propitious from thy throne above
> Look down, and aid our joy.

The verses in the Song Book are from a different version that appears in *Psalms and Hymns ... prepared for the use of the Baptist denomination*, 1858, signed 'Samuel Medley, 1789', but the source of this version has not been traced.

Thy word is like a garden, Lord (658)
Edwin Hodder (1837-1904)

Included in a section headed 'The Word of God', in *The New Sunday School Hymn Book*, 1863, edited by Edwin Hodder.

'Tis good, Lord, to be here (154)
J. Armitage Robinson (1858-1933)

Written in Cambridge in 1888 on the Feast of the Transfiguration (6 August). It was included in *Hymns Ancient and Modern*, New edition, 1904, with the heading: 'Lord, it is good for us to be here' (Matthew 17:4).

'Tis religion that can give (464)
verses 1-3: Mary Masters (*d* 1759?)
verse 4: attributed to John Rippon (1751-1836)
chorus: Anonymous

Verses 1-3 have been derived from a short poem in *Familiar Letters and Poems on Several Occasions*, 1755, by Mary Masters:

> 'Tis Religion that can give,
> Sweetest Pleasures while we live;
> 'Tis Religion must supply,
> Solid Comforts when we die,
> After Death its Joys will be,
> Lasting as Eternity.

The lines:

> Be the living God my Friend,
> Then my bliss shall never end.

were added in *A Selection of Hymns from the Best Authors*, Tenth edition, 1800, compiled by John Rippon, where the hymn was in two four-line verses. The arrangement with the additional lines, 'In the light of God', and the chorus, appeared in the *Athanaeum Collection*, 1863, compiled by Horace Waters, and *The Revivalist*, 1868, compiled by Joseph Hillman.

'Tis the promise of God full salvation to give (392)
verse 1 and chorus: Philip P. Bliss (1838-76)
verses 2-4: Brindley Boon (*b* 1913)

The first verse and chorus are from *Gospel Songs*, 1874, compiled by Philip Bliss. The new verses 2-4 were written for the present Song Book at the request of the Song Book Council, to replace the other verses of the original song.

To God be the glory, a Saviour is mine (640)
Charles Coller (1863-1935)

Entitled 'Emancipation', the song appeared in *The Musical Salvationist*, May 1923, with four verses and a chorus. The chorus, revised as in *Salvation Army Songs*, 1930, has become the second verse.

To God be the glory, great things he hath done (22)
Fanny Crosby (1820-1915)

Published in *Brightest and Best*, 1875, compiled by Robert Lowry and W. Howard Doane.

To leave the world below (901)
verses: William J. Pearson (1832-92)
chorus: attributed to Robert Lowry (1826-99)

This song, entitled 'Marching the Army to Zion', was published in *The War Cry*, 6 March 1880. The chorus appeared earlier in *The Later Songs and Solos*, 1877, compiled by Ira D. Sankey, with the verses 'Come, ye that love the Lord' by Isaac Watts, set to music by Robert Lowry.

To save the world the Saviour came (831)
verses: Richard Slater (1854-1939)
chorus: W. H. Clark

The chorus is from a song beginning 'From mountain top and dreary vale' in *The Wells of Salvation*, 1881, compiled by John R. Sweney and William J. Kirkpatrick. New verses were written by Richard Slater at the request of Herbert Booth to provide 'something more in keeping with the Army spirit'. These verses, beginning 'To save the lost the Saviour came', appeared with the original chorus in *The Musical Salvationist*, June 1889.

To the front! the cry is ringing (702)
Herbert H. Booth (1862-1926)

This song, entitled 'Victory through the Blood', appeared in *The Musical Salvationist*, December 1887, and was then included in *The War Cry*, 4 May 1889, and the author's *Songs of Peace and War*, 1890.

To the hills I lift my eyes (766)
Ernest Rance (1896-1988)

Written at the Salvation Army Conference Centre in Alloa,

Scotland, and published in *The Musical Salvationist*, July-August 1959, with the title 'To the Hills'. The author said:

> During a short stay at Alloa, my room looked out on the Ochills, a range which caught my imagination every day. The hills presented themselves in ever-changing moods and colourings, but the contour remained something fixed and final. One morning, taking a sheet of manuscript paper, I traced the shape of the hills across the stave and then added notes in a rhythmic pattern, keeping to the rise and fall of the contour and trying to capture the genuine Scottish modal sound in the melody. Thus came the little tune to be written. My verses are inspired by the mood and message of Psalm 121.

To the war! to the war! loud and long sounds the cry (703)
Malcolm Stark

This song first appeared in *The War Cry*, 31 January 1880, with the title 'To the war! To the war!' Later, a revised version, with the present chorus, was included in *Salvation Army Songs*, 1899.

To thee, O Lord of earth and sky (933)
Thomas C. Marshall (1854-1942)

Appeared in *The War Cry*, 14 September 1889, and then in *The Musical Salvationist*, July 1891, a special issue of 'Harvest Festival Songs'.

To thee, O Lord, our hearts we raise (934)
William Chatterton Dix (1837-98)

Published in *Hymns for the Services of the Church, and for Private Devotion*, c1864, edited by Arthur H. Ward, and then in *The People's Hymnal*, 1867, compiled by Richard F. Littledale, with a different version of the third verse. (Subsequently the 1868 edition of *The People's Hymnal*, and other hymn books, adopted the version from *Hymns for the Services of the Church*.) The present Song Book incorporates later alterations from *Hymns Ancient and Modern*, 1875, and *The Song Book of The Salvation Army*, 1953.

Touch me with thy healing hand, Lord (531)
Hugh Sladen (1878-1962)

Written in 1919 when the author was the divisional commander for the Newport Division, South Wales. During a period of spiritual revival in the mining communities, he and his wife were receiving rich spiritual blessings every day. One Sunday morning, while thinking of the officers of the division, he wrote this song at his home in Newport, and read it to the officers on the following day at their councils. It was published under the title 'Thy will fulfil in me, Lord', in *The Musical Salvationist*, April 1920, a special issue headed 'Songs from Wales'.

Unfurl the Army banner (781)
William D. Pennick (1884-1944)

Written in Ceylon (now Sri Lanka) during the First World War, for the tune: 'The Farmer's Boy'. The author said that, although the war was dividing nations, the Spirit of Christ bound people of all countries together under the Army flag. Echoing a phrase from Song of Songs 2:4, he wrote: 'Truly, His Banner over us as a people was Love!'. The song was included in *Salvation Army Songs*, 1930.

Unto the hills around do I lift up (767)
John Douglas Sutherland Campbell (1845-1914)

This is the second version of Psalm 121 from the author's *The Book of Psalms: Literally rendered in verse*, 1877.

Unto thee, O Saviour-King (532)
Charles Coller (1863-1935)

Appeared first in *Salvation Army Songs*, 1930, and later included in *The Musical Salvationist*, September-October 1946, in an arrangement for male voices, entitled 'Our Allegiance we bring'.

Unto thee will I cry (641)
Albert Orsborn (1886-1967)

The author described this as a personal song, written in New Zealand when he was chief secretary, at a time of great stress and anxiety. It was written originally to the melody of a Maori slumber song, 'Hine E Hine!' for the male voice party at Auckland Congress Hall. Two verses appear on a typed copy dated 'A.O. 19.10.35' and the third verse, apparently written shortly afterwards, was added at the top of the page. The verses were later revised and were published in *The Musical Salvationist*, July-August 1946, with the tune: 'Shepherd, hear my prayer!' by Ernest Rance.

Valiant soldier, marching to the fray (817)
Alfred H. Vickery (1894-1976)

The author gave two accounts of the circumstances which led him to write this song. In *The Musician*, 16 March 1940, he said: 'An announcement that a special campaign was to be held in the South-East London Division, arranged by our Divisional Commander, now Lieut-Commissioner Orsborn, brought to my mind the theme of "Keep in Step".' Later, in an interview in *The Musician,* 17 March 1951, he said that it was the outcome of a visit to the town of March with the Men's Social Work Headquarters Band, after completing eight open-air meetings during the Sunday morning. Entitled: 'Keep in Step', the song appeared in *The Musical Salvationist,* April 1931.

Walk in the light: so shalt thou know (465)
Bernard Barton (1784-1849)

Published in the author's *Devotional Verses; Founded on, and Illustrative of Select Texts of Scripture,* 1826, with the title 'Walking in the Light'. The verses were based on the text 'But if we walk in the light, as he is in the light, we have fellowship one with another, and the blood of Jesus Christ his Son cleanseth us from all sin' (1 John 1:7). The second verse of the original has now been omitted.

Wanted, hearts baptised with fire (704)
John Lawley (1859-1922)

In her biography, *Commissioner John Lawley* (pages 143-4), Mrs Minnie Carpenter said that the author, after hearing William Booth speaking about heart religion, wrote this song at his home in Clapton, as he was meditating on the General's words: 'Oh, for hearts that burn with love to God! Oh, for hearts that ache for the sins of the people!' Other articles describing the circumstances have also stated that the song was written when Commissioner Lawley was thinking about the scarcity of kind, loving, tender, compassionate hearts. Entitled 'Wanted, Hearts', it was published in *All the World,* January 1892, and was then reprinted in *The Musical Salvationist* Supplement, June 1892. Later, the order of the verses was changed for *The Song Book of The Salvation Army,* 1953, when the third and fourth verses of the original were transposed.

Was it for me, the nails, the spear (134)
Rosina Coull (1876-1957)

Published in *The Musical Salvationist,* September 1919, under the title: 'Was it for me?' and later revised for *The Young People's Song Book of The Salvation Army,* 1963.

We are marching home to Glory (902)
verses: William J. Pearson (1832-92)
chorus: R. F. Hughes

The chorus is from a song beginning 'Onward, children, do not tarry', published in *Song Garland*, 1869, compiled by J. W. Suffern. The verses by William Pearson, with a slightly altered version of the chorus, appeared in *The War Cry*, 10 April 1880, under the title 'The Hallelujah City'.

We are marching on with shield and banner bright (818)
Fanny Crosby (1820-1915)

Written for *Fresh Laurels for the Sabbath School*, 1867, compiled by William B. Bradbury, where it was entitled 'Sunday School Volunteer Song'. There were originally three eight-line verses and the chorus. The present Song Book divides the original verse 1 into two verses, and omits the second half of verse 2 and the first half of verse 3. Several lines have been altered as in *Salvation Army Songs*, 1930.

We are marching up the hillside (903)
Arthur S. Arnott (1870-1941)

Verses 1 and 2 and the chorus appeared in *The Salvation Soloist*, Vol 2 (Australasia), 1918, and *The Officer*, February 1920. The complete song, entitled 'The Homeward Trail', was included in *The Musical Salvationist*, August 1920, a special issue headed 'International Gleanings'—songs collected during Commissioner T. Henry Howard's world tour, 1919. The author said that it was sung by young people at congress meetings in Australia.

We are sweeping through the land (819)
George Scott Railton (1849-1913)

With the title: 'Sweeping through the Land!' it was included in a small booklet, *The Hosanna Songs of The Salvation Army, When the Lord had led them to victory for 14 years and had enabled them to establish the 102nd Corps*, 6 July 1879. The fourth verse has been omitted.

We are the hands of Christ (851)
David R. Fraser (b 1939)

The author said:
> The hymn was written, I think, to fill a gap in a Sunday School Anniversary programme. At the time I was minister of Upper Studley and Southwick Baptist Churches in Trowbridge, Wiltshire.

Each year (from 1964 to 1970) I wrote the entire service for the children at the Upper Studley anniversary. Subsequently the hymn was entered for a TV hymn competition (together with a new tune, written by my brother-in-law, Tony Ware).

It was published by the National Christian Education Council in *Sing New Songs*, 1981.

We are witnesses for Jesus (832)
William D. Pennick (1884-1944)

Written in December 1916, when the author was with a party of missionary officers on furlough in the Nilgiris Hills, South India. His wife said that the song was composed for a quartet of men officers to sing in a meeting conducted by Commissioner Frederick Booth-Tucker in the Union Church, Coonoor, Nilgiris Hills. Apparently it originally commenced with the verse:

> We are witnesses for Jesus
> In the lands beyond the sea.

The chorus began:

> Preach the Word, oh, preach the Word!
> Make the Gospel story heard.

The present form of the song is from *Salvation Army Songs*, 1930, though other versions had appeared earlier in *The Musical Salvationist*, November 1918, and *The Officer*, November 1920.

We find pleasure in the Army (869)
Will J. Brand (1889-1977)

Appeared in *New Songs for Young People*, May 1947, under the title: 'In The Army', and later included in *Sing for Joy*, 1986.

We have a message, a message from Jesus (273)
Rebecca R. Couch (1853-1946)

This song, beginning 'I have a message', appeared in *The War Cry*, 22 December 1881, with the title: 'A message for you'. An altered version, beginning 'We have a message', was included in *Salvation Army Songs*, 1899, omitting the fifth verse of the original, but later the song was extensively revised by Catherine Baird for *The Song Book of The Salvation Army*, 1953.

We have caught the vision splendid (833)
Doris N. Rendell (*b* 1896)

Included in *Songs of His Love*, a collection of the author's songs and poems published privately in about 1972.

We have heard the joyful sound (393)
Priscilla J. Owens (1829-1907)
Written for a Sunday-school mission anniversary. Beginning 'We have heard a joyful sound', it was published in *Songs of Redeeming Love*, 1882, compiled by John R. Sweney, C. C. McCabe, T. C. O'Kane and W. J. Kirkpatrick. Later the first line was altered in *Gospel Hymns, No. 5*, 1887, compiled by Ira D. Sankey, James McGranahan and George C. Stebbins.

We have not known thee as we ought (466)
Thomas B. Pollock (1836-96)
These verses, beginning 'I have not known thee as I ought', appeared anonymously in *The Gospeller*, October 1875, under the title 'Lord, Help Me'. A revised version, as in the present Song Book, was included in *Hymns Ancient and Modern: Supplemental Hymns*, 1889.

We plough the fields, and scatter (935)
Matthias Claudius (1740-1815)
translated by Jane M. Campbell (1817-78)
The German verses, 'Wir pflügen und wir streuen' appeared in the author's *Asmus omnia sua secum portans*, Part 4, 1782, as part of a sketch, 'Paul Erdmann's Fest', in which neighbours came to Paul's house singing this song of thanksgiving. The translation, entitled 'Thanksgiving for the Harvest', was included in *A Garland of Songs*, 1861, edited by Charles S. Bere.

We praise thee, heavenly Father (870)
Walter H. Windybank (1872-1952)
Published for young people in the *Junior's Guide, Attendance Record and Song Book*, 1952, and then in *The Young People's Song Book of The Salvation Army*, 1963.

We praise thee, Lord, with heart and voice (936)
William J. Pearson (1832-92)
Published with other 'Harvest Songs' in *The War Cry*, 10 September 1892, and then included in *The Salvation Soldier's Song Book*, 1893, and *Salvation Army Songs*, 1899. The last line of each verse: 'Shouting the harvest home', was altered to the present version for *The Song Book of The Salvation Army*, 1953, when the original third verse was omitted.

We speak of the realms of the blest (904)
Elizabeth Mills (1805-29)

Written a few weeks before the author's death, after reading a commentary on Psalm 119:44, which said, 'We speak of heaven; but Oh to be there!' (*Exposition of Psalm 119, As Illustrative of the Character of Christian Experience*, 1827, by Charles Bridges, p110). Originally there were six verses, but many hymn books subsequently omitted one or two verses and made various alterations. The version in the present Song Book is derived from *The Christian Mission Hymn Book*, 1870, and *Salvation Army Songs*, 1899.

We thank thee, Lord, for answered prayer (642)
Leslie C. Rusher (b 1905)

Written while the author was editor-in-chief in New Zealand. He said that he felt led to write these verses after attending the final meeting of a successful evangelistic campaign at Wellington South Corps. The corps officer (Lieutenant Dean Goffin) had spoken of the difficulty of finding a suitable song for the meeting on the theme of 'Thanksgiving for answered prayer'. The song was published in *The War Cry*, New Zealand, 14 April 1956, and was later included in *The Musical Salvationist*, October 1961, under the title 'Answered Prayer'.

We the people of thy host (643)
Emma Booth-Tucker (1860-1903)

'Composed for a Council of American Officers held in New York' (*The Consul*, 1927, p 263). The song, which originally began 'We the prophets of Thy host', was published in *The Local Officer*, February 1904, under the title 'Nothing but the Fire'. Later, with the first line altered, it was included in *The Musical Salvationist*, April 1911. The present Song Book includes verses 1, 5, 4 and 6, but with a different chorus, which appeared in *Salvation Army Songs*, 1930.

We wonder why Christ came into the world
See: He came to give us life in all its fulness (274)

We worship thee, O Crucified (135)
Albert Orsborn (1886-1967)

This song is said to have been written for Good Friday meetings at the Congress Hall, Clapton, in about 1914. It was printed in a booklet of *Songs for Use during Special Campaigns in the United Kingdom*, 1923, and, after revision, it was included in *The Beauty of Jesus*, 1947, and *The Song Book of The Salvation Army*, 1953. The verses were derived partly from the author's poem 'The Cross of Christ', published in *The Field Officer*, March 1912. (Another song based on the same poem appeared on 'The Soloist's Page' of *The Musical Salvationist*, December 1913. under the title 'Safe for evermore'.)

Weary of wandering from my God (305)
Charles Wesley (1707-88)

Published in volume 1 of the author's *Hymns and Sacred Poems*, 1749, in a group of hymns headed 'After a Recovery'. (The preceding section is headed 'For One Fallen from Grace'.) The present Song Book includes verses 1-3 from the original six verses, with a few alterations as in *A Collection of Hymns for the Use of the People called Methodists*, 1780, compiled by John Wesley.

Weaver divine, thy matchless skill (644)
Brindley Boon (*b* 1913)

Written at the request of the British Commissioner, William F. Cooper, when the author was editor of *The Musician* for the second time. He was asked to write a song on the subject 'The Divine Weaver', for corps officers' councils at the Regent Hall, London, 6-7 October 1965. During the councils it was sung to the tune 'Saved by grace', but later it was published under the title 'Christ of the Loom', in *The Musical Salvationist*, October 1967, with the author's own tune. The verses were included in *Keep Singing!*, 1976.

Welcome, happy morning (155)
Venantius Fortunatus (c530-609)
translated by John Ellerton (1826-93)

The Latin verses, beginning 'Salve festa dies', are from a poem published in the author's *Opera poetica*, 1881, edited by F. Leo. It was dedicated to Bishop Felix of Nantes, who died in 582, but the earliest surviving manuscripts date from the 8th or 9th century. The translation appeared in *The Supplementary Hymn and Tune Book (With New Appendix)*, Third edition, 1869, edited by Robert Brown-Borthwick. The third and fourth verses of the translation have been omitted.

We'll shout aloud throughout the land (782)
verses: attributed to James C. Bateman (1854-88)
chorus: William T. Giffe (1848-1926)

This song appeared anonymously in *Salvation Music, Volume*

2, December 1883. In *The Musician,* 23 September 1939, Bandmaster Arthur Frost of Hull said that James Bateman wrote the song about 59 years earlier when William Booth presented a flag to the Hull Icehouse Corps. Mrs Horley, an elderly salvationist from Hull, also said that James Bateman was the author of the song, but this information has not been confirmed. The chorus was slightly altered from an earlier song, 'We'll gather from the east and from the west', written by W. T. Giffe for *New Silver Song,* 1872, compiled by W. A. Ogden.

We're a band that shall conquer the foe (820)
William Hodgson (1853-1926)

Although the author said that he wrote this song when he was stationed at Limehouse, it was probably written while he was at Whitby. In a report from Whitby in the first issue of *The War Cry,* 27 December 1879, the author said: 'We are in the "Army" and dare not leave our post. We'll fight until we conquer the foe's most mighty host'. This song, entitled 'In the King's Strength', appeared in *The War Cry,* 7 February 1880, signed 'Capt. Hodgson, The Blood-washed Collier'. Several months later, writing in *The War Cry,* 10 July 1880, immediately after arriving at Limehouse, he reported: 'There are salvation soldiers. Oh, yes! And fighting on in the strength of the King, they mean to go on to greater victories than ever'.

We're an Army fighting for a glorious King (821)
William J. Pearson (1832-92)

Beginning: 'We're an Army fighting for the King of Kings', this song appeared in a special 'Festival Song Book' for Training Home anniversary meetings, 12-13 November 1887, and later in *The Salvation Soldiers' Song Book,* Melbourne, *c*1890. The revised version, omitting the original fourth verse, is found in *Salvation Army Songs,* 1899.

We're bound for the land of the pure and the holy (905)
William Hunter (1811-77)

Apparently written in 1842 and published in the author's *Minstrel of Zion,* 1845. Eight verses and the choruses were included in *Hunter's Songs of Devotion,* 1859, and later the song was No. 1 in *The Revival Hymn Book,* 1866, compiled by William Booth. Verses 3, 4, 7 and 8 have been omitted from the present Song Book.

We're in God's Army and we fight (705)
Catherine Baird (1895-1984)

The author said: 'I wrote this in an effort to make clear that The Salvation Army is exactly the opposite of the armies of violence. To save, not to destroy is our aim. And though we go to battle, it is not with men, but to overthrow by means of God's weapons of love and grace, the evil in the world'. Entitled: 'Our Army', it was included in *New Songs for Young People,* January 1950, and then in *The Song Book of The Salvation Army,* 1953.

We're the soldiers of the Army of salvation (822)
Thomas C. Marshall (1854-1942)

The author said that the song was written at the Citadel, Northampton, while he was a member of the training home staff. Some officers from the training home, with a few local salvationists, had been conducting a meeting in a village a few miles away. As they returned, singing a song about 'sailing in the old ship of Zion', he thought that the tune would be suitable for a marching song. On the following day he wrote these words. The song appeared in a booklet *Songs and Choruses for the Whitsuntide Demonstration at the Congress Hall, Clapton,* 29-30 May 1887, and was later included in *The Musical Salvationist,* December 1887, under the title 'We're the Army that shall conquer'.

We're travelling home to Heaven above (275)
Richard Jukes (1804-67)

Beginning 'We are trav'ling home to heaven above', the song appeared anonymously in *The Primitive Methodist Magazine,* February 1839, but was later included (in a slightly different version) in the author's *Hymns for the Living and the Dying, Volume 1,* Fourth edition, 1852, where it was entitled: 'Will you go?'. The second and fourth verses of the original have been omitted.

What a fellowship, what a joy divine (768)
verses: Elisha A. Hoffman (1839-1929)
chorus: Anthony J. Showalter (1858-1924)

While he was in Hartsells, Alabama, conducting a 'singing-school', Anthony Showalter received news that the wives of two of his former pupils had died. In a letter of sympathy he quoted the verse 'Underneath are the everlasting arms' (Deuteronomy 33:27). Thinking that this was an appropriate theme for a song, he wrote the words and music of the chorus before finishing the letter. He sent the chorus to Elisha Hoffman who added the verses within a few days. The song was published in *The Glad Evangel, for Revival, Camp and Evangelistic Meetings*, 1887, compiled by L. M. Evilsizer, S. J. Perry, and A. J. Showalter.

What a friend we have in Jesus (645)
Joseph Scriven (1819-86)

The words were published in J. B. Packard's *Spirit Minstrel*, 1857, and later appeared anonymously in *Social Hymns, Original and Selected*, 1865, compiled by Horace L. Hastings, and in *Silver Wings*, 1870. Subsequently the words were attributed to Horatius Bonar in *Gospel Hymns and Sacred Songs*, 1875, compiled by P. P. Bliss and Ira D. Sankey, and later to 'Joseph Scriven, c1855' in *Songs of Pilgrimage*, 1886, edited by H. L. Hastings, where there was an additional verse not included in the present Song Book. Apparently, when asked if he was the author, Joseph Scriven said, 'The Lord and I did it between us'. Although the specific circumstances are not known, he is believed to have written the verses in about 1857 to comfort his mother at a time of sorrow.

What a wonderful change in my life has been wrought (394)
Rufus H. McDaniel (1850-1940)

Written in 1914, as an expression of the author's faith, shortly after the death of his youngest son. Having not written any songs for several years, his bereavement prompted him to start writing again. The song was introduced during Billy Sunday's campaign in Philadelphia in 1915 and was published by Homer Rodeheaver in *Songs for Service*, 1915.

What a work the Lord has done (769)
Albert Orsborn (1886-1967)

Written in 1908, when the author was a captain, stationed at Lowestoft II Corps with a lieutenant. During the winter months, when there were no visitors and the congregations were smaller, the corps officers became discouraged. One day, in their morning prayers, the lieutenant said, 'Give us, O Lord, faith for greater things.' Immediately afterwards, the captain wrote this song. Originally beginning 'What a work our God hath done', it was published in *The Field Officer*, April 1909, under the title 'Faith for greater things'. Later it was revised for *The*

Musical Salvationist, March 1924, and *Salvation Army Songs,* 1930.

What can I say to cheer a world of sorrow (706)
Miriam M. Richards (*b* 1911)

The author said that this song was written at a time when she was required to work in a very difficult situation. In 1986, describing the circumstances, she wrote:

> I was returning by train to an appointment not altogether congenial. Family and friends were left behind and adjustment had to be made to what lay before. I had spoken of my unhappiness to the friend who had seen me off at the station and some words she had said lingered in the mind. I began to rough out the lines 'Just where he needs me' and I seemed to be given the answer to my questioning, and the larger outlook of the verses followed. This song which marked the rededication of my life has been blessed around the world—more than any other I have written.

Entitled 'Just where I am', it was published in *The Musical Salvationist,* November 1938, on 'The Soloist's Page'.

What can wash away my sin (306)
Robert Lowry (1826-99)

Published in *Gospel Music,* 1876, compiled by Robert Lowry and W. H. Doane, and then in *Welcome Tidings,* 1877, compiled by Robert Lowry, W. H. Doane and Ira D. Sankey, where the song, beginning 'What can wash away my stain?' was headed 'Without shedding of blood is no remission' (Hebrews 9:22). The fifth and sixth verses of the original have now been omitted.

What is the love of Jesus to thee (276)
Richard Slater (1854-1939)

Written 24 March 1898 and published in *The Musical Salvationist,* January 1900, under the title: 'Oh, remember!'

What shall I do my God to love (55)
Charles Wesley (1707-88)

Published in volume 1 of the author's *Hymns and Sacred Poems,* 1749, in a group of hymns headed 'After a Recovery'. (The preceding section was headed 'For One Fallen from Grace'.) There were originally 18 verses, beginning:

> O what an evil Heart have I,
>   So cold, and hard, and blind,
> With Sin so ready to comply,
>   And cast my God behind.

The present Song Book includes verses 11-13, 15 and 17.

What shall I render to my God (23)
Charles Wesley (1707-88)

From a version of Psalm 116, published in *The Poetical Works of John and Charles Wesley*, Volume 8, 1870. There were 11 eight-line verses, beginning:

> The Lord who saved me by His grace,
>   Who ransom'd the oppress'd,
> My great redeeming Lord I praise,
>   And in His love I rest.

Seven four-line verses, selected from verses 7-11 of the original, were included in *A Collection of Hymns for the Use of the People called Methodists, With a New Supplement*, 1876, and the present Song Book includes verses 1-3 and 5-6 from the 1876 version.

What shall we offer to our Lord (533)
August G. Spangenberg (1704-92)
translated by John Wesley (1703-91)

The German hymn 'Der König ruht, und schauet doch' appeared in the 1737 Appendix to the Herrnhut *Gesangbuch*. The translation, entitled 'God's Husbandry', was published by John and Charles Wesley in *Hymns and Sacred Poems*, 1742, with 13 eight-line verses, beginning:

> High on His everlasting throne,
>   The King of saints His works surveys,
> Marks the dear souls He calls His own,
>   And smiles on the peculiar race.

Later, verses 11-13 of the translation, beginning 'What shall we offer our good Lord', were included in *A Collection of Hymns for the Use of the People called Methodists*, 1780, compiled by John Wesley, divided into six four-line verses.

What various hindrances we meet (646)
verses 1-3: William Cowper (1731-1800)
verse 4: Anonymous

Verses 1-3 are from a hymn with six verses, entitled 'Exhortation to prayer', in the second part of the *Olney Hymns*, 1779. The final verse was added by the compilers of the 1868 Appendix to *Hymns Ancient and Modern*.

What wondrous gifts are in my care (871)
Catherine Baird (1895-1984)

Written in 1961, by request, for *The Young People's Song Book of The Salvation Army*, 1963. The author said that she wrote the verses for young people at school, having in mind particularly the schoolboys in the band at Balham:

> The band numbers 13 hard-working musicians. Some of them are at grammer school and are thinking of what they will do in future days. We have potential farmers, teachers, engineers, and musicians, but best of all, a group of boys whose great desire is to possess the greatest of all gifts—knowledge of God. For these young people, and all like them, the song was penned.

When all my labours and trials are o'er (906)
Charles H. Gabriel (1856-1932)

The inspiration for this song came from Ed Card, the superintendent of the Sunshine Rescue Mission in St Louis, Missouri, who was known as 'Old Glory Face'. His prayers usually ended with the phrase, 'And that will be glory for me!' The song appeared in *Make His Praise Glorious*, 1900, compiled by Edwin O. Excell.

When Christ drew near to dwell with men (102)
Miriam M. Richards (*b* 1911)

First published in *The Musical Salvationist*, July 1967, under the title: 'The Nearness of Christ', and then included in *Keep Singing!*, 1976, where the original chorus became the fourth verse.

When from sin's dark hold thy love had won me (534)
Will J. Brand (1889-1977)

Written for 'Day of Renewal' meetings conducted by General Albert Orsborn in the Central Hall, Westminster, 19 October 1949. The song, entitled 'Renewal', with music by Colonel Bramwell Coles, was introduced during the morning meeting by cadets of the 'Standard Bearers' session. Later it was published in *The Musical Salvationist*, July-August 1951.

When he cometh, when he cometh (852)
William O. Cushing (1823-1902)

This song, entitled 'Jewels', was published in *The Red Bird . . . the Summer Number of 'Our Song Birds', A Juvenile Musical Quarterly*, 1866, by George F. Root and B. R. Hanby, and in *Fresh Laurels for the Sabbath School*, 1867, compiled by William B. Bradbury. It was headed 'And they shall be mine, saith the Lord of hosts, in that day when I make up my jewels' (Malachi 3:17).

When, his salvation bringing (853)
John King (1789-1858)

Headed 'The Hosannas of Children', with the reference Matthew 21:15, in *The Psalmist, A Selection of Psalms and Hymns, for Divine Worship*, 1830, compiled by Henry and John Gwyther. Each verse had a short refrain:
verse 1—'Hosanna to Jesus' their theme.
verse 2—'Hosanna to Jesus' we'll sing.
verse 3—'Hosanna to Jesus our King.'
In the index the author of this hymn was named as 'I. King', but after further research he was identified in Julian's *Dictionary of Hymnology*, p1595, as John King.

When I ponder o'er the story (770)
Cornelie Booth (1864-1920)

Published at the time of the author's marriage to Herbert Booth, in their collection *Songs of Peace and War*, 1890, where it was entitled: 'A Perfect Trust'.

When I survey the wondrous cross (136)
Isaac Watts (1674-1748)

From the third part of the author's *Hymns and Spiritual Songs*, 1707, where it was headed: 'Crucifixion to the World by the Cross of Christ; Gal 6:14'. The first verse began:
> When I survey the wondrous Cross
> Where the young Prince of Glory dy'd,

but the author changed the second line to its present form in the second edition (1709) of his *Hymns and Spiritual Songs*. The original fourth verse has been omitted.

When Jesus from Calvary called me (553)
Will J. Brand (1889-1977)

Written, by request, to the tune 'Crugybar', for *The Song Book of The Salvation Army*, 1953, when another song was needed for the 'Holiness Enjoyed' section. The author said that he found the rhythm very difficult to set.

When Jesus looked o'er Galilee (103)
Catherine Baird (1895-1984)

First appeared anonymously in *The Young Soldier*, 20 April 1935, with the title: 'When Jesus Walked by Galilee'. Later, a revised version (with the same title) was published in *The Musical Salvationist*, Young People's Supplement, September 1938. Subsequently, it was included in the author's *The Sword of God, and other poems*, 1950, entitled 'Easter Hymn', and then in *The Song Book of The Salvation Army*, 1953. The author said: 'It belongs to those moments of reverie when one tries to see into the mind of our Lord'.

When Jesus was born in the manger (137)
Anonymous

This song, beginning 'When Jesus was born in a manger', appeared anonymously in *The Officer*, May 1893, with the following note: ' "To save a poor sinner", our "Song of the Month" was composed in America by a soldier, and first sung by the late Mrs Major Dale. It was introduced in England by Major Aspinall, and taken up by Colonel Lawley, who has moved thousands in the General's recent meetings while singing it over and over again'. In this version, there were four verses and the chorus. A revised version, published in *The War Cry*, 6 May 1893, omitted the second verse of the original and added a new fourth verse. The fifth verse was added later, in *Salvation Army Songs*, 1899. Subsequently, the first line was altered in *Salvation Army Songs*, 1930, and there were other minor alterations for *The Song Book of The Salvation Army*, 1953, where the fourth and fifth verses were attributed to John Lawley. In *Commissioner John Lawley*, p 147, Mrs Carpenter said that Lawley wrote three new verses for this song when he was travelling in Queensland, Australia, with William Booth. (Apparently the General liked the first verse and chorus of the original, but not the other verses.) Unfortunately, this account cannot be reconciled with the published versions of the song, or the dates of William Booth's visits to Queensland, so it is not possible to identify which verses were written by Lawley.

When morning gilds the skies (187)
Anonymous
translated by Edward Caswall (1814-78)

The German hymn, 'Beim frühen Morgenlicht', appeared anonymously in Sebastian Pörtner's *Katholisches Gesangbuch*, 1828. The translation, entitled 'The Praises of Jesus', with 28 couplets and the refrain 'May Jesus Christ be praised', was published in *The Masque of Mary, and other poems*, 1858, by Edward Caswall. Six verses had appeared earlier in a *Collection of Catholic Hymns*, 1853, edited by H. Formby and J. Lambert, and subsequently eight verses were included in the 1868 Appendix to *Hymns Ancient and Modern*. The present Song Book includes verses 1, 2, 5, 7 and 8 from the 1868 version.

When mothers of Salem (797)
William M. Hutchings (1827-76)

Written originally in six verses for an anniversary service at St Paul's Chapel Sunday-school, in Wigan, Lancashire, and subsequently revised by the author in five verses, with a missionary emphasis, for *The Juvenile Missionary Magazine*, June 1850. Later, four verses, slightly altered, were included in *The Child's Own Hymn Book*, 1865, edited by John Curwen. For the present Song Book, the first half of verse 3 has been combined with the second half of verse 4 to form a new third verse.

When my heart was so hard (395)
verses: Herbert H. Booth (1862-1926)
chorus: Anonymous

The chorus appeared in *The War Cry*, 23 June 1883, with verses by Captain Hadden, beginning: 'Once I was bound a slave to sin'. Subsequently, it was published with the verses by Herbert Booth in the anniversary report of Salvation Army work in Scotland, August 1882-August 1883, and in *Salvation Music, Volume 2*, December 1883. The origin of the chorus is unknown, though the tune 'At the cross' was adapted from a secular song, 'Take me home to the place where I first saw the light', published in New York in 1853, with music by W. L. Bloomfield, and later re-arranged by John Hill Hewitt in an edition published in Augusta, Georgia, in 1864. (Further information about the song 'Take me home' is given in *The Hymn*, July 1980, the journal of the Hymn Society of America.)

When peace like a river attendeth my way (771)
Horatio G. Spafford (1828-88)

Although it is not known exactly when this song was written, it was apparently related to the following circumstances in the author's life. His wife and four daughters were travelling to Europe from America when their ship, the *Ville du Havre*, sank on 22 November 1873, after a collision, and his daughters were lost at sea. Mrs Spafford was rescued and made her way to Paris to await the arrival of her husband. In her book, *Our Jerusalem*, 1951, p 53, the author's daughter, Bertha Spafford Vester (born in 1878) said that when her father crossed the Atlantic immediately after the tragedy he wrote the hymn 'on the high seas, near the place where his children perished'. However, Ira D. Sankey, in *My Life and Sacred Songs*, 1906, p 127, said that in 1876 he visited Mr and Mrs Spafford in their home in Chicago and that Mr Spafford wrote the hymn during that time, to commemorate the death of his children. Four verses and the chorus appeared in *Gospel Songs No. 2*, 1876, compiled by Ira D. Sankey and P. P. Bliss. Later, a different version, with five verses and the chorus, was included in *Sacred Songs and Solos*, 1877, compiled by Ira D. Sankey. The present Song Book includes verses 1, 2, 4 and 5 from the later version.

When shall I come unto the healing waters (647)
Albert Orsborn (1886-1967)

This song was apparently written in 1934, while the author was Chief Secretary for New Zealand, awaiting the arrival of a new territorial commander. After visiting Te Aroha, an area noted for its hot springs and medicinal waters, he wrote the song in Wellington, as he thought about the hill of Calvary, and the cleansing stream flowing for the healing of the nations. It was published in *The War Cry*, 6 June 1936, with the title: 'Healing Waters'. In his autobiography, *The House of my Pilgrimage* (p 136), he wrote: '. . . I am normally a very happy man. Nevertheless, I have been permitted to endure extremely heavy and bitter sorrows'. He said that three of his songs were the outcome of such experiences: 'I know thee who thou art' (59), 'Unto thee will I cry' (641), and this song. (Later, a meditation, 'Healing Waters', by General Orsborn, based on this song, appeared in *The Officer*, July 1969, in the series 'Outlines and Expositions'.)

When shall thy love constrain (307)
Charles Wesley (1707-88)

Entitled 'The Resignation', in *Hymns and Sacred Poems*, 1740, by John and Charles Wesley. There were originally 22 verses, beginning:

> And wilt Thou yet be found?
> And may I still draw near?
> Then listen to the plaintive sound
> Of a poor sinner's prayer.

The present Song Book includes verses 9, 11, 12 and 16.

When the trumpet of the Lord shall sound (907)
James M. Black (1856-1938)

The author said that, when he was president of a young people's society, a 14-year-old girl attended the meetings for a while, but one evening, when the roll of members was called, she was absent. He spoke about the importance of being present when our names are read from the 'Lamb's book of life' (Revelation 21:27) and prayed, 'O God, when my own name is called up yonder, may I be there to respond'. He looked for a song on this theme, but could find nothing suitable, so he wrote this song after the meeting, when he arrived home. It was published in *Songs of the Soul,* 1894, compiled by Joseph F. Berry and J. M. Black, and in *Pentecostal Hymns,* 1894, compiled by Henry Date.

When upon life's billows you are tempest-tossed (396)
                                   Johnson Oatman (1856-1922)
Published in *Songs for Young People,* 1897, compiled by Edwin O. Excell, who composed the tune, 'Count your blessings'.

When we cannot see our way (772)
                                   Thomas Kelly (1769-1855)
Published in *Hymns by Thomas Kelly Not Before Published,* 1815, with the heading: 'I will trust, and not be afraid' (Isaiah 12:2).

When we gather at last over Jordan (908)
                                   Francis A. Blackmer (1855-1930)
Based on the text 'Yet the number of the children of Israel shall be as the sand of the sea, which cannot be measured nor numbered' (Hosea 1:10). The song appeared originally in the author's *Gospel in Song,* 1884, beginning 'When we enter the portals of Glory', but was subsequently altered to the present version in *Gospel Hymns No. 5,* 1887, compiled by Ira D. Sankey, James McGranahan and George C. Stebbins, and in *Sacred Songs and Solos,* 1888, compiled by Ira D. Sankey.

When we walk with the Lord (397)
                                   John H. Sammis (1846-1919)
In meetings conducted by D. L. Moody in Brockton, Massachusetts, a young man said in his testimony, 'I am not quite sure—but I am going to trust and I am going to obey'. Daniel B. Towner, who was singing in the meetings, noted these words and sent them to J. H. Sammis, who wrote the chorus and then the verses of the song. It was published in *Hymns Old and New,* 1887, with music by D. B. Towner.

When wise men came seeking for Jesus from far (92)
                                   Richard Slater (1854-1939)
Written in October 1892 and published in *All the World,*

December 1892, as 'A Christmas Song for Children', entitled: 'The Birthplace of Jesus'. There were four verses and a chorus, and the song was reprinted without alteration in *The Musical Salvationist,* June Supplement, 1893. The first two verses of the original were included in *Salvation Army Songs,* 1899, but later the present version of the second verse appeared in *The Song Book of The Salvation Army,* 1953, based on lines from the original second and third verses.

When wondrous words my Lord would say (398)
Albert Orsborn (1886-1967)

Appeared in *The War Cry,* 28 March 1931, with the title: 'In Childlike Speech'. In an article, 'Love Came Down', in *The War Cry,* 24 December 1949, the author said that the chorus came to his mind many years before, when he was walking through a London park on his way to a meeting. He wrote: 'It was very near the Christmas season. Meditating on the wonder of His coming, and having in my head at the same time a little French tune, I sang aloud: "He came right down to me!" '

When you feel weakest, dangers surround (773)
Lucy M. Booth-Hellberg (1868-1953)

Published under the title 'Keep on believing' in *The Musical Salvationist,* January 1889, where the words were attributed to Staff-Captain Mildred Duff. Subsequently they were attributed to Commissioner Mrs Booth-Hellberg in *The War Cry,* 8 August 1896, but to Brigadier Duff in *The War Cry,* 20 February 1897. Mrs Booth-Hellberg, who had composed the tune when she was unwell, at the age of about 17 or 18, later explained, 'Commissioner Duff helped me with the rhyming of the words, but the thought contained in them was quite my own' (*The Bandsman and Songster,* 4 September 1937).

When you find the cross is heavy (790)
Frederick A. Trevillian (c1858-1925)

Published in *The War Cry,* 21 October 1893, under the heading 'Holiness' and then in *The Musical Salvationist,* January 1894, as a song for the 'swearing-in of recruits'. The verses (without the chorus) were included in *Salvation Army Songs,* 1899, but a new chorus (based on the second half of verse 1) was added for *Salvation Army Songs,* 1930. The verses and the later chorus were revised by Will J. Brand for *The Song Book of The Salvation Army,* 1953.

Where are now those doubts that hindered (399)
Ruth F. Tracy (1870-1960)

Written at the request of Commissioner Thomas Coombs, for the tune 'Where is now the merry party?' The author said, 'He suggested the theme and I wrote the verses. They truly expressed, and express, my own experience, too'. The first and second verses appeared anonymously in *The Young Soldier*, 30 June 1900, with a verse 'Where are now those chains that bound me' from a similar song by Lorelle Damon, which originally began 'Where are now the golden fancies'. Later the three verses by Ruth Tracy were published anonymously in *The Deliverer*, September 1905, but were signed 'R. T.' in *The Deliverer*, November 1911 and June 1913. The chorus was added to these verses in *Salvation Army Songs*, 1930.

Where lowly spirits meet (648)
Albert Orsborn (1886-1967)

Written on 27 July 1939, by request, for special prayer meetings held around the world on 10/11 August 1939, in response to General Evangeline Booth's call to prayer for God's blessing on the High Council. The song was published in *The War Cry*, 5 August 1939, under the heading: 'Prayer for The Salvation Army and the 1939 High Council'. It was later sung in the Royal Albert Hall (24 April 1946) at the London welcome to the 1946 High Council, which elected Albert Orsborn as General.

While here before thy cross I kneel (649)
William H. Hutchins (1870-1945)

The verses, without the chorus, first appeared in *The War Cry*, 2 September 1893. A few months later, the complete song was included in *The Musical Salvationist*, May 1894, under the title 'Seeking Holiness'. In a letter to Arch Wiggins (4 December 1936), about 45 years after writing the song, the author said:

> I remember quite well how one day I had experienced one of those delightful Visions of Jesus, and His sacred Cross, His great sacrifice, His compassion, and His wondrous love—extended to a lost and ruined World; my soul was stirred. I had caught something of His Spirit. I wanted to be filled with His Spirit. I wanted to be more like Jesus. I felt an intense longing and passion for souls. It was while under the influence of the Holy Spirit, that the words of the song, 'Lord, fill my craving heart', came to me—by divine inspiration.

While shepherds watched their flocks by night (93)
Nahum Tate (1652-1715)
This hymn, based on Luke 2:8-15, was published in *A Supplement to the New Version of Psalms by N. Tate and N. Brady*, 1700, under the heading 'Song of the Angels at the Nativity of our Blessed Saviour'.

Who are these arrayed in white (909)
Charles Wesley (1707-88)
Based on Revelation 7:13-17. Originally beginning 'What are these array'd in white', it was published by John and Charles Wesley in *Hymns on the Lord's Supper*, 1745. The third verse of the original has been omitted.

Who comes to me, the Saviour said (277)
William Kitching (1837-1906)
Apparently written during the author's later years, based on four texts from John's gospel: verse 1—John 11:25; verse 2—John 6:35; verse 3—John 4:14; and verse 4—John 8:12. Entitled 'Life in Jesus', it was published in *The Musical Salvationist*, January 1913, with music by the author's grandson, Deputy Bandmaster (later General) Wilfred Kitching (New Barnet). The verses and chorus were altered slightly for *Salvation Army Songs*, 1930, and the chorus was revised again for *The Song Book of The Salvation Army*, 1953.

Who is he in yonder stall (104)
Benjamin R. Hanby (1833-67)
This song, with eight verses and the chorus, was published in *The Dove . . . the Fall Number of 'Our Song Birds', A Juvenile Musical Quarterly*, 1866, compiled by George F. Root and B. R. Hanby. Later, an altered version of the song, with 10 verses and the chorus, appeared in *Sacred Songs and Solos, No. 2*, 1881, compiled by Ira D. Sankey. The present Song Book includes verses 1, 2, 4, 8-10 from the later version.

Who is it tells me what to do (204)
John Gowans (b 1934)
This song, from the final section of the musical *Spirit!*, is sung during a scene based on Acts 9:10-19, where Ananias is told to go to the house of Judas, to see Saul of Tarsus. After a pilot production at the Regent Hall, London, on 23 July 1973, the full-length version of the musical was presented at the Kelvin Hall, Glasgow, on 2 September 1974.

Who is on the Lord's side (707)
Frances Ridley Havergal (1836-79)

Written on 13 October 1877 and published under the title 'On the Lord's Side', in the author's *Loyal Responses; or Daily Melodies for the King's Minstrels,* 1878, where it was headed: 'Thine are we, David, and on thy side, thou son of Jesse' (1 Chronicles 12:18). Originally there were five eight-line verses, each with a four-line 'response'. The choruses in the present version were originally the responses to verses 3 and 5.

Who shall dare to separate us (554)
Arch R. Wiggins (1893-1976)

This paraphrase of Romans 8:35-39 was written for the tune 'St Oswald' after hearing Dr Howard Williams (minister of Bloomsbury Central Baptist Church) read from this chapter during a television epilogue on 21 October 1966, following the disaster at the Welsh mining village of Aberfan, Glamorgan. It was published in *Keep Singing!,* 1976.

Who the child of God shall sever (555)
Albert Orsborn (1886-1967)

This song, entitled 'Shines the Glory', appeared in *The Musical Salvationist,* July 1968, with the tune 'Cedar Hill' by Albert E. Dalziel. The first verse is a paraphrase of Romans 8:35. The third and fourth verses are based on the third verse and chorus of an earlier song, 'Faith is not afraid of darkness', which the author wrote for his first wife, apparently when he was divisional commander in Norfolk, 1919-22. Their son (later Commissioner Howard Orsborn) sang 'Faith is not afraid of darkness' at his mother's memorial service at the Regent Hall, London, 11 October 1942. Two verses and the chorus were then printed in *The Deliverer,* December 1942-January 1943, and the complete song was included in *The Beauty of Jesus,* 1947, beginning 'Have you read the declaration'.

Who, who are these beside the chilly wave (910)
Tullius C. O'Kane (1830-1912)

From *Precious Hymns,* c1870, published by the Bethany Sabbath School, Philadelphia.

Who'll be the next to follow Jesus (278)
Annie S. Hawks (c1835-1918)

This song, published by Bethany Sabbath School,

Philadelphia, in *Precious Hymns,* c1870, appeared later in *The Christian Mission Magazine,* August 1876.

Who'll fight for the Lord everywhere (708)
George Scott Railton (1849-1913)

Included in *The Hosanna Songs of The Salvation Army,* 6 July 1879, with the title: 'Fight Everywhere', The verses were revised for *The Song Book of The Salvation Army,* 1953.

Whosoever heareth! shout, shout the sound (279)
Philip P. Bliss (1838-76)

Written after hearing Henry Moorhouse, an English evangelist, preach seven sermons on John 3:16 in Chicago, during the winter of 1869-70. The song appeared in *The Prize,* 1870, compiled by George F. Root.

Why are you doubting and fearing (467)
Herbert H. Booth (1862-1926)

Written in June 1883, the song appeared in *Salvation Music, Volume 2,* December 1883, beginning with the verse:

> When in the tempest He'll hide us,
> When in the storm He'll be near;
> All the way 'long He will carry us on,
> Now we have nothing to fear.

The verses were in their present order in *Salvation Songster's Songs, Part 2,* 1884, but later the fourth verse was altered slightly for *The Song Book of The Salvation Army,* 1953 and the second verse was revised for the 1986 Song Book.

Why should I be a slave to sin (468)
William Baugh (1852-1942)

When the author was a captain, at the Regent Hall Corps, London, a young woman came to the penitent form, seeking full salvation. He said that she was afraid to 'get out of Romans 7 into Romans 8'. This song gave the answer to her questions. It was published in *The War Cry,* 19 October 1895, and then in *Salvation Army Songs,* 1899.

Why should life a weary journey seem (400)
Emma Johnson

Published in *The Sacred Trio,* 1892, compiled by John R. Sweney and William J. Kirkpatrick, and then included anonymously in *The Officer,* March 1895, and *The Musical Salvationist,* October 1896.

Will your anchor hold in the storms of life (280)
Priscilla J. Owens (1829-1907)

Published in *Songs of Triumph*, 1882, compiled by John S. Inskip, and in *Songs of Joy and Gladness*, 1885, compiled by W. McDonald, Joshua Gill, John R. Sweney and W. J. Kirkpatrick. Originally there were five verses and the chorus, but later the song was extensively rewritten, omitting the second verse of the original, for *New Hymns and Solos*, 1888, compiled by Ira D. Sankey.

With joy of heart I now can sing (401)
Anonymous

This song, entitled 'Jesus saves', appeared in *The Musical Salvationist*, June 1910, and was later slightly altered in *Salvation Army Songs*, 1930.

With my faint, weary soul to be made fully whole (469)
William H. Burrell (1822-1909)

This song, beginning 'With my sin-wounded soul', appeared in *Gems of Praise*, 1876, compiled by John R. Sweney. The first line was altered to the present version in *The Hallelujah Book*, 1878, compiled by William Booth.

With my heart so bright in the heavenly light (402)
Herbert H. Booth (1862-1926)

Appeared under the title: 'It doesn't matter now', in *The War Cry*, 23 December 1882, to be sung to the tune 'Far away down South'. The chorus began:
> My soul is full of joy,
> Old Satan can't destroy.

With my heart so full of sadness (470)
Herbert H. Booth (1862-1926)

Appeared anonymously in *Salvation Music, Volume 2*, December 1883, under the title: 'Oh, Saviour, I am coming', but then included with the author's initials in *Salvation Songster's Songs, Part 2*, February 1884, compiled by Herbert Booth. The fourth verse has been omitted.

With stains of sin upon me (403)
Henry Allen (1865-1943)

This is one of many songs which the author is said to have introduced with his testimony during Sunday evening meetings at New Brompton (later Gillingham) Corps in Kent. Entitled 'That means me', it was published in *The Musical Salvationist*, October 1895, beginning 'With loads of sin upon me'. The verses were extensively revised for *The Song Book of The Salvation Army*, 1953, with further alterations in the third verse for the 1986 Song Book. The second verse of the original has been omitted.

With steady pace the pilgrim moves (911)
Richard Jukes (1804-67)

Published in *The Primitive Methodist Revival Hymn Book*, 1861. The seventh verse of the original has now been omitted.

Within my heart, O Lord, fulfil (138)
Herbert H. Booth (1862-1926)

These verses, with the chorus 'It was on the Cross' (now linked with the song: 'On Calvary's brow my Saviour died'), appeared in the booklet *Songs of the Nations*, prepared for the International Congress, 1886. (A revised version of the song, with a different chorus, was included in the author's *Songs of Peace and War*, 1890, but did not come into general use.)

Wonderful story of love (139)
John M. Driver (1858-1918)

Published in *Songs of the Soul*, 1885, compiled by Bolton and Driver.

Would Jesus have the sinner die (140)
Charles Wesley (1707-88)

Published in the author's *Hymns on God's Everlasting Love*, 1741, with the title 'Jesus Christ, the Saviour of all Men'. There were originally 18 verses, beginning:

> See, sinners, in the gospel glass,
>   The Friend and Saviour of mankind!
> Not one of all the apostate race
>   But may in Him salvation find:
> His thoughts, and words, and actions prove—
> His life and death—that God is love.

Verses 12, 14, 16-18 were included as a separate hymn, beginning 'Would Jesus have the sinner die', in *A Collection of Hymns for the Use of the People called Methodists*, 1780, compiled by John Wesley.

Would you be free from your burden of sin (281)
Lewis E. Jones (1865-1936)

Written during a camp meeting at Mountain Lake Park, Maryland. The song was published in *Songs of Praise and Victory,* 1899, compiled by William J. Kirkpatrick and H. L. Gilmour, and in *Gospel Praises,* 1899, compiled by W. J. Kirkpatrick, H. L. Gilmour and J. L. Hall.

Would you know why I love Jesus (404)
Anonymous

The words were attributed to George A. Robertson in *Songs of Gratitude,* 1877, compiled by James H. Fillmore, but then appeared anonymously (set to music by Elisha Hoffman) in *Spiritual Songs for Gospel Meetings and the Sunday School,* 1878, compiled by Elisha A. Hoffman and J. H. Tenney. Subsequently the words were sometimes attributed to Elisha Hoffman, and occasionally to George Robertson, about whom nothing is known.

Would you of our banner know the meaning (783)
William D. Pennick (1884-1944)

In *A Singing Missionary,* 1949, a service of song, Mrs Lieut-Commissioner Pennick said that her husband wrote this song in India in August 1916, on the Nilgiris Hills, when he was on furlough at Windermere, the officers' home of rest. Shortly afterwards, it was used by the children of the Salvation Army boarding schools at Trivandrum, South India, as the basis for a Salvation Army flag drill. The song, entitled 'The Message of the Flag', was published in *The Musical Salvationist,* October 1917, and was then reprinted in *The Officer,* February 1918, with details of the accompanying flag drill. The fifth verse of the original has now been omitted.

Ye servants of God, your Master proclaim (24)
Charles Wesley (1707-88)

This was the first of four 'Hymns to be sung in a Tumult', published in a pamphlet, *Hymns for Times of Trouble and Persecution,* 1744. Frank Baker said:

> The troubled months preceding and following the Jacobite Rebellion of 1745 were also months of extreme anti-Methodist persecution, when the followers of the Wesleys were slandered, plundered, and mobbed. In spite of genuine protestations of loyalty to the Crown, Methodists were often dubbed Papists and Jacobites,

just as John Wesley was reputed to be the Young Pretender in disguise. This redoubled the fury of the attacks.

(*Representative Verse of Charles Wesley*, 1962, p 50)

The second and third verses, which have now been omitted, were particularly relevant to the original circumstances:

> The Waves of the Sea Have lift up their Voice,
> Sore troubled that we In Jesus rejoice;
> The Floods they are roaring, But Jesus is here,
> While we are adoring, He always is near.
>
> Men, Devils engage, The Billows arise,
> And horribly rage, And threaten the Skies:
> Their Fury shall never Our Steadfastness shock,
> The weakest Believer Is built on a Rock.

Ye valiant soldiers of the cross (912)

Anonymous

Appeared anonymously in the *Republican Hymn Book*, 1845, compiled by Thomas Herbert, and in *The Wesleyan Sacred Harp*, 1855, compiled by W. McDonald and S. Hubbard, with a chorus beginning 'Let us never mind the scoffs or the frowns of the world'. The present chorus appeared in *Salvation Army Music*, 1880, with the verse 'There is a land of pure delight' by Isaac Watts, and was later linked with 'Ye valiant soldiers of the cross' in *Salvation Army Songs*, 1899.

Years I spent in vanity and pride (405)

William R. Newell (1868-1956)

Written at the Moody Bible Institute, Chicago, when the author was on his way to a lecture. He gave the words to Dr Daniel B. Towner, the director of music at the Institute, who composed the music. The song was published in *Famous Hymns*, 1895.

Yes, there flows a wondrous river (471)

Richard Slater (1854-1939)

Written 14 January 1893, based on Revelation 22:1. It was published in *The Salvation Soldier's Song Book*, 1893, and then in *Salvation Army Songs*, 1899. The second verse was altered slightly for *The Song Book of The Salvation Army*, 1953.

Yet once again, by God's abundant mercy (173)

Albert Orsborn (1886-1967)

The second and third verses of this song are derived from a

poem, 'From Lands Afar', which the author wrote for the International Congress Number of *All the World*, June 1914, beginning:

> When the proud empires of the world have crumbled,
>   Sharing oblivion with the lost and dead
> When the small vanities of men are humbled,
>   And over all forgetfulness has spread;
>
> We shall behold a nobler empire rising,
>   Vaster than any mortal eyes have seen;
> Throned in what state, above man's vain despising,
>   Shall we behold the lowly Nazarene!

The complete song, headed 'The British Commissioner's Song', was printed on the cover of a booklet of songs and choruses selected for the 'Light at Midnight' campaign in Britain, 1940-41.

Yield not to temptation, for yielding is sin (823)
Horatio R. Palmer (1834-1907)

The author said that he received the inspiration for the song while he was working on the dry subject of 'Theory'. Putting aside his work, he quickly wrote the words and music. Later, he made a few changes to the third verse. The song was published in *The National Sunday-School Teachers' Magazine;* in the author's *Sabbath School Songs*, 1868, and in *Notes of Joy*, 1869, compiled by Mrs J. F. Knapp, where the first verse began 'Yield not to temptation, for weakness is sin'.

You can't stop rain from falling down (854)
John Gowans (*b* 1934)

From the musical *Hosea*, which was previewed during officers' councils at Bognor Regis, Sussex, in October 1969, and was first presented in public at Lewisham Town Hall on 12 November 1969. In the musical this song is sung by Bill and Peter to underline Bill's comment: 'You'll never stop God from loving you'. The refrain of the original has now become the third verse.

You may sing of the joys over Jordan (406)
Alfred H. Saker-Lynne (1867-1948)

Appeared in *The War Cry*, 29 March 1890, when the author was bandmaster at Kennington, and later revised by Catherine Baird for *The Song Book of The Salvation Army*, 1953.

You must have your sins forgiven (913)

Fred W. Fry (1859-1939)

Written for the tune 'Ere the sun goes down', as a solo for Cadet (later Colonel) Richard Adby, from High Wycombe. He apparently brought the tune with him to the training home at Clapton and became a member of the singing brigade being formed for a new tour. The song, originally beginning 'You must get your sins forgiven', was included in *Salvation Songster's Songs, Part 2*, February 1884, compiled by Herbert Booth for the third campaign of the Salvation Singing Brigade. The first line was altered for *The Song Book of The Salvation Army*, 1953.

Your garments must be white as snow (914)

Anonymous

Appeared anonymously in *Salvation Music, Vol 2*, December 1883; in *The Salvation Songster,* 1885, and *Highway Songs for Gospel Meetings*, 1886, compiled by E. E. Nickerson.

PART TWO

Notes on authors

ACKLEY, Alfred Henry

b Spring Hill, Pennsylvania, 21 January 1887
d Whittier, California, 3 July 1960

After graduating from Westminster Theological Seminary, Maryland, he was ordained as a presbyterian minister in 1914 and subsequently served as pastor of churches in Elmhurst and Wilkes-Barre, Pennsylvania and in Escondido, California. For several years he assisted the evangelist Billy Sunday and for a time he was assistant pastor at Shadyside Presbyterian Church in Pittsburgh, Pennsylvania. Following early musical training from his father, Stanley F. Ackley, he studied under other teachers including the cellist Hans Kronold. He composed about 1,500 gospel songs, sometimes with his brother Bentley D. Ackley, and helped to compile hymnals and song books for the Rodeheaver Publishing Company.

Song: I serve a risen Saviour (334)

ADAMS, Sarah Fuller (*née* FLOWER)

b Harlow, Essex, 22 February 1805
d St Martin-in-the-Fields, Middlesex, 14 August 1848

The daughter of a political journalist, Benjamin Flower. In 1834, she married William Bridges Adams, a civil engineer. She wrote poetry and prose for *The Repository*, a periodical edited by William Johnson Fox, the minister at South Place Unitarian Church, Finsbury, London, where she was a member. She contributed 13 hymns to the collection *Hymns and Anthems*, 1841, which he compiled. Her other publications included *Vivia Perpetua*, 1841, a religious dramatic poem in five acts; and *The Flock at the Fountain*, 1845, a catechism for children, with hymns.

Song: Nearer, my God, to thee (617)

AGNEW, May

See: **STEPHENS, May Agnew**

ALDERSLEY, Nathan Atkinson

b Carlton, Yorkshire, 26 May 1826
d Wellington, New Zealand, 19 October 1899

Converted as a young man, he was a methodist local preacher, but joined The Salvation Army in about 1879 and became a sergeant in the corps at Keighley, Yorkshire, where he was a dealer in earthenware. In 1884, he went to New Zealand, where he lived in Christchurch and later in Wellington. Severely crippled with rheumatism for many years, he wrote prose and poetry, including several songs. He contributed a number of songs to *The War Cry* during 1883.

Song: Of all in earth or Heaven (65)

ALEXANDER, Cecil Frances (*née* HUMPHREYS)

b Redcross, County Wicklow, Ireland, 1818
d Londonderry, Ireland, 12 October 1895

The daughter of Major John Humphreys, of the Royal Marines. Before her marriage to the Reverend William Alexander in 1850, she had already published *Verses for Holy Seasons*, 1846 and her *Hymns for Little Children*, 1848, which included most of her well-known hymns. Her husband was Bishop of Derry and Raphoe and, after her death, Archbishop of Armagh and Primate of All Ireland. Her later publications included *Narrative Hymns for Village Schools*, 1853, and *Hymns Descriptive and Devotional*, 1858.

Songs: All things bright and beautiful (25)
Jesus calls us; o'er the tumult (428)
Once, in royal David's city (87)
Spirit of God, that moved of old (202)
There is a green hill far away (133)

ALEXANDER, James Waddell

b Hopewell, Virginia, 13 March 1804
d Sweetsprings, Virginia, 31 July 1859

Educated at the College of New Jersey (now Princeton University) and at the Princeton Theological Seminary, he was ordained in 1827 and was pastor of the First Presbyterian Church, Trenton, New Jersey, 1829-32. He was then, successively, professor of rhetoric at the College of New Jersey, 1832-44; pastor of the Duane Street Presbyterian Church, New York City, 1844-49; professor of church history, at Princeton Theological Seminary, 1849-51; and pastor of the Fifth Avenue Presbyterian Church, New York City, 1851-59. His collected translations were published posthumously in *The Breaking Crucible and other translations*, 1861.

Song: O sacred head once wounded (123)

ALFORD, Henry

b Bloomsbury, Middlesex, 7 October 1810
d Canterbury, Kent, 12 January 1871

Educated at Ilminster Grammar School and Trinity College, Cambridge. After his ordination in 1833, he served as curate at Winkfield, Wiltshire, and at Ampton, and then became vicar of Wymeswold, Leicestershire, in 1835. He was there for 18 years, and after four years at Quebec Chapel, in London, he became Dean of Canterbury in 1857. His hymns and translations mainly appeared in *Psalms and Hymns*, 1844, in his *Poetical Works*, 1845 (and later editions) and *The Year of Praise*, 1867. He wrote a commentary on the Greek New Testament in four volumes, 1844-61.

Songs: Come, ye thankful people, come (924)
Forward! be our watchword (682)
Ten thousand times ten thousand (167)

ALLEN, Henry

b Gillingham, Kent, 18 February 1865
d Gillingham, Kent, 2 February 1943

A salvationist from about 1882 to 1899, he was bandmaster of the New Brompton (later Gillingham) Corps for about seven years and afterwards was junior soldiers' sergeant-major. He played a variety of musical instruments, including the clarinet, concertina, violin and flute, and formed a flute band, mandolin band and cornet band, for young people. He often introduced a new song as part of his testimony in Sunday evening meetings. After leaving The Salvation Army, he was active in young people's mission work, and, in later years, joined the Christian Scientists.

Song: With stains of sin upon me (403)

ANDERSON, Harry (or Henry)

b ?
d ?

Apparently a native of Belfast, he is believed to have been the organist at the Carlisle Circus Methodist Church there. When his song appeared in *The Musical Salvationist* in 1887 he was designated 'Auxiliary H. Anderson', and his father, William Anderson, of Queen Street, Belfast is said to have helped in Salvation Army meetings when the Academy Street Corps opened in Belfast.

Song: Saviour, I want thy love to know (455)

ARNOTT, Arthur Smith

b Newcastle, New South Wales, Australia, 17 June 1870
d Melbourne, Australia, 1 May 1941

Son of William Arnott, a baker (later, a biscuit manufacturer), he grew up in the methodist church, where his father was a Sunday-school superintendent, but after his conversion he became a salvationist at the Central Corps in Newcastle. After training in 1898, he soon became private secretary to Commandant Herbert Booth, Territorial Commander for Australia and New Zealand. He spent most of his subsequent service as head of the Subscribers' Department in Melbourne, but in addition he was Men's Social Secretary, 1906-12; Special Efforts Secretary 1912-21 and 1933-35; and Young People's Secretary, 1921-23. He retired as a colonel in 1935, and lived in Canterbury, Victoria. Many of his songs were written for young people's demonstrations which he organised for over 30 years at annual congress meetings in Melbourne.

Songs: Home is home, however lowly (663)

Jesus, tender lover of my soul (600, chorus)
O how I'd like to see his face (884)
Tell them in the east and in the west (829)
We are marching up the hillside (903)

ARNOTT, Catherine Bonnell

b St John, New Brunswick, Canada, 27 March 1927

Daughter of the Reverend John Sutherland Bonnell, a presbyterian minister, she was educated at McMaster University, Hamilton, but moved to Claremont, California, after her marriage to the Reverend Robert Arnott. In 1971, she obtained a doctor of philosophy degree in sociology at the University of California. She is a specialist in family problems and has lectured for several years at La Verne University, California, under her professional name, Dr Catherine Cameron. She started to write poetry as a child, at the age of seven.

Song: O Christ, who came to share our human life (181)

ASHBY, Elizabeth (*née* ASPINALL)

b Warrington, Lancashire, 20 January 1881
d Dulwich, London, 29 April 1988

Daughter of Brigadier Frank Aspinall, who pioneered Salvation Army work in the western United States. As a child she travelled with her parents to the United States in 1883, and on returning to England moved to Maidstone, Plymouth, Hull, Ipswich and other towns according to her father's divisional appointments. She left school in Ipswich at the age of 14 and went to work in her father's office. One of her songs appeared in *The Musical Salvationist* at that time, in September 1895. She worked as secretary to her father until she entered training for officership. In 1903 she married Captain William A. Ashby in Elgin, Scotland and served with him as an officer in the north of Scotland. He later became a baptist minister in Scotland and then in London.

Song: Beautiful Jesus, bright star of the earth (175)

AUBER, Henriette

b Spitalfields, Stepney, Middlesex, 4 October 1773
d Hoddesdon, Hertfordshire, 22 January 1862

Daughter of James Auber (later rector of Tring, Hertfordshire), who was descended from a French Huguenot family. Although at her baptism and death her name is recorded as Henriette, she was often later known as Harriet. She apparently lived most of her life at Broxbourne and Hoddesdon. She wrote devotional and other poetry, some of which was published in her collection *The Spirit of the Psalms*, 1829.

Song: Our blest redeemer, ere he breathed (200)

BABCOCK, Maltbie Davenport

b Syracuse, New York, 3 August 1858
d Naples, Italy, 18 May 1901

Educated at Syracuse University and Auburn Theological Seminary, he was ordained in 1882 as a minister in the Presbyterian Church and was pastor of the First Presbyterian Church, Lockport, New York, and then pastor of the Brown Memorial Church in Baltimore for 14 years. He succeeded Henry Van Dyke as pastor of the Brick Presbyterian Church, New York City in 1899. He died while travelling to the Holy Land and his collected writings were published shortly afterwards in *Thoughts for Every-day Living*, 1901.

Song: This is my Father's world (42)

BAIRD, Catherine Elizabeth Cain

b Sydney, Australia, 12 October 1895
d London, 28 April 1984

Daughter of Salvation Army officers in Australia, she was born on the day the hymn writer, Mrs C. F. Alexander, died.

At the age of eight she moved with her parents to South Africa, where she became an officer in 1915. After service in corps and headquarters appointments, she was transferred to the United States, where she was editor of *The Young Soldier* in Chicago for 11 years. In 1934 she came to London as editor of *The Young Soldier* at International Headquarters. Later she had additional responsibilities as editor of *The Warrior* and in 1953 she was appointed Literary Secretary. She retired as a colonel in 1957. Her publications included *The Sword of God, and other poems*, 1950; *Evidence of the Unseen*, 1956; and *Reflections*, 1975; and she also compiled a *Book of Salvationist Verse*, 1963.

Songs: A boy was born in Bethlehem (855)
Brief is our journey through the years (874)
Eternal God, our song we raise (5)
Jesus, lead me up the mountain (429, verse 3)
Jesus, Lord, we come to hail thee (595)
Let thy heart be at rest (739)
Never fades the name of Jesus (63)
O bright eternal One (36)
O Father, friend of all mankind (796)
O Love, revealed on earth in Christ (449)
Spirit of God, thou art the bread of Heaven (631)
The Son of God goes forth to war (701, chorus)
We're in God's Army and we fight (705)
What wondrous gifts are in my care (871)
When Jesus looked o'er Galilee (103)

BAKER, Henry Williams

b Vauxhall, Surrey, 27 May 1821
d Monkland, Herefordshire, 12 February 1877

Son of Sir Henry Loraine Baker, a captain in the Royal Navy (later a vice-admiral). He was educated privately and then at Trinity College, Cambridge. After his ordination in 1844 he was assistant curate of Great Hockesley, near Colchester, Essex, and became vicar of Monkland, near Leominster, Herefordshire, in 1851. He succeeded to the baronetcy on his father's death in 1859. Appointed secretary to the committee which first met to prepare *Hymns Ancient and Modern* in September 1858, he was chairman of the Proprietors of Hymns Ancient and Modern, 1860-77. He contributed hymns and translations to the original edition in 1861, the 1868 Appendix and the revised edition in 1875.

Songs: Lord, thy word abideth (655)
The King of love my shepherd is (53)

BAKEWELL, John

b Brailsford, Derbyshire, 1721
d Lewisham, Kent, 18 March 1819

Converted at the age of 18, partly through reading the *Fourfold State* by Thomas Boston, he began to preach in his home neighbourhood in 1744 and became a methodist preacher in 1749 after he had moved to London. For some years he was in charge of the Greenwich Royal Park Academy, and, after leaving Greenwich, he apparently lived temporarily in various places where there was no other methodist preacher. His tombstone at the methodist City Road Chapel, in London, says: 'He adorned the doctrine of God our Saviour eighty years and preached His glorious Gospel about seventy years.'

Song: Hail, thou once despisèd Jesus (109)

BALE, Malcolm James

b Parkstone, Dorset, 7 May 1934

He grew up in the corps at Branksome and, after two years' national service in the RAF, entered the International Training College from Branksome in 1954. After training, he was appointed to youth work and then served as a corps officer before he was transferred to the editorial department at International Headquarters in 1964. He was editor of *All the World,* 1967-68, and of *Vanguard,* 1968-72; assistant editor of *The War Cry,* 1972-74, and editor of *The Musician,* 1974-77. Subsequently he has served as a corps officer, at Rochdale, 1977-78; Editor-in-Chief in Australia, 1978-83; and Divisional Secretary in North London Division, 1983-85. He was appointed Editor-in-Chief at International Headquarters, as a lieutenant-colonel, in 1985. His first poem, written at the age of eight, won a prize in an arts and crafts exhibition in the Southampton Division, and he has since contributed several compositions to *The Musical Salvationist* and the band journals.

Song: O Lord, whose human hands were quick (518)

BARING-GOULD, Sabine

b Exeter, Devon, 28 January 1834
d Lew Trenchard, Devon, 2 January 1924

Son of Edward Baring-Gould, he spent much of his early life in France and Germany. He was educated at Clare College, Cambridge, and then taught at St Barnabas Choir School, Pimlico and at Hurstpierpoint College in Sussex. After his ordination in 1864, he was curate at Horbury, Yorkshire, then moved to Dalton, near Thirsk, and in 1871 became rector of East Mersea, Essex. In 1872 he inherited the family estate at Lew Trenchard and in 1881 became rector there. He was a collector of English folk-songs and compiled *Songs and Ballads of the West*, 1889-91 with H. Fleetwood Shepherd, and *A Garland of Country Song*, 1894. His other publications included *Lives of the Saints*, in 15 volumes, 1872-77.

Songs: Now the day is over (673)
Onward, Christian soldiers (690)
Through the night of doubt and sorrow (765)

BARNARD, Samuel

b ?
d Sheffield, Yorkshire, 6 June 1807

He trained for the ministry at Trevecca College, in South Wales, founded by the Countess of Huntingdon, and was apparently ordained in London before serving first at the Countess's church at Berkhampstead, and later at another of her churches, in New Dagger Lane, Hull. He is believed to have ministered at a meeting house built for him in Hope Street, Hull, from 1797 to about 1800, and finally was minister at Howard Street, Sheffield for several years from about 1803 until his death. He compiled a collection of hymns, *Spiritual Songs for Zion's Travellers*, 1799, to which he contributed several of his own hymns anonymously.

Song: Jehovah is our strength (9)

BARTON, Bernard

b Carlisle, Cumberland, 31 January 1784
d Woodbridge, Suffolk, 19 February 1849

Educated at a Quaker school in Ipswich. As a young man, he was apprenticed to a shopkeeper in Halstead, Essex, but in 1806 he moved to Woodbridge, in Suffolk, where he joined his brother in a corn and coal business. For a year, after his wife died, he worked as a private tutor in Liverpool, but he returned to Woodbridge in 1810 and was a bank clerk there for almost 40 years. He wrote prose and poetry, his published works including *Devotional Verses*, 1826 and *Household Verses*, 1849.

Songs: Lamp of our feet, whereby we trace (654)
Walk in the light: so shalt thou know (465)

BATEMAN, James Conner

b Hull, Yorkshire, 18 November 1854
d Pentre, South Wales, 5 June 1888

The son of James Bateman, a flax-dresser, he became a music-hall entertainer, singing and playing the banjo. He worked at an oil mill and seriously injured his leg in an accident at work. Apparently a friend suggested that he should join The Salvation Army, as a cure for his depression, and, one day, he followed the sound of a drum from a public house to the Salvation Army hall in Sculcoates. Following his conversion and a short period as a soldier, he became an officer in 1882, and in six years served in about 14 corps appointments, including Cradley Heath, Northampton, Manchester Openshaw, Hanley and Middlesbrough. He contributed a number of songs to *The Musical Salvationist*.

Songs: Come, shout and sing, make Heaven ring (798)

Come, with me visit Calvary (413, chorus)
March on, salvation soldiers (810)
Once I was far in sin (374)
Sinner, see yon light (260)
Though I wandered far from Jesus (391)
We'll shout aloud throughout the land (782)

BAUGH, William

b Laverstock, near Salisbury, Wiltshire, 29 May 1852
d Penge, London, 9 July 1942

Son of James Baugh, a farm labourer, he was apparently the eldest of 10 children. Converted through a methodist campaign, he later became a salvationist in Barnsley. As a corps officer he served at Hartlepool, Sheffield, New Radford and Whitechapel, then opened the Regent Hall Corps, and had other corps appointments in South Wales and the north of England. He was a divisional commander in Canada, for four years, and then in England, where he became a spiritual special and later Provincial Young People's Secretary for South London. He often assisted William Booth in his campaigns and retired as a brigadier in 1914. His song: 'I was a slave for many years', written for the tune 'Champagne Charlie', first appeared in *The War Cry*, Christmas 1881.

Songs: Blessèd Saviour, now behold me (477)
Why should I be a slave to sin (468)

BAXTER, Lydia

b Petersburg, New York, 2 September 1809
d New York, 22 June 1874
Her birthday is sometimes given as 8 or 9 September.

Converted through the preaching of a baptist missionary, the Reverend Eben Tucker, she and her sister helped to commence the baptist church in their home town of Petersburg. After her marriage she moved to New York, and, although she was an invalid for many years, her home was often a meeting place for Christian leaders seeking advice and inspiration. She published a book of devotional poetry: *Gems by the Wayside*, 1855.

Song: Take the name of Jesus with you (66)

BAYLISS, Wilfrid

b Portsea, Hampshire, 12 August 1882
d Wolverhampton, Staffordshire, 6 October 1952

Son of Edward Swayn Bayliss, an Admiralty inspector. As a boy he moved to Pontypridd and grew up under the influence of Welsh nonconformist preachers. A marine engineer in Newcastle upon Tyne until 1910, he then became manager (and later managing director) of Messrs Joseph Wright Ltd, of Tipton, Staffordshire. He retired at the age of 44 because of illness and after a serious operation, spent 20 years in hospital, returning home only about seven years before his death. His main activity in hospital was writing new hymns and poems, which he published under the name of 'W. B. Coton'. Several of his hymns were published in *Prize and Accepted Settings of the Hymn Tune Association,* 1947.

Song: Plan our life, O gracious Saviour (863)

BAYLY, Albert Frederick

b Bexhill, Sussex, 6 September 1901
d Chichester, Sussex, 26 July 1984

Educated at Hastings Grammar School, and later at Mansfield College, Oxford, preparing for the congregational ministry. Previously he had trained briefly as a shipwright at the Royal Dockyard School in Portsmouth, but he left because working on warships was against his pacifist views. From 1928, he served as a congregational minister in the north of England, at Whitley Bay, Morpeth, Burnley, Swanland (East Yorkshire) and St Helens, and then moved to Thaxted, Essex, in 1962, serving as minister there until his retirement in 1972. In retirement, he lived in Springfield, Chelmsford and was active in the United Reformed Church locally. His hymns and poems were mainly published in a series of booklets: *Rejoice, O people*, 1950; *Again I say Rejoice*, 1967; *Rejoice Always*, 1971; *Rejoice in God*, 1977; and *Rejoice Together*, 1982.

Songs: O Lord of every shining constellation (38)
Praise and thanksgiving (927)

BENNARD, George

b Youngstown, Ohio, 4 February 1873
d Reed City, Michigan, 10 October 1958

Son of a coal miner, he moved as a child with his family to Albia, Iowa, and later to Lucas, Iowa, where he was converted in a Salvation Army meeting. At the age of 16, he worked in the coal mines to support his widowed mother and four sisters. After his marriage he served as a Salvation Army officer for several years, and then he became an interdenominational evangelist, leading revival meetings in the United States and Canada. He was also connected with the Chicago Evangelistic Institute in city mission work and evangelism. He composed more than 300 gospel songs.

Song: On a hill far away stood an old rugged cross (124)

BENNETT, Sanford Fillmore

b Eden, New York, 21 June 1836
d Richmond, Illinois, 12 June 1898

Educated at Waukegan Academy and the University of Michigan. He was converted during a methodist revival. For two years he was superintendent of schools in Richmond, Illinois, and then became associate editor of a weekly newspaper, *The Independent*, at Elkhorn, Wisconsin. During the American Civil War he was a second lieutenant in the Fortieth Wisconsin Volunteers, but, after the war, he returned to Elkhorn and opened a drugstore. He began to study medicine, and graduated from Rush Medical College in 1874. He practised medicine for 22 years. His first poems appeared in the Waukegan *Gazette* in the 1850s and he later wrote extensively in prose and verse.

Song: There's a land that is fairer than day (900)

BERNARD of Clairvaux

b Les Fontaines, near Dijon, France, *c*1091
d Clairvaux, France, 20 August 1153

Son of a knight, Tesselin, he was educated at Chatillon. With a number of companions, he entered the Cistercian monastery at Citeaux, *c* 1112. In 1115, he was sent with a group of monks to found the monastery of Clairvaux, and remained as abbot there throughout his life. He was a preacher and theologian, and became involved in the controversy surrounding papal elections in 1130 and an unsuccessful crusade which he promoted in 1146-47.

Songs: Jesus, the very thought of thee (61)
Jesus, thou joy of loving hearts (602)
O sacred head once wounded (123)

BETHAM-EDWARDS, Matilda Barbara

See: **EDWARDS, Matilda Barbara Betham**

BEVAN, Emma Frances (*née* SHUTTLEWORTH)

b Oxford, 25 September 1827
d Cannes, France, 13 February 1909

Daughter of the Reverend Philip Shuttleworth, warden of New College, Oxford (later Bishop of Chichester). In 1856, she married Robert Cooper Lee Bevan, a banker in the City of London, and, after her marriage, was associated with the Brethren movement in Barnet, Hertfordshire. She translated German verse into English and published her translations in several books, including *Songs of Eternal Life,* 1858 and *Songs of Praise for Christian Pilgrims,* 1859.

Song: Sinners Jesus will receive (262)

BICKERSTETH, Edward Henry

b Islington, Middlesex, 25 January 1825
d Paddington, London, 16 May 1906

Son of the Reverend Edward Bickersteth, compiler of *Christian Psalmody*, 1833, which had an early influence on the hymnody of the Church of England. He was educated at Trinity College, Cambridge, and, after his ordination, was curate of Banningham, Norfolk; curate of Christ Church, Tunbridge Wells; rector of Hinton Martell; and vicar of Christ Church, Hampstead, 1855-85, before becoming Dean of Gloucester for a few months, and Bishop of Exeter, 1885-1900. He compiled *Psalms and Hymns*, 1858, and the *Hymnal Companion to the Book of Common Prayer*, 1870 (and later editions) which was widely used by evangelical anglican churches.

Songs: Come ye yourselves apart and rest awhile (564)
Peace, perfect peace, in this dark world of sin (752)

BINNEY, Thomas

b Newcastle upon Tyne, 30 April 1798
d Upper Clapton, Hackney, Middlesex, 24 February 1874

Son of a presbyterian elder, he worked as an apprentice to a bookseller, and then studied for the congregational ministry at the Coward Trust seminary, Wymondley, Hertfordshire. He served as a minister at the New Meeting, Bedford, for about a year; at an independent chapel in Newport, Isle of Wight, 1824-29; and then at the King's Weigh House Chapel, in London, 1829-69. He was chairman of the Congregational Union in 1845, and visited Australia, 1857-59. His publications included a sermon on the use of music in worship, *The Service of Song in the House of the Lord*, 1848, and also more than 50 other works, including a few hymns.

Song: Eternal Light! Eternal Light (414)

BLACK, James Milton

b South Hill, Sullivan County, New York, 19 August 1856
d Williamsport, Pennsylvania, 21 December 1938

After studying singing and organ playing, he became a teacher in singing schools, and for some years he edited collections of gospel songs for the Methodist Book Concern, McCabe Publishing Company and the Hall-Mack Company. One of the most popular books was *Songs of the Soul*, 1894, which apparently sold more than 400,000 copies in its first two years. He was a member of Pine Street Methodist Church, Williamsport, 1904-38, and served on the joint commission which prepared the *Methodist Hymnal*, 1905.

Song: When the trumpet of the Lord shall sound (907)

BLACKMER, Francis Augustus

b Ware, Massachusetts, 17 February 1855
d Somerville, Massachusetts, 8 October 1930

Son of August and Jane Blackmer, who were influenced by the Millerite (Adventist) Movement, he was baptised at an adventist camp-meeting in Springfield, Massachusetts. He was educated at Wilbraham Academy, but was largely self-taught in harmony and musical composition; he spent most of his life in Somerville, Massachusetts, a suburb of Boston, where he had a pianoforte business. For many years he served as choirmaster and song leader in the Advent Christian Church, in Somerville, and he was also an elder of the church, and a song leader at the Alton Bay camp-meetings each summer at Lake Winnepesaukee, New Hampshire, 1914-30. He wrote his first gospel song at the age of 16, and later composed more than 300 songs and compiled several gospel song books, including *The Gospel Awakening*, 1888; *Singing by the Way*, 1895; and *Songs of Coming Glory*, 1926.

Songs: Once I thought I walked with Jesus (549)
        When we gather at last over Jordan (908)

BLISS, Philip Paul

b Clearfield County, Pennsylvania, 9 July 1838
d near Ashtabula, Ohio, 29 December 1876

He was educated at Susquehanna Collegiate Institute, Towanda, and, in summer 1860, studied music for six weeks at the Normal Academy of Music, in Geneseo, New York. After becoming a music teacher, he wrote songs for the music publishers Root and Cady, of Chicago. In 1870 he was appointed choir-leader and Sunday-school superintendent at the First Congregational Church, Chicago. Encouraged by Dwight L. Moody, he became a singing evangelist in 1874, and often assisted Major Daniel W. Whittle in revival meetings. After Christmas 1876, he was travelling by train to an engagement in Chicago, when the train crashed near Ashtabula and he died trying to rescue his wife from the wreckage. He was involved in compiling a number of collections of gospel songs, including *The Prize*, 1870; *The Charm*, 1871; and *Gospel Songs, A Choice Collection of Hymns and Tunes, New and Old*, 1874.

Songs: Almost persuaded now to believe (226)
Brightly beams our Father's mercy (478)
Have you on the Lord believed (418)
Ho, my comrades, see the signal (804)
I am so glad that our Father in Heaven (323)
I will sing of my redeemer (180)
Man of sorrows! what a name (118)
Sing them over again to me (258)
Standing by a purpose true (847)
'Tis the promise of God full salvation to give (392)
Whosoever heareth! shout, shout the sound (279)

BLOMBERG, Gösta

b Stockholm, Sweden, 5 April 1905
d Stockholm, Sweden, 27 May 1981

Converted at the age of 12, he entered the International Training College in 1923 from Östersund Corps, Sweden. After corps appointments in England and Sweden, he became private secretary to two territorial commanders in Sweden and then to General Evangeline Booth in London, 1938-39. He then served in the United States of America as a corps officer, youth secretary and general secretary for Scandinavian work. Returning to Sweden, he became Editor-in-Chief and Literary Secretary in 1946 and Training Principal in 1949. His subsequent appointments were as Chief Secretary, Finland; International Youth Secretary, at International Headquarters; Chief Secretary, Sweden, 1957-60; and Territorial Commander for Denmark, 1960-61, for Germany, 1961-66 and for Sweden, 1966-73. He retired as a commissioner in 1973.

Song: I love to sing of the Saviour (178)

BOADEN, Edward

b Helston, Cornwall, 1 May 1827
d Leamington Spa, Warwickshire, 2 June 1913

In 1849 he became a minister in the Wesleyan Methodist Association (later the Methodist Free Church), serving first at Gosport, Hampshire, and subsequently in various towns and cities, including Manchester, 1867-71 and 1885-91; Harrogate, 1874-85; Southport, 1891-1902; and Leamington, 1902-7. He was president of the Methodist Free Church in 1871, and first president of the United Methodist Church in 1907. Among other responsibilities, he was secretary of the Chapel Fund, 1864-1901, and assisted in compiling *Methodist Free Church Hymns*, 1889. For many years he was actively interested in the Temperance Movement.

Song: Here, Lord, assembled in thy name (581)

BOBERG, Carl Gustaf

b Mönsterås, Sweden, 16 August 1859
d Kalmar, Sweden, 7 January 1940

Son of a shipyard carpenter, he was a sailor for several years. He was converted at the age of 19 and, after attending a Bible school in Kristinehamn for two years, he became a preacher in Mönsterås. For 13 years he represented Mönsterås in the Upper House of the Swedish Parliament, and was editor of the weekly *Sanningsvittnet* (Witness of the Truth), 1890-1916. He published several books of poetry and hymns, and assisted in compiling two hymn books for the Swedish Covenant Church.

Songs: O Lord my God, when I in awesome wonder (37)
O mighty God! When I thy works consider (39)

BODE, John Ernest

b St Pancras, Middlesex, 23 February 1816
d Castle Camps, Cambridgeshire, 6 October 1874

Son of William Bode, head of the foreign department of the General Post Office, he was educated at Eton College, Charterhouse School and Christ Church, Oxford. He was a tutor at Christ Church for six years and, after his ordination, became rector of Westwell, Oxfordshire, in 1847, and then rector of Castle Camps, Cambridgeshire, in 1860. His publications included *Short Occasional Poems,* 1858, and *Hymns from the Gospel of the Day, for each Sunday and the Festivals of our Lord*, 1860.

Song: O Jesus, I have promised (862)

BONAR, Horatius

b Edinburgh, 19 December 1808
d Edinburgh, 31 July 1889

Son of James Bonar, second Solicitor of Excise, he was educated in Edinburgh at the High School and University, where he studied under Dr Thomas Chalmers, the professor of divinity. He became assistant to the minister at Leith, and in 1837 was ordained at Kelso, as minister of the North Parish. In 1843 he joined Dr Chalmers in founding the Free Church of Scotland, but remained in Kelso as minister of the Free Church. In 1866 he became minister of the Chalmers Memorial Church in Edinburgh, and in 1883 he was elected Moderator of the General Assembly of the Free Church. He edited the quarterly *Journal of Prophecy*, 1848-73 and was for some time joint-editor of the Free Church newspaper *The Border Watch*. Many of his hymns were published in *Songs for the Wilderness*, 1843; *The Bible Hymn Book*, 1845; and three volumes of *Hymns of Faith and Hope*, 1857, 1861 and 1866.

Songs: Fill thou my life, O Lord my God (7)
Go, labour on, spend and be spent (683)
I heard the voice of Jesus say (332)
No, not despairingly (296)
Not what these hands have done (297)

BOON, Brindley John Railton

b Willesden, Middlesex, 11 August 1913

Although he was the son and grandson of salvationists, he attended Cricklewood Methodist Sunday School and was organist there at the age of 15. Shortly afterwards he became a salvationist at Child's Hill, and served as songster leader there and at Chalk Farm. After training as a cadet, 1949-50, he spent much of his officership in the Editorial Department at International Headquarters, including periods as editor of *The Musician*, 1955-61 and 1965-66, and editor of *The War Cry*, 1972-76, and later as Editor-in-Chief. He was assistant editor and then editor of *The War Cry* in Canada, 1961-63, and National Secretary for Bands and Songster Brigades in the British Territory, 1966-72. His last appointment was as Executive Officer for the 1978 International Congress, and he retired as a colonel in 1978. He has contributed songs to *The Musical Salvationist* for more than 50 years, and wrote *Play the Music, Play*, 1966; *Sing the Happy Song*, 1978; and *ISB*, 1985, a history of the International Staff Band.

Songs: Greatest joy is found in serving Jesus (857)
I would be thy holy temple (786)
Lord of my youth, teach me thy ways (861)
Spirit divine, come as of old (218)
Thou art holy, Lord of Glory (528)
Thou hast called me from the byway (463)
'Tis the promise of God full salvation to give (392, verses 2-4)
Weaver divine, thy matchless skill (644)

BOOTH, Ballington

b Brighouse, Yorkshire, 28 July 1857
d Blue Point, Long Island, New York, 5 October 1940

Second son of William and Catherine Booth, founders of The Salvation Army. He was educated at home, at schools in Bristol and Taunton, and at the Institute for Theological and Missionary Training, in Nottingham. At the age of 23 he was in charge of the first Salvation Army training home for men officers. In 1883 he went to Australia as joint-commander of The Salvation Army there, and after two years returned to England, where he married in 1886. He went to command Salvation Army work in the United States in 1887, but resigned after eight years because of policy differences and conflicts within the Booth family. In 1896 he founded Volunteers of America, a religious and social welfare organisation similar in concept to The Salvation Army, and was its general and commander-in-chief for 44 years. He played several musical instruments and composed a number of songs. His publications included *From Ocean to Ocean*, 1891, and *The Prayer that Prevails*, 1920.

Song: The cross that he gave may be heavy (758)

BOOTH, Cornelie Ida Ernestine (*née* SCHOCH)

b Bois-le-Duc, 13 October 1864
d Selsey, Sussex, 31 May 1920

Daughter of C. F. Schoch, a Dutch artillery officer, who later helped to establish the work of The Salvation Army in Holland and Germany. In 1890 she married Herbert Booth, third son of William and Catherine Booth. She contributed a few songs to the collection *Songs of Peace and War*, published at the time of their marriage.

Songs: Have you heard the angels singing (242)
When I ponder o'er the story (770)

BOOTH, Evangeline Cory

b Hackney, Middlesex, 25 December 1865
d Hartsdale, New York, 17 July 1950

Seventh child of William and Catherine Booth, founders of The Salvation Army. Her birth was registered as Eveline Cory, but she was generally known as Evangeline, or Eva. At the age of 18, she was an assistant at the training home for women, giving oversight to the Cellar, Gutter and Garret Brigade, and in 1886 she was appointed corps officer at the Great Western Hall, Marylebone. Later, she became field commissioner, responsible for the Army's work in London, including the training homes. Subsequently, she served as Territorial Commander for Canada, 1896-1904, and as Commander for the United States, 1904-34. As the fourth General of The Salvation Army, 1934-39, she travelled extensively throughout Britain and on international tours, and after her retirement she returned to live in the United States. She wrote a number of songs which were published as *Songs of the Evangel*, 1927 (enlarged edition 1937).

Songs: Dark shadows were falling (237)
Father of love, of justice and of mercy (486)
I bring thee my cares and my sorrows (288)
The world for God! The world for God (830)

BOOTH, Herbert Howard

b Penzance, Cornwall, 26 August 1862
d Yonkers, New York, 25 September 1926

Fifth child of William and Catherine Booth, founders of The Salvation Army. (At his birth and marriage he was registered as Herbert Henry, but he was usually known as Herbert Howard.) He was educated at Allesley Park College and the Congregational Institute in Nottingham. He helped pioneer Army work in France, 1880-82, and started to write songs in French during this period. In 1883, the Army's musical department was established at Clapton under his supervision, and for several years he formed groups of singers among the cadets at the training homes. Subsequently, after an overseas tour in 1888, he was in charge of Army work in Britain, in Canada, 1892-95, and in Australia, 1896-1901, where he compiled *The Salvation Soldiers' Song Book*, 1897. In 1901, he moved to the Army's farm colony at Collie, in Western Australia, but the following year he resigned from the Army and went to the United States. He then travelled extensively on lecture tours in North America, South Africa, Australia and New Zealand, first with a film *Soldiers of the Cross*, prepared in Australia in 1899-1900, and later promoting a scheme to establish an undenominational 'Christian Confederacy' which he had outlined in 1915. At the time of his marriage to Cornelie Schoch in 1890, a collection of 86 of their songs, *Songs of Peace and War*, was published.

Songs: All I have, by thy blood thou dost claim (473, chorus)
As I am before thy face (285)
Before thy face, dear Lord (409)
Blessèd Lord, in thee is refuge (713)
From every stain made clean (415)
I bring my heart to Jesus, with its fears (420)
I bring to thee my heart to fill (489)
Let me hear thy voice now speaking (502)
Let me love thee, thou art claiming (503)
Lord through the blood of the Lamb that was slain (437)
Love of love so wondrous (250)
My mind upon thee, Lord, is stayed (513)
O wanderer, knowing not the smile (253)
Saviour, hear me while before thy feet (303)
Summoned home! the call has sounded (894)
There are wants my heart is telling (460)
To the front! the cry is ringing (702)
When my heart was so hard (395)
Why are you doubting and fearing (467)
With my heart so bright in the heavenly light (402)
With my heart so full of sadness (470)
Within my heart, O Lord, fulfil (138)

BOOTH, William

b Sneinton, Nottingham, 10 April 1829
d Hadley Wood, Hertfordshire, 20 August 1912

Son of Samuel Booth, a builder. At the age of 15 he was converted, and two years later became a local preacher. He was influenced by visiting revivalists, including Isaac Marsden and the American evangelist, James Caughey. In 1849 he moved to London, working as a pawnbroker until 1852, when he became a preacher at Binfield House, a methodist reform chapel in Clapham. Later that year he was appointed to Spalding, Lincolnshire. In 1854, he joined the Methodist New Connexion, serving as an assistant minister in London, and then for two years as an evangelist. In 1857 he was appointed to Brighouse, Yorkshire, and then served in Gateshead, 1858-61. Subsequently, he conducted mission meetings as an independent evangelist, 1862-65, leading revivals in various places, including Cornwall, Cardiff, Walsall, Leeds and London. A series of tent meetings in East London in July and August 1865 led to the development of the East London Christian Mission, which became The Christian Mission in 1869 and The Salvation Army in 1878. By 1912, Army work was established in 58 countries. He compiled a number of song books, from *The Revival Hymn Book*, used by the East London Christian Mission, to *Salvation Army Songs*, 1899. His extensive publications included *In Darkest England and the Way Out*, 1890, in which he outlined his scheme for social service and salvation.

Songs: Jesus, my Lord, through thy triumph I claim (543)
O boundless salvation! deep ocean of love (298)
O Christ of pure and perfect love (440)
O Jesus, Saviour, Christ divine (447)
Thou Christ of burning, cleansing flame (203)

BOOTH, William Bramwell

b Halifax, Yorkshire, 8 March 1856
d Hadley Wood, Hertfordshire, 16 June 1929

The eldest child of William and Catherine Booth, founders of The Salvation Army, he was named after the holiness preacher William Bramwell (1759-1818). Educated by private tutors and briefly at the City of London School, at the age of 13 he took part in Children's Mission meetings in Bethnal Green, and in subsequent years became involved in various aspects of Christian Mission work. He was appointed Travelling Secretary of The Christian Mission in 1877, and served as Chief of the Staff of The Salvation Army, 1880-1912. Succeeding his father as General in 1912, he travelled widely, supporting and developing the work of the Army in 82 countries and colonies by 1929. He was associated with W. T. Stead in the campaign which led to the Criminal Law Amendment Act 1885, raising the age of consent to 16. An administrator and a teacher of holiness, he wrote articles and books, including *Our Master*, 1908; *Papers on Life and Religion*, 1920; *Echoes and Memories*, 1925; and *These Fifty Years*, 1929. He contributed poems and songs to the monthly *Christian Mission Magazine* and *The Salvationist*, and had overall responsibility for the preparation of *Salvation Army Songs*, 1930.

Songs: Come in, my Lord, come in (562)
Living in the fountain (352)
My faith looks up to thee (742)
O when shall my soul find her rest (454)
Oft have I heard thy tender voice (749)

BOOTH-CLIBBORN, Arthur Sydney

b Moate, County Westmeath, 20 February 1855
d Islington, London, 12 February 1939

Son of James Clibborn, owner of linen mills at Bessbrook in Armagh. He was educated in France and Switzerland, graduating from Lausanne University. He grew up in the Society of Friends, but, after meeting The Salvation Army at Bessbrook, offered to help the Army in France. In 1881, with the rank of colonel, he went to Paris, where he edited the paper *En Avant*, and in 1882 commenced Army meetings in Geneva. He adopted the name Booth-Clibborn in 1887 shortly before his marriage to Catherine Booth (La Maréchale). They served together in France and Switzerland until 1896 and then as Territorial Commanders for Holland and Belgium. In 1901, he joined a mission founded by Dr John A. Dowie, an American evangelist and faith healer, and resigned from the Army. In 1905, while preaching in Paris, he was attacked and his leg was seriously injured. His later years were spent mainly at his home on Highbury Hill, in London. He wrote over 300 hymns and songs, and, with his wife, compiled a French song book, *Chants de l'Armée du Salut*, 1892.

Song: O God of light, O God of love (446)

BOOTH-CLIBBORN, Catherine

b Gateshead, Durham, 18 September 1858
d Ilsington, Devon, 9 May 1955

Eldest daughter of William and Catherine Booth, founders of The Salvation Army. At the age of 17, she became a travelling evangelist in The Christian Mission, and in 1881 she led a small group of pioneers to commence Salvation Army work in France, where she soon became known as 'La Maréchale'. In September 1883, during a period of intense opposition to The Salvation Army in Switzerland, she was imprisoned for 12 days at Neuchâtel. She married Arthur Booth-Clibborn in 1887 and served with him in France and Switzerland, 1887-96, and then in Holland and Belgium, 1896-1901. After the First World War, she resumed her preaching tours, speaking at revival meetings in England, Ireland, Canada, the United States, Australia and New Zealand. In 1948, she made her last visit to Switzerland and France, at the age of 90. She compiled a collection of gospel songs, *Wings of Praise,* which included several songs by members of the Booth-Clibborn family. Among other publications she also wrote *They Endured,* 1934, the story of The Salvation Army in France and Switzerland, and contributed to *A Poet of Praise,* 1939, a tribute to Arthur Booth-Clibborn.

Songs: O Lamb of God, thou wonderful sin-bearer (448)
O spotless Lamb, I come to thee (450)

BOOTH-HELLBERG, Lucy Milward

b Hackney, Middlesex, 28 April 1868
d Stockholm, Sweden, 18 July 1953

Youngest child of William and Catherine Booth, founders of The Salvation Army. After the marriage of her sister Emma in 1888, she was for some time in charge of the training home in London, and was then appointed to India in 1890, where she was known as Colonel (later Commissioner) Ruhani. In 1894 she married a Swedish officer, Colonel Emanuel D. Hellberg. They adopted the surname Booth-Hellberg and served together as Territorial Commanders for India, 1894-96; France, 1896-1901; and Switzerland, 1896-1904. After the promotion to Glory of her husband in 1909, she was Territorial Commander for Denmark, 1910-1920, and then for Norway, 1920-28. Following a short period as an international travelling commissioner she was Territorial Commander for South America (East), 1929-33, with oversight of South America (West) and Brazil. Returning to London in 1933, she was admitted to the Order of the Founder, and retired in 1934.

Songs: Sins of years are all numbered (893)
When you feel weakest, dangers surround (773)

BOOTH-TUCKER, Emma Moss

b Gateshead, Durham, 8 January 1860
d near Marceline, Missouri, 28 October 1903

Fourth child of William and Catherine Booth, founders of The Salvation Army. She was Training Home Mother, responsible for women cadets, 1880-1888, and in 1884 established the Cellar, Gutter and Garret Brigade to work in the London slums. Later, while helping to choose officer reinforcements to send to India in 1887, she met Commissioner Frederick Tucker. They were married in 1888, adopted the name Booth-Tucker, and served together in India, 1888-91, where she was known as Commissioner Raheeman (or Rahiman). They were appointed to London in 1891, as commissioners for Foreign Affairs, and then went to the United States as joint territorial commanders in 1896. He was known as the Commander and she was called 'The Consul'. While travelling from Kansas City to Chicago in 1903, she was seriously injured in a train crash at Dean Lake, and died shortly afterwards, while continuing the journey on a relief train.

Songs: O my heart is full of music and of gladness (369)
We the people of thy host (643)

BOOTH-TUCKER, Frederick St George de Lautour

b Monghyr, India, 21 March 1853
d Stoke Newington, London, 17 July 1929

Son of William Thornhill Tucker, a deputy commissioner in the Indian Civil Service. He was educated at Cheltenham

College, and in 1875 was converted during the Moody and Sankey campaigns in London. He served in the Indian Civil Service, 1876-81, but while on leave in England in 1881 he joined The Salvation Army and worked in the legal department at International Headquarters. In 1882, he led a group of pioneer officers to India, where he became known as 'Fakir Singh'. He married Emma Booth in 1888 and adopted the name Booth-Tucker. They served in India until 1891 when they were appointed to London as commissioners for Foreign Affairs. Subsequently he was Territorial Commander in the United States, 1896-1904; Foreign Secretary, in London, 1904-7; Special Commissioner for India and Ceylon, 1907-19; and Travelling Commissioner until his retirement in 1924. He wrote a number of poems and songs, and compiled a collection of *One Hundred Favorite Songs of The Salvation Army*, 1899, in the United States. He was the first editor of *The Officer* magazine in 1893, and was the author of several books, including a *Life of Catherine Booth*, 1892; *The Consul*, 1903; and *Muktifauj*, 1923, the story of the first 40 years of the Army in India and Ceylon.

Songs: I bring thee, dear Jesus, my all (422)
They bid me choose an easier path (780)

BOTTOME, Francis

b Belper, Derbyshire, 26 May 1823
d Gunnislake, Cornwall, 29 June 1894

After moving to the United States, he entered the ministry of the Methodist Episcopal Church in 1850. He was awarded the honorary Doctor of Divinity degree from Dickinson College, Carlisle, Pennsylvania in 1872. He wrote a number of gospel songs and assisted in compiling R. P. Smith's *Gospel Songs*, 1872. His other publications included *Centenary Singer*, 1869, and *Round Lake*, 1872.

Songs: Come, Holy Ghost, all sacred fire (208)
Full salvation, full salvation (540)
Let us sing of his love once again (808)
O bliss of the purified, bliss of the free (364)
Precious Jesus, O to love thee (520)

BOURIGNON, Antoinette

b Lisle, France, 13 January 1616
d Franeker, Friesland, 30 October 1680

After her conversion, apparently through the influence of a Huguenot preacher, she is said to have left home in 1640 on the eve of her intended wedding, when her parents tried to force her into marriage against her will. Later she entered a convent for a short period and was briefly in charge of an orphanage. She travelled widely on a personal mission for spiritual reform and renewal, and attracted followers in France, Holland, England and Scotland. Her extensive writings, in more than 20 volumes, were published in Amsterdam, 1679-84.

Song: Come, Saviour Jesus, from above (480)

BOURNE, Hugh

b Stoke-on-Trent, Staffordshire, 3 April 1772
d Bemersley, Staffordshire, 11 October 1852

After his conversion in 1799, he joined the methodists in the Burslem Circuit, becoming a class leader and preacher in 1801. With a small group of friends, he arranged a series of prayer meetings which culminated in a camp-meeting on Mow Cop, near Burslem, on Sunday 31 May 1807. Although subsequent camp-meetings were opposed by the Wesleyan Methodists, he continued to help organise a growing number of supporters, who became known in 1812 as the Society of Primitive Methodists. He published the first issue of the *Primitive Methodist Magazine* in 1818 and was subsequently editor for more than 20 years. He compiled a small *General Collection of Hymns and Spiritual Songs, for Camp-Meetings, Revivals, etc*, in 1809, and prepared other hymn books for the Primitive Methodists, 1818-25. He wrote a number of hymns, sometimes with William Sanders, for the later collections.

Songs: Hark! the gospel news is sounding (239)
My soul is now united to Christ, the living vine (361)

BOVAN, Arthur White

b c1869
d Hackney, London, 17 March 1903

In 1891, he was homeless in London and came to The Salvation Army seeking employment. Given shelter and work, he was later converted in the Salvation Army hostel in Quaker Street. He became an officer and served in the Men's Social Work, latterly, with the rank of adjutant, in the statistical department at the Men's Social Work Headquarters. Several of his songs and poems appeared in *The War Cry* and other publications.

Song: There's a crown laid up in Glory (899)

BOWRING, John

b Heavitree, Exeter, Devon, 17 October 1792
d Heavitree, Exeter, Devon, 23 November 1872

At the age of 14 he left the grammar school in Moretonhampstead, Devon, to work with his father, a manufacturer of woollen goods. By the age of 16, he could speak six languages and later claimed to be able to read 200 and converse in 100 languages. He apparently intended to become a unitarian minister, but his interest in politics developed and he became editor of the radical *Westminster Review*, in 1825. He served as Commissioner to France on commercial matters, 1834-35, and as Member of Parliament for Kilmarnock, 1835-37, and for Bolton, 1841-49. In 1849 he was appointed Consul-General at Canton, and was later Governor of Hong Kong, 1854-59. Knighted in 1854, his publications included two collections of hymns: *Matins and Vespers, with Hymns and Devotional Pieces*, 1823, and *Hymns as a Sequel to the Matins*, 1825.

Song: In the cross of Christ I glory (112)

BRADY, Nicholas

b Bandon, County Cork, 25 October 1659
d Richmond, Surrey, 20 May 1726

Educated at Westminster School, Christ Church, Oxford and Trinity College, Dublin. After his ordination, he held several appointments in Cork before he came to London, where he served as incumbent of St Catherine Cree, 1691-96, lecturer of St Michael's, Wood Street, and Chaplain to King William III, and later to Queen Anne. Sometimes holding more than one appointment simultaneously, he was also incumbent of Stratford-on-Avon, 1702-05, and incumbent of Richmond, Surrey, from 1696. With Nahum Tate, he compiled the *New Version of the Psalms of David*, 1696, a complete metrical version of the psalms, intended to replace the *Old Version* of Sternhold and Hopkins, dating from *c*1560.

Songs: As pants the hart for cooling streams (557)
Through all the changing scenes of life (21)

BRAND, William John

b Chatham, Kent, 17 August 1889
d Hastings, Sussex, 26 May 1977

At the age of about seven, he started learning to play the harmonium, and developed an interest in church music as a choir boy at Christ Church, Dover. He attended Salvation Army meetings in Dover at the invitation of a friend, and became a junior soldier and corps cadet. Later, after his marriage, he was deputy songster leader at Catford during the First World War. At the age of 18, he worked in the Stationery Department at International Headquarters, but subsequently was employed for 42 years by J. and E. Hall and Co Ltd, refrigeration engineers, at Dartford. He began writing poetry regularly in about 1937, and wrote over 350 songs and 150 sonnets, many of which have been included in *The Musical Salvationist* and in his anthology, *With Sword and Song*, 1975.

Songs: Above the world-wide battlefield (774)
Earthly kingdoms rise and fall (799)
Jesus, thou hast won us (788)

Lord, as we take our chosen way (688)
O Holy Ghost, on thee we wait (198)
O soul, consider and be wise (885)
Rise up, O youth! for mighty winds are stirring (864)
Set forth within the sacred word (656)
Sing we many years of blessing (939)
There is beauty in the name of Jesus (70)
There's a road of high adventure (868)
This, our time of self-denial (922)
We find pleasure in the Army (869)
When from sin's dark hold thy love had won me (534)
When Jesus from Calvary called me (553)

BRIDGERS, Luther Burgess

b Margaretsville, North Carolina, 14 February 1884
d Atlanta, Georgia, 27 May 1948

He started preaching at the age of 17, and after studying at Asbury College, Wilmore, Kentucky, he was a methodist pastor for about 12 years. His wife and three sons died in a fire at her father's home at Harrodsburg, Kentucky, in 1910. Subsequently, except for a period after the First World War when he was involved in mission work in Belgium, Czechoslovakia and Russia, he was an evangelist in the Methodist Episcopal Church, South. After 1932, he served as pastor at churches in Georgia and North Carolina, and retired in 1945 at Gainesville, Georgia.

Song: There's within my heart a melody (390)

BRIDGES, Matthew

b Maldon, Essex, 14 July 1800
d Sidmouth, Devon, 6 October 1894

Son of John Bridges, of Wallington House, Surrey. He grew up in the Church of England and developed an interest in poetry and church history. His early publications included a book *The Roman Empire under Constantine the Great*, 1828. Later, he was influenced by the Oxford Movement, and, in 1848, he became a Roman catholic. For a number of years he lived in Quebec, Canada, but at least for a few months before he died, he and his wife were living at Convent Villa, a small guest house attached to the Convent of the Assumption, in Sidmouth. His hymns were published in *Hymns of the Heart*, 1848 (enlarged edition, 1851) and *The Passion of Jesus*, 1852.

Song: Crown him with many crowns (156)

BROOKS, Phillips

b Boston, Massachusetts, 13 December 1835
d Boston, Massachusetts, 23 January 1893

Educated at Boston Latin School, Harvard University, and the Episcopal Theological Seminary in Alexandria, Virginia. After his ordination in 1859, he began his ministry at the Church of the Advent, Philadelphia, and in 1862, he became rector of Holy Trinity Church, Philadelphia. He was appointed rector of Trinity Church, Boston, in 1868, and served there until 1891 when he was consecrated Bishop of Massachusetts. Many of his sermons have been published, together with his *Lectures on Preaching*, delivered at Yale Divinity School in 1877.

Song: O little town of Bethlehem (86)

BROWN, Arnold

b Tottenham, Middlesex, 13 December 1913

Son of corps officers at Tottenham, his family emigrated to Belleville, Ontario, Canada in 1923. On leaving school, he became a clerk and secretary in a railway office, and, after visiting England in 1933, trained for Salvation Army officership, 1934-35. He wrote the words for the cadets' sessional song that year. For two years he was a corps officer at Bowmanville and then served in the editorial department in Toronto for almost 10 years. Later, as Territorial Publicity Representative, he developed the radio series *This is my Story* and the television series *The Living Word*, which were transmitted throughout the United States and Canada. After two years as Territorial Youth Secretary in Canada, he was Secretary for Public Relations, at International Headquarters, 1964-69; Chief of the Staff, 1969-74; Territorial Commander for Canada and Bermuda, 1974-77; and General, 1977-81. He wrote: *What hath*

God wrought?, a history of the first 50 years of Salvation Army work in Canada, his autobiography, *The Gate and the Light*, 1984, and *Yin: The Mountain the Wind Blew Here*, 1988.

Songs: Descend, O Holy Spirit, thou (211)
       On God's word relying (222)

BROWNE, Simon

b Shepton Mallet, Somerset, 1680
d Shepton Mallet, Somerset, 1732

He studied for the congregational ministry at the academy of the Reverend John Moore, in Bridgwater, Somerset and served as pastor of a chapel in Portsmouth, later becoming minister of the Independent Chapel in Old Jewry, London. In later years he suffered from serious mental delusions, possibly the result of an encounter with a highwayman (who died during a violent struggle), and the death of his wife and son shortly afterwards. He published more than 20 books, including a dictionary, theological works, and his *Hymns and Spiritual Songs, designed as a Supplement to Dr Watts,* 1720.

Song: Come, gracious Spirit, heavenly dove (190)

BROWNING, Elizabeth Barrett

b Coxhoe Hall, Durham, 6 March 1806
d Florence, Italy, 30 June 1861

Daughter of Edward Moulton, who later adopted the surname Barrett. She grew up at Hope End, near Ledbury, Herefordshire, but, after her mother died, the family moved to Sidmouth, and in 1828 came to London. In 1846, she married the poet Robert Browning, against her father's wishes, and shortly afterwards went to Paris and then to Italy, first to Pisa and finally to Florence. She wrote verses from childhood and published *The Battle of Marathon,* 1820 (when she was aged 14); *The Seraphim and Other Poems,* 1838; and many other volumes of collected poems, including her *Sonnets from the Portuguese.*

Song: The little cares which fretted me (41)

BUCK, Joseph

b Uxbridge, Middlesex, 12 July 1889
d Aberdeen, 13 March 1945

He was converted on Christmas Eve, 1906, and entered the training college from Southall in 1909. His first appointment, to Misterton, Lancashire, was followed by several corps appointments, including Bridlington, Durham, Middlesbrough, Edinburgh, Paisley and Darlington. He was sectional officer at Findochty during the Moray Firth Revival in 1921. Subsequently, he served as Divisional Young People's Secretary in North East London and South Yorkshire; as Chancellor in the North-West and Northern Divisions; and as Assistant Divisional Commander in the Durham Division. He was appointed Divisional Commander in the North Scottish Division in 1942. He wrote a number of songs which appeared in *The Musical Salvationist*. He was a brigadier when he was promoted to Glory as a result of injuries received in a motoring accident.

Song: Love has a language, all its own making (51)

BUDRY, Edmond Louis

b Vevey, Switzerland, 30 August 1854
d Vevey, Switzerland, 12 November 1932

After studying theology and philosophy at Lausanne, he served as pastor at Cully and St Croix, 1881-89. In 1889 he moved to Vevey, where he was pastor of the free church for almost 35 years, until his retirement in 1923. He wrote poetry and chorale texts and translated hymns from Latin, German and English. Some of his hymns were published in *Chants Évangéliques*, 1885 (Lausanne).

Song: Thine is the glory (152)

BUELL, Harriet Eugenia Peck

b Cazenovia, New York, 2 November 1834
d Washington, DC, 6 February 1910

Until 1898 she lived in Manlius, New York, where she was a member of the Methodist Episcopal Church. Apparently, after moving to Washington, DC in 1898, she continued to live at Thousand Island Park, New York, during the summer. For 50 years she contributed poetry regularly to the *Northern Christian Advocate*, in Syracuse, New York.

Song: My Father is rich in houses and lands (354)

BUNYAN, John

b Elstow, Bedfordshire, 1628
d London, 31 August 1688

Son of a tinker (a maker and mender of kettles, pots and pans), he was baptised on 30 November 1628. He followed his father's trade for some time, but, during the Civil War period, he was drafted into the Parliamentary army, 1644-47. He later joined an independent congregation in Bedford, whose minister, John Gifford, was a former Royalist major. He moved to Bedford in 1655 and began preaching in 1656. As a nonconformist preacher, he was imprisoned in Bedford, 1660-72 and again in 1676-77. Probably during this second period of imprisonment he started to write the first part of *The Pilgrim's Progress*, 1678 (Part 2, 1684). He became pastor of the Bedford congregation in 1672. His extensive writings included poetry and other books, including *Grace Abounding*, 1666 and *The Holy War*, 1682.

Song: He who would valiant be (685)

BURNS, James Drummond

b Edinburgh, 18 February 1823
d Mentone, France, 27 November 1864

Educated in Edinburgh, at the High School and the university. In 1843, he became a member of the Free Church and was ordained as a minister in 1845 at Dunblane. He went abroad in 1847 because of ill health and took charge of the Free Church congregation in Funchal, Madeira. When his health improved, he became minister of a new congregation at Hampstead, London, in 1855, but, with recurring illness, he moved to southern France in 1863. His publications included *The Vision of Prophecy and Other Poems*, 1854 (enlarged 1858), and *The Evening Hymn*, 1857 which contained an original hymn and prayer for every evening of the month. He contributed a short article on 'Hymns' to the *Encyclopaedia Britannica*, 8th edition.

Song: Hushed was the evening hymn (839)

BURRELL, William H.

b Sandy Stone, Sussex County, New Jersey, 13 October 1822
d Camden, New Jersey, 14 October 1909

He was active in the methodist ministry for 31 years, and spent the latter part of his life in Camden, New Jersey.

Song: With my faint, weary soul to be made fully whole (469)

BURTON, John (junior)

b Stratford, Essex, 23 July 1803
d Stratford, Essex, 22 January 1877

For about 50 years he was in business as a cooper and basket-maker, in Stratford. He was a deacon at the congregational chapel he attended, and for 27 years taught in a Sunday-school at Plaistow. He contributed hymns to the *Evangelical Magazine*, the *Child's Companion* and other periodicals, and also to the *Union Hymn Book for Scholars*, 1840. His own publications included *One Hundred Original Hymns for the Young*, 1850; *Hymns for Little Children*, 1851; and *The Book of Psalms in English Verse*, 1871.

Songs: I often say my prayers (588)
Saviour, while my heart is tender (865)

BURTON, John (senior)

b Nottingham, 26 February 1773
d Leicester, 24 June 1822

A member of the Baptist Church, he lived in Nottingham until 1813, when he moved to Leicester. He wrote his first hymns for his Sunday-school children, and was one of the compilers of the *Nottingham Sunday School Union Hymn Book*, 1812. He published *The Youth's Monitor in Verse, a series of Little Tales, Emblems, Poems and Songs*, 1803.

Song: Holy Bible, book divine (652)

BYROM, John

b Manchester, 29 February 1692
d Manchester, 26 September 1763

Son of a linen-draper, he was educated at Merchant Taylors' School, London, and Trinity College, Cambridge. In 1716, he went to Montpellier, France, to study medicine, but he did not qualify as a doctor. Returning to London, he invented a system of shorthand, which he taught to John and Charles Wesley, among other people. He was elected a Fellow of the Royal Society in 1724. His poetry was published posthumously in his *Poems*, 1773, and an enlarged edition in 1814.

Song: Christians awake, salute the happy morn (78)

CAMPBELL, Jane Montgomery

b Paddington, Middlesex, 1817
d Bovey Tracey, Devon, 15 November 1878

Daughter of the Reverend A. Montgomery Campbell, rector of St James's Church, Paddington. She taught music in the parish school there and published some of her musical exercises in *A Handbook for Singers*. Later, while living at Bovey Tracey, she translated a number of German hymns which she contributed to *A Garland of Songs*, 1862, and *Children's Choral Book*, 1869, compiled by the Reverend Charles S. Bere. Apparently, she died as a result of a carriage accident on Dartmoor.

Song: We plough the fields, and scatter (935)

CAMPBELL, John Douglas Sutherland

b Westminster, Middlesex, 6 August 1845
d East Cowes, Isle of Wight, 2 May 1914

Educated at Eton, St Andrews and Trinity College, Cambridge. As the Marquis of Lorne, he was Member of Parliament for Argyllshire, 1868-78, and for three years was also private secretary to his father. In 1871, he married Princess Louise, fourth daughter of Queen Victoria, and served as Governor-General of Canada, 1878-83. Later he was appointed Governor and Constable of Windsor Castle, in 1892, and was MP for Manchester South from 1895 until he became Ninth Duke of Argyll in 1900. His many publications included *The Book of Psalms, literally rendered in verse*, 1877; *Canadian Life and Scenery*, 1886; and *The Governor's Guide to Windsor Castle*, 1895.

Song: Unto the hills around do I lift up (767)

CARTER, Russell Kelso

b Baltimore, Maryland, 18 November 1849
d Catonsville, Maryland, 23 August 1926

After graduating from the Pennsylvania Military Academy in Chester, he became an instructor there, and later, professor of chemistry and natural sciences, in 1872, and professor of civil engineering and higher mathematics, in 1881. For a short while, 1873-76, he was engaged in sheep rearing in California. He was ordained as a methodist minister in 1887 and was active in the Holiness movement and camp meetings, but subsequently he studied medicine and became a physician in Baltimore. He contributed hymns and tunes to *Hymns of the Christian Life*, 1891 which he edited with the Reverend Albert B. Simpson, for the Christian and Missionary Alliance.

Songs: Once I was far in sin (374, chorus)
Standing on the promises of Christ my King (757)

CARTER, Ruth

b Clapton, London, 22 August 1900
d Clacton-on-Sea, Essex, 4 November 1982

Educated at Farringtons School, in Kent, and later, at Westhill Training College, Birmingham. Her family moved to Buckhurst Hill, Essex, in 1909, and she became a member of the Congregational (later United Reformed) Church there in 1919, becoming involved in a number of church activities, including Sunday-school. Until her retirement in 1975 she was a teacher, and, for about 20 years, did remedial teaching for individual children at her home.

Song: For your holy book we thank you (856)

CASSON, Hodgson

b Workington, Cumberland, 1788
d Birstal, Yorkshire, 23 November 1851

He was the eldest in a family of 11 children. After about five years as a local preacher in the Whitehaven circuit, he became a methodist minister in 1815, and walked more than 120 miles to his first appointment, in the Ayr and Kilmarnock circuit. Subsequently he served in Kendal, 1817-19; Brough and Penrith, 1819-21; Dumfries, 1821-24; Richmond and Reeth, 1824-27; Gateshead, 1827-30; Durham, 1830-33; North and South Shields, 1833-36; and Birstal, 1836-39. He retired in 1839, but continued to preach in Birstal and in neighbouring circuits for several years.

Song: My Saviour suffered on the tree (360)

CASWALL, Edward

b Yately, Hampshire, 15 July 1814
d Edgbaston, Warwickshire, 2 January 1878

Son of the Reverend Robert Clarke Caswall, vicar of Yately. He was educated at Chigwell Grammar School, Marlborough School and Brasenose College, Oxford. After his ordination in

1838, he served as curate at Bishop's Norton and Milverton, Somerset; St Dunstan's, Fleet Street, London; and Shenley, Hertfordshire. He was perpetual curate at Stratford-sub-Castle, near Salisbury, 1840-46, but joined the Roman Catholic Church in 1847. After his wife died in 1849 he entered the Oratory of St Philip Neri, at Edgbaston, Birmingham, and was ordained as a Roman catholic priest in 1852. His translations of Latin hymns appeared in several publications, including *Lyra Catholica*, 1849 and *The Masque of Mary, and other poems*, 1858.

Songs: I met the good shepherd (111)
Jesus, the very thought of thee (61)
See, amid the winter's snow (88)
When morning gilds the skies (187)

CHANDLER, John

b Witley, Surrey, 16 June 1806
d Putney, Surrey, 1 July 1876

Son of the Reverend John F. Chandler, vicar of Witley, Godalming, Surrey. He was educated at Corpus Christi College, Oxford, and was ordained in 1831. He succeeded his father as vicar of Witley in 1837. His *Hymns of the Primitive Church*, 1837, included translations of 108 Latin hymns, mainly from the *Paris Breviary*, 1736. His other publications included *Life of William of Wykeham*, 1842; and *Horae Sacrae: Prayers and Meditations*, 1844.

Song: Christ is our corner-stone (940)

CHARLES, Elisabeth (*née* RUNDLE)

b Tavistock, Devon, 2 January 1828
d Hampstead, London, 28 March 1896

Daughter of John Rundle, a banker and a Member of Parliament. In 1851 she married a barrister, Andrew Paton Charles, and was later sometimes known as Elisabeth Rundle Charles (or Rundle-Charles). She was a member of the Church of England, and was a poet, a translator, a musician, a painter and the author of more than 25 books, including *The Voice of Christian Life in Song*, 1858; *The Three Wakings, with Hymns and Songs*, 1859; and *Songs Old and New*, 1882.

Song: Come and rejoice with me (311)

CHESHAM, Albert E.

b Scunthorpe, Lincolnshire, 7 June 1886
d Falls Church, Virginia, 16 September 1971

His family moved to Canada when he was a boy, and he grew up on the Prairies in western Canada. Later he was one of 10 'cowboys' who represented America at the International Congress in London in 1914. Converted in Spokane, Washington in 1905, he was commissioned as a Salvation Army officer in Chicago in 1907. He served as a corps officer in the Western States and then at headquarters in Minneapolis, where he became divisional commander in 1925. Subsequently he was the field secretary, 1938-41 and chief secretary, 1941-47, in the Central Territory; and territorial commander, 1947-52, in the Southern Territory. He retired as a lieut-commissioner in 1952.

Song: O Father and Creator (221)

CHISHOLM, Thomas Obediah

b near Franklin, Simpson County, Kentucky, 29 July 1866
d Ocean Grove, New Jersey, 29 February 1960

At the age of 16 he was a teacher in the country school he had attended, and five years later became editor of the weekly newspaper the *Franklin Favorite*. He was converted in 1893, in revival meetings conducted by Dr Henry Morrison and moved to Louisville as editor of Morrison's *Pentecostal Herald*. After ordination as a methodist minister in 1903, he served for a year at Scottsville, Kentucky, but because of illness moved to a farm near Winona Lake, Indiana. He became an insurance agent in Winona Lake, and later in Vineland, New Jersey, and he retired to the methodist home in Ocean Grove in 1953. He wrote more than 1,200 poems and gospel songs.

Songs: Great is thy faithfulness, O God my Father (33)
O to be like thee! blessèd Redeemer (623)

CLARK, W. H.

b ?
d ?

Little is known about the author, though he was probably American, *c*1880, and may also have written the hymn 'All praise to him who reigns above', attributed to W. H. Clark, *c* 1888, in *The Mennonite Hymnal*, 1969, and an anthem, by William H. Clark, in *The Church Bell*, 1867, compiled by W. O. Perkins.

Songs: Give to Jesus glory (952)
To save the world the Saviour came (831, chorus)

CLAUDIUS, Matthias

b Reinfeld, near Lübeck, Germany, 15 August 1740
d Hamburg, Germany, 21 January 1815

Son of Matthias Claudius, Lutheran pastor at Reinfeld, he was educated at the University of Jena, studying theology, law and languages. After a short period as a private secretary in Copenhagen, he became a journalist and newspaper editor in Hamburg in 1768, and then in Wandsbeck, near Hamburg, in 1771. He was appointed as a Commissioner of Agriculture and Manufactures of Hesse-Darmstadt, in 1776, and in the following year became editor of the official Hesse-Darmstadt newspaper. After a serious illness in 1777, he returned to Wandsbeck, as editor of the *Wandsbecker Bote*, and continued to live at Wandsbeck when he was appointed auditor of the Schleswig-Holstein Bank at Altona, in 1788. He moved to live with a daughter in Hamburg shortly before he died.

Song: We plough the fields, and scatter (935)

CLAYTON, Norman John

b Brooklyn, New York, 22 January 1903

Converted in the South Brooklyn Gospel Church, he has served as a church organist for more than 50 years. In his early years, he worked on a dairy farm, then in an office in New York City, and later in the construction business, with his father, and for a commercial bakery manufacturer. In 1942 he joined the staff of Jack Wyrtzen, as organist and vibraharpist for the 'Word of Life' rallies in New York City. At this time he was also associated with the Sunday Morning Radio Bible Class and with Bellerose Baptist Church. He published gospel song books, 1945-59, and when his publishing company merged with the Rodeheaver Company in 1959, he became a writer, editor and arranger for the company. He has lived in Centreport, New York since 1960.

Song: Jesus my Lord will love me for ever (349)

CLEPHANE, Elizabeth Cecilia Douglas

b Edinburgh, 18 June 1830
d Melrose, Roxburghshire, 19 February 1869

Daughter of Andrew Douglas Clephane, Sheriff Principal of Fife and Kinross. She was a member of the Free Church of Scotland and, after the death of her father, lived at Ormiston, East Lothian, and later at Bridgend House, near Melrose. She was known as 'Sunbeam' for her humanitarian work in Melrose. Her hymns were published posthumously in a magazine, *The Family Treasury*, 1872-74.

Song: Beneath the cross of Jesus (476)

COBB, A. P.

b ?
d ?

Little is known about the author, who was probably American, *c*1890.

Song: Do you know the song that the angels sang (80)

CODNER, Elizabeth (*née* HARRIS)

b Dartmouth, Devon, 1823
d Croydon, Surrey, 28 March 1919

Daughter of Robert Harris, of Dartmouth. In 1849 she married the Reverend Daniel Codner, who was for some time curate of Peterborough. For several years she was associated with the work of the Reverend William Pennefather at the Mildmay Protestant Mission in London, and edited the monthly magazine *Woman's Work in the Great Harvest Field*, published by the mission. She wrote a number of pamphlets and books, including *Among the Brambles*, 1880, and *Behind the Cloud*, 1885.

Song: Lord, I hear of showers of blessing (295)

COLES, Bramwell

b Cambridge, 22 February 1887
d Folkestone, Kent, 9 August 1960

Son of Salvation Army officers, he worked as a junior clerk at International Headquarters and entered the International Training College from Chalk Farm, in 1914. After service as a corps officer at Middlesbrough North Ormesby, New Barnet and Hendon, he worked in the Editorial Department at International Headquarters, 1921-23, and in the Music Editorial Department, 1923-25. He was then appointed to the editorial staff in Toronto, and served in Canada until 1936, when he became Head of the Music Editorial Department in London. He retired from that appointment as a colonel in 1952. Often known as 'the Army's Sousa', after the American march composer, John Philip Sousa, he won first prize for his march 'Chalk Farm' in a music competition in 1909. He subsequently contributed more than 100 compositions to the band journals, as well as many songs to *The Musical Salvationist*.

Song: How can I better serve thee, Lord (488)

COLLER, Charles

b Romford, Essex, 5 March 1863
d Edmonton, Middlesex, 21 March 1935

Son of Wellesley Mason Coller, a shoemaker. He grew up in Woodford, but, after starting work in London, he became a salvationist at Regent Hall in 1885. He was a member of the Household Troops Band on its first campaign in 1887 and was later a trombone player in the International Staff Band. From

1895 he worked in various Salvation Army trade depots and then in the Trade Department (later Salvationist Publishing and Supplies, Ltd) in London. His last appointment was in charge of the music publications department, and he retired as a major in 1928. In 1880 he won a copy of Heber's *Poems* as a prize for a temperance acrostic, and, from 1895, he contributed more than 200 songs to *The Musical Salvationist*.

Songs: From the heart of Jesus flowing (539)
Hark! the sounds of singing (803)
Joyful news to all mankind (249)
Make the world with music ring (809)
Our Father, who in Heaven art (624)
Salvation! Shout salvation (828)
To God be the glory, a Saviour is mine (640)
Unto thee, O Saviour-King (532)

COLLINS, William Giles

b Kingswood, Gloucestershire, 11 September 1854
d Guildford, Surrey, 1 June 1931

Son of William Giles Collins, a farmer. He served his apprenticeship in Cardiff and in 1876 moved to Guildford, where he was an ironmonger for more than 50 years. When the Army opened in Guildford in 1881, he became a salvationist, serving for some time as corps secretary and band secretary and then as corps sergeant-major until his retirement early in 1931. He contributed a number of songs to *The War Cry* and *The Musical Salvationist*.

Songs: Before I found salvation (309)
Once I was lost, on the breakers tossed (375)

COLLYER, William Bengo

b Deptford, Kent, 14 April 1782
d Peckham, Surrey, 9 January 1854

Educated for the ministry at Homerton College, he served as pastor of a congregational church at Peckham for more than 50 years. He was also pastor of a congregation which met in Salters' Hall, London, 1814-26. He compiled *Hymns partly collected and partly original, designed as a Supplement to Dr*

Watts's Psalms and Hymns, 1812, which included 57 of his hymns, and many others were published in the *Evangelical Magazine*, in his *Services suited to the Solemnization of Matrimony, Baptism, etc*, 1837, and appended to his published sermons.

Song: Return, O wanderer, return (256)

CONDER, Josiah

b London, 17 September 1789
d Hampstead, Middlesex, 27 December 1855

Son of Thomas Conder, an engraver and bookseller, he went to work in his father's bookshop at the age of 13 and became the owner in 1811, when his father retired. He was proprietor and editor of the *Eclectic Review*, 1814-37, and editor of *The Patriot*, a nonconformist newspaper established in 1832. He wrote hymns and poems, and contributed 56 hymns to *The Congregational Hymn Book: a Supplement to Dr Watts's Psalms and Hymns*, 1836, which he edited. His other publications included *The Star in the East*, 1824; a *Dictionary of Ancient and Modern Geography*, 1834; a *Life of Bunyan*, 1835; and *The Choir and the Oratory; or Praise and Prayer*, 1837.

Song: Day by day the manna fell (566)

COOKE, Oliver Mark

b Little London, Kennington, Berkshire, 13 July 1873
d West Ashford, Kent, 5 March 1945

Son of Mark Cooke, a farm labourer. His family moved to London, where he studied music, gaining the London College of Music certificate for organ playing. He learnt to play a cornet at the Borough Corps, and later served as bandmaster at Peckham, and then as songster leader, first at Nunhead, and then at Lewisham. He contributed his first song to *The War Cry* in October 1888, and wrote regularly for *The Musical Salvationist* during the next 50 years.

Song: Say, are you weary? Are you heavy laden (257)

COOPER, F. S.

b ?
d ?

Nothing is known about the author.

Song: Take thou my hand and guide me (635)

COUCH, Rebecca Rhoda (*née* FOSTER)

b Gillingham, Kent, 14 March 1853
d Barming Heath, Kent, 21 May 1946

Daughter of Richard T. Foster, a writer at HM Dockyard, Chatham. In 1875, she married Mark Couch, a lance-corporal in the Royal Engineers. In 1881 they lived in Cross Street, New Brompton, Kent, and later at 2 Albany Terrace, Gillingham, Kent. The song now attributed to her appeared in *The War Cry*, 22 December 1881, under the name 'R. R. Couch, New Brompton', so at that time she may have been a salvationist in the New Brompton (later Gillingham) corps.

Song: We have a message, a message from Jesus (273)

COULL, Rose or Rosina (*née* NICOL)

b Battersea, Surrey, 29 July 1876
d Greenock, Renfrewshire, 4 February 1957

For many years she served as an officer in the Australia Southern Territory, latterly with the rank of major. She was Divisional Secretary in the Northam Division (Western Australia) and later in Melbourne East Division, and for a time she was territorial guard organiser. Following her retirement she married a former bandmaster from Hamilton (Scotland). After moving to Scotland she was a soldier at the Dunoon Corps. She contributed a number of songs to *The Musical Salvationist* in the period 1912-40.

Song: Was it for me, the nails, the spear (134)

COUSIN, Anne Ross (*née* CUNDELL)

b Kingston-upon-Hull, Yorkshire, 27 April 1824
d Edinburgh, 6 December 1906

Daughter of Dr David Ross Cundell, a physician. She grew up in the Anglican Church, but became a presbyterian and married William Cousin, a presbyterian minister, in 1847. He served at churches in Chelsea, London, and later in Irvine and Melrose, in Scotland. After retirement they lived in Edinburgh. She was a musician and a linguist, and contributed a number of hymns and poems to *The Christian Treasury*, and other periodicals. Many of these were included in her anthology *Immanuel's Land, and other pieces*, 1876.

Song: The sands of time are sinking (896)

COWPER, William

b Great Berkhampstead, Hertfordshire, 15 November 1731
d East Dereham, Norfolk, 25 April 1800

Son of Dr John Cowper, chaplain to King George II and rector of Great Berkhampstead. He was educated at Westminster School, and was called to the Bar in 1754, but did not practise as a barrister. He was nominated as Clerk to the Journals of the House of Lords, but declined the position because he feared appearing before the House for examination. He suffered periods of depression throughout his life, but he received encouragement and support from friends with whom he lived: Dr Nathaniel Cotton, at St Albans, 1763-65; the Reverend and Mrs Morley Unwin, at Huntingdon, 1765-68; and the widowed Mrs Unwin, at Olney, 1768-86, Weston Underwood, 1786-95 and East Dereham. At Olney, he assisted the curate, the Reverend John Newton, with parish work and contributed to the *Olney Hymns*, 1779, compiled by John Newton. After John Newton had moved to London in 1780, Cowper published his first volume of *Poems*, 1782, and wrote some of his best-known poetry, including 'The Task' and 'John Gilpin'.

Songs: All scenes alike engaging prove (556)
God moves in a mysterious way (29)
Hark, my soul! it is the Lord (110)

Jesus, where'er thy people meet (604)
O for a closer walk with God (442)
The Spirit breathes upon the word (657)
There is a fountain filled with blood (132)
What various hindrances we meet (646)

COX, Sidney Edward

b Northampton, 29 June 1887
d Birmingham, Alabama, 22 September 1975

He emigrated to Canada in 1907 and was educated at the Garbutt Business College and the Cooper Institute of Accountancy. Converted in the Central Methodist Church in Calgary in 1908, he immediately joined The Salvation Army there, entering the training college in Toronto in 1909. He served for several years in Canada, at the Toronto training college, in corps appointments, and at divisional and territorial headquarters. Subsequently, after a period as education director of Moody Bible Institute in Chicago, he served in the USA Southern Territory as education secretary; territorial young people's secretary (eight years); principal of the training college (four years): and territorial revivalist (three years). In 1944 he became an independent evangelist, conducting campaigns throughout the USA and Canada, and also teaching in Bible colleges, in Miami, Florida and Atlanta, Georgia. In later years he recorded tapes for home Bible study groups. His early song writing was encouraged by William A. Hawley, in Calgary, and his first published song appeared in *The Musical Salvationist* in June 1915.

Songs: Are you seeking joys that will not fade (227)
By the peaceful shores of Galilee (680)
God's love to me is wonderful (48)
I am amazed when I think of God's love (319)
I am drinking at the fountain (320, chorus)
I want to tell what God has done (335)
In my heart there's a gladsome melody (340)
In the love of Jesus I have found a refuge (341)
It was love reached me when far away (342)
Jesus came to save me (347)
One golden dawning, one glorious morning (888)
Tell out the wonderful story (384)
The Saviour sought and found me (386)
There's a path that's sometimes thorny (462)
There's a road of high adventure (868, chorus)
There's a song that's ringing in my heart today (389)

CRAFTS, Wilbur Fisk

b Fryeburg, Maine, 12 January 1850
d Washington, DC, 27 December 1922

Son of the Reverend Frederick A. Crafts, a methodist minister. He was educated at Wesleyan University, Connecticut and at Boston University. He served as a methodist minister for several years and then as pastor of congregational and presbyterian churches. Later, he founded the American Sabbath Union in 1889, and for more than 25 years he was superintendent of the International Reform Bureau, which he founded in 1895. He contributed extensively to magazines and wrote numerous books, including *Trophies of Song*, 1874; *Song Victories*, 1877; *Bible Stories and Poems*, 1914; and a *History of National Prohibition*, 1920. (He was a member of a national commission to frame a constitutional amendment on prohibition, 1915-16.)

Song: I stand all bewildered with wonder (542)

CROSBY, Fanny

b Southeast, Putnam County, New York, 24 March 1820
d Bridgeport, Connecticut, 12 February 1915

Named Frances Jane, but usually known as Fanny, she was blind almost from birth because an early eye infection was incorrectly treated by an unqualified doctor. She attended the New York Institution for the Blind, became a teacher there, and in 1858 married Alexander Van Alstine (or Van Alsteine), who had been a music instructor at the Institution. At the age of eight she started writing poetry, and published her first book, *The Blind Girl, and Other Poems*, in 1844. Later she wrote about 9,000 hymns and gospel songs for various composers, using more then 200 pen names. Almost 6,000 songs were written for the publishers Biglow and Main, of New York. As she could actually write only her name, she composed the verses in her mind and dictated them to a friend or a secretary. She lived for many years in Manhattan, but moved to Brooklyn in 1896, and later to Bridgeport, Connecticut, in 1900, after 65 years in New York.

Songs: A wonderful Saviour is Jesus, my Lord (710)
Behold me standing at the door (229)

Blessèd assurance, Jesus is mine (310)
Come with happy faces (836)
God's trumpet is sounding: To arms! is the call (684, chorus)
Hold thou my hand! so weak I am, and helpless (726)
I am praying, blessèd Saviour (584)
I am thine, O Lord; I have heard thy voice (585)
I must have the Saviour with me (731)
Jesus is tenderly calling thee home (248)
Jesus, keep me near the cross (115)
O soldier, awake, for the strife is at hand (689)
Only a step to Jesus (255)
Pass me not, O loving Saviour (301)
Praise him! Praise him! Jesus our blessèd redeemer (184)
Rescue the perishing, care for the dying (691)
Safe in the arms of Jesus (889)
Sinner, how thy heart is troubled (259)
Sinner, whereso'er thou art (261)
So near to the Kingdom! yet what dost thou lack (263)
Tell me the story of Jesus (99)
Though your sins be as scarlet (272)
To God be the glory, great things he hath done (22)
We are marching on with shield and banner bright (818)

CUSHING, William Orcutt

b Hingham Center, Massachusetts, 31 December 1823
d Lisbon, New York, 19 October 1902

A minister of the Christian Church (Disciples of Christ), he served as pastor of churches in Searsburg, Auburn, Brookley, Buffalo and Sparta, New York, but retired in 1870 because of ill health, following the death of his wife. He developed an interest in writing and wrote more than 300 hymns which were set to music by Ira D. Sankey, George F. Root, Robert Lowry and other composers.

Songs: Down in the valley with my Saviour I would go (483)
Ring the bells of Heaven, there is joy today (550)
When he cometh, when he cometh (852)

DALZIEL, Albert Ernest

b Islington, London, 10 April 1892
d Toronto, Canada, 29 December 1974

Son of Alexander Dalziel, a foreman builder and a salvationist at King's Cross Corps. He became corps secretary and then deputy bandmaster there before he entered the training college in 1912. In the following year he was commissioned as assistant cadets' sergeant-major and became conductor of the cadets' band. After several corps and divisional appointments, he served on the training college staff, 1923-30, and then moved to Canada as Training Principal (Canada West) in Winnipeg, 1930-32; Divisional Commander for British Columbia, and Training Principal in Toronto, 1937-39. Returning to Britain, he was Chief Side Officer for Men at the International Training College, and subsequently General Secretary for Scotland and Ireland; Staff Secretary for the British Territory; Director of the European Relief Work, 1946-49; Chief Secretary for South Africa for five years; and finally Provincial Commander in Newfoundland. He retired as a colonel in 1957. He wrote poetry, choruses and songs, sometimes in collaboration with General Albert Orsborn. In retirement he helped to compile *Songs of Faith*, 1971, published in Canada.

Song: Eternal God, unchanging (6)

DARWOOD, William McKendree

b c1835
d Little River, Connecticut, 27 April 1914

After serving as pastor of several methodist episcopal churches in Indiana, he moved to New York, where he was minister at Bedford Street Church for three years, followed by three years at Washington Heights Church and five years in Yonkers. He was then pastor of the Eighteenth Street Church, New York, from 1899 until he retired from active ministry, five years before he died.

Song: On Calvary's brow my Saviour died (125)

DAVIES, Howard

b Melbourne, Australia, 12 November 1940

Son of salvationists. He started to learn the violin at the age of seven and later obtained the Associate Musician of Australia (violin) diploma. Before entering the training college in Melbourne in 1964 he was bandmaster at the Camberwell (Victoria) Corps and worked as a bank clerk. After commissioning in 1966 he served on the training college staff for a year and was then a corps officer for six years at Broadford and Shepparton, Victoria. In 1972 he was appointed to the International Music Editorial Department in London and was also a member of the International Staff Band (baritone) for four years. Returning to Australia in 1976 he again served as a corps officer and in 1984 was appointed to the training college in Melbourne, where he was senior training officer, and then became assistant training principal in 1986. He has composed musicals about the lives of William Booth and George Scott Railton, and has contributed songs regularly to *The Musical Salvationist*, as well as brass band compositions and arrangements for the band journals.

Song: Many are the things I cannot understand (52)

DAVIES, Marjorie Beryl (*née* SMITH)

b Portslade, Sussex, 27 July 1920

The daughter of salvationists at Portslade, she was converted at the age of nine. In 1935 her family moved to Carshalton, where she became young people's singing company leader and then corps secretary. She entered the training college in 1941 and, after her commissioning in the following year, served in corps appointments in the Cardiff and Swansea Divisions. In 1949 she married 2nd Lieutenant William Davies and they have since served together as corps officers (at Port Talbot; in South Yorkshire; and at Brighton Edward Street) and then at Penang Boys' Home, 1960-65, where she was matron of the boys' home and English school. Returning to England they again served in corps appointments, including Welling, Winton, Penge and Bromley, subsequently becoming County Evangelists in South Somerset, 1983-87, and then in Lincolnshire. Encouraged by the song-writer Will J. Brand, at Welling, she has contributed songs and poems to various Salvation Army publications.

Song: Lord, with joyful hearts we worship (795)

DAVIS, Frank M.

b near Marcellus, Onondaga County, New York, 23 January 1839
d Chesterfield, Indiana, 1 August 1896

The youngest of a family of 10 children, he started to compose songs as a boy, and attended village singing schools. At home, he learnt to play the melodeon and, later, the piano. He travelled extensively, living in various places, including Baltimore, Maryland; Cincinnati, Ohio; and Burr Oak and Findley, Michigan. He taught vocal and instrumental music, conducted choirs and performed as a soloist. His first book for Sunday-schools, *New Pearls of Song*, 1877, was followed by other song books for Sunday-schools and the temperance movement, including *Notes of Praise* and *Brightest Glory*.

Song: Saviour, lead me, lest I stray (627)

DAVIS, William Henry

b Wanstead, Essex, 19 April 1854
d Balham, London, 6 November 1918

Known as Harry Davis, he was the son of William Davis, a coachman. By trade, he was a packing-case maker, and became a salvationist in Whitechapel, where he was apparently a member of the brass band formed there in 1880. Later he transferred to Stepney, and subsequently to Balham Congress Hall. He wrote 300-400 songs, the majority of which were published in *The War Cry* and *The Musical Salvationist*. His first song appeared in *The War Cry* in January 1880.

Songs: Jesus, precious Saviour, thou hast saved my soul (499)
        Lord, for a mighty revival we plead (608)
        Thou Lamb of God, whose precious blood (638)

DEARMER, Percy

b Kilburn, Middlesex, 27 February 1867
d Westminster, 29 May 1936

Educated at Westminster School, at Vevey, in Switzerland, and at Christ Church, Oxford. After his ordination in 1891, he served as curate in several London parishes, and was vicar of

St Mary's, Primrose Hill, 1901-15. (Martin Shaw became organist there in 1908.) He was secretary of the London branch of the Christian Social Union, 1891-1912, and, during the First World War, served as chaplain to the British Red Cross in Serbia, and then as a lecturer for the YMCA. In 1919, he was appointed professor of ecclesiastical art at King's College, London, and in 1931 he was made a canon of Westminster. He edited the *English Hymnal*, 1906, with Ralph Vaughan Williams as music editor, and later compiled *Songs of Praise*, 1925 and 1931, and the *Oxford Book of Carols*, 1928, with Vaughan Williams and Martin Shaw. He also wrote the handbook *Songs of Praise Discussed*, 1933.

Songs: He who would valiant be (685)
Jesus, good above all other (97)
Let us rejoice, the fight is won (146)

DITMER, Stanley E.

b Youngstown, Ohio, 6 November 1924

Son of Salvation Army officers, he served in the US Navy for three years as a radio instructor and then studied at Oberlin College Conservatory of Music, before entering the school for officers' training in New York in 1948, from Toledo, Ohio. He served in corps appointments and on the training college staff, and also in various appointments as a divisional and territorial youth leader. Subsequently he has been Divisional Commander for Eastern New York; Territorial Secretary for Program, USA Eastern; Chief Secretary, USA Southern; and Territorial Commander, USA Central Territory. He was appointed Territorial Commander for the USA Eastern Territory in 1986. About 30 of his vocal and instrumental compositions have been published.

Song: I shall not fear though darkened clouds may gather round me (732)

DIX, William Chatterton

b Bristol, 14 June 1837
d Cheddar, Somerset, 9 September 1898

Son of a surgeon, William John Dix, who wrote a biography of the poet, Thomas Chatterton. He was educated at Bristol

Grammar School, and later became manager of a marine insurance company in Glasgow. He wrote hymns and poems, and versified translations from Greek hymns and other sources. His publications included *Hymns of Love and Joy*, 1861; *Altar Songs, Verses on the Holy Eucharist*, 1867; *A Vision of All Saints*, 1871; and *Seekers of a City*, 1878.

Songs: As with gladness men of old (76)
To thee, O Lord, our hearts we raise (934)

DOANE, George Washington

b Trenton, New Jersey, 27 May 1799
d Burlington, New Jersey, 27 April 1859

He studied law at Union College, Schenectady, New York, and theology at the General Theological Seminary, New York City. After his ordination in 1821 he served as assistant priest at Trinity Church, New York, and in 1824 became professor of rhetoric and belles-lettres at Washington College, Hartford, Connecticut. Subsequently, he was assistant minister, and later rector, of Trinity Church, Boston, and in 1832 he was consecrated Bishop of New Jersey. He promoted the church missionary movement and the establishment of church schools, and founded St Mary's Hall, Burlington, for girls, in 1837 and Burlington College, for men, in 1846. Some of his many hymns were published in *Songs by the Way, Chiefly Devotional*, 1824.

Song: Thou art the way: to thee alone (100)

DOANE, William Howard

b Preston, Connecticut, 3 February 1832
d South Orange, New Jersey, 24 December 1915

He attended Woodstock Academy, where he conducted the school choir at the age of 14. As a young man, he worked for three years in his father's cotton manufacturing business, but he then joined J. A. Fay & Co, manufacturers of woodworking machinery, and moved with the firm to Cincinnati, in 1860, where he later became president of the firm. He was superintendent of the Mount Auburn Baptist Sunday-school, in Auburn, Ohio, for about 25 years. He composed more than

2,000 gospel song tunes, many for verses by Fanny Crosby, and published at least 35 collections of songs for Sunday-schools and mission meetings, including *Sabbath Gems*, 1861; *Songs of Devotion*, 1870; and *Royal Diadem*, 1873.

Song: On to the conflict, soldiers, for the right (813)

DODDRIDGE, Philip

b London, 26 June 1702
d Lisbon, Portugal, 26 October 1751

Son of an oilman, the youngest of 20 children, though only two survived infancy, he was educated at Kingston Grammar School, and then at St Albans and at the nonconformist academy at Kibworth, Leicestershire. He preached his first sermon at the age of 20 and became pastor of the independent congregation at Kibworth, in 1723. Six years later, he opened an academy at Market Harborough, to train young men for the ministry, but, in the following year, he moved the academy to Northampton when he was appointed pastor of the Castle Hill Meeting. He served there until 1751 when he travelled to Lisbon, because of illness, shortly before he died. He wrote many books on theology, notably *The Rise and Progress of Religion in the Soul*, 1745. His hymns were published posthumously, by his friend Job Orton, in *Hymns founded on Various Texts in the Holy Scriptures*, 1755, and by his great-grandson, John Doddridge Humphreys, in *Scriptural Hymns by the Rev Philip Doddridge*, 1839.

Songs: Eternal Source of every joy (925)
Hark the glad sound! the Saviour comes (81)
O God of Bethel, by whose hand (918)
O happy day that fixed my choice (365)

DOWNTON, Henry

b Pulverbatch, Shropshire, 12 February 1818
d Hopton, Suffolk, 8 June 1885

Son of John Downton, sub-librarian of Trinity College, Cambridge. He was educated at Trinity College, Cambridge, and, after his ordination in 1843, served as curate of Bembridge, Isle of Wight, and then Holy Trinity, Cambridge, before becoming perpetual curate of St John's, Chatham, in 1849. He went to Geneva in 1857, as British Chaplain, then after returning to England, was appointed rector of Hopton, in 1873. He contributed hymns to the *Church of England Magazine* and also translated some French hymns, which were included in his *Hymns and Verses*, 1873.

Song: For thy mercy and thy grace (937)

DRAPER, William Henry

b Kenilworth, Warwickshire, 19 December 1855
d Clifton, Bristol, 9 August 1933

Educated at Cheltenham College and Keble College, Oxford. After his ordination in 1880, he served as curate of St Mary's, Shrewsbury, 1880-83; vicar of Alfreton, 1883-89; vicar of the Abbey Church, Shrewsbury, 1889-99; and rector of Adel, Leeds, 1899-1919. He was then Master of the Temple, in London, until 1930, when he became vicar of Axbridge, Somerset. He translated a number of hymns from Latin and Greek, and published *The Victoria Book of Hymns*, 1897, and *Hymns for Holy Week*, 1899.

Song: All creatures of our God and King (2)

DRIVER, John Merritte

b 1858
d 6 June 1918

Son of James R. Driver, he was educated at Illinois Agricultural College and Boston University. Becoming a minister in the Methodist Episcopal Church, he was pastor of People's Church, Chicago, 1902-07. He published several books and was joint editor of *Songs of the Soul*, 1885.

Song: Wonderful story of love (139)

DUFF, Mildred Blanche

b Westminster, 26 January 1860
d Westwick, Norfolk, 8 December 1932

Daughter of Colonel James Duff, who had served in the Crimean War and was later Member of Parliament for North Norfolk. She grew up at Westwick House, Norfolk, and her family's home in Upper Brook Street, London, and attended her first Salvation Army meetings at the Exeter Hall, London, and later at North Walsham, Norfolk. After the first International Congress in 1886, she accompanied Major Hanna Ouchterlony to Sweden, and, following two months' training in London, served as Training Home Mother in Stockholm and as a corps officer in Malmö. Returning to England in 1888, she was on the staff of the training home for five years and then took charge of the London Slums Division in 1894. Shortly afterwards, she was appointed editor of *All the World*, later becoming editor of *The Young Soldier, The Warrior, The Life-Saving Scout and Guard*, and the *International Company Orders*. She also travelled as *aide-de-camp* with Mrs General Bramwell Booth. She retired as a commissioner in 1926.

Song: The heart that once has Jesus known (267)

DUFFIELD, George

b Carlisle, Pennsylvania, 12 September 1818
d Bloomfield, New Jersey, 6 July 1888

Educated at Yale College and Union Theological Seminary, New York. He became a presbyterian minister in 1840 and served as pastor of churches in Brooklyn, 1840-47; Bloomfield, New Jersey, 1847-52; Philadelphia, 1852-61; Adrian, Michigan, 1861-65; Galesburg, Illinois, 1865-69; Saginaw City, Michigan, in 1869; and Ann Arbor and Lansing, Michigan, 1869-84. For some years, he was editor of the presbyterian newspaper, the *Christian Observer*. After his retirement in 1884, he lived in Detroit and latterly in Bloomfield, New Jersey, with his son, the Reverend Samuel W. Duffield, author of *English Hymns, Their Authors and History*, 1886.

Song: Stand up, stand up for Jesus (699)

DUNKERLEY, William Arthur ('John Oxenham')

b Cheetham, Manchester, 12 November 1852
d High Salvington, Worthing, Sussex, 23 January 1941

Educated at Old Trafford School and Victoria University, Manchester, he travelled extensively on business in Europe and North America. Returning to England, he published a London edition of the *Detroit Free Press* and other periodicals, with Robert Barr and Jerome K. Jerome. Under the pseudonym 'John Oxenham' (derived from a character in *Westward Ho!*) he wrote more than 40 novels and several small books of verse, including *Bees in Amber*, 1913; *The King's High Way*, 1916; and *The Vision Splendid*, 1917. He was a Bible class teacher and a deacon at Ealing Congregational Church, West London.

Songs: In Christ there is no east or west (826)
'Mid all the traffic of the ways (615)
Peace in our time, O Lord (827)

EDGAR, Mary Susanne

b Sundridge, Ontario, Canada, 23 May 1889
d Toronto, Canada, 17 September 1973

Educated at Havergal College and the University of Toronto, and also by correspondence with the University of Chicago. She was a graduate of the YWCA National Training School, New York City, and was associated with the YWCA and camp work in Canada for many years. In 1922, she founded Camp Glen Bernard for Girls, in northern Ontario. She was a member of the Anglican Church and lived in Toronto after her retirement in 1955. She published collections of poems and essays, including *Woodfire and Candlelight*, 1945; *Under Open Skies*, 1955; and *A Christmas Wreath of Verse*, 1965.

Song: God who touchest earth with beauty (32)

EDMESTON, James

b Wapping, Middlesex, 10 September 1791
d Homerton, Middlesex, 7 January 1867

He was an architect and surveyor, and for a time Sir George Gilbert Scott (1811-78) was one of his pupils. He served as a churchwarden and held various other offices at St Barnabas' Church, Homerton. He supported the work of the London Orphan Asylum, founded by the Reverend Andrew Reed at Clapton, and wrote a number of hymns for the children there, and for his family devotions. Altogether he wrote about 2,000 hymns which were published in the *Evangelical Magazine* and in his various collections, including *Sacred Lyrics*, 1820-22; *One Hundred Hymns for Sunday Schools*, 1821; *Infant Breathings*, 1846; and *Sacred Poetry*, 1847.

Song: Lead us, heavenly Father, lead us (607)

EDWARDS, Alice Georgina (*née* PURDUE)

b Battersea, Surrey, 24 October 1878
d Rochford, Essex, 22 October 1958

In 1882 her family moved to Notting Hill, where she was converted in a Salvation Army meeting at the age of 12. She had music lessons and learnt to play the piano, mandolin and cornet. Before she entered the training home in 1896 she was a music teacher and was also the pianist in a musical group led by Richard Slater which conducted meetings in the London area. She married Captain (later Major) Robert W. Edwards in 1899, and they served together in various corps appointments, including Portsmouth Citadel, Birmingham Citadel, Govan, Perth and Norland Castle. They were appointed to the Public Relations Bureau in 1925 and retired in 1932. She served as young people's sergeant-major at Croydon Citadel, and was home league secretary at Birmingham Sparkhill and, later, at Southend Citadel for nearly 20 years.

Song: Saviour, my all I'm bringing to thee (523)

EDWARDS, Matilda Barbara Betham

b Westerfield, Suffolk, 4 March 1836
d Hastings, Sussex, 4 January 1919

Daughter of Edward Edwards, a farmer, and his wife Barbara (*née* Betham). She was educated mainly at home, but for a short while attended schools in Ipswich and Peckham. After the death of her unmarried sister in 1865, she moved to London, but she travelled widely, particularly in France and Germany. From 1884, she lived in Hastings. She wrote poems and novels, including *The White House by the Sea*, 1857; *Dr Jacob*, 1864; *Kitty*, 1869; and *Lord of the Harvest*, 1899.

Song: God make my life a little light (838)

ELGINBURG, James L.

b ?
d ?

The identity of this author has not yet been established. It seems likely that his name was James Lawson, and that Elginburg was not a surname but was possibly a place with which he was associated.

Song: Jesus, I my cross have taken (498, chorus)

ELLERTON, John

b Clerkenwell, Middlesex, 16 December 1826
d Torquay, Devon, 15 June 1893

Educated at King William's College, Isle of Man, and at Trinity College, Cambridge. He was ordained in 1850 and served as curate of Easebourne, near Midhurst, Sussex, 1850-52; curate of St Nicholas', Brighton and lecturer at St Peter's, Brighton, 1852-60; vicar of Crewe Green and chaplain to Lord Crewe, 1860-72; rector of Hinstock, Shropshire, 1872-76; and rector of Barnes, Surrey, 1876-84. After travelling to Switzerland and Italy, to rest and recover from illness, he became rector of White Roding, Essex, in 1886. He was editor of *Hymns for School and Bible Classes*, 1859, joint-editor of SPCK *Church Hymns*, 1871, and later wrote notes on the authors and translators for the folio edition of *Church Hymns*, in 1881. His other publications included *The Holiest Manhood*, 1882, and *Our Infirmities*, 1883.

Songs: Saviour, again to thy dear name we raise (674)
The day thou gavest, Lord, is ended (677)
This is the day of light (669)
Welcome, happy morning (155)

ELLIOTT, Charlotte

b Clapham, Surrey, 18 March 1789
d Brighton, Sussex, 22 September 1871

She spent her early life mainly in Clapham, and in 1821 suffered a severe illness from which she never fully recovered. In the following year, Dr César Malan, an evangelist from Geneva, visited her home, and she subsequently corresponded with him, as her spiritual guide, for 40 years. In 1823, she went to live with her brother in Torquay and later in Brighton. She wrote letters, essays and poetry, and edited the annual *Christian Remembrancer Pocket Book* for 25 years from 1834. Her 150 hymns were mainly published in *Psalms and Hymns for Public, Private and Social Worship*, 1835-48, compiled by her brother, the Reverend Henry Venn Elliott, and in other books which she compiled, including *The Invalid's Hymn Book*, 1834-54, and *Hours of Sorrow Cheered and Comforted*, 1836.

Songs: I want that adorning divine (589)
　　　　Just as I am, without one plea (293)

ELLIOTT, Emily Elizabeth Steele

b Brighton, Sussex, 22 July 1836
d Islington, London, 3 August 1897

Daughter of the Reverend Edward Bishop Elliott, rector of St Mark's Church, Brighton, and niece of the hymn writer, Charlotte Elliott. She was interested in the work of the Mildmay Park Mission, and for six years edited *The Church Missionary Juvenile Instructor*. She wrote a number of hymns for St Mark's Church, Brighton, and later published hymns and poems in *Chimes of Consecration and their Echoes*, 1873, and *Chimes for Daily Service*, 1880 (the second part of which was also published separately, with the title *Under the Pillow*, for use in hospitals and infirmaries).

Songs: A needy sinner at thy feet (282, chorus)
　　　　O for a heart to praise my God (444, chorus)
　　　　Thou didst leave thy throne and thy kingly crown (101)

EWENS, George Phippen Reeves

b Taunton, Somerset, 4 January 1841
d Uphill, Somerset, 19 June 1926

He served his apprenticeship as a printer and became a reporter and compositor on *The Mercury* newspaper in Clevedon, Somerset. Subsequently he undertook other printing work, including setting a hymn book in type for an evangelist in Tottenham. For several years he worked in the Great Western Railway offices at Paddington, and then for the Mexican Railway. He travelled to Venezuela as agent for the South American Missionary Society, before returning to work in the Society's headquarters in London. From there he set up in business as a printer. He joined The Salvation Army after seeing an open-air meeting at Westbourne Park, and became secretary of the Notting Hill Corps. William Booth appointed him as editor of *The War Cry* from the second issue (3 January 1880), but in 1886 he was sent to the Devon Division, where he established several corps in Devon and West Somerset villages. In 1895 he was appointed to open Salvation Army work in Gibraltar, and he then returned to work in the office of the Chief of the Staff at International Headquarters until his retirement. He wrote extensively, usually using the pen-name 'Grace, Peace, Evermore' (based on his initials).

Song: If you want pardon, if you want peace (427)

EXCELL, Edwin Othello

b Stark County, Ohio, 13 December 1851
d Louisville, Kentucky, 10 June 1921

Son of a German Reformed pastor. As a young man, he worked as a plasterer and bricklayer, but at the age of 20 he became a teacher in singing schools. He later studied music, 1877-83, under George F. Root and his son, Frederick W. Root. He was converted during a revival in the Methodist Episcopal Church, East Brady, Pennsylvania, and after moving to Chicago, in 1883, he published about 90 collections of gospel songs. He composed the music for more than 2,000 gospel songs, and for 20 years assisted the evangelist, Sam P. Jones, as a congregational song leader in his revival meetings.

Song: My robes were once all stained with sin (359)

FABER, Frederick William

b Calverley, Yorkshire, 28 June 1814
d Brompton, Kensington, Middlesex, 26 September 1863

Educated at Shrewsbury and Harrow Schools and Balliol College, Oxford. He became a Fellow of University College, and after his ordination in the Church of England in 1837, he was rector of Elton, Huntingdonshire, 1843-45, and was a strong supporter of the Oxford Movement. After a visit to Rome and Florence in 1845 he became a Roman catholic. He founded a community called 'Brothers of the Will of God', and in 1849 came to London, where he established the London 'Oratorians', or 'Priests of the Congregation of St Philip Neri'. The Oratory moved to Brompton in 1854. He wrote about 150 hymns, using the simplicity and fervour of the 'Olney Hymns' and the hymns of John and Charles Wesley as his models. A collected edition of his hymns was published in 1862.

Songs: Hark, hark, my soul, what warlike songs are swelling (802)
O come and look awhile on him (121)
Souls of men! why will ye scatter (265)

FAIRCLOUGH, Colin

b Leyland, Lancashire, 17 March 1937

He grew up in the Methodist Church, attending a Sunday-school in Fleetwood, and was later converted during national service in the Royal Navy. He became a salvationist in Gibraltar in 1957 and entered the International Training College from Blackpool Citadel in the following year. After serving in corps appointments, 1960-64, at New Seaham and Ryhope, Tow Law and Seaton Delavel, he was appointed to St Helena in the South Atlantic. Subsequently he was commanding officer at Port Elizabeth Central Corps (South Africa), 1968-69, and Training Principal in the Philippines, 1970-74. After further corps work at Salisbury Citadel, Rhodesia (Zimbabwe) and Canterbury, in

Britain, he was appointed to the Social Services (Investigation Department) in 1983, becoming head of the department in 1986.

Song: Christ of Glory, Prince of Peace (479)

FAIRHURST, John

b ?
d ?

Little information about his life is available. He worked as a pattern-maker in Sheffield, and it is believed that he may have been a sergeant in the Attercliffe Corps, *c*1884. His daughter, Mary Fairhurst (1868-1914), became a Salvation Army officer in 1886 and married Captain (later Major) John Cooper in 1899. (Subsequently their four children became Salvation Army officers.)

Song: On Calvary's brow my Saviour died (125, chorus)

FARJEON, Eleanor

b Westminster, 13 February 1881
d Hampstead, London, 5 June 1965

Daughter of Benjamin Farjeon, a novelist. She was educated privately and became a writer of poetry, novels, plays and books for children. She wrote the libretto for the opera *Floretta*, composed by her brother Harry Farjeon (1878-1948). Her first book, *Nursery Rhymes of London Town*, 1916, was followed by other publications, including *The Glass Slipper*, 1944, and *The Last Four Years*, 1958. She was awarded the Carnegie Medal and the Hans Andersen International Medal for her book *The Little Bookroom*, 1955, and, in 1959, she received the Regina Medal in recognition of her work for children. At the age of 70 she became a Roman catholic.

Song: Morning has broken (35)

FARNINGHAM, Marianne

See: **HEARN, Mary Anne**

FAWCETT, John

b Lidget Green, Yorkshire, 6 January 1740
d Hebden Bridge, Yorkshire, 25 July 1817

At the age of 16, he was converted through the preaching of George Whitefield, and in 1758 he joined the Baptist Church in Bradford. In 1763 he became a baptist minister at Wainsgate, near Hebden Bridge, and in 1777 a new chapel was built for the congregation at Hebden Bridge. He declined an invitation to become pastor of Carter Lane Baptist Chapel, London, in 1772, and to be President of the Baptist Academy in Bristol, in 1793. He founded the Northern Education Society, later known as Rawdon College. His publications included a *Devotional Commentary on the Holy Scriptures*, 1811, and *Hymns adapted to the Circumstances of Public Worship and Private Devotion*, 1782.

Song: Blest be the tie that binds (660)

FEATHERSTON, William Ralph

b Montreal, Canada, 23 July 1846
d Montreal, Canada, 20 May 1873

Son of John and Mary Featherston. He and his parents were apparently members of the Wesleyan Methodist Church (later known as St James United Church) in Montreal. No other information about his life is available.

Song: My Jesus, I love thee, I know thou art mine (357)

FLINT, Annie Johnson

b Vineland, New Jersey, 24 December 1866
d Clifton Springs, New York, 8 September 1932

Daughter of Eldon Johnson. Her parents apparently died before she was aged six, and she was adopted, with her sister, by a family named Flint. After attending a school at Trenton, she became a teacher, but a few years later she was affected by arthritis and in less than five years she was unable to walk.

She went to live near Clifton Springs Sanitarium, where she enjoyed the company of visiting missionaries, ministers and teachers. She started to write verses at the age of nine, learnt to play the piano and set several poems to music. Her poems were published on a series of cards, as well as in magazines and books, including *By the Way: Travelogues of Cheer*.

Song: He giveth more grace as our burdens grow greater (579)

FORTUNATUS, Venantius Honorius Clementianus

b Ceneda, near Treviso, Italy, *c*530
d Poitiers, France, 609

He studied as an orator and poet in Milan and Ravenna. While he was a student, he became almost blind, but recovered his sight after anointing his eyes with oil, from a lamp burning before the altar of St Martin of Tours, in a church in Ravenna. He made a thanksgiving pilgrimage to the shrine of St Martin, at Tours, in 565, and, during his travels, he formed a friendship with Queen Rhadegunda, who had founded the convent of St Croix, at Poitiers. He decided to settle at Poitiers and was ordained, and, in 599, he became Bishop of Poitiers. He wrote a *Life of St Martin of Tours* and many poems and hymns, including *Hymns for all the Festivals of the Christian Year*.

Song: Welcome, happy morning (155)

FOSDICK, Harry Emerson

b Buffalo, New York, 24 May 1878
d Bronxville, New York, 5 October 1969

Educated at Buffalo, at Colgate University, Union Theological Seminary and Columbia University. He was ordained in 1903 and served as pastor of the First Baptist Church, Montclair, New Jersey, 1904-15. At Union Theological Seminary, he lectured on baptist principles and homiletics, 1908-15, and was professor of practical theology, 1915-46. During this time, he was associate minister at the First Presbyterian Church, Manhattan, 1919-25, and pastor of Park Avenue Baptist Church (later Riverside Church), 1926-46. His publications included *A Guide to Understanding the Bible*, 1938; an autobiography, *The Living of These Days*, 1956; and *A Book of Public Prayers*, 1960.

Song: God of grace and God of glory (577)

FRANCIS of Assisi

b Assisi, Italy, c1182
d Assisi, Italy, 3 October 1226

Son of Pietro Bernardone, a cloth merchant. As a young man, he was imprisoned for a year during a civil war between Assisi and Perugia, 1202-03. Subsequently he was on his way to join the army in southern Italy when he heard a 'heavenly voice' telling him to return to Assisi. After other visions, he left home to live a life of poverty and devoted himself to repairing three churches near Assisi, including a chapel known as 'the Portiuncula'. A small group of followers joined him there, increasing to more than 5,000 by the year 1220. The friars went out on preaching missions, returning each year (at Whitsun) for an assembly at the Portiuncula. In 1219 he led a mission to the Holy Land and Egypt, where he visited the Sultan's camp and preached for several days to the Saracens. When he returned from the Holy Land his health was deteriorating, and he retired from the leadership of the Franciscan Order. He lived for a short while at Mount La Verna, in 1224, and then near San Damiano before returning finally to the Portiuncula.

Song: All creatures of our God and King (2)

FRANCIS, Samuel Trevor

b Cheshunt, Hertfordshire, 19 November 1834
d Worthing, Sussex, 28 December 1925

He spent his early life in Hull, where he was a member of the parish church choir, but he later moved to London, where he joined the brethren assembly in Kennington. He was an evangelist and open-air preacher, and travelled extensively. He accompanied R. C. Morgan, editor of *The Christian*, on a visit to North Africa, and assisted in the Moody and Sankey campaigns, 1873-75. His hymns and poems were published in

The Life of Faith and other newspapers and magazines, and in several books, including *O the Deep, Deep Love of Jesus, and other poems*, 1926, which appeared posthumously.

Song: O the deep, deep love of Jesus (182)

FRASER, David Rutherford

b Oxted, Surrey, 1 June 1939

The son of Quaker parents, he was educated at Sidcot School, Somerset, and then at Exeter University and Regent's Park College, Oxford. At the age of 16 he had become a Quaker, but three years later he was baptised and became a baptist. Ordained in 1964, he served as pastor of Upper Studley and Southwick Baptist Churches, near Trowbridge, Wiltshire, 1964-70, and Hearsall Baptist Church, Coventry, 1970-73. He then became a management training consultant in Manchester, and in 1978 established his own management consulting company. He attends the baptist church in Wigan, where he assists the minister, and also preaches in other free churches in the area.

Song: We are the hands of Christ (851)

FRY, Charles William

b Alderbury, Wiltshire, 30 May, 1838
d Polmont, Stirlingshire, 24 August 1882

Son of Abraham Fry, a journeyman bricklayer. (He was registered at birth as William Charles Fry, but he married in 1858 as Charles William Fry.) Converted at the age of 17 in a Sunday evening prayer meeting at the Wesleyan chapel in Alderbury, he soon became a local preacher. He played the violin, cello, piano and harmonium, led a small orchestra at the chapel and formed a brass band there for special occasions. He also played solo cornet in a local volunteer military band. He worked as a bricklayer and later established his own business as a builder. In 1878 he and his three sons (with their brass instruments) assisted the Christian Mission evangelists in Salisbury at their open-air meetings, and then, for several years, they travelled as a family band, accompanying William Booth on his campaigns. In May 1880 they moved to London and joined the headquarters staff, continuing to assist in meetings as a brass or string quartet. He wrote a number of songs which appeared in *The War Cry* in 1880 and 1881. After an illness in March 1882, he went to stay in the home of Mr and Mrs T. Livingstone Learmoth at Park Hall, Polmont, where a few months later he died.

Songs: Come, thou burning Spirit, come (481)
God gave his Son for me (45)
I've found a friend in Jesus (344)

FRY, Fred William

b Alderbury, Wiltshire, 3 July 1859
d Gillingham, Kent, 24 June 1939

Son of Charles William Fry, the first Salvation Army bandmaster (see above). As a boy he played a cornet in the Wesleyan chapel orchestra in Alderbury, and at the age of eight played the harmonium. When he was 14 he went to work in Whiteparish, but after about four years came home to Fisherton to work with his father in the building trade. He was a member of the Fry family band, which was formed in Salisbury in 1878 and toured Britain extensively until 1882, when his father died. He was then appointed secretary to Herbert Booth and for several years travelled on musical campaigns with the Training Home Songsters, various groups of officers and cadets, and then the Household Troops Band. He worked in the Music Editorial Department preparing band music and the music typesetting for *The Musical Salvationist*, 1886-92. For a time he was William Booth's private secretary. In 1891 he was appointed bandmaster of the International Staff Band, and in the following year went to Canada as private secretary to Commandant Herbert Booth. Returning to England, he worked for many years in the Town Clerk's Department in Gillingham. He became a methodist local preacher in 1895 and was, at various times society and chapel steward and secretary of the local preachers' meeting.

Songs: God's anger now is turned away (317)
In the Army of Jesus we've taken our stand (687)
You must have your sins forgiven (913)

GABRIEL, Charles Hutchison

b near Wilton, Iowa, 18 August 1856
d Los Angeles, California, 15 September 1932

Son of Isaac Gabriel. At home, he learnt to play the reed organ, and at the age of 16 started to teach in singing schools and to write gospel songs. He was music director for the Sunday-school at Grace Methodist Episcopal Church, in San Francisco, 1889-90, and in 1892 moved to Chicago, where he worked as a song writer and editor of gospel song collections. He often used the pseudonym 'Charlotte G. Homer' for his gospel song texts. He compiled 35 books of gospel songs, eight Sunday-school song books, 19 collections of anthems and 23 cantatas, and also wrote other books, including *Gospel Songs and their Writers*, 1915.

Songs: I stand amazed in the presence (179)
  In loving kindness Jesus came (339)
  When all my labours and trials are o'er (906)

GAY, Edwin

b Black Torrington, Devon, 11 April 1860
d Portsmouth, Hampshire, 1 May 1952

He was converted in 1881 at Devonport Morice Town, and, before entering the training home at Clapton in 1883 he took charge of the corps at Barnstaple for two months, when the officer there was unwell. After 11 weeks' training he served in corps appointments at Stratford (Essex), Truro, Luton and Oxford. While he was in Oxford he received a telegram from the Chief of the Staff, Bramwell Booth, asking if he was willing to go to America. Within a few days, he sailed to New York where he was appointed to open a corps in Chicago. Later he served in Boston and did pioneering work in the Western States for several years. Returning to England, he had appointments in various divisions, latterly as chancellor in the Southampton Division. He retired as a brigadier in 1926 after 43 years' service.

Song: I am saved, blessedly saved, by the blood (321)

GERHARDT, Paulus

b Gräfenhainichen, near Wittenberg, 12 March 1607
d Lübben, Saxe Merseburg, 7 June 1676

Son of Christian Gerhardt, burgomaster of Gräfenhainichen. He was educated at Grimma and the University of Wittenberg, and then moved to Berlin as tutor to the family of Andreas Barthold, a lawyer, whose daughter he later married. In 1651 he was ordained as pastor at Mittenwalde, near Berlin, and in 1657 he became a deacon at the Church of St Nicholas, in Berlin, where Johann Crüger was choirmaster. In the midst of theological controversy, he was deposed in 1666, but he remained in Berlin until he was appointed archdeacon at Lübben, in 1669. His hymns mainly appeared in various editions of Crüger's *Praxis pietatis melica* and in *Geistliche Kirchen-Melodien*, 1649.

Songs: All my heart this night rejoices (73)
Commit thou all thy griefs (715)
Give to the winds thy fears (721)
O sacred head once wounded (123)

GHYSEN, Hendrik

b 1660
d 1693

He was a goldsmith and silversmith, and was precentor at the Amstel Church, in Amsterdam. He was also a poet, who compiled a new version of the metrical psalms, *Den Hoonigraat der psalmdichten*, 1686 (Amsterdam), based on 17 earlier versions of the psalms.

Song: O Father, let thy love remain (958)

GIBBY, Arthur Robert

b London, *c*1862
d Pembroke Dock, Pembrokeshire, 7 October 1932

Son of Robert Gibby, a shipwright. He was converted in 1883 at Pembroke Dock, where he worked for some time as a skilled labourer in HM Dockyard. At Pembroke Dock Corps, he served for eight years as corps sergeant-major and as young people's sergeant-major for nine years. Later, he was young people's treasurer and corps correspondent. He wrote over 500 songs, many of which were published in *The War Cry* and *The Young Soldier*.

Song: There is a mercy seat revealed (269)

GIFFE, William Thomas

b Portland, Indiana, 28 June 1848
d Seattle, Washington, 13 July 1926

At the age of 16, he became a soldier and served in the Union Army during the last year of the Civil War. He was educated at Liber College, and later studied music with various teachers, including George F. Root, W. A. Ogden and Horatio R. Palmer. A concert singer and choral conductor, he was for some years a supervisor of music in schools, before he became owner of the Home Music Company, in Logansport, Indiana. He wrote a number of gospel songs, and published music for male voices, and other anthems. He was the author of *A Practical Course in Harmony and Musical Composition,* and for several years was editor of the *Home Music Journal*.

Songs: Salvation! O the joyful sound (382, chorus)
We'll shout aloud throughout the land (782, chorus)

GILMORE, Joseph Henry

b Boston, Massachusetts, 29 April 1834
d Rochester, New York, 23 July 1918

Educated at Phillips Academy, Brown University and Newton Theological Seminary. He was ordained as a baptist minister in 1862 and served as pastor at Fisherville, New Hampshire, 1862-64 and Rochester, New York, 1865-67. During the Civil War, he was private secretary to his father, Joseph A. Gilmore, governor of New Hampshire, and, for a short while, he edited the *Daily Monitor* in Concord, New Hampshire. He was professor of logic, rhetoric and English literature at the University of Rochester, 1868-1908. His publications included

The Art of Expression, 1876; *He Leadeth Me, and Other Religious Poems*, 1877; and *Outlines of English and American Literature*, 1905.

Song: He leadeth me! O blessèd thought (725)

GLADDEN, Washington

b Pottsgrove, Pennsylvania, 11 February 1836
d Columbus, Ohio, 2 July 1918

Educated at Owego Academy and Williams College. He became a congregational minister in 1860, and served as pastor at Brooklyn, New York, 1860-61; Morrisania, New York, 1861-68; North Adams, Massachusetts, 1868-71; Springfield, Massachusetts, 1871-82; and First Congregational Church, at Columbus, 1882-1914. From 1904 to 1907 he was Moderator of the National Council of Congregational Churches. For some time he was editor of the New York *Independent* and the magazine *Sunday Afternoon*. He was also author of various books, including *The Christian Way*, 1877; *Who Wrote the Bible?*, 1891; and *Recollections*, 1909.

Song: O Master, let me walk with thee (519)

GOWANS, John

b Blantyre, Lanarkshire, 13 November 1934

Son of Salvation Army officers. After completing his national service in the Royal Army Educational Corps in Germany he entered the International Training College from Grangetown in 1954. Following several corps appointments, he served as Divisional Youth Secretary (Hull and Lincs), 1970-71; commanding officer, Nottingham Memorial Halls, 1971-73; national stewardship secretary, 1973-75; Divisional Commander (Manchester), 1975-77; and Chief Secretary for France, 1977-81. He was appointed to USA Western Territory in 1981, where he was Secretary for Program and then Divisional Commander for Southern California. In 1986 he became Territorial Commander for France with the rank of colonel. Since 1967 he has written a series of musicals with Colonel John Larsson, including *Take-*

Over Bid, Hosea, Jesus Folk, Spirit!, Glory!, White Rose, The Blood of the Lamb, Son of Man, and *Man Mark II.*

Songs: Burning, burning, brightly burning (206)
Do you sometimes feel that no one truly knows you (238)
Don't assume that God's dismissed you from his mind (44)
For the mighty moving of thy Spirit (192)
For thine is the Kingdom (951)
Have you ever stopped to think how God loves you (49)
He came to give us life in all its fulness (274)
I believe that God the Father (324)
If human hearts are often tender (50)
In your heart of hearts are you a trifle weary (244)
Kneeling in penitence I make my prayer (605)
Knowing my failings, knowing my fears (294)
Once in misery I walked alone (376)
Out of my darkness God called me (378)
There are hundreds of sparrows, thousands, millions (850)
There is a message, a simple message (270)
There's no other name but this name (71)
They shall come from the east (170)
Who is it tells me what to do (204)
You can't stop rain from falling down (854)

GRAHAM, Sarah Jean

b c1854
d c1889

She was a salvationist in the corps at Lindsay, Ontario (Canada). Apparently her fiancé died of consumption as a young man and she never fully recovered from the shock. She was aged about 35 when she died.

Song: On the cross of Calvary (128)

GRANT, Robert

b Bengal, 1779
d Dalpoorie, India, 9 July 1838

Son of Charles Grant, a director of the East India Company, he was educated at Magdalene College, Cambridge, and was called to the Bar in 1807. He entered Parliament in 1818 and was successively MP for Elgin Burghs, Inverness Burghs,

Norwich and Finsbury. Appointed Judge Advocate General in 1832, he was knighted in 1834, when he went to India as Governor of Bombay. He contributed hymns to the *Christian Observer,* 1806-15 and to *Psalms and Hymns,* 1835, compiled by H. V. Elliott. His brother, Lord Glenelg, published 12 of his hymns and poems in *Sacred Poems,* 1839.

Song: O worship the King, all glorious above (16)

GRIGG, Joseph

*b c*1720
d Walthamstow, Essex, 29 October 1768

The son of poor parents, he is said to have been 'brought up to mechanical pursuits'. In 1743, he apparently left his trade and became assistant minister to the Reverend Thomas Bures, of the presbyterian church, Silver Street, London. In 1747, he retired from the ministry when Thomas Bures died, and went to live at St Albans. His hymns and poems were collected by Daniel Sedgwick and published, with a memoir, in *Hymns on Divine Subjects,* 1861.

Song: Jesus, and shall it ever be (592)

GROVES, Alexander

b Newport, Isle of Wight, 18 March 1842
d Henley-on-Thames, Oxfordshire, 30 August 1909

Son of James Groves, a grocer. In 1860, he moved to Henley, where he worked for a while as a grocer, and later became an accountant. He was a member of Henley Charity Trustees, 1885-1909 and was secretary of Henley Salisbury Club, 1888-1906. He served as a member of the Board of Guardians from 1890 and was appointed JP for the borough in 1901. He became a trustee of Henley Savings Bank in 1887, auditor in 1897, and was actuary for the bank, 1898-1909. For some time he was organist at Henley Wesleyan Chapel, but he was subsequently associated with the parish church for several years, becoming a sidesman there in 1898.

Song: Break thou the bread of life (650, verses 2 and 3)

GROZINSKY, Gustave Adolf Alexander Augustine

b Moscow, c1870
d Edmonton, Alberta, 21 December 1936

Son of Julius Grozinsky, a tailor. From Russia (where his father had earlier been exiled to Siberia as a political offender) his family came to England via North Germany, and settled in Camberwell. There he followed the Salvation Army band to the hall, and a few weeks later was converted. He trained as a cadet in Leicester, Hitchin and Hammersmith, and served in several corps appointments, including Northampton, Wandsworth, Catford, Dorking and Thurso. Later, he moved to Canada, where he was a soldier at Edmonton Citadel. He played the violin, banjo and guitar, and contributed a number of songs to *The War Cry* and *The Musical Salvationist*, 1888-93.

Song: 'Neath our standard, we're engaging (778)

GURNEY, Dorothy Frances (*née* BLOMFIELD)

b Finsbury Circus, London, 4 October 1858
d Notting Hill, London, 15 June 1932

Daughter of the Reverend Frederick George Blomfield, rector of St Andrew Undershaft, London. She married Gerald Gurney in 1897, and with her husband joined the Roman Catholic Church at Farnborough Abbey in 1919. She published two volumes of *Poems*, and *A Little Book of Quiet*.

Song: O perfect Love, all human thought transcending (948)

GUYON, Jeanne Marie Bouvières de la Mothe

b Montargis, France, 13 April 1648
d Blois, France, 9 June 1717

Daughter of Claude Bouvières, Seigneur de la Mothe Vergonville. She grew up mainly in Ursuline, Benedictine and Dominican convents, and in 1664 married Jacques Guyon. After he died in 1676, she travelled extensively in France, Switzerland and Italy, writing and speaking about faith and prayer, and assisting in charitable work. She faced allegations that her teaching was heretical and in 1688 she was arrested and imprisoned in the Convent of St Marie, near Paris, for about eight months. A few years later she was imprisoned in the Castle of Vincennes, 1695-96; in a convent at Vaugirard, 1696-98; and in the Bastille, 1698-1702. She wrote letters to her spiritual advisers, Francis de la Combe (a Barnabite monk) and Francis Fenelon (Archbishop of Cambrai), and also published about 40 books, including *A Short Method of Prayer* and *Poésies et Cantiques Spirituels*, 1722, a collection of almost 900 poems and spiritual songs, many of them written during her imprisonment.

Song: All scenes alike engaging prove (556)

HALL, William John

b London, 31 December 1793
d Tottenham, Middlesex, 16 December 1861

Educated at Corpus Christi College, Cambridge. After ordination, he became a minor canon of St Paul's Cathedral, London, in 1826; priest-in-ordinary of the Chapel Royal, St James's, in 1829; and vicar of Tottenham, in 1851. He published *Sermons*; *Prayers for the Use of Families* and other works. With Edward Osler, he compiled *Psalms and Hymns adapted to the Services of the Church of England*, 1836 (known as the *Mitre Hymn Book*).

Song: Blest are the pure in heart (411, verses 2 and 4)

HAMILTON, Eliza H.

b ?
d ?

No information about the author is available. Her song seems to have appeared first in the United States.

Song: Jesus, my Lord, to thee I cry (291)

HAMMOND, Edward Payson

b Ellington, Connecticut, 1 September 1831
d Hartford, Connecticut, 14 August 1910

Son of Elijah Hammond, a teacher. He was educated at Phillips Academy, Andover, Massachusetts; Williams College; Union Seminary, New York; and Free Church College, Edinburgh. While he was studying in Edinburgh he conducted revival meetings in Edinburgh, Glasgow, London and Liverpool, and, after returning to America he was ordained as an evangelist by the Presbytery of New York in 1862. Subsequently he led revival meetings in Chicago, Detroit, Philadelphia and other American cities, as well as in Britain in 1867 and again later, when he also visited Scandinavia. He compiled *Hymns especially adapted for seasons of deep religious interest*, 1867, and *Hymns of Salvation*, 1867, and published several other books, including *The Conversion of Children*, 1878.

Song: I feel like singing all the time (326)

HANBY, Benjamin Russell

b Rushville, Ohio, 22 July 1833
d Chicago, 16 March 1867

Son of the Reverend William Hanby, a minister of the United Brethren Church. He was educated at Otterbein University, and after graduation served as an agent for the college, and then as principal of an academy at Seven Mile, in Butler County, Ohio. He was pastor of a church at Lewisburg, for two years, and, for a short while, at New Paris, where he later opened a singing school for children. Subsequently, he worked for the music publishers, John Church Company, in Cincinnati, and from 1865, for Root and Cady, in Chicago. He helped to compile several song books and wrote 68 songs, many of which appeared in *Our Song Birds,* a music quarterly for children.

Song: Who is he in yonder stall (104)

HANKEY, Arabella Catherine

b Clapham, Surrey, 1834
d Westminster, 9 May 1911

Daughter of Thomas Hankey, a banker, who was a member of the evangelical 'Clapham Sect', associated with William Wilberforce. She was often known as Katherine, or Kate. As a girl, she taught in a Sunday-school in Croydon, and at the age of 18 she commenced a Bible class for girls working in shops in the West End of London. After travelling to South Africa, to bring home an invalid brother, she became particularly interested in mission work in Africa. Her publications included *The Old, Old Story*, 1866 and *Heart to Heart*, 1870 (enlarged 1873 and 1876).

Song: Tell me the old, old story (98)

HARLAND, Edward

b Ashbourne, Derbyshire, 1810
d Stafford, 8 June 1890

Educated at Wadham College, Oxford. After his ordination, he was curate of Newborough, 1833-36, and of Sandon, 1836-51. He became vicar of Colwich, Staffordshire, in 1851, and a prebendary of Lincoln Cathedral, in 1873. He compiled *A Church Psalter and Hymnal*, 1855, with a supplement in 1863, an undated enlarged edition, and another supplement in 1876.

Song: O for a humbler walk with God (445)

HART, Joseph

b London, *c*1712
d London, 24 May 1768

The son of Christian parents, he apparently received a classical education and became a teacher of languages. After many years of spiritual uncertainty, he was converted on Whit Sunday 1757 through hearing a sermon in the Moravian chapel, Fetter Lane, on the text: 'Because thou hast kept the word of my patience, I also will keep thee from the hour of temptation. . . .' (Revelation 3:10). He preached his first sermon at the old meeting house, St John's Court, Bermondsey, and in 1760 he became minister at Jewin Street Chapel, London. He published his *Hymns composed on Various Subjects, with the Author's Experience*, 1759 (with additional supplements in 1762 and 1765).

Song: This, this is the God we adore (962)

HARTSOUGH, Lewis

b Ithaca, New York, 31 August 1828
d Mount Vernon, Iowa, 1 January 1919

He was educated at Cazenovia Seminary and entered the ministry of the Methodist Episcopal Church. For 15 years, he served churches in the Oneida Conference, New York, and then became first superintendent of the Utah Mission. He was later appointed presiding elder of the Wyoming District, and, after two years as pastor in Epworth, Iowa, he transferred to the Northwest Iowa Conference in 1874. He is said to have travelled about 400,000 miles during his ministry. He was music editor of *The Revivalist*, 1868, compiled by Joseph Hillman.

Song: I hear thy welcome voice (423)

HASTINGS, Thomas

b Washington, Connecticut, 15 October 1784
d New York, 15 May 1872

Son of Dr Seth Hastings, a physician. He taught himself music, and at the age of 18 started to conduct choirs. He became a music teacher in 1806 and was active in the Oneida County Musical Society. In Utica, he edited the *Western Recorder*, 1823-32, in which he published articles on improving church music. In 1832, he moved to New York, where he conducted several church choirs and assisted Lowell Mason with compiling *Spiritual Songs for Social Worship*, 1831-32. He wrote 600 hymns and 1,000 tunes, and compiled 50 collections, including *The Mother's Hymn-Book*, 1834 and 1850, and *Devotional Hymns and Poems*, 1850.

Song: Father, we for our children plead (791)

HATCH, Edwin

b Derby, 4 September 1835
d Headington, Oxford, 10 November 1889

Educated at King Edward's School, Birmingham, and Pembroke College, Oxford. Shortly after his ordination, he went to Canada, where he was professor of classics at Trinity College, Toronto, and then rector of a high school in Quebec. He returned to England as vice-principal of St Mary's Hall, Oxford, in 1867, and became rector of Purleigh, in 1883, and University Reader in Ecclesiastical History, at Oxford, in 1884. He gave the Bampton Lectures (1880) and the Hibbert Lectures (1888) on the history of the Early Church.

Song: Breathe on me, Breath of God (189)

HAUSMANN, Julie Katharina von

b Riga, Latvia, 1825 or 1826
d near Wösso, Estonia, 1901

Daughter of a preparatory school teacher, she grew up in Mitau, Kurland, where her father had apparently moved to become a government councillor. She worked for short periods as a governess, but later devoted herself to caring for her father, who had become blind. After he died, in 1864, she lived mainly with various relatives in Germany, France, Switzerland, St Petersburg (now Leningrad), and Estonia. She published a devotional book, *Hausbrot,* and a collection of poems, *Maiblumen, Lieder einer Stillen im Lande.*

Song: Take thou my hand and guide me (635)

HAVERGAL, Frances Ridley

b Astley, Worcestershire, 14 December 1836
d Oystermouth, Glamorgan, 3 June 1879

Daughter of the Reverend William Henry Havergal, vicar of Astley. Her name Ridley came from her godfather, the Reverend William H. Ridley, though she liked to associate it with Bishop Ridley, the Reformation martyr. She was educated at home, at small private schools, and at the Louisenschule in Düsseldorf, and she also studied for some months with Pastor Schulze-Berge, at Obercassel. Her family moved to Henwick House, Hallow, near Worcester, in 1842, and to St Nicholas' Rectory, Worcester, in 1845. She taught in the Sunday-school at St Nicholas', from the age of nine, and kept a record of her scholars, 1846-60. She was governess to the children of her sisters, at Oakhampton, 1860-67, and at Winterdyne, near Bewdley, during 1868, and then moved to Leamington. A helper in missions at Bewdley and in Liverpool, she also spoke at YWCA meetings, and supported the work of the Mildmay Institution in London. She contributed poetry to *Good Words, Home Words* and *The Sunday Magazine;* prepared an edition of her father's music, *Havergal's Psalmody,* 1871; and helped the Reverend Charles B. Snepp to compile *Songs of Grace and Glory,* 1872 (and later editions). Her own publications included: *The Ministry of Song,* 1869; *Under the Surface,* 1874; *Loyal Responses,* 1878; and *Under His Shadow,* 1879.

Songs: I am trusting thee, Lord Jesus (727)
    I bring my sins to thee (421)
    I could not do without thee (325)
    Lord, speak to me, that I may speak (612)
    Master, speak: thy servant heareth (614)
    Take my life, and let it be (525)
    Who is on the Lord's side (707)

HAWEIS, Hugh Reginald

b Egham, Surrey, 3 April 1838
d St Marylebone, London, 29 January 1901

Son of the Reverend John Oliver Willyams Haweis, Canon of Chichester. He was educated at Trinity College, Cambridge, and then travelled in Italy, where he served under Garibaldi in the Italian War of Independence, 1860. After his ordination in 1861, he served as a curate in Bethnal Green, Westminster and Stepney, and then became perpetual curate of St James, Marylebone, in 1866. His publications included *Music and*

Morals, 1871; *My Musical Life,* 1884; *Travel and Talk,* 1897; and *Old Violins,* 1898.

Song: The homeland! the homeland (895)

HAWKES, Frederick George

b Good Easter, Essex, 6 February 1869
d Ashurst, Hampshire, 24 November 1959

He was converted at the age of 14, became a salvationist in 1886, and was for a time a bandsman at Chelmsford. In 1887, after applying to become an officer, he was appointed to the Household Troops' Band for its first tour. He then worked in the Music Publishing Department at Clapton before returning to the Household Troops' Band (playing bass trombone and later solo euphonium). In 1892 he joined the Music Editorial Department, and served there until his retirement as a colonel in 1936. He was head of the department for more than 20 years, after the retirement of Richard Slater, and was also bandmaster of the Trade Headquarters Band, 1895-96, and bandmaster at Penge Corps for several years. He composed more than 150 marches and selections for the band journals, as well as other vocal and instrumental works. His first song appeared in *The Musical Salvationist* in April 1891. He wrote articles on music for *The Musical Salvationist, The War Cry, The Bandsman and Songster* and *The Musician,* and also several books, including *Studies for Band Training,* 1905.

Song: Give me a restful mind (574)

HAWKINS, Hester Periam (née LEWIS)

b Wantage, Berkshire, 13 November 1846
d Reigate, Surrey, 18 May 1928

Married Joshua Hawkins, of Bedford. With Edwin Moss, she compiled *The Home Hymn Book, A Manual of Sacred Song for the Family Circle,* 1885. She was also the author of several books on astronomy, including *The ABC Guide to Astronomy,* 1912; *Ourselves and the Universe,* 1920; and *Astronomy for Busy People,* 1922.

Song: Heavenly Father, thou hast brought us (938)

HAWKS, Annie Sherwood

b Hoosick, New York, 25 or 28 May 1835 or 1836
d Bennington, Vermont, 3 January 1918

She married Charles H. Hawks in 1859 and for many years lived in Brooklyn, New York. She was a member of the Hanson Place Baptist Church, where the pastor, Robert Lowry, encouraged her to write hymns. After her husband died in 1888, she lived with a daughter in Bennington. She wrote over 400 hymns, which were published in various Sunday-school collections, including *Pure Gold*, 1871, and *Royal Diadem*, 1873.

Songs: I am saved, I am saved (322)
I need thee every hour (587)
Who'll be the next to follow Jesus (278)

HAWLEY, William A.

b Campbellford (or Belleville), Ontario, c1870(?)
d Calgary, Alberta, 9 August 1929

He grew up in Campbellford, Ontario, where at the age of 11 he was organist at the methodist church and five years later became leader of the choir. After a year at medical college in Toronto, he studied at Boston Conservatory of Music, and in later years was often known as Professor Hawley. An injury to his left hand apparently led him to abandon music as a profession and he became a piano tuner, though for several years he was organist of the First Baptist Church in Charlottetown, Prince Edward Island. He then joined The Salvation Army there, assisting with various activities, including junior meetings and the Band of Love. Subsequently he served at the Rupert Avenue Corps, in Winnipeg, for two years, and then at Calgary Citadel Corps for 12 years. He also helped to launch the No. 2 corps in Calgary. He wrote anthems and other music and later composed a number of Salvation Army songs.

Song: A light came out of darkness (94)

HEARN, Mary Anne ('Marianne Farningham')

b Farningham, Kent, 17 December 1834
d Barmouth, Merioneth, 16 March 1909

After short periods in Bristol and Gravesend, she lived for many years in Northampton, where she was a member of the College Street Baptist Church. She contributed to *The Christian World* newspaper, from its foundation in 1857, and for some years was editor of *The Sunday School Times*. She wrote under the name 'Marianne Farningham' and published about 20 books, including *Morning and Evening Hymns for the Week*, 1870 and *Songs of Sunshine*, 1878.

Song: Just as I am, thine own to be (860)

HEATH, George

b c1750
d 1822

Educated at the Dissenting Academy in Exeter, he became pastor of a presbyterian church in Honiton, Devon, in 1770, but was later a unitarian minister. He published *Hymns and Poetic Essays Sacred to the Public and Private Worship of the Deity*, 1781, and *A History of Bristol*, 1797.

Song: My soul, be on thy guard (812)

HEATHCOTE, Agnes Parker (née McDOUALL)

b Lanark, Scotland, 2 April 1862
d ?

Daughter of a minister, the Reverend James Douglas McDouall, she was converted while at boarding school and four years later joined The Salvation Army in Banff. She came to the training home in London in 1883, and after a few weeks' training was appointed to Cellar, Gutter and Garret work. From there she went on a tour with the Salvation Songsters, and then for about 18 months worked in the training home nursery. Subsequently she served on midnight rescue work, and on the training home staff, latterly as secretary to Mrs Emma Booth-Tucker. In 1888 she married Staff-Captain Wyndham S. Heathcote, who had been a curate in the Church of England before becoming an officer in 1886. He returned to the anglican church as curate of St Andrew, Streatham, 1890-93, and later served in South Africa and Australia, where he became a unitarian minister. He died in 1956, but nothing is known about his wife's later years.

Songs: I heard a voice so gently calling (490)
Pleasures sought, dearly bought (379)

HEBER, Reginald

b Malpas, Cheshire, 21 April 1783
d Trichinopoly, India, 3 April 1826

He was educated at Whitchurch Grammar School, then under a private tutor at Neasden, and at Brasenose College, Oxford. At Oxford, he won the Newdigate Prize for his poem 'Palestine', in 1803, and he was elected a Fellow of All Souls College, in 1804. He then travelled for two years, through Norway, Sweden, Russia, Poland and Hungary. After his ordination in 1807, he was rector of Hodnet, Shropshire, until 1823, when he became Bishop of Calcutta. While he was at Hodnet, a number of his hymns appeared in the *Christian Observer*, 1811-16, and he compiled a collection of hymns which was published posthumously as *Hymns, written and adapted to the Weekly Church Service of the Year*, 1827. This included some hymns contributed by Henry Hart Milman and other authors.

Songs: Holy, holy, holy, Lord God Almighty (220)
The Son of God goes forth to war (701)

HEDGE, Frederic Henry

b Cambridge, Massachusetts, 12 December 1805
d Cambridge, Massachusetts, 21 August 1890

Educated in Germany and at Harvard, he served as minister of unitarian churches in West Cambridge, 1829-35; Bangor, Maine, 1835-50; Providence, Rhode Island, 1850-56; and Brookline, Massachusetts, 1856-72. He was also professor of ecclesiastical history at Harvard, 1857-76, and professor of German, 1872-81. He edited the unitarian *Hymns for the Church of Christ*, 1853, with Dr F. D. Huntington.

Song: A mighty fortress is our God (1)

HENLEY, John

b Torquay, Devon, 28 March 1800
d Weymouth, Dorset, 10 May 1842

He was converted in 1813, and a few years later became a local preacher. After serving temporarily as a preacher in the South Petherton circuit in 1824, he was appointed as a methodist minister in the Dunster circuit. He offered for missionary work in 1826, but was sent to the Witney circuit, and subsequently served in Sherborne, 1828-30; Lancaster, 1830-32; Derby, 1832-35; Dudley, 1835-38; Sheffield, 1838-41; and Manchester, from September 1841. Having been in poor health for several years, he was seriously ill in April 1842, and travelled to Weymouth shortly before he died.

Song: Children of Jerusalem (834)

HENSLEY, Lewis

b Bloomsbury, Middlesex, 20 May 1824
d Walsingham, Norfolk, 1 August 1905

Educated at Trinity College, Cambridge, where he was later a Fellow and assistant tutor, 1846-52. After ordination in 1851, he was curate of Upton with Chalvey, Buckinghamshire; vicar of Ippolyts with Great Wymondly, Hertfordshire; and then vicar of Hitchin, Hertfordshire, from 1856. He was appointed an honorary canon of St Albans in 1881. His publications included: *Hymns for the Sundays after Trinity*, 1864; *Hymns for the Minor Sundays from Advent to Whitsunday*, 1867; and *The Scholar's Algebra*, 1875.

Song: Thy kingdom come, O God (172)

HERBERT, Daniel

b Sudbury, Suffolk, 10 April 1751
d Sudbury, Suffolk, 29 August 1833

There is little definite information about the author's life. It seems that in early life he was a servant in London, and then returned to Sudbury, where he worked as a bunting manufacturer. For some years, he was minister of the Little Meeting, Sudbury, which had apparently seceded from the Sudbury Congregational Church. He published several editions of his *Hymns and Poems* between 1801 and 1827.

Song: Ten thousand thousand souls there are (266)

HERBERT, George

b Montgomery, 3 April 1593
d Bemerton, Wiltshire, 1 March 1633

Educated at Westminster School and Trinity College, Cambridge. He became a Fellow of Trinity College in 1615 and Public Orator for the University in 1619. After his ordination, in 1626, he was appointed to the parish of Leighton Bromswold, Huntingdonshire, but three years later, he moved to his brother's home at Woodford, Essex, because of illness. In 1630, he became rector of Fugglestone, with Bemerton, near Salisbury. Three weeks before he died, he gave a manuscript collection of his poems, *The Temple*, to his friend Nicholas Ferrar, who published it shortly afterwards.

Song: Let all the world in every corner sing (11)

HERKLOTS, Rosamond Eleanor

b Mussoorie (Masuri), India, 22 June 1905
d Greenwich, London, 21 July 1987

She grew up in Kendal, Shipley and Leeds, the daughter of an anglican vicar, and was educated at Leeds Girls' High School, Leeds University and the London Day Training College. She became a teacher, but, after teaching for a while, she took up secretarial work, for some years in Unilever House and then for more than 20 years as secretary to the neurologist, Dr C. Worster-Drought. Later she worked in the head office of the Association for Spina Bifida and Hydrocephalus. After starting to write hymns in about 1940 she wrote more than 70, some of which have been used in Sunday-schools.

Song: Forgive our sins as we forgive (572)

HEWITT, Eliza Edmunds (*née* STITES)

b Philadelphia, Pennsylvania, 28 June 1851
d Philadelphia, Pennsylvania, 24 April 1920

Daughter of Captain James S. Stites, she was a cousin of the hymn writer Edgar Page Stites. She lived throughout her life in Philadelphia, where she was superintendent of the Sunday-school of the Northern Home for Friendless Children and was a member of the Olivet Presbyterian Church. Later she moved to another part of the city and served as superintendent of the primary department of the Calvin Presbyterian Church. Many of her poems were set to music by John R. Sweney and William J. Kirkpatrick.

Songs: How firm a foundation (653, chorus)
O for a heart that is whiter than snow (443)
Sing the wondrous love of Jesus (892)
There is sunshine in my soul today (387)

HILL, V.

b ?
d ?

No information about the author is available.

Song: Jesus, so dear to us (955)

HINCHSLIFFE, Joseph

b Sheffield, 1760
d Dumfries, 1807

He was a silversmith and cutler, and was apparently a member of the methodist society at Norfolk Street, Sheffield, and later at Dumfries.

Song: This is the field, the world below (932)

HINE, Stuart Wesley Keene

b Hammersmith, London, 25 July 1899

He was dedicated as a baby under the Salvation Army flag at Hammersmith, and heard William Booth preach in 1912 at the Ilford Hippodrome. He was educated at Coopers' Company School, and at the age of 14 was converted after hearing a solo by Annie Ryall and her explanation of John 3:14-15. After serving in the British army, in France and Belgium, 1917-19, he worked as a missionary in Volhynia, in eastern Poland, 1923-32, and then in Ruthenia (or Sub-Carpathian Russia), in Czechoslovakia, 1932-39. In 1939 he returned to England where he carried out evangelistic work among children evacuated from London, Polish prisoners-of-war, and later, Russian and Ukranian refugees. He held weekly meetings for Slavs in Earls Court, 1950-59, and then moved to Burnham-on-Sea, Somerset, and later to Walton-on-the-Naze, Essex. In 1927 he started translating hymns, and published *The Story of 'How Great Thou Art!'*, 1958; and *Not You, but God: A Testimony to God's faithfulness*, 1982.

Song: O Lord my God, when I in awesome wonder (37)

HODDER, Edwin

b Staines, Middlesex, 13 December 1837
d Chichester, Sussex, 1 March 1904

He went to New Zealand in 1856 with a group of pioneers, as a sociological experiment, but in 1861 returned to England where he became a civil servant and, after his retirement in 1897, lived at Henfield, Sussex. He compiled the *New Sunday School Hymn Book*, 1863 (enlarged edition, 1868) and published other books, including *Memories of New Zealand Life*, 1862, and *The Life of a Century*, 1900.

Song: Thy word is like a garden, Lord (658)

HODGES, Samuel Horatio

b Street, Somerset, 5 February 1841
d Flushing, New York, 12 August 1922

Son of Samuel Hodges, a cordwainer. He is said to have been a lawyer in America before joining the Army. He served for several years as an officer during the 1880s, and for a time travelled with William Booth, leading congregational songs and singing solos. In later years, he joined the Society of Friends (Quakers).

Song: Tell me what to do to be pure (459, verse 3?)

HODGSON, William

b Escomb, Durham, 20 July 1853
d Walthamstow, Essex, 8 June 1926

Son of William Hodgson, a coal miner. From the age of 11 he worked at the mine, first as a trapper boy, and then as a miner. In later years he was known as 'The Blood-washed Collier'. After his conversion he became a methodist local preacher. In 1879 he joined The Salvation Army in Spennymoor and, three days after meeting William Booth, he was appointed as an officer to Seaham Harbour. Subsequently he served in several corps appointments, including Whitby, North Shields, Limehouse, Chelsea and Hexham, and then in provincial centres, including Newcastle, Plymouth and Bristol. He then became 'Grace-before-Meat' representative in Brighton and Exeter, and served finally in the Subscribers' Department at International Headquarters. He retired in 1911 as a staff-captain. He contributed a number of songs to *The War Cry*.

Song: We're a band that shall conquer the foe (820)

HOFFMAN, Elisha Albright

b Orwigsburg, Pennsylvania, 7 May 1839
d Chicago(?), 25 November 1929

Son of the Reverend Francis A. Hoffman, a preacher and conference leader in the Evangelical Association. He was educated at Union Bible Seminary, New Berlin, Pennsylvania, and in 1868 was ordained by the East Pennsylvania Conference of the Evangelical Association. For some years he was involved in church and mission work and music publishing in Napoleon and Cleveland, Ohio. He then served as pastor of congregational churches in Cleveland and Grafton, Ohio, 1881-92; and as pastor of presbyterian churches in Vassar, Michigan, 1892-97; Benton Harbor, Michigan, 1897-1911; and Cabery, Illinois, 1911-22. He wrote more than 2,000 gospel songs and edited about 50 song books, including *The Evergreen*, 1873, and *Spiritual Songs for Gospel Meetings and the Sunday School*, 1878, with J. H. Tenney.

Songs: Down at the cross where my Saviour died (315)
Have you been to Jesus for the cleansing power (417)
What a fellowship, what a joy divine (768)

HOGGARD, Robert

b Beverley, Yorkshire, 16 November 1861
d Hadleigh, Essex, 13 August 1935

At the age of nine he was a barge boy and worked on the waterways near Beverley for about seven years. He became a Salvation Army officer after William Booth had visited Hull to present a flag to the Icehouse Corps, and served in corps appointments, including Bristol Circus and Scarborough, and later in divisional work and as a provincial officer. Subsequently he was Candidates' Secretary and then Commander of the Southern Province in Southampton. In 1908 he was appointed to pioneer Army work in Korea, and after several years there he served successively as Territorial Commander for Scotland, South Africa and New Zealand, and as an international travelling commissioner. His last appointment was as Territorial Commander for Canada (West) and he retired as a commissioner in 1932. He contributed several songs to *The Musical Salvationist*.

Song: Saviour of light, I look just now to thee (628)

HOLBROOK, Olive Leah (*née* GILL)

b Hebburn-on-Tyne, Durham, 8 June 1895
d Camberwell, London, 10 March 1986

Daughter of Major and Mrs W. Gill, she entered the training college from Leeds New Wortley in 1915 and was commissioned as a sergeant in the following year. After corps appointments at Kennington Lane, Gravesend and Plumstead, she was a brigade officer at the training college for two sessions. She married Captain (later Commissioner) Theodore Holbrook in 1921. They served together for 46 years, in corps, training college and divisional appointments in Britain, and subsequently in Central America and West Indies, in Rhodesia, and Western India, and finally at International Headquarters (where her husband was International Secretary for Asia and Africa). They retired in 1967. She started writing verses occasionally when she was a cadet, and later wrote articles for various Salvation Army publications. For about four years she wrote regularly for *The Musician* under the pen-name 'Greta Friend'.

Song: Deep were the scarlet stains of sin (176)

HOPPER, Edward

b New York, 17 February 1816 or 1818
d New York, 23 April 1888

Educated at New York University and Union Theological Seminary, New York. He served as pastor of presbyterian churches in Greenville, New York, and Sag Harbor, Long Island, for about 11 years, and was then pastor at the Church of the Sea and Land, in the New York harbour area.

Song: Jesus, Saviour, pilot me (598)

HOPPS, John Page

b London, 6 November 1834
d Shepperton, Middlesex, 6 April 1911

Educated at the baptist college, Leicester. He served for a short while as baptist minister at Hugglescote and Ibstock,

Leicestershire, and then became assistant minister at the Church of the Saviour, Birmingham, in 1856. After 1860, he ministered to unitarian congregations in Sheffield, Dukinfield and Glasgow, and subsequently in Leicester, 1876-92, and in London, 1905-1909. He edited a monthly periodical, *The Truthseeker*, 1863-87, and compiled several hymn books, including *Hymns for Public Worship and the Home*, 1858, and *The Children's Hymn Book*, 1879.

Song: Father, lead me day by day (837)

HORNE, Charles Silvester

b Cuckfield, Sussex, 15 April 1865
d Toronto, Canada, 2 May 1914

Educated at Glasgow University and Mansfield College, Oxford. He was pastor of the Allen Street Congregational Church, Kensington, 1889-1903, and then superintendent of Whitefield's Central Mission, Tottenham Court Road, London. He was Chairman of the Congregational Union of England and Wales, 1910-11, and was elected MP for Ipswich in 1909.

Song: Sing we the King who is coming to reign (166)

HOW, William Walsham

b Shrewsbury, Shropshire, 13 December 1823
d Leenane, County Mayo, Ireland, 10 August 1897

Son of a solicitor, William Wybergh How. He was educated at Shrewsbury School, at Wadham College, Oxford, and at Durham. After ordination in 1846, he was curate of St George's, Kidderminster, 1846-48 and curate of Holy Cross, Shrewsbury, 1848-51. He became rector of Whittington, Shropshire, in 1851, and served for a few months during 1865 as chaplain of the English church in Rome. In 1879, he was appointed rector of St Andrew Undershaft, London, and Bishop of Bedford (suffragan bishop for East London), and in 1888 he became the first Bishop of Wakefield. He wrote about 60 hymns, and published other books, including *Daily Prayers for Churchmen*, 1852. He compiled *Psalms and Hymns*, 1854, with the

Reverend Thomas B. Morrell, and was also joint editor of *Church Hymns*, 1871.

Songs: For all the saints who from their labours rest (876)
       O Jesus, thou art standing (299)
       Soldiers of the cross, arise (697)
       Summer suns are glowing (40)

HOWE, Julia Ward

b New York, 27 May 1819
d Middletown, Rhode Island, 17 October 1910

In 1843, she married Dr Samuel G. Howe, who was for some years Director of the Perkins Institute for the Blind, in Boston. She was an active supporter of many humanitarian causes, including work among the blind, the abolition of slavery, women's suffrage and a world-wide campaign to end war. She often preached in unitarian and other churches. Her publications included several volumes of poetry: *Passion Flowers*, 1854; *Words of the Hour*, 1856; and *Later Lyrics*, 1866.

Song: Mine eyes have seen the glory of the coming of the Lord (162)

HOYLE, Richard Birch

b Cloughfold, Lancashire, 8 March 1875
d Wimbledon, Surrey, 14 December 1939

He studied for the baptist ministry at Regent's Park College, London, and served as pastor of churches in Sudbury, Aberdeen and London, 1900-17, and in Belvedere, Kent, 1923-26. He was editor of the *Red Triangle* magazine published by the YMCA, 1918-23, and was later professor of systematic theology at Western Theological Seminary in Pittsburgh, Pennsylvania, 1934-36. Apparently, on his return to England, he was pastor of Kingston-on-Thames Baptist Church. He translated hymns from a number of languages and contributed to *Cantate Domino*, 1925, the hymn book of the World Student Christian Federation.

Song: Thine is the glory (152)

HUBBARD, Sidney Robert

b Stepney, London, 29 April 1898
d Tunbridge Wells, Kent, 4 December 1984

His parents were salvationists at Whitechapel Corps and later at Stepney. He became a junior soldier at Mile End Corps and then transferred to Limehouse where he was appointed bandmaster at the age of 16. He entered the training college in 1923, and, after a year as a cadet-sergeant, served for about 20 years in corps appointments including Sowerby Bridge, Kirkburton, Clacton-on-Sea, Folkestone, Luton Citadel and Barking. During the Second World War he was on war work for two years. In 1947 he was transferred to the Public Relations Bureau at International Headquarters and later served in the Secretary's Department (Publicity Section) for more than 10 years. He retired as a brigadier in 1963. For several years he studied music by correspondence course with Bandmaster George Marshall. His first song was published while he was a cadet, and he later composed music for bands and contributed a number of songs to *The Musical Salvationist*.

Song: Jesus saved me! O the rapture (350)

HUGHES, R. F.

b ?
d ?

No information about the author is available, though he was apparently living in the United States, *c*1870.

Song: We are marching home to Glory (902, chorus)

HULL, Anna Matilda

b Marpool Hall, Exmouth, Devon, *c*1812
d Eastbourne, Sussex, 29 August 1882

Daughter of William Thomas Hull, a magistrate. She published a collection of her hymns in 1850, and also *Heart*

Melodies, 1864, and other books. Some of her hymns appeared in H. W. Soltau's *Pleasant Hymns for Boys and Girls*, 1860, and *The Enlarged London Hymn Book*, 1873.

Song: There is life for a look at the crucified one (271)

HUMPHREY, Alfred

b Kingston-on-Thames, Surrey, 18 August 1864
d Winton, Hampshire, 20 February 1933

Son of William Humphrey, a gardener. Before joining The Salvation Army he was a Bible class leader and local preacher but, when a corps opened in Kingston he was bandmaster and corps treasurer for two years, and then entered the Battersea Training Garrison in 1889. Subsequently he served in several corps appointments, including Stratford, Camberwell, Highgate and Regent Hall, and was later transferred to divisional work in 1903. After nine years as Chancellor of the Training Territory (East London), he was Divisional Commander for Notts and Derby, and West London, and then became Staff Secretary at National Headquarters. He retired as a colonel in 1929.

Song: I sought for love and strength and light (541)

HUNT, John

b Bardsley, near Oldham, Lancashire, 18 August 1897
d Ilford, Essex, 20 February 1982

After military service in France during the First World War he entered the training college in 1919 from Oldham Citadel, where he was a cornet soloist. Before training he had been in charge of corps at Whitstable and Sandwich, and subsequently he served in corps appointments including Gillingham, Manchester Star Hall and Rochdale Citadel. In 1940 he was transferred to The Salvation Army Assurance Society, where he later became Assistant Staff Secretary. For a few years, during the Second World War, he was a member of the Assurance Songsters and he was also for a time editor of the *Assurance* magazine. In 1948 he was appointed to International Headquarters as Assistant Education Secretary, becoming

Education Secretary in 1953. He retired as a colonel in 1962. He contributed a number of songs to *The Musical Salvationist*, several with music by Harry Kniveton.

Song: Those first disciples of the Lord (760)

HUNTER, William

b near Ballymoney, County Antrim, 26 May 1811
d Cleveland, Ohio, 18 October 1877

Son of John Hunter. His family emigrated to America in 1817 and settled in York, Pennsylvania. He studied at Madison College and was ordained as a methodist minister. He edited the *Pittsburgh Conference Journal*, 1836-40, and the *Christian Advocate*, 1844-52 and 1872-76, and he was professor of Hebrew at Allegheny College, 1855-70. His hymns were published in his *Select Melodies*, 1838-51; *The Minstrel of Zion*, 1845; and *Songs of Devotion*, 1859.

Songs: The great physician now is near (67)
We're bound for the land of the pure and the holy (905)

HUNTINGTON, De Witt Clinton

b Townshend, Vermont, 27 April 1830
d Lincoln, Nebraska, 8 February 1912

Educated at Syracuse University, New York. After his ordination as a methodist episcopal minister in 1853, he served as pastor of churches in Rochester, 1861-71 and 1876-79; Syracuse, 1873-76; and Olean, New York, 1885-89; in Bradford, Pennsylvania, 1882-85 and 1889-91; and in Lincoln, Nebraska, 1891-96. He was also presiding elder in Rochester, 1871-73 and 1879-82, and in Lincoln, 1896-98. Subsequently he was chancellor of Nebraska Wesleyan University, 1898-1908, and then became professor of English Bible there in 1908.

Song: O think of the home over there (886)

HUSSEY, Jennie Evelyn

b Henniker, New Hampshire, 8 February 1874
d Concord, New Hampshire, 1958

She grew up on a farm where her family had apparently lived for four generations. She was a member of the Society of Friends. At the age of eight she started writing poems, and later wrote more than 150 hymns, as well as poems, stories for children, and articles about flowers, for various periodicals. She spent her later years in a home for the aged, at Concord, New Hampshire.

Song: King of my life, I crown thee now (117)

HUTCHINGS, William Medlen

b Devonport, Devon, 28 August 1827
d Camberwell, Surrey, 21 May 1876

Son of William Hutchings. He was apparently a congregationalist, and was for some time a printer and publisher in London.

Song: When mothers of Salem (797)

HUTCHINS, William Henry

b Dunstable, Bedfordshire, 6 November 1870
d Dunstable, Bedfordshire, 17 September 1945

He grew up in Dunstable, where he attended the methodist church, but in 1889 he went to live in Luton and served as a bandsman at Luton II Corps for about three years. He then returned to Dunstable and became a methodist local preacher and a mission-band leader and also held other responsibilities in the church. He sometimes spelt his surname 'Hutchings', and was probably the author of a song, 'Cleanse me now', by W. H. Hutchings, Dunstable, in *The War Cry*, 18 June 1887.

Song: While here before thy cross I kneel (649)

INGEMANN, Bernhardt Severin

b Thorkildstrup, Falster, Denmark, 28 May 1789
d Sorö, Zealand, Denmark, 24 February 1862

Son of a Lutheran pastor, he was educated at the University of Copenhagen. He spent two years travelling in France, Germany, Switzerland and Italy, and became professor of Danish language and literature at Sorö Academy, in 1822. He wrote lyric poetry, historical novels, stories for children, hymns and songs, including *High-Mass Hymns*, 1825, for each of the Christian festivals. His collected works were published in 34 volumes in 1851.

Song: Through the night of doubt and sorrow (765)

IRONS, Genevieve Mary

b Brompton, Middlesex, 28 December 1855
d Eastbourne, Sussex, 13 December 1928

Daughter of Dr Williams J. Irons. She contributed poems to the *Sunday Magazine*, and published *Corpus Christi*, 1884, a manual for Holy Communion.

Song: Drawn to the cross which thou hast blest (287)

IZZARD, John Colquhoun

b Glasgow, 19 March 1924

He became a Salvation Army officer in 1947 from Parkhead, Glasgow. After serving in corps appointments, and then at International Headquarters, and as national youth crusader, he was appointed to Cardiff as divisional young people's secretary in 1963. Subsequently he was national organiser for torchbearer groups and youth centres, 1966-69; assistant national youth secretary, 1969-72; and territorial youth secretary for Scotland, 1972-74. In 1974 he returned to corps work in the Birmingham Division, and since 1982 he has been commanding officer at

Birmingham Harborne Corps. He retired in June 1989. He has contributed several poems to the *Assurance* magazine and *The Officer*.

Song: Dear Lord, I lift my heart to thee (717)

JACKSON, George Galloway

b Fairfax, Tokomairiro, New Zealand, 28 December 1866
d Weston, Oamaru, New Zealand, 27 October 1893

He came from a presbyterian family in Weston, near Oamaru, South Island. He was educated at Otago Boys' High School and became a Salvation Army officer in 1888. He served at territorial headquarters in various positions, latterly with the rank of ensign. His responsibilities included the preparation of early issues of the New Zealand *Band Journal*. He played the concertina, banjo, cornet, euphonium and organ. For a time he was bandmaster of the Oamaru Band, and he also trained other brass and vocal groups, including the 'Beulah Land Singers' and the Lasses' Brass, String and Timbrel Band.

Song: I want, dear Lord, a heart that's true and clean (426)

JAMES, Annie L.

b ?
d ?

No information about the author is available. Her song seems to have appeared first in the United States in 1887.

Song: Is there a heart that is waiting (247)

JAMES, Mary Dagworthy

b 10 August 1810
d 1883

Little is known about the author, except that she was apparently a close friend of Mrs Phoebe Palmer of New York City, and contributed regularly to the *Guide to Holiness*. She also wrote a number of biographies, including *The Soul Winner: A Sketch of Edmund J. Yard*, 1883, her brother, who was a class leader and hospital visitor in Philadelphia, Pennsylvania, for 65 years.

Song: My body, soul and spirit (511)

JARVIS, Maureen Elsa (*née* MILLARD)

b Dunedin, New Zealand, 1 April 1928

Daughter of salvationists, Arthur and Janet Millard, who contributed songs to *The Musical Salvationist*. Her family moved to Palmerston North in 1944 and from there she entered the training college in 1952. She was commissioned in the following year and married Lieutenant (later Lieutenant-Colonel) Victor Jarvis in 1955. After five years in corps appointments they served for more than 20 years at territorial headquarters where she was for a time secretary of the league of mercy. Subsequently they were appointed to the Central North Division and then in 1986 to the Northern Division in Auckland, where she is divisional director of women's organisations. While serving at territorial headquarters she was young people's singing company leader at Wellington South Corps for nine years, and also completed a bachelor of music degree at the Victoria University of Wellington. She has written a few songs for *The Musical Salvationist* and *New Songs for Young People*.

Song: O God of love eternal (943)

JEFFERSON, William

b Blyth, Northumberland, 17 April 1806
d Ripley, Derbyshire, 13 April 1870

At the age of nine, he left school and went to work in a coal mine. He later showed an aptitude for music and was a member of his chapel choir. After his conversion, aged 23, he attended evening classes and became a local preacher, superintendent of the Sunday-school, and a class leader. Called to the primitive methodist ministry, he served in the Leicester circuit for two years, and then in a succession of appointments, including

Chesterfield, Burton-upon-Trent, Nottingham, Barnsley, Sheffield, Lincoln, Derby and Ripley.

Song: Come, sinners, to Jesus, no longer delay (233)

JENKINS, William Vaughan

b Bristol, 6 September 1868
d Bitton, Gloucestershire, 30 June 1920

Son of Frederick Augustus Jenkins, an accountant, he was educated at Bristol Grammar School and became a chartered accountant. He was active in mission work, and, at various times, was associated with the Tyndale Baptist Church, Highbury Congregational Church and the parish church in Bitton, where he lived in later years. He was secretary of the Adult School Union, in Bristol, and was a member of the National Council of the Adult School Movement. He was also a choir leader and was one of the compilers of the *Fellowship Hymn Book*, 1909.

Song: O God of love, to thee we bow (947)

JOHNSON, Emma

b ?
d ?

No information about the author is available. Her song seems to have appeared first in the United States, *c*1892.

Song: Why should life a weary journey seem (400)

JOHNSON, Gustaf Kaleb

b Ornuga, near Borås, Sweden, 19 January 1888
d Duluth, Minnesota, 25 November 1965

At the age of 15 he emigrated to the United States. After three months as a soldier, he entered the training college in New York in 1909, from the corps in Ridgway, Pennsylvania. He served in corps appointments in the USA Eastern Territory, 1910-24 and then in the USA Central Territory, where he commanded several corps, including Duluth, Chicago

(Roseland), Minneapolis Cedar Avenue and Minneapolis Central. With the rank of senior-major, he retired in 1953. He started writing songs when he was 15 and later wrote hundreds of songs in Swedish and English, mostly with his own melodies. He also played the violin.

Song: Songs of salvation are sounding (383)

JOHNSON, Joseph

b Basingstoke, Hampshire, 31 March 1848
d Sale, Cheshire, 12 December 1926

Educated at Cheshunt College, he became a congregational minister in 1875. For some years, from 1877, he was minister of a church in Ashton on Mersey, Cheshire. He wrote several hymns; stories for young people, including *Ruth's Life-work,* 1885, *The Master's Likeness,* 1885 and *Dibs: a Story of Young London Life,* 1887; and a biographical study, *George MacDonald,* 1906.

Song: God speaks to us in bird and song (31)

JOHNSON, Robert

b Scotland
d ?

After his conversion he became a Salvation Army officer in Scotland, and then transferred to the London training home, where he was a member of the singing brigade. He was a singer and a violinist, and wrote a few songs which appeared in *The War Cry* and *The Musical Salvationist* in the period 1882-87.

Songs: Marching on in the light of God (811)
Soldiers of our God, arise (696)

JOLLIFFE, Fanny (*née* PEGG)

b 18 September 1862 (?)
d Islington, London, 10 February 1943

She was converted in a Salvation Army meeting in a disused carriage factory in Leamington, and in 1886 trained as a cadet at the Great Western Hall, Marylebone. She served as a training officer in Northampton, Bath, Oxford and Battersea, and in corps appointments at Leamington and Sheffield. For six months she was in charge of a revival brigade of lieutenants and later returned to training garrison work at several centres in London. In 1895 she married Major (later Commissioner) George Johnson Jolliffe, whose subsequent appointments included Head of the Subscribers' Department, International Secretary for Europe, and Governor of the Men's Social Work. They retired in 1939. (Although she was usually known as Fanny or Fannie, her name was registered as Frances when she married.)

Song: I do not ask thee, Lord (586)

JONES, Lewis Edgar

b Yates City, Illinois, 8 February 1865
d Santa Barbara, California, 1 September 1936

Educated at Moody Bible Institute, Chicago. He worked for the YMCA in Davenport, Iowa, and Fort Worth, Texas, and latterly as general secretary in Santa Barbara, 1915-25. He wrote a number of hymns, some of which appeared under various pseudonyms, including Lewis Edgar, Edgar Lewis and Mary Slater.

Song: Would you be free from your burden of sin (281)

JONES, Richard Granville

b Dursley, Gloucestershire, 26 July 1926

Educated at Truro School and St John's College, Cambridge (where he studied mechanical sciences) and later at Hartley Victoria College, Manchester. He has been minister of methodist churches in Sheffield, 1955-64; Birkenhead, 1964-69; and Fakenham and Wells, 1982-83, and became chairman of the Methodist Church, East Anglia District, in 1983. He was area secretary for the Student Christian Movement in Nottingham,

1953-55, and was for several years on the staff of Hartley Victoria College: as tutor, 1969-73; senior tutor, 1973-78; and principal, 1978-82. He has served on various methodist connexional committees, including Faith and Order, Church Membership, the Division of Ministries, and the committee which prepared *Hymns and Psalms*, 1983. His publications include: *How goes Christian Marriage?* 1978, and *Groundwork of Worship and Preaching*, 1980.

Song: God of concrete, God of steel (30)

JOY, Dorothy Olive

b Leeds, Yorkshire, 19 September 1903
d Croydon, Surrey, 17 December 1982

Daughter of Colonel Edward H. Joy. She was converted in a home league meeting led by her mother at Hanwell, and later became a songster at Penge. In 1924 she moved to Canada with her parents and after a time at Winnipeg Citadel transferred to Fort Rouge Corps, where she was corps cadet guardian. In Winnipeg she joined the staff of the editorial department, serving eventually as editor of *The Young Soldier*. Moving to South Africa she was songster leader and drama group leader at Cape Town Citadel. In 1939 she returned to England and held various responsibilities at Croydon Citadel. For about eight years she was secretary to the corps stewardship council and for many years prepared a quarterly corps newsletter, also writing to officers serving overseas. She was employed in the Ministry of Food and later the Ministry of Pensions, retiring in 1963. She wrote stories, poems and plays, and contributed several songs to *The Musical Salvationist*.

Song: For every rule of life required (785)

JOY, Edward Henry

b Canterbury, Kent, 16 November 1871
d Cheam, Surrey, 16 February 1949

He became a salvationist in Canterbury, but was later a bandsman at Folkestone before becoming an officer in 1894.

After one corps appointment (at Tunstall, where he was responsible for Golden Hill outpost), he served in provincial and divisional appointments until 1917, when he was transferred to International Headquarters, as Under Secretary in the Foreign Office. In 1919 he accompanied Commissioner T. Henry Howard on an international tour, visiting the United States, Canada, New Zealand, Australia and India. Subsequently he served in Western Canada, as Immigration Secretary, and then Editor-in-Chief, and in 1932 became editor of *The War Cry* in South Africa. He retired as a colonel in 1938 and in the following year returned to England. His first verses were published in *The Little Soldier* in 1887, and his first song 'We March to Victory' appeared in *The Musical Salvationist*, April 1892. The musical *Glory!* (written by John Gowans and John Larsson in 1975) was based on his book *The Old Corps*, 1944, which described early corps activities at Folkestone.

Songs: Is there a heart o'erbound by sorrow (246)
Jesus, tender lover of my soul (600)
O that in me the mind of Christ (451)
There was a Saviour came seeking his sheep (388)

JUKES, Richard

b Clungunford, Shropshire, 9 October 1804
d West Bromwich, 10 August 1867

Son of Richard Jukes, of Goathill, Shropshire. After his conversion in 1825 he became an exhorter and then a local preacher, and subsequently served as a primitive methodist minister for 32 years. He retired in 1859 and spent his later years in West Bromwich. A large number of his hymns and poems were first published on circuit plans, in the *Primitive Methodist Magazine* and in various small booklets. Most of his hymns were later included in *The Book that will Cheer You: or, Hymns for the Living and Dying*, 1862. James Pritchard wrote his biography, *The Poet of the Million*, 1868.

Songs: Behold! behold the Lamb of God (107)
I'm a soldier bound for Glory (338)
My heart is fixed, eternal God (356)
We're travelling home to Heaven above (275)
With steady pace the pilgrim moves (911)

KAUFMAN, Mrs S. Z.

b ?
d ?

No information about the author is available. Her song seems to have appeared first in the United States in 1885.

Song: Have you ever heard the story (96, verses 1-3)

KEBLE, John

b Fairford, Gloucestershire, 25 April 1792
d Bournemouth, Hampshire, 29 March 1866

Son of the Reverend J. Keble, vicar of Coln St Aldwyn's, Gloucestershire. He was educated at home and at Corpus Christi College, Oxford. He became a Fellow of Oriel College in 1811 and was a college tutor there, 1818-23. After his ordination in 1816, he served for short periods as curate of East Leach and Burthorpe, and later as curate of Southrop and as curate of Hursley, in 1825. He published *The Christian Year: or Thoughts in Verse for the Sundays and Holy Days throughout the Year,* 1827, and was appointed professor of poetry at Oxford in 1831. He preached the Assize Sermon at Oxford in 1833 on 'National Apostasy', which is usually considered the beginning of the Oxford Movement. He became vicar of Hursley in 1836, and served there for 30 years. His other publications included *Lyra Innocentium,* 1846; *Academical and Occasional Sermons,* 1847; and *Tracts for the Times,* Nos. 4, 13, 40 and 89.

Songs: Blest are the pure in heart (411, verses 1 and 3)
New every morning is the love (668)
Sun of my soul, thou Saviour dear (676)
The voice that breathed o'er Eden (949)

KELLY, Thomas

b Kellyville, Stradbally, Queen's County, 13 July 1769
d Dublin, 14 May 1855

Son of Thomas Kelly, a judge. He was educated at Trinity College, Dublin, and came to the Temple, in London, intending to become a lawyer. After his conversion, he was ordained in the Irish Episcopal Church, in 1792, but the Archbishop of Dublin prevented him from preaching there, because of his evangelical doctrines. He preached for some time in unconsecrated buildings, but left the Established Church and built places of worship at Athy, Portarlington, Wexford and elsewhere. He wrote 765 hymns which he published in *A Collection of Psalms and Hymns extracted from Various Authors*, 1802, and in successive editions of his *Hymns on Various Passages of Scripture*, 1804-53.

Songs: Happy we who trust in Jesus (722)
Jesus comes! Let all adore him (159)
Look, ye saints! The sight is glorious (147)
O joyful sound! O glorious hour (149)
The head that once was crowned with thorns (168)
When we cannot see our way (772)

KEN, Thomas

b Little Berkhampsted, Hertfordshire, July 1637
d Longbridge Deverill, Wiltshire, 19 March 1711

Educated at Winchester College, and New College, Oxford. After his ordination in 1661 he was rector of Little Easton, 1663; incumbent of St John-in-the-Soke, Winchester, 1665; rector of Brighstone, Isle of Wight, 1667-69; and prebendary of Winchester and rector of East Woodhay, from 1669. He served briefly as chaplain to Princess Mary (later Queen Mary II) at The Hague, in 1679, and in 1685 he was appointed Bishop of Bath and Wells. He was one of seven bishops imprisoned in the Tower of London for opposing the Declaration of Indulgence, 1688, but after trial he was acquitted. In 1691, he was deprived of his See (removed from office) when he refused to take the Coronation Oath at the accession of King William III. He published *A Manual of Prayers for the Use of the Scholars of Winchester College*, 1674, adding hymns for morning, evening and midnight in later editions. His other poems, including *Hymns for all the Festivals of the Year*, were published posthumously in four volumes in 1721.

Songs: Awake, my soul, and with the sun (665)
Glory to thee, my God, this night (671)
Praise God, from whom all blessings flow (959)

KETHE, William

b ?
d Dorset, 1594

Little definite information about his life is known. He is sometimes said to have been born in Scotland, but this is uncertain. He was in exile in Frankfurt and Geneva, 1555-57, during a period of persecution in the reign of Queen Mary, and may have been one of the translators of the Geneva Bible, published in 1560. He was apparently rector of Childe Okeford, near Blandford, Dorset, from about 1565, probably until his death.

Song: All people that on earth do dwell (3)

KIDDER, Mary Ann (*née* PEPPER)

b Boston, Massachusetts, 16 March 1820
d Chelsea, Massachusetts, 25 November 1905

As a teenager she lost her sight, but several years later she fully recovered. She lived for many years in New York City and was a member of the Methodist Episcopal Church. She wrote a number of hymns.

Songs: Above the waves of earthly strife (872)
Lord, I care not for riches, neither silver nor gold (883)

KING, John

b Kingston upon Hull, Yorkshire, 1789
d Kingston upon Hull, Yorkshire, 12 September 1858

Educated at Queens' College, Cambridge. He was ordained in 1814 and was apparently curate of Wellington with Eyton, Shropshire, before becoming perpetual curate of Christ Church, Hull, in 1822. His publications included *Sermons*, 1832; *A Treatise on Conscience*, 1838; and a *Memoir of the Reverend Thomas Dykes, of Hull*, 1849.

Song: When, his salvation bringing (853)

KITCHING, Theodore Hopkins

b Ackworth, Yorkshire, 29 December 1866
d Paris, 10 February 1930

Son of William Kitching, a schoolmaster (see below). He was educated at Ackworth School, and at the age of 16 was converted in a Salvation Army meeting while on holiday in Bristol. In 1888 he became an officer and served in secretarial, training and other appointments in Britain, France and Switzerland, and Belgium. In 1906 he compiled the first edition of *The Salvation Army Year Book*. Subsequently he was Secretary to the Founder, William Booth, 1909-12; Secretary to General Bramwell Booth, 1912-14; and International Secretary for Europe, 1914-16. He became the General's Secretary again in 1916, and was later Editor-in-Chief, 1921-29, and finally head of the Literary Department and Translations Bureau. In February 1930 he was travelling to Geneva as the General's ambassador, but died suddenly in a station restaurant in Paris. His son, Wilfred (1893-1977), became the Army's seventh General in 1954.

Song: How wonderful it is to walk with God (583)

KITCHING, William

b Gainsborough, Lincolnshire, 1 June 1837
d Clevedon, Somerset, 24 December 1906

Son of William Kitching, a grocer. He was educated at Ackworth School, Yorkshire, and Bootham School, York, and later became a master at Sidcot School, Somerset, 1860-62, and at Ackworth School, 1862-80. He then moved to Southport, where he opened a school for boys. He was a member of the Society of Friends (Quakers), but his home in Southport, and later in Clevedon, was always open to visiting salvationists and he contributed verses occasionally to Salvation Army periodicals. One of his songs was included in *Sacred Songs and Solos*, compiled by Ira D. Sankey, and his poems were published in *Verses for my Friends*.

Song: Who comes to me, the Saviour said (277)

LAINCHBURY, James

b Keresley, Warwickshire, 15 March 1861
d ?

Son of William Lainchbury, a gardener. After leaving school, he worked as a cabinet maker in Wellingborough until October 1881 when he entered the training home at Clapton. Following two months' training, he served in several corps appointments, including Sunderland I, Hull II, Leeds I and Liverpool V, always taking a special interest in children's work. In 1885 he was appointed Little Soldiers' Adjutant in the London Division and subsequently held a similar appointment in the Kent and Sussex Division until September 1888. He contributed songs and articles regularly to *The Little Soldier* during 1886.

Song: Children, sing for gladness (835)

LANGE, Joachim

b Gardelegen, 26 October 1670
d Halle, 7 May 1744

Son of Mauritius Lange, senior councillor at Gardelegen. He was educated at the University of Leipzig and became a private tutor in Berlin, in 1693. Subsequently he was rector of a school at Cöslin, in Pomerania; rector of the Friedrichswerder Gymnasium, at Berlin; pastor of the Friedrichstadt church, 1699-1709; and professor of theology at Halle, from 1709. He published more than 100 theological works, including a seven-volume commentary on the Bible: *Biblisches Licht und Recht*, 1730-38.

Song: O God, what offering shall I give (516)

LARSSON, Flora Ethel Mildred (*née* BENWELL)

b Buenos Aires, Argentina, 31 May 1904

Daughter of Commissioner Alfred J. Benwell. She entered the training college in 1926 from Copenhagen Temple Corps.

After training and a year as a cadet-sergeant she served in France and at International Headquarters, and then married Captain (later Commissioner) Sture Larsson in 1934. They served together at Loughborough Junction Corps, and subsequently in Sweden, Denmark, South America, France, Finland and Norway. Latterly he was International Secretary for Europe and retired in 1974. Her publications include *My Best Men are Women*, 1974, and books of devotional readings and prayers. She has written a number of songs, including several for children, and has also translated some Scandinavian songs into English.

Songs: Each day is a gift supernal (666)
Gentle arms of Jesus (792)
I'm going to make my life into a melody (858)
Thank you, Lord, for all your goodness (552)

LATHBURY, Mary Artemisia

b Manchester, New York, 10 August 1841
d East Orange, New Jersey, 20 October 1913

Daughter of a methodist minister or local preacher. She was a writer, a poet and a professional artist. She edited and contributed to magazines published by the Methodist Sunday School Union, and founded the 'Look-up Legion' for young people in methodist Sunday-schools. For some years she was associated with the annual Chautauqua Assembly meetings at Lake Chautauqua, New York. She apparently joined the Church of the New Jerusalem, in Orange, New Jersey, in 1895. She wrote *The Child's Story of the Bible*, 1898.

Song: Break thou the bread of life (650, verse 1)

LATTA, Eden Reeder

b near Ligonier, Noble County, Indiana, 24 March 1839
d ?

There is little information available about the life of the author. Apparently, as a boy he was a close friend of William A. Ogden, who later composed music for many of his Sunday-school songs. He wrote more than 1,600 songs and hymns for various publishers and composers, including E. S. Lorenz, J. H. Fillmore and James McGranahan.

Song: Tell me what to do to be pure (459, chorus)

LAWLEY, John

b Foulden, Norfolk, 31 December 1859
d Watford, Hertfordshire, 9 September 1922

Son of John Lawley, a farm labourer. As a boy he helped with farm work until his family moved to Bradford, where he became an engine-lad. He was converted in a Christian Mission meeting in Pullan's Theatre, Bradford, and nine months later, he became a Christian Mission evangelist. In 1878 he was stationed at Jarrow-on-Tyne where he wrote the first of his many songs. He later served in other corps and divisional appointments, and as Candidates' Secretary (National Headquarters). He was ADC to the Founder, General William Booth, for more than 20 years, and subsequently to General Bramwell Booth, assisting in their meetings as a soloist and leader of congregational singing.

Songs: Come, with me visit Calvary (413)
Give us a day of wonders (575)
Have you seen the crucified (243)
Near thy cross assembled, Master (197)
O happy, happy day (366)
Though thunders roll and darkened be the sky (761)
Wanted, hearts baptised with fire (704)
When Jesus was born in the manger (137)

LEESON, Jane Eliza

b Wilford, Nottinghamshire, 1808
d Leamington, Warwickshire, 18 November 1881

Little is known about the author, except that she is said to have been a member of the Catholic Apostolic Church until late in life when she became a Roman catholic. She published *Hymns and Scenes of Childhood, or a Sponsor's Gift*, 1842; *Paraphrases and Hymns for Congregational Singing*, 1853; and other poetry, songs and ballads. She also contributed some hymns and translations to Henry Formby's *Catholic Hymns*, 1851, and to *Hymns for the Use of the Churches*, 1864 (the hymn book of the Catholic Apostolic Church).

Song: Saviour, teach me day by day (846)

LEIDZÉN, Erik William Gustaf

b Stockholm, Sweden, 25 March 1894
d New York, 18 December 1962

He was born on Easter Day, four months after his father, Staff-Captain Erik W. Leidzén, had died. He studied music in Copenhagen and at the Royal Conservatory of Music in Stockholm. He emigrated to the United States in 1915, and became widely known as a composer, pianist, lecturer and conductor. For some years he was arranger for the Edwin Franko Goldman Band in New York. He lectured at various schools and colleges, including New York University, the University of Michigan, the Ernest Williams School of Music and the National Music Camp at Interlochen, Michigan. He was instructor for many years at the annual Salvation Army summer camp at Star Lake, New Jersey. His first contribution to the band journals was the march 'Stockholm I', published in 1915, and his first composition in the *Festival Series* was the festival march 'Pressing Onward' in 1925. His other compositions included an 'Irish Symphony' dedicated to his mother, Elinor Kelly Leidzén. He also wrote the book *An Invitation to Band Arranging*.

Song: Peace, perfect peace, far beyond all understanding (751)

LEIGHTON, Thomas Henry Collett

b c1858
d ?

Son of Thomas Leighton, a nailmaker. He became an officer in 1884 from Halifax I Corps, and served in several corps appointments, including Raunds and Ringstead, Kettering, and Leyton. In 1887 he was appointed village adjutant in charge of the Cambridge District, and he later served in Canada, becoming a major in 1890. Sometimes signing himself 'Tommy the Nailer', he contributed a number of poems and songs to *The War Cry* and early volumes of *The Musical Salvationist*.

Song: Praise God, I'm saved (960)

LLOYD, William Freeman

b Uley, Gloucestershire, 22 December 1791
d Kings Stanley, Gloucestershire, 22 April 1853

In 1810, he was appointed one of the secretaries of the Sunday School Union, and in 1816 became associated with the Religious Tract Society. He commenced the *Sunday School Teacher's Magazine* and for several years edited the *Child's Companion* and the *Weekly Visitor*. He wrote books and tracts for Sunday-school teachers and children, and published his collected poetry in *Thoughts in Rhyme*, 1853.

Song: My times are in thy hand (917)

LONGFELLOW, Henry Wadsworth

b Portland, Maine, 27 February 1807
d Cambridge, Massachusetts, 24 March 1882

Son of Stephen Longfellow, a lawyer, and brother of the hymn writer Samuel Longfellow. He was educated at Bowdoin College and then studied in France, Spain, Italy and Germany for four years, before becoming professor of modern languages and librarian at Bowdoin College, 1829-35. After further study in Europe he was professor of modern languages and belles-lettres at Harvard, 1835-54. His first published poem appeared in the *Gazette of Maine* in 1820, and his first book of verse, *Voices of the Night* was published in 1839. His later poetry included *The Golden Legend,* 1851; *The Song of Hiawatha,* 1855; and *The Courtship of Miles Standish, and Other Poems,* 1858.

Song: Let nothing disturb thee (956)

LONGFELLOW, Samuel

b Portland, Maine, 18 June 1819
d Portland, Maine, 3 October 1892

Educated at Portland Academy, Harvard University and Harvard Divinity School. He became a unitarian minister and served as pastor at Fall River, Massachusetts, 1848-51; Brooklyn, New York, 1853-60; and later at Germantown, Pennsylvania, 1878-83. With Samuel Johnson, he compiled *A Book of Hymns for Public and Private Devotion*, 1846, and *Hymns of the Spirit*, 1864. He also wrote a biography of his brother, Henry Wadsworth Longfellow, which was published in 1886.

Song: Holy Spirit, truth divine (194)

LONGSTAFF, William Dunn

b Sunderland, 28 January 1822
d Sunderland, 2 April 1894

Son of a ship owner and land owner. He was treasurer of the Bethesda Free Chapel, in Sunderland, established by the Reverend Arthur A. Rees, and he was also a friend of General William Booth and the evangelists Moody and Sankey. A number of songs by William D. Longstaff, or W. D. Longstaff, of Sunderland, which appeared in *The War Cry*, 1883-89, were probably written by the same author.

Song: Take time to be holy, speak oft with thy Lord (458)

LOWRY, Robert

b Philadelphia, Pennsylvania, 12 March 1826
d Plainfield, New Jersey, 25 November 1899

Son of Crozier Lowry, a tavern keeper. He was educated at the University of Lewisburg (later Bucknell University) and then became a baptist pastor, serving at West Chester, Pennsylvania, 1854-58; Bloomingdale Baptist Church, New York City, 1859-61; Hanson Place Baptist Church, Brooklyn, 1861-69; and the First Baptist Church, Lewisburg, Pennsylvania, 1869-75, where he was also professor of rhetoric at the University of Lewisburg. Subsequently he was pastor of Park Avenue Baptist Church at Plainfield, New Jersey, for nine years. He composed music for about 500 gospel songs, mainly for verses written by other authors, and he was joint editor of several collections of Sunday-school songs, including *Happy Voices*, 1865; *Bright Jewels*, 1869; *Royal Diadem*, 1873; and *Welcome Tidings*, 1877.

Songs: Give me the wings of faith to rise (879, chorus)
I need thee every hour (587, chorus)
Low in the grave he lay (148)
Once I heard a sound at my heart's dark door (373, chorus)
Shall we gather at the river (891)
To leave the world below (901, chorus)
What can wash away my sin (306)

LUDGATE, Joseph C.

b London
d Wheaton, Illinois, 1 November 1947

He was brought up in the Roman Catholic Church, but, as a boy, sometimes attended meetings at a gospel mission hall, where he was later converted. He went to some Salvation Army meetings in Whitechapel and at the new International Headquarters, but then emigrated to Canada in 1882, apparently 'to get away from the Army'. In London, Ontario, he soon met a salvationist from England, Jack (later Colonel) Addie, and in May 1882 they held an open-air meeting in Victoria Park, from which Salvation Army work in Canada developed. He was commissioned as a lieutenant in Brooklyn, and served in a succession of appointments in New Jersey, New York, Toronto, and other divisions. Later, as a brigadier, he was Divisional Officer in the Rocky Mountains Division and Secretary for Field Affairs in the Department of the West. During the First World War he was apparently a military chaplain and is said to have been attached for a time to the staff of Wheaton Military College as a spiritual adviser. He started to write songs after reading an appeal for new songs in *The War Cry* in 1882, and later tried to write at least one song for publication each week.

Song: A friend of Jesus! O what bliss (709)

LUKE, Jemima (*née* THOMPSON)

b Islington, Middlesex, 19 August 1813
d Newport, Isle of Wight, 2 February 1906

Daughter of Thomas Thompson, one of the founders of the British and Foreign Sailors' Society. She first contributed to the *Juvenile Magazine* at the age of 13, and was later the editor of *The Missionary Repository*, 1841-45, a missionary magazine for children. In 1843 she married Samuel Luke, a congregational minister who became pastor of Hope Chapel, Clifton, in 1853, and then minister of Pembroke Chapel, Clifton, in 1866. Sometime after his death in 1868, she moved to Newport. Her publications included *The Female Jesuit*, 1851, and *A Memoir of Eliza Ann Harris, of Clifton*, 1859.

Song: I think, when I read that sweet story of old (794)

LUTHER, Martin

b Eisleben, Saxony, 10 November 1483
d Eisleben, Saxony, 18 February 1546

Son of Hans Luther, a miner. He was educated at schools at Magdeburg and Eisenach, and at the University of Erfurt. In 1505, he entered an Augustinian monastery at Erfurt, and in 1507 he was ordained as a priest. After lecturing and teaching at Wittenberg and Erfurt, he was appointed professor of theology at the University of Wittenberg. There he became increasingly involved in theological and ecclesiastical controversy. In 1517 he declared his opposition to the sale of indulgences, and his continued disputes with Papal authority led to his excommunication. He was given refuge at Wartburg Castle, near Eisenach, in 1521, but a year later returned to Wittenberg, where he became one of the outstanding leaders of the Reformation. He translated the Bible into German, 1521-34, and wrote a number of hymns and paraphrases, often adapting tunes from folksong sources.

Song: A mighty fortress is our God (1)

LYNCH, Thomas Toke

b Dunmow, Essex, 5 July 1818
d Camden Town, Middlesex, 9 May 1871

Son of John Burke Lynch, a surgeon. He studied for a short while at Highbury Independent College, and served as minister of congregations in Highgate, 1847-49, and in London, 1849-56. After a period of illness he resumed his ministry in 1860 in a room in Gower Street and then in the new Mornington Church, Hampstead Road, London, which opened in 1862. His hymns were published in *The Rivulet,* 1855, with additional hymns in the enlarged edition, 1868, and his other publications included *Thoughts on a Day,* 1844, and *The Mornington Lecture,* 1870.

Song: Gracious Spirit, dwell with me (212)

LYTE, Henry Francis

b Ednam, Roxburghshire, 1 June 1793
d Nice, France, 20 November 1847

Son of an Army officer, Captain Thomas Lyte. He was educated at Portora Royal School, Enniskillen, and at Trinity College, Dublin. After studying medicine for a while, he changed to theology and was ordained in 1815. He served briefly as curate at Taghmon, near Wexford, and later at Marazion, Cornwall, and at Charlton, near Kingsbridge, Devon, before becoming perpetual curate of Lower Brixham, Devon, in 1823. In Brixham he lived at Berry Head House which was presented to him by King William IV, but in later years, when his health was deteriorating, he spent much of his time in Naples, Switzerland, the Tyrol and Rome, hoping to find a climate which suited him. Most of his hymns and poems were published in *Tales on the Lord's Prayer in Verse,* 1826; *Poems, chiefly Religious,* 1833 (enlarged 1845); and *The Spirit of the Psalms,* 1834 (enlarged 1836).

Songs: Abide with me; fast falls the eventide (670)
        Jesus, I my cross have taken (498)
        Praise, my soul, the King of Heaven (17)

LYTH, John

b York, 13 March 1821
d York, 13 March 1886

He became a methodist minister in 1843 and served in Stroud, Gloucester, Deptford, Nottingham, Halifax and Burnley, until 1859, when he was appointed to Germany, and worked there for six years, before returning to England in 1865. Continuing in circuit work in Redruth, Liverpool, Sheffield, Hull, Nottingham and Sunderland, he retired in 1883. He edited *Wild Flowers; or a Selection of Original Poetry*, 1843, which included some of his own poems, and also wrote *The Blessedness of Religion in Earnest*, 1861 (a biography of his mother), and *Glimpses of Early Methodism in York*, 1885.

Song: There is a better world, they say (268)

McALONAN, William John

b Ligoniel, near Belfast, 12 June 1863
d Winchmore Hill, Middlesex, 1 May 1925

His first contact with The Salvation Army was through an open-air meeting in Ligoniel in 1880, and, three months later, he was converted. In 1882 he left his employment as a clerk and cashier and entered the Devonshire House training home in Hackney. After four months' training, he was appointed to the Lancashire Division as ADC to the divisional commander. Subsequently he was in charge of the Worcester and Hereford District, followed by the Swansea District, and then served in the trade department for seven years, and in other headquarters appointments for a further seven years. He became a territorial commander in 1901, serving successively in Sweden, Switzerland, Germany, and Holland. Afterwards he was appointed International Secretary for Missionary Countries, and finally, for three years, he was Managing Director of The Salvation Army Assurance Society.

Songs: All have need of God's salvation (824)
I have seen his face in blessing (330)

McDANIEL, Rufus Henry

b near Ripley, Ohio, 29 January 1850
d Dayton, Ohio, 13 February 1940

Educated at Parker's Academy, Claremont County, Ohio. At the age of 19 he was licensed to preach and in 1873 was ordained in the Christian Church (Disciples of Christ). He served as pastor of several churches in Ohio, including Hamersville, Higginsport, Centerburg and Sugar Creek, and after a pastorate at Cincinnati, he retired to Dayton. He wrote more than 100 hymns, many of which were published by The Rodeheaver Company.

Song: What a wonderful change in my life has been wrought (394)

MACDONALD, George

b Huntly, Aberdeenshire, 10 December 1824
d Ashtead, Surrey, 18 September 1905

Educated at King's College, Aberdeen, and Highbury College, London, where he studied for the congregational ministry. He was minister of Trinity Congregational Church, Arundel, 1850-53, and for short periods during 1854 and 1855 ministered to small congregations in Manchester and Bolton, subsequently devoting himself to lecturing and writing. He was professor of English language and literature at Bedford College, London, 1859-67, and went on lecture tours in Scotland, in 1869, and the United States, 1872-73. He wrote novels, short stories and poetry, including *Within and Without*, 1855; *David Elginbrod*, 1863; *Robert Falconer*, 1868; and *A Threefold Cord*, 1883. He contributed some hymns to *Hymns and Sacred Songs for Sunday Schools and Sacred Worship*, 1855, edited by George Bubier.

Song: They all were looking for a king (91)

MACKENZIE, Elizabeth Ann (*née* RUMSBY)

b Saxmundham, Suffolk, 18 July 1853
d London, Ontario, 1943

Daughter of Samuel Rumsby, a currier. She became an officer from Woodbridge, Suffolk in 1884 and was stationed at various corps including Hendon, Woolwich and Battersea II. She married Staff-Captain (later Colonel) George Alfred Mackenzie in 1887. He was Chief Secretary in Canada, 1892-96, but then resigned because of illness. Afterwards he became a congregational minister, serving as pastor for 20 years at Stratford, Ontario. He retired in 1937.

Song: Love divine, from Jesus flowing (439)

McKIE, Thomas

b Newcastle upon Tyne, 25 March 1860
d Wylam, Northumberland, 26 August 1937

Son of Thomas McKie, a cartman. After attending Salvation Army meetings in Gateshead for several months, he was converted at Newcastle Corps in 1880. Five months later he became an officer, serving in several corps appointments, including Bristol Circus, Hull Icehouse, and Clapton Congress Hall. Subsequently he was vice-principal at the training home, conducted campaigns around the world (as an international travelling commissioner), and then served successively as Territorial Commander for Germany, Australia and Sweden. He was Principal of the International Training College, 1912-17, but, during this time, took command temporarily in Canada after the *Empress of Ireland* disaster in 1914. He resigned his officership in 1917.

Song: Precious Saviour, we are coming (201)

MACLEOD, Norman

b Campbeltown, Argyllshire, 3 June 1812
d Glasgow, 16 June 1872

Educated at the University of Glasgow and Edinburgh. He became a minister of the Church of Scotland in 1838, serving in Loudoun, Ayrshire, and then in Dalkeith, before moving to the Barony Parish, Glasgow, in 1851. He was Moderator of the General Assembly in 1869. He commenced the first penny savings bank in Glasgow and for several years edited the *Edinburgh Christian Instructor,* and the magazine *Good Words,* founded in 1860.

Song: Courage, brother, do not stumble (716)

MACMILLAN, Margaret Lodge

b Bell Island, Newfoundland, 2 September 1923

Daughter of Major and Mrs J. N. Lodge, Salvation Army officers for many years in Newfoundland. She graduated as a registered nurse in 1946 from the Salvation Army Grace General Hospital in St John's, Newfoundland, and after graduation moved to Toronto. She married Wallace G. MacMillan and served for several years in the North Toronto Corps, where she was organist. Returning to nursing, she spent 12 years working on programmes and services related to cancer: with the Canadian Cancer Society and Princess Margaret Hospital, Toronto, and presenting a programme on the early detection of cancer to government departments and industry. In 1986 she was living in Don Mills, Ontario, where she assisted as organist in a local evangelical church.

Song: In the depths of my soul's greatest longing (493)

MANN, Frederick (or Frederic)

b Tavistock, Devon, 1 April 1846
d Croydon, Surrey, 20 July 1928

Son of John Mann, a Wesleyan minister. He was educated at the University of London. Having apparently been a methodist minister, he was ordained in the Church of England in 1882. He served as curate at Woodford, Essex, 1882-91; curate-in-charge at Woodford Bridge, 1891-93; chaplain at the London County Asylum, Claybury, 1893-1901; and vicar of Temple Ewell, near Dover, 1901-17. In retirement he lived in Croydon, where he was chairman of the Croydon branch of the Guild of Health.

Song: My God, my Father, make me strong (744)

MARRIOTT, John

b Cottesbach, Leicestershire, 1780
d St Giles-in-the-Fields, Middlesex, 31 March 1825

Educated at Rugby School and Christ Church, Oxford. After his ordination in 1804, he served as private tutor in the family of the Duke of Buccleuch and was then appointed rector of Church Lawford, Warwickshire in 1807. Although he retained this post, he lived in Devon for many years, apparently for the sake of his wife's health. He was successively curate of St James, Exeter; St Lawrence, Exeter; and Broadclyst. He did not allow his hymns to be published during his lifetime.

Song: Thou, whose almighty word (224)

MARSHALL, Thomas Charles

b Marylebone, Middlesex, 7 September 1854
d Jersey City, New Jersey, 7 October 1942

Son of Thomas D. Marshall, a boot maker. He went to America in 1873 and lived for five years in Illinois, Kansas and Missouri, before going to China where he was a proof-reader in the Imperial Maritime Customs Service in Shanghai. After returning to England in 1882, he became a salvationist at the Regent Hall Corps (where his father was corps treasurer) and in January 1883 joined the staff of *The War Cry*. He served as an officer until 1898, in various appointments in London and New York. He was successively personal secretary to General William Booth; a member of the training home staff; editor of *The Conqueror* magazine in the United States for several years; and editor of the monthly magazine *All the World*. He started to write songs at the suggestion of William Booth and later wrote about 450 songs, also contributing poetry to *The War Cry* until a few days before he died.

Songs: O Jesus, Saviour, hear my cry (620)
To thee, O Lord of earth and sky (933)
We're the soldiers of the Army of salvation (822)

MARTIN, W. C.

b ?
d ?

Nothing is known about the author, except that he was apparently an evangelist or minister in the United States, *c*1900.

Song: The name of Jesus is so sweet (68)

MASON, John

b Northamptonshire (?) *c*1640
d Water Stratford, Buckinghamshire, 1694

The son of a dissenting minister, he was educated at Strixton School, Northamptonshire, and at Clare Hall, Cambridge. He was appointed curate of Isham, Northamptonshire, and in 1668 became vicar of Stantonbury, Buckinghamshire. About five years later, he became rector of Water Stratford. Near the end of his life, he preached a sermon, 'The Midnight Cry', in which he declared the imminent return of Christ. Crowds gathered from the surrounding villages, expecting Christ to appear at Water Stratford, and there were extraordinary scenes of singing and dancing. After he died, testifying that he had seen the Lord, his followers apparently continued to hold meetings in the village for several years. He wrote *Spiritual Songs; or Songs of Praise to Almighty God*, 1683, and also contributed poems to *Penitential Cries*, 1693, compiled by his friend Thomas Shepherd.

Songs: I've found the pearl of greatest price (346)

MASON, Lowell

b Medfield, Massachusetts, 8 January 1792
d Orange, New Jersey, 11 August 1872

As a child he learnt to play several instruments and at the age of 16 led the village choir and conducted singing schools. He lived in Savannah, Georgia, 1812-27, where he worked in a bank, studied music, and served for seven years as organist at the First Presbyterian Church. After moving to Boston in 1827 he was president of the Handel and Haydn Society, 1827-32, and choir director of Bowdoin Street Church for 14 years. He established the Boston Academy of Music in 1832, and subsequently travelled extensively to promote church music and music education. He published more than 1,000 hymn tunes, almost 500 tune arrangements, and over 80 music collections, including the *Boston Handel and Haydn Society Collection of Church Music*, 1821; *The Juvenile Psalmist*, 1829; and *Carmina Sacra*, 1852.

Song: Lord, I make a full surrender (504)

MASTERS, Mary

b ?
d 1759?

Little is known about the author, except that she published a collection of *Poems,* 1733, and later *Familiar Letters and Poems on Several Occasions,* 1755.

Song: 'Tis religion that can give (464)

MATHAMS, Walter John

b Bermondsey, Surrey, 30 October 1853
d Swanage, Dorset, 29 January 1931

After spending his early years at sea, he studied at Regent's Park Baptist College, and became pastor of a church at Preston, Lancashire. In 1879 he travelled to Australia, and on his return became minister at Falkirk, Scotland, in 1883 and then in Birmingham in 1888. He joined the Church of Scotland in 1900 and was chaplain to the Scottish forces in Egypt, 1900-02, and then served as assistant minister in Stronsay, Orkney, 1906-09 and in charge of Mallaig Mission Church, 1909-19. His publications included *At Jesus' Feet,* 1876; *Fireside Parables,* 1879; and *Sunday Parables,* 1883.

Songs: God is with us, God is with us (158)
Jesus, friend of little children (842)

MATHESON, George

b Glasgow, 27 March 1842
d North Berwick, East Lothian, 28 August 1906

Educated at Glasgow Academy and Glasgow University. In his early years his sight began to deteriorate and from the age of 18 he was almost completely blind. He was licensed as a presbyterian preacher in 1866, and served for two years as assistant at Sandyford Church, Glasgow, and then as minister at Innellan, Argyllshire, for 18 years, after which he moved to St Bernard's Church, Edinburgh, in 1886, serving there until his retirement in 1899. He published several books on theology, spiritual life and devotion, and one book of poetry, his *Sacred Songs*, 1890.

Songs: Make me a captive, Lord (508)
O Love that wilt not let me go (621)

MATSON, William Tidd

b West Hackney, Middlesex, 17 October 1833
d Portsea, Hampshire, 23 December 1899

Educated at St John's College, Cambridge, and the Agricultural and Chemical College, Kennington. He joined the Methodist New Connexion in 1853, but trained for the congregational ministry at Cotton End Academy, near Bedford, in 1857. He became pastor at Havant, Hampshire, in 1859, moving to Gosport Old Meeting in 1862, for about nine years. He was then pastor of churches at Rothwell and Stratford; minister of Highbury Chapel, Portsmouth, 1879-85; and minister at Sarisbury Green from 1885 until he retired in 1897. A new chapel (1931) at Sarisbury Green was named the 'William Tidd Matson Memorial Church'. His published poetry included *Pleasures of the Sanctuary*, 1865; *The Inner Life*, 1866; *Sacred Lyrics*, 1870, and other publications.

Song: Lord, I was blind! I could not see (353)

MAWBY, Hilda Ivy Alice (*née* MEMMOTT)

b Chelsea, London, 9 December 1903
d Camberwell, London, 30 March 1983

Daughter of Frederick Memmott, a master painter and decorator. She entered the training college at the age of 18, and after service in France returned to Britain, where she married Captain (later Major) Arthur H. Mawby in 1929. They served in several corps appointments, including Bargoed, Edinburgh Congress Hall, Hastings and Mansfield, and were then appointed to the South-West Scottish Division, where her husband (the divisional young people's secretary) was promoted to Glory in 1943. Subsequently she was commanding officer at Woking Corps, and then served in the editorial department where she later became editor of *The Deliverer* and *All the World*. She was appointed National Home League Secretary

(British Territory) in 1955 and retired as a colonel in 1963. In addition to many songs and poems, she wrote *On My Desert Island*, 1968, a book of talks for women.

Songs: Like to a lamb who from the fold has strayed (740)
       Softly the shadows fall o'er land and sea (675)
       There is strength in knowing Jesus (759)

MEDLEY, Samuel

b Cheshunt, Hertfordshire, 23 June 1738
d Liverpool, Lancashire, 17 July 1799

Son of Guy Medley, a school teacher. At the age of 14 he was apprenticed to an oilman, in London, but in 1755 he joined the navy. He was wounded off Cape Lagos, Portugal, in 1759, and returned to London. After his recovery, he was converted and joined the Eagle Street Baptist Church in 1760. He opened a school in London, but in 1766 he was called to preach and, in the following year, he became pastor of a baptist church in Watford, Hertfordshire. In 1772 he moved to Liverpool as pastor of the Byrom Street Baptist Church. Most of his hymns were first printed in magazines or on leaflets and later appeared in various editions of his collected hymns, 1785-1800.

Songs: I know that my redeemer lives (144)
       O what amazing words of grace (254)
       Thy presence and thy glories, Lord (946)

MEHLING, Charles

b 22 May 1889
d Marlboro, New Jersey, 11 January 1969

He was converted in 1905, and shortly afterwards became a bandsman. He entered training from Philadelphia II Corps, and after his commissioning in 1911 served in the USA Eastern Territory, in corps appointments, as a divisional youth secretary and later as territorial evangelist. He retired as a lieut-colonel in 1952. He played the trombone and presented vocal and instrumental duets with his wife. After retirement he lived for many years at the retired officers' residence at Asbury Park, New Jersey.

Song: The Lord's command to go into the world (700)

MIDLANE, Albert

b Carisbrooke, Isle of Wight, 23 January 1825
d Newport, Isle of Wight, 27 February 1909

He was apprenticed to a printer, but he later worked for many years as an ironmonger. As a young man he was a member of St James's Street Congregational Church, but at the age of 23 he joined the Brethren congregation at the Gospel Hall in Newport. His Sunday-school teacher encouraged him to write poetry and his first hymn was published in 1842 in *The Youth's Magazine*. Subsequently he wrote more than 1,000 hymns which were published in magazines, mission hymn books and his various collections, including *The Bright Blue Sky Hymn Book*, 1904, and *The Gospel Hall Hymn Book*, 1904.

Songs: Hark! the voice of Jesus calling (240)
Revive thy work, O Lord (626)

MILLER, Emily Huntington

b Brooklyn, Connecticut, 22 October 1833
d Northfield, Minnesota, 2 November 1913

Daughter of the Reverend Thomas Huntington, a methodist minister. She was educated at Oberlin College, Ohio, and married Professor John E. Miller, of Greentown, Ohio, in 1860. For some years she was joint-editor of a children's magazine, *The Little Corporal*, and she was Dean of Women Students at North-Western University, Illinois, 1891-98. Her publications included *Captain Firth, Little Neighbors* and *From Avalon, and other poems*.

Song: I love to hear the story (840)

MILLS, Elizabeth (*née* KING)

b Stoke Newington, Middlesex, 1805
d Finsbury Place, Middlesex, 21 April 1829

Daughter of Philip King. She was the wife of Thomas Mills, a Member of Parliament.

Song: We speak of the realms of the blest (904)

MILMAN, Henry Hart

b St James's, Middlesex, 10 February 1791
d Sunninghill, Berkshire, 24 September 1868

Son of Sir Francis Milman, physician to King George III. He was educated at Eton, and Brasenose College, Oxford. After his ordination in 1816, he was vicar of St Mary's, Reading, 1818-35, and during that period was also professor of poetry at Oxford, 1821-31. He became rector of St Margaret's, Westminster, and a canon of Westminster in 1835, and was appointed Dean of St Paul's Cathedral in 1849. He contributed 13 hymns to *Hymns*, 1827, compiled by Reginald Heber, and also edited *A Selection of Psalms and Hymns, adapted to the Use of the Church of St Margaret, Westminster*, 1837. He was author of a *History of the Jews*, 1829, and a *History of Latin Christianity*, 1854.

Song: Ride on, ride on in majesty (150)

MILTON, John

b London, 9 December 1608
d St Giles without Cripplegate, Middlesex, 8 November 1674

Son of John Milton, a freeman of the Scriveners' Company. He was educated at St Paul's School, London, and Christ's College, Cambridge. After graduating, he lived at Horton, Buckinghamshire, 1632-38, travelled to Italy, 1638-39, and then moved to London, where he was tutor to his sister's children and other boys. In 1649 he was appointed Secretary for Foreign Tongues, in the Council of State, with responsibility for translating government letters. For some years his sight had been deteriorating, and by the end of 1652 he was totally blind. He published *Paradise Lost* in 1667, and *Paradise Regained* and *Samson Agonistes* in 1671. His earlier poetry included 19 psalm paraphrases.

Song: Let us with a gladsome mind (34)

MINGAY, Albert Ernest

b near Newmarket, Suffolk, 11 December 1904

He was converted at the age of 11, came from the Congregational Church to The Salvation Army when he was 15, and entered the training college in 1923, from Newmarket Corps. He served for about 13 years in corps appointments and then for two years at the Glasgow Instructional Centre. During the Second World War he was divisional young people's secretary in Glasgow and Manchester, and afterwards became a divisional commander (in the Tees Division and in Hull and Lincs). Subsequently he was National Candidates' Secretary, 1950-54; Chief Side Officer at the International Training College, 1954-57; Chief Secretary, Australia Southern, 1957-62; Territorial Commander for Scotland 1962-67; and Governor of the Men's Social Services in Great Britain and Ireland, 1967-69. He was British Commissioner, 1969-72 and then Principal of the International College for Officers, before retiring at the end of 1973. A member of the Shortlands Poetry Circle, he was, for two years, secretary of the writers' group. He has contributed a number of songs to *The Musical Salvationist* and published an anthology of his poetry, *My Day for Living*, 1970.

Songs: Come, Holy Spirit, thou guest of the soul (209)
Is it nothing to you that one day Jesus came (245)

MOHR, Joseph

b Salzburg, Austria, 11 December 1792
d Wagrein, near St Johann, Austria, 4 December 1848

A chorister in the cathedral choir at Salzburg, he was later ordained as a Roman catholic priest in 1815. He was assistant priest at Ramsau and Laufen, and at St Nicholas's Church, Oberndorf, 1817-19, and also served in other churches in the diocese of Salzburg, including Kuchl, Golling, Authering and Hof. He was vicar-substitute at Hintersee, and was then appointed vicar there in 1828, and priest-in-charge at Wagrein, in 1837.

Song: Silent night! Holy night (89)

MONOD, Theodore

b Paris, 6 November 1836
d Paris, 26 February 1921

Educated at the University of Paris and the Western Theological Seminary, in Pennsylvania. He was licensed to preach in 1861 and served as pastor of the Second Presbyterian Church, Kankakee, Illinois, for two years. Returning to France, he was pastor of the Chapelle du Nord, in Paris, 1864-75. He travelled extensively as an evangelist, preaching at Mildmay, Keswick and other meetings in Britain. He was editor of *Le Libérateur*, and published a number of his sermons and other books, including *The Gift of God*, 1876; *Denying Self*, 1878; and *Life more Abundant*, 1881.

Song: O the bitter shame and sorrow (548)

MONSELL, John Samuel Bewley

b St Columb's, County Derry, 2 March 1811
d Guildford, Surrey, 9 April 1875

Son of the Reverend Thomas Bewley Monsell, archdeacon of Londonderry. He was educated at Trinity College, Dublin. After his ordination in 1834 he was chaplain to Bishop Richard Mant, and later rector of Ramoan, before becoming vicar of Egham, Surrey, in 1853. He was appointed rector of St Nicholas, Guildford, Surrey, in 1870. He died as a result of an accident during building work at the church. He wrote about 300 hymns and poems, which appeared in his various publications, including *Hymns of Love and Praise*, 1863 and 1866, and *The Parish Hymnal*, 1873.

Songs: Fight the good fight with all thy might (718)
O worship the Lord in the beauty of holiness (183)
Sing to the Lord of harvest (929)

MONTGOMERY, James

b Irvine, Ayrshire, 4 November 1771
d Sheffield, Yorkshire, 30 April 1854

Son of John Montgomery, a Moravian minister. In 1776 he moved with his parents to Grace Hill, a Moravian settlement near Ballymena, County Antrim. He studied at the Moravian seminary at Fulneck, near Leeds, and then worked as a shop assistant at Mirfield, near Wakefield, and later at Wath, near Rotherham. In 1792 he moved to Sheffield, as assistant to Mr Gales, publisher of the *Sheffield Register* newspaper, and, two years later, he became the editor, changing the name of the paper to the *Sheffield Iris*. He was editor for 31 years and was twice imprisoned (once for printing a song commemorating the fall of the Bastille, and once for reporting a riot in Sheffield). He defended the freedom of the press, and supported many causes, including the Bible Society, foreign missions and the abolition of slavery. He began writing poetry at the age of 10, and later wrote more than 400 hymns, which were published in various collections, including *Greenland, and Other Poems*, 1819; *The Christian Psalmist*, 1825; *The Poet's Portfolio*, 1835; and *Original Hymns for Public, Private and Social Devotion*, 1853.

Songs: Angels, from the realms of Glory (75)
       For ever with the Lord (877)
       Lord God, the Holy Ghost (196)
       Prayer is the soul's sincere desire (625)
       Servant of God, well done (890)
       Stand up and bless the Lord (20)
       This stone to thee in faith we lay (945)

MOORCOCK, Miss R.

b ?
d ?

No information about the author is available. Gordon Avery apparently found her song in 'an old gospel tune book' but he did not record its title or date.

Song: Beautiful land, so bright, so fair (873)

MOORE, Thomas

b Dublin, 28 May 1779
d Chittoe, Wiltshire, 25 February 1852

Son of John Moore, a grocer. He was educated at Trinity College, Dublin, and came to London in 1799, intending to study law at the Middle Temple, but he decided instead to devote himself to literature. In 1803, he was appointed Registrar to the Court of Admiralty in Bermuda, but, in the following year, he appointed a deputy and returned to England, after travelling in America. Later, in 1818, he was answerable for a debt of £6,000 when his deputy left the post. He started writing verses before he was 14, and published several volumes of poetry and other works, including *Odes and Epistles*, 1806; *Sacred Songs*, 1816; *Lalla Rookh*, 1817; and *Odes upon Cash, Corn, Catholics and Other Matters*, 1828.

Song: Come, ye disconsolate, where'er ye languish (236)

MORRIS, Lelia Naylor

b Pennsville, Ohio, 15 April 1862
d Auburn, Ohio, 23 July 1929

In 1866, after the Civil War, her family moved to Malta, Ohio, and later, when her father died, her mother opened a millinery shop in McConnelsville. She was a member of the Methodist Protestant Church, but after her marriage in 1881 to Charles H. Morris, she joined the Methodist Episcopal Church, and regularly attended methodist camp-meetings in Ohio and Maryland. She wrote more than 1,000 gospel songs, in later years writing on a large blackboard because her sight was poor.

Song: Holy Ghost, we bid thee welcome (213)

MOTE, Edward

b London, 21 January 1797
d Horsham, Sussex, 13 November 1874

As a young man he was influenced by the preaching of John Hyatt, of Tottenham Court Road Chapel. After working as a cabinet-maker, he became pastor of the baptist church at Horsham, Sussex, in 1852, where he served for 21 years. He wrote more than 100 hymns, which were included in his *Hymns of Praise, A New Selection of Gospel Hymns*, 1836.

Song: My hope is built on nothing less (745)

MOUNTAIN, Jessie (*née* GILBERTHORPE)

b Sheffield, Yorkshire, 1 December 1895
d Blackpool, Lancashire, 28 May 1981

As a child she was a member of the junior singing brigade and young people's legion in Sheffield, and later became leader of a Bible class and a founder member of Sheffield Citadel Songster Brigade. In 1920 she married Deputy Bandmaster (afterwards Bandmaster) Herbert A. Mountain, and subsequently visited many corps with his musical party, 'The Melody Makers'. In 1940 they moved to Blackpool Citadel where she again led a Bible class. For a few years (1945-50) they lived in Boscombe, before returning to Blackpool. She wrote a number of poems and songs, many of which were published in *The Musical Salvationist*, with music by her husband.

Song: Kneeling before thee, Lord, I am praying (501)

MUNDELL, Thomas Hodgson

b Maryport, Cumberland, 25 November 1849
d South Croydon, Surrey, 15 November 1934

Son of James Mundell, a school teacher. He was a godson of Dean Archibald Tait (later Archbishop of Canterbury) and, after his parents died, he was brought up by an aunt and uncle in Carlisle, where he worked for a time in the Dean and Chapter Registry. He practised as a solicitor in Carlisle and Bristol before moving to London, where he was a Salvation Army officer, 1893-95, serving for a short while as secretary to Commissioner Carleton, in the Legal Section at International Headquarters. Subsequently he had a London office in Godliman Street, near St Paul's, and lived for more than 35 years in Croydon, He was known as 'The Poor Man's Lawyer', because he often gave advice at nominal charges to people in need. In his later years he had a particular interest in missionary work.

Songs: Blessèd and glorious King (561)
       Saviour and Lord, we pray to thee (692)

NEALE, John Mason

b St Pancras, Middlesex, 24 January 1818
d East Grinstead, Sussex, 6 August 1866

Educated at Blackheath, Sherborne, and Trinity College, Cambridge. At Cambridge, he was a tutor at Downing College and in 1839 was one of the founders of the Camden Society. He won the Seatonian Prize for a sacred poem 11 times. After his ordination, in 1841, he was briefly chaplain at Downing College and incumbent of Crawley, Sussex, but because of illness he then spent about three years in Madeira. In 1846, he became warden of Sackville College, almshouses at East Grinstead, and in 1854 he founded the Community of St Margaret, a nursing sisterhood which two years later became established in a house near Sackville College. For several years he was leader-writer for the *Morning Chronicle*. He had a knowledge of about 20 languages, including Russian, Greek, Syriac and Portuguese. His hymns and translations appeared in his various publications, including *Medieval Hymns and Sequences*, 1851, and *Hymns of the Eastern Church*, 1862. Many of them became more widely known through *The Hymnal Noted*, 1851, and *Hymns Ancient and Modern*.

Song: Art thou weary, art thou languid (228)

NEANDER, Joachim

b Bremen, Germany, 1650
d Bremen, Germany, 31 May 1680

Son of Johann Joachim Neander, a master at the Paedagogium at Bremen. He was educated at the Paedagogium and the Academic Gymnasium in Bremen, and was converted in 1670 through the preaching of Theodore Under-Eyck, pastor of St Martin's Church, Bremen. In 1671, he became a private tutor at Frankfurt-am-Main, and in 1674 was appointed rector of the Latin school at Düsseldorf. He returned to Bremen in 1679, as assistant to Theodore Under- Eyck, but died less than a year later. He wrote about 60 hymns, mostly while he was at Düsseldorf, and they were collected and published in his *Glaub- und Liebesübung*, 1680, and other posthumous editions.

Song: Praise to the Lord, the Almighty, the King of creation (19)

NEUMARK, Georg

b Langensalza, Thuringia, 7 or 16 March 1621
d Weimar, 8 or 18 July 1681

Son of Michael Neumark, a clothier. He was educated at the Gymnasium at Schleusingen and at Gotha. He left Gotha in 1641, intending to go to the University of Königsberg, but his possessions were stolen by highwaymen on the Gardelegen Heath. Left with only his prayer book and a little money sewn up in his clothes, he became a tutor in a family at Kiel, until he was able to go to Königsberg in 1643. He studied law and poetry there for five years and then spent some time in Warsaw, Thorn, Danzig and Hamburg. He was appointed court poet, librarian and registrar to the Duke of Weimar in 1652, and was later secretary of the Ducal Archives. His hymns appeared mainly in his *Fortgepflantzter Musikalisch-Poetischer Lustwald*, 1657.

Song: Leave God to order all thy ways (738)

NEUMEISTER, Erdmann

b Uechteritz, near Weissenfels, 12 May 1671
d Hamburg, 18 August 1756

Son of Johann Neumeister, a schoolmaster and organist. He was educated at the University of Leipzig and lectured there for a short time, until he became assistant pastor at Bibra, in 1697, and pastor, in 1698. He went to Weissenfels in 1704 as tutor to the daughter of Duke Johann Georg and as court preacher, but he moved to Sorau in 1706, to become senior court preacher and superintendent. In 1715, he was appointed pastor of St James's Church, Hamburg. He wrote more than 650 hymns, which were published in various collections, including his *Evangelischer Nachklang*, 1718.

Song: Sinners Jesus will receive (262)

NEWELL, William Reed

b Savannah, Ohio, 22 May 1868
d DeLand, Florida, 1 April 1956

Son of David Ayers Newell. He was educated at the University of Wooster, Ohio, and Princeton Theological Seminary. In

1895 he moved to Chicago, where he was pastor of Bethesda Congregational Church, 1895-96, and assistant superintendent of the Moody Bible Institute, 1896-98. Subsequently he conducted interdenominational Bible classes for many years in various cities, including Chicago, St Louis, Detroit, Toronto and London. His publications included *Old Testament Studies*, 1905; *The Book of Revelation*, 1935, and other biblical commentaries.

Song: Years I spent in vanity and pride (405)

NEWMAN, John Henry

b London, 21 February 1801
d Edgbaston, Warwickshire, 11 August 1890

Educated at school in Ealing and at Trinity College, Oxford. He was elected a Fellow of Oriel College in 1822, and became a tutor there in 1826. Having been ordained in 1824, he served as curate at St Clement's, and later as vicar of St Mary's, Oxford, 1828-43. After a six-month tour in southern Europe, including Rome, he heard John Keble's sermon in Oxford on 'National Apostasy' (July 1833), which is regarded as the beginning of the Oxford Movement. He contributed to the series *Tracts for the Times*, notably as author of Tract 90: *Remarks on Certain Passages in the Thirty-Nine Articles*, 1841. In 1845 he became a Roman catholic, and two years later was ordained as a Roman catholic priest. In 1848 he established an oratory at Maryvale, near Birmingham, which moved to Alcester Street, Birmingham, in the following year, and to Edgbaston in 1852. He was rector of the new Catholic University at Dublin, 1854-58, and became a cardinal in 1879. Among other publications, he wrote an account of his life and work, *Apologia pro Vita Sua*, 1864, and his published poetry included *Lyra Apostolica*, 1836; *Verses on Religious Subjects*, 1853; and *Verses on Various Occasions*, 1865 and 1868.

Songs: Lead, kindly Light, amid the encircling gloom (606)
   Praise to the holiest in the height (18)

NEWTON, John

b London, 24 July 1725
d London, 21 December 1807

Son of John Newton, a master mariner. At the age of 11 he went to sea with his father, and sailed on several voyages,

1736-43. Early in 1744 he was conscripted into the Royal Navy, serving on HMS *Harwich* during 1744, but in the following year he transferred to a merchant ship bound for Africa, where he became a slave trader. Returning to England in 1748 on a cargo ship, *The Greyhound*, he read the New Testament and a translation of *The Imitation of Christ* by Thomas à Kempis, which led to his conversion. The ship survived a violent storm on 10 March 1748, a date which he always remembered as the day of his deliverance. After other voyages as a slave trader, 1748-54, he was appointed Tide Surveyor in the Customs and Excise Department in Liverpool in 1755. He studied Greek and Hebrew in preparation for ordination, and, though his first application was rejected, he was ordained in 1764 and served as curate of Olney, Buckinghamshire, 1764-79, and rector of St Mary Woolnoth, in London, 1780-1807, where he campaigned vigorously for the abolition of slavery. He wrote 280 hymns for the *Olney Hymns*, 1779, which also included 68 hymns by his friend, William Cowper.

Songs: Amazing grace! how sweet the sound (308)
Approach, my soul, the mercy seat (284)
Begone, unbelief (712)
Behold the throne of grace (560)
Come, my soul, thy suit prepare (563)
Day of judgment! Day of wonders (875)
Glorious things of thee are spoken (157)
How sweet the name of Jesus sounds (58)
How tasteless and tedious the hours (318)
Though troubles assail (763)

NICHOLSON, James L.

b Ireland, *c*1828
d Washington, DC, 6 November 1876

He emigrated to America in about 1850 and settled in Philadelphia, where he became a member of Wharton Street Methodist Episcopal Church. He was active in evangelism and Sunday-school work. In 1871 he moved to Washington, DC, where he worked as a postal clerk, and continued to teach Sunday-school classes and to lead singing in his church.

Song: Lord Jesus, I long to be perfectly whole (436)

NICOL, Rose

See: **COULL, Rose (*née* NICOL)**

NIELSEN, Mads

b Langaa, Denmark, 27 February 1879
d Aabyhøj, Denmark, 8 December 1958

He was a chemist, but also wrote poetry and short stories. He published several books of poetry, and other poems appeared in Christian newspapers and magazines. He was a member of the Danish Lutheran Church.

Song: Each day is a gift supernal (666)

NILES, Nathaniel

b South Kingston, Rhode Island, 15 September 1835
d Madison, New Jersey, 29 June 1917

Son of the Reverend William Watson Niles, he was educated at Phillips Andover Academy and was admitted to the New York bar in 1857. He became speaker of the New Jersey assembly in 1872, and government director of Union Pacific Railroad in 1879. He was president of Tradesmen's National Bank, New York, 1884-89. In the New Jersey legislature, he introduced laws relating to school finance and free school libraries.

Song: Precious promise God hath given (753)

NISBETT, Ada Mary (*née* GARNETT)

b London (?), Ontario, 14 (or 21) November 1866 or 1867
d London (?), Ontario, 5 May 1931

She became a cadet in 1885 from Lindsay, Ontario, and served as an officer in several corps in Quebec and Ontario. She resigned in 1889 because of her mother's illness, and in 1893 married John Nisbett. She wrote about 25 songs, many of which were published anonymously in *The War Cry* in Canada.

Song: I have a home that is fairer than day (881)

NITSCHMANN, Anna

b Kunewald, Moravia, 24 November 1715
d Herrnhut, Germany, 21 May 1760

Daughter of David Nitschmann, a cartwright, and sister of Johann Nitschmann. The family moved to the Moravian settlement at Herrnhut in 1725, and she was appointed as an elder in 1730, apparently with responsibility for the unmarried women. In 1735, she became companion to Benigna, daughter of Count von Zinzendorf, and accompanied her to England in 1737. During 1740, she went to Pennsylvania, where she joined in mission work among the Indians, but she returned to Germany in 1743. She married Count von Zinzendorf, at Berthelsdorf, in 1757, a year after the death of his first wife. Her hymns were published in various appendices to the *Herrnhut Gesang-Buch*, 1735.

Song: I thirst, thou wounded Lamb of God (424, verse 4)

NITSCHMANN, Johann

b Kunewald, Moravia, 25 September 1712
d Sarepta, Russia, 30 June 1783

Son of David Nitschmann, a cartwright, and brother of Anna Nitschmann, he moved with his family to Herrnhut in 1725. He studied theology at Halle, and later returned there to study medicine. In 1733, he came back to Herrnhut, where he was private secretary to Count von Zinzendorf for a year. He was then involved mainly in mission work until 1745 when he became a deacon in the Moravian community, at Herrnhaag, and later at Herrnhut, in 1750. He was consecrated as a bishop in 1758, and was appointed superintendent of the Moravian communities in England and Ireland in 1761. Five years later, he took charge of a new settlement at Sarepta, in Russia.

Song: I thirst, thou wounded Lamb of God (424, verse 3)

NOEL, Caroline Maria

b Teston, Kent, 10 April 1817
d St Marylebone, Middlesex, 7 December 1877

Daughter of the Reverend Gerard T. Noel, who compiled *A Selection of Psalms and Hymns,* 1810, which included a number of his own hymns. She wrote a few hymns when aged 17-20 and, more than 20 years later, published *The Name of Jesus and Other Verses for the Sick and Lonely,* 1861. (Subsequent enlarged editions had the title *The Name of Jesus and Other Poems.)*

Song: At the name of Jesus (141)

NUNN, Mary Ann

b Colchester, Essex, 17 May 1778
d Colchester, Essex, 27 February 1847

Daughter of John Nunn, a wine merchant. She was the sister of the Reverend John Nunn who compiled *Psalms and Hymns from the most Approved Authors,* 1817. She wrote a number of books, including *The Benevolent Merchant.*

Song: One there is above all others (377)

NUTTALL, Richard

b Blackpool, Lancashire, 2 April 1891
d Madras, India, 2 May 1946

Son of Richard Nuttall, a butcher. His parents were salvationists in Blackpool where he learnt to play the piano, euphonium and cornet, and later became bandmaster at Blackpool Citadel. During the First World War, while on military service in France, he conducted the band at the hostel for servicemen in Rouen. After the war he entered the training college with his wife, served for four years in corps appointments in Britain, and then, in 1923, went to India, where he was known as 'Anand Das' (Happy Servant). During 23 years in India and Ceylon, his appointments included divisional commander, training officer and finance and property secretary. Latterly he was General Secretary for the Madras and Telegu Territory, with the rank of brigadier.

Song: God is our light and God is our sunshine (316)

OAKELEY, Frederick

b Shrewsbury, Shropshire, 5 September 1802
d Islington, Middlesex, 29 January 1880

Son of Sir Charles Oakeley, sometime Governor of Madras. He was educated at Christ Church, Oxford, and was ordained in the Church of England in 1826. Subsequently, he became a prebendary of Lichfield Cathedral in 1832, preacher at Whitehall in 1837, and minister of Margaret Chapel, Margaret Street, in London, in 1839. He joined the Roman Catholic Church in 1845 and was appointed a canon of Westminster Procathedral in 1852. He published theological pamphlets and several collections of poetry, including *Lyra Liturgica: Reflections in Verse for Holy Days and Seasons,* 1865.

Song: O come, all ye faithful (85)

OAKEY, Emily Sullivan

b Albany, New York, 8 October 1829
d Albany, New York, 11 May 1883

Educated at Albany Female Academy, where she became a teacher of languages and English literature. She wrote extensively for newspapers and magazines.

Song: Sowing the seed by the dawn-light fair (931)

OATMAN, Johnson

b near Medford, New Jersey, 21 April 1856
d Norman, Oklahoma, 25 September 1922

Educated at Herbert's Academy, Vincentown, New Jersey, and the New Jersey Collegiate Institute, in Bordentown. He was ordained in the Methodist Episcopal Church, but apparently continued as a local preacher. For some years he worked with his father, but he later established an insurance business at Mount Holly, New Jersey. He wrote words for more than 5,000 gospel songs, many of which were set to music by John R. Sweney, William J. Kirkpatrick, Edwin O. Excell, and other composers.

Song: When upon life's billows you are tempest-tossed (396)

OBERLIN, John Frederic

b Strasbourg, France, 31 August 1740
d Walderbach, Bavaria, 1 June 1826

Educated at the University of Strasbourg. For some time he was a teacher and he then became a Lutheran minister at Walderbach (Ban de la Roche) in 1767. In addition to his pastoral responsibilities, he established village schools and pioneered kindergarten work, and also introduced lending and savings banks, promoted improved farming techniques, and initiated road and bridge building. A few hymns have been attributed to him, though apparently without much evidence.

Song: O Lord, thy heavenly grace impart (517)

O'KANE, Tullius Clinton

b Fairfield County, Ohio, 10 March 1830
d Delaware, Ohio, 10 February 1912

Educated at Ohio Wesleyan University. He was mathematics tutor there until 1857, when he became principal of a school in Cincinnati. He worked for the piano firm of Philip Phillips & Company, 1864-67, and after moving to Delaware, Ohio, in 1867, he was travelling representative for the Smith American Organ Company of Boston for six years. During this time, he regularly attended Sunday-school conventions and started publishing Sunday-school song books, including *Fresh Leaves,*

1868; *Jasper and Gold*, 1877; *Joy to the World*, 1878; and *Songs of Redeeming Love* (No. 1, 1882, and No. 2, 1887).

Song: Who, who are these beside the chilly wave (910)

OLIPHANT, William Elwin

b Dover, Kent, 30 March 1860
d San Remo, Italy, 17 February 1941

Son of John Elwin Oliphant (or Olifent), a pilot. He was educated at the London College of Divinity and, after ordination in the Church of England, served as curate of St Paul's Church, Onslow Square, 1883-84. He became a salvationist in 1884, trained as a cadet, and was appointed to Marylebone and then to take charge of the East London Division. After other divisional appointments and a period as private secretary to the Chief of the Staff, he was Territorial Commander for Holland, and subsequently for Sweden, Germany, and Switzerland and Italy. He retired as a commissioner in 1930, following extended furlough. His publications included *Gerhard Tersteegen*, 1905; *The Life and Work of Oberlin*, 1906; and *The Story of German Song*, 1909.

Song: I kneel beside thy sacred cross (729)

OLIVERS, Thomas

b Tregynon, Montgomery, 1725
d London, March 1799

His parents died when he was aged four, and he grew up in various places, with little education. At the age of 18 he was apprenticed to a shoemaker, but he did not become established in the trade. He was converted through hearing a sermon by George Whitefield, in Bristol, on the text: 'Is not this a brand plucked from the burning?' After a few months he went to live at Bradford-on-Avon, Wiltshire, later becoming a member of the methodist society and a local preacher. In 1753, he became an itinerant preacher in Cornwall, and during the next 25 years he apparently travelled 100,000 miles in England and Ireland, on one horse. For some years, he assisted John Wesley with editing the *Arminian Magazine.*

Songs: O thou God of my salvation (370)
The God of Abraham praise (223)

ORSBORN, Albert William Thomas

b Maidstone, Kent, 4 September 1886
d Boscombe, Hampshire, 4 February 1967

Son of Salvation Army officers who helped pioneer Army work in Norway in 1888. He worked at International Headquarters, 1899-1905, and at the age of 16 won first prize in a song competition organised by *The War Cry.* After training, 1905-06, he served in corps appointments at Chelmsford, Lowestoft South and Ipswich Citadel. He was then appointed Brigade Officer at the training college, and during the First World War was Divisional Young People's Secretary in the East London Division. He wrote about 250 songs for holiness meetings at the Congress Hall, Clapton, 1912-19. He was Divisional Commander, in Norwich, 1919-22, and in South London, 1922-25, and then Chief Side Officer for Men at the International Training College for eight years. Subsequently he was Chief Secretary in New Zealand, 1933-36; Territorial Commander, Scotland and Ireland, 1936-40; and British Commissioner, 1940-46. Elected General in 1946, he served for eight years until his retirement in 1954. He published an anthology of his songs and poems, *The Beauty of Jesus,* 1947, and his autobiography, *The House of my Pilgrimage,* 1958.

Songs: Army flag! Thy threefold glory (776)
Believe him! Believe him! the holy one is waiting (410)
Earnestly seeking to save and to heal (484)
Have we not known it, have we not heard it (724)
I have no claim on grace (290)
I know thee who thou art (59)
In the secret of thy presence (591)
In the shadow of the cross (145)
In their appointed days (494)
Life is a journey; long is the road (351)
Many thoughts stir my heart as I ponder alone (119)
My life must be Christ's broken bread (512)
Not unto us, O Lord (163)
O God, if still the holy place (619)
O Lord, how often should we be (747)

O Lord, regard thy people (944)
O Love upon a cross impaled (122)
On every hill our Saviour dies (127)
Once, on a day, was Christ led forth to die (129)
Others he saved, himself he cannot save (130)
Saviour, if my feet have faltered (522)
Say but the word, thy servant shall be healèd (456)
Silent and still I stand (131)
Since the Lord redeemed us from the power of sin (755)
Son of God! Thy cross beholding (185)
Spirit of eternal love (630)
The Saviour of men came to seek and to save (527)
Though thy waves and billows are gone o'er me (762)
Unto thee will I cry (641)
We worship thee, O Crucified (135)
What a work the Lord has done (769)
When shall I come unto the healing waters (647)
When wondrous words my Lord would say (398)
Where lowly spirits meet (648)
Who the child of God shall sever (555)
Yet once again, by God's abundant mercy (173)

OTTAWAY, Victor

b East Brixton, London, 18 October 1892
d Toronto, Canada, 4 March 1968

Son of Arthur K. Ottaway, a commercial traveller, he attended West Norwood Corps in England, but emigrated to Canada in 1923. He worked as a salesman for the Canada Bread Company for 30 years, and was corps sergeant-major at Wychwood Corps, Toronto. After winning a song-writing competition in 1966, he published 40 of his songs in a booklet, *Canadian Songs of Devotion.*

Song: Make me aware of thee, O Lord (613)

OWENS, Priscilla Jane

b Baltimore, Maryland, 21 July 1829
d Baltimore, Maryland, 5 December 1907

Daughter of Isaac Owens, she spent her life in Baltimore, where she was a school teacher for 49 years. She also taught in the Sunday-school at the Union Square Methodist Episcopal Church, and wrote most of her hymns for Sunday-schools. She contributed poetry and prose to the *Methodist Protestant* and the *Christian Standard*.

Songs: We have heard the joyful sound (393)
Will your anchor hold in the storms of life (280)

OXENHAM, John

See: **DUNKERLEY, William Arthur**

PALMER, Horatio Richmond

b Sherburne, New York, 26 April 1834
d Yonkers, New York, 15 November 1907

He studied music in New York, Berlin and Florence, and became director of Rushford Academy of Music, New York, in 1857. He also served as organist and choir director at the baptist church in Rushford. In 1861 he moved to Chicago, where he established a monthly musical journal *Concordia* in 1866. Returning to New York in 1874, he organised the Church Choral Union in New York City, and for several years he was dean of the summer school of music at Chautauqua, New York. His publications included *The Song Queen, The Song King,* and *The Song Herald*.

Song: Yield not to temptation, for yielding is sin (823)

PALMER, Ray

b Little Compton, Rhode Island, 12 November 1808
d Newark, New Jersey, 29 March 1887

Son of the Hon. Thomas Palmer, a judge in Rhode Island, he was educated at Phillips Academy, Andover, and at Yale University. He became pastor of the Central Congregational Church, in Bath, Maine, in 1835, and in 1850 was appointed to the First Congregational Church, at Albany, New York. He was corresponding secretary to the American Congregational Union, 1865-78, and spent his later years in Newark. He contributed hymns and translations to the *Sabbath Hymn Book,* 1858, and also published *Hymns and Sacred Pieces,* 1865; *Hymns of my Holy Hours,* 1868; and his *Poetical Works,* 1876.

Songs: Jesus, thou joy of loving hearts (602)
My faith looks up to thee (743)

PALSTRA, William Frederik

b Utrecht, Netherlands, 9 November 1904
d Amsterdam, Netherlands, 17 April 1973

At the age of 16 he accompanied his parents to the Dutch East Indies when his father was appointed Divisional Officer for Mid-Celebes. In 1925 he became an officer from Weltevreden Corps, in Batavia, and subsequently served in corps appointments, in military homes and relief work, and with various responsibilities at Territorial Headquarters in Bandoeng. With the territorial commander and other staff officers he was arrested in 1942 and was interned for three years. In 1946 he was transferred to Holland, where he was Field Secretary, 1950-53; Chief Secretary, 1953-60; and Territorial Commander for the Netherlands, 1960-66. He was appointed International Secretary for Europe in 1966, and retired as a commissioner in 1969.

Song: O Father, let thy love remain (958)

PARKER, William Henry

b Basford, Nottingham, 4 March 1845
d Basford, Nottingham, 2 December 1929

He was apprenticed in the machine-construction department of a New Basford lace-maker, but later became head of an insurance company. A member of Chelsea Street Baptist Church, in Nottingham, he was involved there in Sunday-school work, and wrote a number of hymns for Sunday-school anniversaries. He published a small collection of poetry, *The Princess Alice, and Other Poems,* 1882.

Songs: Holy Spirit, hear us (193)
Tell me the stories of Jesus (848)

PARR, Ernest Henry

b Exeter, Devon, 19 May 1909

Son of Wesleyan methodist parents. During the First World War his family moved to Scotland, where he was converted as a boy at Govan. He played soprano cornet in Govan Band at the age of 15, and in February 1927 assisted the International Staff Band on a visit to Southend Citadel. In 1928 he emigrated to Winnipeg, Canada, and six years later moved to Toronto, where he was a proof reader in the territorial headquarters printing department before entering the training college in 1938. After training he was appointed to Gravenhurst Corps in Northern Ontario, but within a year he returned to territorial headquarters, working in the printing, trade and youth departments. His subsequent appointments were as divisional youth secretary, divisional secretary and divisional commander; General Secretary and, later, Training Principal at the training college in Toronto; and finally Staff Secretary. He retired as a lieut-colonel in 1975. He served for a time as Executive Officer of the Canadian Staff Band. He has written a number of songs and, for 10 years, has contributed a new Christmas song to *The War Cry* in Canada each year.

Song: All our hearts rejoice this morning (74)

PEACEY, John Raphael

b Hove, Sussex, 16 July 1896
d Brighton, Sussex, 31 October 1971

Educated at St Edmund's School, Canterbury, and later (after serving in the army in France) at Selwyn College and the Clergy Training School, in Cambridge. He was ordained in 1922, and was then assistant master at Wellington College, 1922-23, and fellow, dean, and precentor of Selwyn College, 1923-27. Moving to India, he became headmaster of Bishop Cotton School, Simla, 1927-35, and principal of the Bishop's College, Calcutta, 1935-45. After returning to England he was canon residentiary of Bristol Cathedral, 1945-66, with various responsibilities in the diocese, including Diocesan Missioner, 1956-66. He retired to Hurstpierpoint in 1967 and served as rural dean of Hurst from 1969.

Songs: Awake, awake! Fling off the night (408)
O Lord, we long to see your face (748)

PEARSON, William James

b Derby, 1832
d Hackney, London, 17 October 1892

He grew up in Derby, where his mother was a class leader at the Traffic Street Primitive Methodist Chapel. Converted at the age of 14, he later became a local preacher. He moved to London in 1874 to join The Christian Mission and served as superintendent of the Shoreditch Circuit and then as an evangelist in Hastings, Whitechapel, Wellingborough, Manchester and Bradford. (He was stationed in Bradford in 1878 when The Christian Mission became known as The Salvation Army.) After a short period in charge of the corps at East Hartlepool, he returned to London in 1879, as manager of the Salvation Army Book Stores. Subsequently he travelled widely as a representative of *The War Cry* and as a quarterly collection officer. He was well known for his ministry of faith healing. For a number of years he wrote a new song each week, contributing regularly to *The War Cry* and occasionally to *The Musical Salvationist*.

Songs: All round the world the Army chariot rolls (775)
Christ of self-denial (921)
Come, join our Army, to battle we go (681)
God is keeping his soldiers fighting (800)
God's trumpet is sounding: To arms! is the call (684, verses)
I want the faith of God (733)
I'm set apart for Jesus (495)
It is the blood that washes white (113)
Jesus, give thy blood-washed Army (593)
Jesus, lead me up the mountain (429)
Jesus, save me through and through (430)
Jesus, thy fulness give (431)
Jesus, thy purity bestow (432)
Joy! joy! joy! there is joy in The Salvation Army (807)
Lord, give me more soul-saving love (609)
O thou God of every nation (622)
O thou God of full salvation (452)

To leave the world below (901, verses)
We are marching home to Glory (902, verses)
We praise thee, Lord, with heart and voice (936)
We're an Army fighting for a glorious King (821)

PENNEFATHER, William

b Dublin, 5 February 1816
d Muswell Hill, Middlesex, 30 April 1873

Son of Richard Pennefather, Baron of the Irish Court of Exchequer, he was educated at Westbury College, near Bristol, and at Trinity College, Dublin. Following his ordination in 1841, he was curate at Ballymacugh and then vicar of Mellifont, near Drogheda. Subsequently, after moving to England, he served at Trinity Church, Walton, Aylesbury, 1848-52; Christ Church, Barnet, 1852-64; and St Jude's, Mildmay Park, from 1864. At Barnet, he commenced a series of annual Christian conferences which continued at Mildmay, where he also established the Mildmay Religious and Benevolent Institution. Most of his hymns were written for the Mildmay Conferences, and were published on leaflets or pamphlets, including *Hymns Original and Selected* for the 1872 conference, and in his *Original Hymns and Thoughts in Verse*, 1873.

Song: Jesus, stand among us (599)

PENNICK, William Drake

b Fulham, Middlesex, 1 January 1884
d Shoreditch, London, 8 July 1944

Son of Shepherd D. Pennick, a sergeant in the Metropolitan Police and also band sergeant at the Congress Hall, Clapton, for 25 years. He entered the training home from the Clapton Congress Hall in 1903, and, after corps appointments in Britain, served in India and later in China, 1918-28. He then became Sub-Territorial Commander for Belgium, before returning to India in 1933. His last appointment was as Territorial Commander for Northern India, with the rank of lieutenant-commissioner. Seriously ill when he left Lahore in June 1944, he was promoted to Glory from Mildmay Mission Hospital a week after arriving in Britain. He wrote verses when he was a boy and later started to write songs while he was serving overseas.

Songs: King of love so condescending (500)
There is a holy hill of God (461)
Unfurl the Army banner (781)
We are witnesses for Jesus (832)
Would you of our banner know the meaning (783)

PERRONET, Edward

b Sundridge, Kent, 1725 or 1726
d Canterbury, Kent, 2 January 1792

Son of the Reverend Vincent Perronet, vicar of Sundridge. He grew up in the Church of England and for some years supported the work of John Wesley. He was apparently a Methodist preacher until about 1755, but subsequently he became minister at the Countess of Huntingdon's chapel in Watling Street, Canterbury. At the end of his life he was pastor of a small independent congregation in Canterbury. He published his poetry and hymns in *Select Passages of the Old and New Testament versified,* 1756; *A Small Collection of Hymns,* 1782; and *Occasional Verses, Moral and Sacred,* 1785.

Song: All hail the power of Jesus' name (56)

PETERS, Mary (*née* BOWLY)

b Cirencester, Gloucestershire, 17 April 1813
d Clifton, Bristol, 29 July 1856

Daughter of Richard Bowly, of Cirencester. She married the Reverend John M. Peters, who was vicar of Langford, Berkshire. He died in 1834. She wrote *The World's History from the Creation to the Accession of Queen Victoria,* in seven volumes. Her 58 hymns were published in *Hymns intended to Help the Communion of Saints,* 1847, though some had previously appeared in the Plymouth Brethren *Psalms, Hymns and Spiritual Songs,* 1842.

Song: Through the love of God our Saviour (764)

PETERSON, John Willard

b Lindsborg, Kansas, 1 November 1921

He came from a musical family who were members of the Mission Covenant Church and were active in Christian broadcasting. He served as a pilot in the US Army Air Force in Asia, during the Second World War. He studied in Chicago at Moody Bible Institute and the American Conservatory of Music, and was then a staff musician for WMBI (the radio station of the Moody Bible Institute), 1950-54. In 1954 he joined Singspiration, Inc. as an editor and composer, and in 1963 he became president of the company when it was acquired by Zondervan Publishing House. He has written and composed more than 1,000 gospel songs, cantatas and musicals, including *Night of Miracles, Born a King* and *Jesus is Coming,* and his other publications include *A Book of Favourite Poems,* 1963, and *Great Hymns of our Faith,* 1968.

Song: O what a wonderful, wonderful day (371)

PHELPS, Sylvanus Dryden

b Suffield, Connecticut, 15 May 1816
d New Haven, Connecticut, 23 November 1895

Educated at Connecticut Literary Institute, Brown University and Yale Divinity School. He served as pastor of the First Baptist Church, New Haven, 1846-74 and then at Jefferson Street Baptist Church, in Providence, Rhode Island, 1874-76. Subsequently he was editor of the journal *The Christian Secretary.* He published poetry and prose, including *The Holy Land, with Glimpses of Europe and Egypt,* 1862.

Songs: Once I heard a sound at my heart's dark door (373)
Saviour, thy dying love (524)

PIERPOINT, Folliott Sandford

b Bath, Somerset, 7 October 1835
d Newport, Monmouthshire, 10 March 1917

Son of William Horne Pierpoint, of Bath. He was educated at the Grammar School, Bath, and at Queens' College, Cambridge. For a time he was master of classics at Somersetshire College but subsequently he lived in various places, including Babbacombe, Devon. He contributed hymns to the *Churchman's Companion* and Orby Shipley's *Lyra Eucharistica* (2nd edition, 1864), and published his poetry in *Songs of Love, The Chalice of Nature, and Lyra Jesu*, 1878.

Song: For the beauty of the earth (28)

PIGGOTT, William Charter

b Leighton Buzzard, Bedfordshire, 9 August 1872
d Epsom, Surrey, 5 November 1943

Educated at Highfield College, Huddersfield, and Headingley Wesleyan College. He was minister at the Brotherhood Church, Harrow Road, London, 1896-1900, and then served as a congregational minister at Greville Place, Kilburn, 1901-04; Bunyan Meeting, Bedford, 1905-12; Whitefield's Tabernacle, Tottenham Court Road, London, 1912-16; and Streatham, 1917-37. He was Chairman of the Congregational Union of England and Wales, 1931-32.

Song: For those we love within the veil (878)

PIGOTT, Jean Sophia

b Ireland, 1845
d Leixlip, Lucan, County Kildare, 12 October 1882

Little is known about the author, except that she contributed a few hymns to early editions of *Hymns of Consecration and Faith* and published an anthology, *A Royal Service, and other poems*, 1877.

Song: Lord Jesus, thou dost keep thy child (741)

PLANT, Thomas William

b Bicester, Oxfordshire, 2 January 1866
d Upwood, Huntingdonshire, 29 October 1944

Son of Thomas Plant, a cordwainer. He was a member of a large musical family and often took part in chapel services and concerts. After a Salvation Army officer on furlough had visited Bicester, he helped to continue revival meetings there and became an officer in 1888. He served as secretary to the divisional officer in Reading, and later to William Booth, Commissioner Thomas McKie, and territorial commanders in Canada and Germany. Subsequently he conducted meetings in Britain as a 'spiritual musical special' for many years, and then retired as a brigadier in 1929. During the First World War he had worked in clubs for servicemen and in 1941 he again volunteered for war work, taking charge of Upwood Red Shield Club for three years. He played more than 20 instruments, including the banjo, concertina, piano and tubular bells, and wrote many songs, which he often used as solos.

Song: I have found a great salvation (328)

POLLARD, Adelaide Addison

b Bloomfield, Iowa, 27 November 1862
d New York City, 20 December 1934

Originally named Sarah, she later adopted the name Adelaide. After attending schools in Denmark, Iowa and Valparaiso, Indiana, she studied elocution and physical culture at Boston School of Oratory. She taught at several schools in Chicago and later at the Christian and Missionary Alliance Training School in Nyack, New York, 1905-07. She was interested in missionary work and faith healing, and assisted Dr John Alexander Dowie in some of his healing services. Before the outbreak of the First World War she spent several months in Africa, but when the war began she moved to Scotland and afterwards returned to New York.

Song: Have thine own way, Lord, have thine own way (487)

POLLOCK, Florence Lilian (or Lillian)

b Wolverhampton, Staffordshire, 27 January 1899
d Waltham Forest, London, 8 January 1981

The daughter of Salvation Army officers, she was corps cadet guardian at Watford Citadel before entering the training garrison from Norwich I Corps. After her commissioning in

1922, she was a cadet-sergeant for a year and then served in corps appointments at Buntingford and Eaton Bray. She transferred to The Salvation Army Assurance Society in 1928. Latterly she was secretary to the General Manager and retired as a brigadier in 1961.

Song: On Calvary's tree the King of Glory languished (126)

POLLOCK, Thomas Benson

b Strathallan, Isle of Man, 28 May 1836
d Bordesley, Warwickshire, 15 December 1896

Educated at Trinity College, Dublin, he gained the Vice-Chancellor's Prize for English Verse there in 1855. He was ordained in 1861 and served as curate of St Luke's, Leek, Staffordshire and than at St Thomas's, Stamford Hill, London. In 1865, he became curate to his brother, the Reverend J. S. Pollock, at St Alban's Mission, Birmingham, and 30 years later succeeded his brother as vicar, but died a few months afterwards. He published *Metrical Litanies for Special Services and General Use,* 1870, and was chairman of the committee of *Hymns Ancient and Modern,* in 1895-96.

Song: We have not known thee as we ought (466)

POTT, Francis

b Southwark, Surrey, 29 December 1832
d Speldhurst, Kent, 26 October 1909

Educated at Brasenose College, Oxford. After his ordination in 1856, he served as a curate in Bishopworth, Gloucestershire, 1856-58; Ardingly, Sussex, 1858-61; and Ticehurst, Sussex, 1861-66; and then as rector of Northill, Bedfordshire, 1866-91. He was a member of the committee which prepared *Hymns Ancient and Modern,* 1861, and he also edited *Hymns fitted to the Order of Common Prayer,* 1861, and *The Free Rhythm Psalter,* 1898.

Song: The strife is o'er, the battle done (151)

POWELL, Walter Mason

b Islington, Middlesex, 29 August 1867
d Bidborough, Kent, 29 January 1956

He was converted as a boy at Wesley's Chapel, City Road, London, and later became a methodist local preacher. He started to attend Salvation Army meetings when a corps opened at Upper Norwood, and became an officer in 1888. After three years in corps, divisional and provincial appointments in Britain, he was appointed to Holland as Chief Secretary, and subsequently served in Norway, Japan, Northern India and Denmark, before returning to divisional work in England. In 1910 he became assistant staff secretary at International Headquarters and then served in the Subscribers' Department and the Emigration Department until 1926, when he was appointed to Salvationist Publishing and Supplies Ltd. He retired as a lieut-colonel in 1932.

Song: O mighty God! When I thy works consider (39)

RAILTON, George Scott

b Arbroath, 6 July 1849
d Cologne, Germany, 19 July 1913

Son of the Reverend Launcelot Railton, a methodist minister who had earlier been a missionary in Antigua. He was converted in 1860 at the age of 10, at his home in Wigton, Cumberland. He attended Woodhouse Grove School, Leeds, but after his parents died in 1864 he moved to London. Having learnt Spanish while working for a shipping firm he went on a mission to Morocco in 1868. When he returned, he worked for a time in Cornwall and then in Stockton-on-Tees and Middlesbrough where he was a methodist local preacher. He became Secretary of The Christian Mission in 1873, after reading the Mission report *How to Reach the Masses with the Gospel*, 1872. In 1880 he led a group of pioneers to commence Salvation Army work in New York and then established his headquarters in Philadelphia and later in St Louis. Early in 1881 he was recalled to London. Subsequently he travelled extensively, campaigning in South Africa, Holland, South America, the West Indies, the Far East, West Africa, China, Russia and Turkey, and many other countries. He was in charge of Salvation Army work in Germany, 1890-94, and later was Territorial Commander for France, 1901-02. He was promoted to Glory while returning from Switzerland, when he changed trains in Cologne. He wrote a number of Salvation Army songs and was the author of several books, including *Soldiers of Salvation*, 1909, and a biography, *General Booth*, 1912.

Songs: Hark, hark, my soul, what warlike songs are swelling (802)
   No home on earth have I (362)
   Shout aloud salvation, and we'll have another song (815)
   Soldier, rouse thee! War is raging (693)
   Tell me what to do to be pure (459, verses 1, 2)
   We are sweeping through the land (819)
   Who'll fight for the Lord everywhere (708)

RANCE, Ernest Edward

b Gloucester, 9 June 1896
d Orpington, Kent, 3 February 1988

Before entering the training garrison in 1919 he was corps secretary at Gillingham. After corps and training college appointments, he served for 20 years at Men's Social Work Headquarters, where for a short while he was bandmaster of the headquarters band. At this time he also conducted the East London Chorus in divisional meetings at Clapton. During the Second World War he was Salvation Army Services Officer in the Western and South-Eastern Military Commands. Subsequently he served at National Headquarters, in the Northern and Birmingham Divisions (as chancellor), and then as National Secretary for Bands and Songster Brigades, 1950-60. For a year he was director of the Migration and Settlement Department, and retired as a lieut-colonel in 1961. He composed songs as well as music for the band journals, and played the concertina, piano, organ and trombone.

Song: To the hills I lift my eyes (766)

RANKIN, Jeremiah Eames

b Thornton, New Hampshire, 2 January 1828
d Cleveland, Ohio, 28 November 1904

Educated at Middlebury College, Vermont, and at Andover

Theological Seminary. He was ordained in 1855 and served as minister of congregational churches in New York; St Albans, Vermont; and Charlestown, Massachusetts. He then became pastor of the First Congregational Church, Washington, DC, in 1869, and moved to the Valley Congregational Church, Orange, New Jersey, in 1884. In 1889, he returned to Washington, DC, as president of Howard University. He published several volumes of sermons and other books, including the *Gospel Temperance Hymnal*, 1878; *Gospel Bells*, 1883, and *German-English Lyrics, Sacred and Secular*, 1897.

Song: God be with you till we meet again (954)

READ, Eliza (?)

b ?
d ?

Little is known about the author (Mrs Read) except that she was apparently a soldier at Shankhill Road Corps in Belfast, 1880-81, when the corps officer was Captain Annie E. Lockwood (later Mrs Commissioner Richard Wilson).

Song: I heard of a Saviour whose love was so great (331)

READ, Harry

b Teesville, Middlesbrough, Yorkshire, 17 May 1924

After serving in the British Army during the Second World War, he entered the International Training College from Edinburgh Gorgie Corps in 1947. He has served in corps appointments at Dorking, Chichester, Eastbourne Old Town, Portslade and Hanwell; in divisional appointments in South-West Scotland, 1964-66, and Nottingham, 1975-78; and on the staff of the International Training College, as sectional officer (1954-62), field training officer (1966-69), second side officer (1969-72) and training principal (1978-81). He was also Director of Information Services at International Headquarters, 1972-75; Chief Secretary, Canada and Bermuda, 1981-84; and Territorial Commander, Australia Eastern, 1984-87 before being appointed

British Commissioner in 1987. He wrote a number of songs for the annual commissioning of cadets during the years he was on the staff of the training college.

Songs: God's soldier marches as to war (801)
Lord of all glory and of grace (957)

REED, Andrew

b St Clement Danes, Middlesex, 27 November 1787
d Cambridge Heath, Middlesex, 25 February 1862

Son of Andrew Reed, a watchmaker. He learnt his father's trade, but later studied at Hackney College, for the congregational ministry. He became minister at New Road Chapel, St George-in-the-East in 1811 and served for exactly 50 years, there and at the new 'Wycliffe Chapel' built for the growing congregation in 1831. He founded the London Orphan Asylum at Clapton in 1825, and subsequently established other orphanages and asylums at Wanstead, in Essex, and at Reedham, Earlswood and Putney, in Surrey. (The building at Clapton became the Salvation Army Congress Hall and Training Home in 1882.) In 1817 he prepared a supplement to Isaac Watts's *Psalms and Hymns,* and later compiled *The Hymn Book,* 1842, to which he contributed 19 hymns.

Song: Spirit divine, attend our prayers (217)

REED, Elizabeth or Eliza (*née* HOLMES)

b London, 4 March 1794
d St Leonards-on-Sea, Sussex, 4 July 1867

Daughter of Jasper T. Holmes, of Castle Hall, Reading. In 1816, she married the hymn writer, the Reverend Andrew Reed. She assisted her husband in his extensive charitable work and contributed 21 hymns to *The Hymn Book,* 1842, which he compiled. She also published *Original Tales for Children* and *The Mother's Manual for the Training of her Children,* 1865.

Song: O do not let thy Lord depart (251)

REES, Bryn Austin

b Chelsea, London, 21 September 1911
d Epping, Essex, 4 August 1983

Son of the Reverend Thomas Mardy Rees, a congregational minister. He was educated at Neath Grammar School, and Hackney and New College, London. After his ordination in 1935, he was congregational minister at Sawbridgeworth, Hertfordshire, 1935-40; Ipswich, Suffolk, 1940-41; Felixstowe, Suffolk, 1945-48; Muswell Hill, Middlesex, 1950-62; and the United Free Church, Woodford Green, Essex, 1962-72. In 1972 he moved to Epping, Essex, where he was minister of the United Reformed Church in Lindsey Street and also Free Church chaplain at St Margaret's Hospital. He had earlier served as a chaplain in the Royal Air Force, 1941-45 and 1948-50.

Song: Have faith in God, my heart (723)

RENDELL, Doris Nicol

b Knottingley, Yorkshire, 31 January 1896

Daughter of Staff-Captain Thomas Rendell, who assisted General William Booth in some of his campaign meetings, 1904-08, and on his North Scottish motorcade. She was converted at the age of eight after a junior meeting at Shepherds Bush, and entered the training garrison in 1921 from Regent Hall Corps, where she had been cradle roll sergeant and assistant young people's sergeant-major. Before becoming a cadet she worked in the Ministry of Health. Subsequently she served in the East London Division as a corps officer and as divisional helper, and then in the office of the Chancellor at International Headquarters for 20 years. She retired as a lieut-colonel in 1959, after 10 years as Applicants' Secretary at Women's Social Work Headquarters. Her first song was published in 1930 and she later contributed more than 100 songs to *The Musical Salvationist* and other publications.

Songs: Emblem of a thousand battles (777)
For thy sweet comfort in distress (719)
God of comfort and compassion (576)
In days long past the mercy seat (590)
In this hour of dedication (787)

Lord of life and love and power (789)
Soldiers of King Jesus (866)
We have caught the vision splendid (833)

RICHARDS, Miriam Mary

b New Barnet, Hertfordshire, 12 April 1911

Daughter of Brigadier and Mrs William J. Richards. She grew up in Java, and in Korea where her father was promoted to Glory in 1920. Before entering the training college in 1932 she worked for five years at International Headquarters in the Editorial Department. After a year as a cadet-sergeant she was appointed to Chester-le-Street and then to the Young People's Department at National Headquarters in 1935, and to Northern Territorial Headquarters in Leeds in 1936. Subsequently she served at the International Training College, 1938-44; on Women's Social Work, 1944-55; and as editor of the *Home League Exchange*, 1955-71. She retired as a lieut-colonel in 1971. More than 125 of her songs have been published, including a number written for *The Young People's Song Book*, 1963. She has written a history of Salvation Army medical work, *It Began with Andrews*, 1972, and other books.

Songs: Beyond the farthest bounds of earth (27)
Not only, Lord, on that great day (618)
What can I say to cheer a world of sorrow (706)
When Christ drew near to dwell with men (102)

RINKART, Martin

b Eilenburg, Saxony, 23 April 1586
d Eilenburg, Saxony, 8 December 1649

Son of Georg Rinkart, a cooper. He was educated at the Latin School in Eilenburg, at St Thomas's School, Leipzig, and the University of Leipzig. After serving as pastor at Erdeborn and Lyttichendorf, near Eisleben, he became archdeacon at Eilenburg in 1617. He served there throughout the Thirty Years War (1618-48), when the walled town became overcrowded with refugees from the surrounding area. He is said to have buried almost 4,500 people who died through disease and famine in 1637. He wrote extensively, including poetry and drama. Many of his hymns were published in his *Jesu Hertz-Buchlein*, 1636 (second edition, 1663) and other collections.

Song: Now thank we all our God (12)

RIPPON, John

b Tiverton, Devon, 29 April 1751
d Surrey, 17 December 1836

He studied for the ministry at the Baptist College, Bristol, and in 1775 became pastor of the baptist church in Carter Lane, London, where he served for more than 60 years until he died. He was editor of the *Baptist Annual Register*, 1790-1802. He compiled *A Selection of Hymns from the Best Authors, Intended as an Appendix to Dr Watts' Psalms and Hymns*, 1787, which was enlarged in subsequent editions, and was widely used in Britain and America.

Song: 'Tis religion that can give (464, verse 4)

ROBINSON, George Wade

b Cork, Ireland, 1838
d Southampton, 28 January 1877

Educated at Trinity College, Dublin and New College, London. He became a congregational minister, serving as co-pastor at York Street Chapel, Dublin, and later as pastor at St John's Wood, London, at Dudley, and Union Street, Brighton. He published two books of poetry: *Songs in God's World* and *Loveland*.

Song: Loved with everlasting love (545)

ROBINSON, Joseph Armitage

b Keynsham, Somerset. 9 January 1858
d Upton Noble, Somerset, 7 May 1933

Educated at Christ's College, Cambridge. After his ordination in 1881 he was domestic chaplain to the Bishop of Durham, 1883-84, dean of Christ's College, 1884-90, and also assistant curate of Great St Mary's, Cambridge, 1888-92. He was appointed professor of divinity at Cambridge in 1893, and prebendary of Wells in 1894, and then became rector of St Margaret's, Westminster, and a canon of Westminster in 1899. Subsequently he was dean of Westminster, 1902-11, and dean of Wells from 1911 until he died. His many publications on theology and church history included a *Commentary on the Epistle to the Ephesians*, 1904.

Song: 'Tis good, Lord, to be here (154)

ROBINSON, Robert

b Swaffham, Norfolk, 27 September 1735
d Showell Green, Warwickshire, 8 or 9 June 1790

In 1749 he was apprenticed to a barber in London, though he apparently left before completing his training. He heard George Whitefield preach in 1752 on Matthew 3:7 and three years later, after a spiritual struggle, he was converted. During 1758 he was in charge of a Calvinistic methodist chapel at Mildenhall, Suffolk and then of an independent congregation in Norwich. In the following year, he was called to preach at Stone Yard Baptist Church in Cambridge and became pastor there in 1761. He also worked as a farmer and merchant, and retired to Birmingham in 1790. His publications included *A Plea for the Divinity of our Lord Jesus Christ*, 1776, and a *History of Baptism and Baptists*, 1790.

Song: Come, thou Fount of every blessing (313)

ROLFE, Emmanuel

b Berwick St James, Wiltshire, 3 December 1853
d Chickerell, Dorset, 15 February 1914

He worked for several years on a farm before moving to London and then to Middlesbrough, where he heard William Booth preach at the Middlesbrough Theatre. He was converted in 1875 and joined The Christian Mission, becoming a Salvation Army officer in 1879 from North Ormesby. After several corps appointments in Britain (including Manchester, Salisbury, Dudley and Birmingham), he served in Australia (1882-89) and

New Zealand (1889-92) and then returned to Britain, where he was stationed in the Brighton and Oxford Divisions. He was appointed to the West Indies in 1894 to take charge of Army work in Jamaica, and subsequently served at International Headquarters (1901-03) in the Staff Department and the Foreign Office.

Song: Jesus came down my ransom to be (114)

ROOT, George Frederick

b Sheffield, Massachusetts, 30 August 1820
d Bailey's Island, Maine, 6 August 1895

In 1839 he became assistant organist at Winter Street and Park Street churches in Boston, and for several years assisted Lowell Mason as a music teacher in Boston schools. He moved to New York in 1844 and taught music at schools and colleges, including Union Theological Seminary and the New York Institute for the Blind, where Fanny Crosby was one of his students. She wrote the text for his cantata *The Flower Queen*. After moving to Chicago in 1858 he worked for the music publishers Root and Cady until 1871, and then with the John Church Company of Cincinnati. He composed several hundred songs and compiled and edited at least 75 collections of songs and ballads.

Songs: Come to the Saviour, make no delay (235)
She only touched the hem of his garment (304)

ROTH, Elton Menno

b Berne, Indiana, 27 November 1891
d Glendale, California, 31 December 1951

He was converted in a **Mennonite** revival meeting at the age of 12, and was baptised in the Wabash River. He apparently intended to be a commercial artist, but later attended Fort Wayne Bible School and Moody Bible Institute. By the time he was 14, he was director of a church choir, and for several years he travelled with evangelists, as a singer and choir director. He subsequently taught music at the Alliance Bible School in New York and at other colleges in Los Angeles. In 1931, he founded the Ecclesia Choir, which toured extensively throughout the United States.

Song: I have a song that Jesus gave me (327)

ROTHE, Johann Andreas

b Lissa, near Görlitz, Silesia, 12 May 1688
d Thommendorf, near Bunzlau, 6 July 1758

Son of Aegidius Rothe, pastor at Lissa. He was educated at the University of Leipzig, and was licensed to preach in 1712. He became tutor in a family at Leube, near Görlitz, in 1718, and preached in various churches. Count von Zinzendorf heard him preach in 1722 and appointed him pastor at Berthelsdorf, where the Moravian community of Herrnhut was within his parish. Later, he apparently offended Zinzendorf, and became pastor at Hermsdorf, near Görlitz, in 1737, assistant pastor at Thommendorf, in 1739, and chief pastor there in 1742.

Song: Now I have found the ground wherein (746)

ROUSE, Louise M.

b ?
d ?

Nothing is known about the author.

Songs: Come, thou Fount of every blessing (313, chorus)
Precious Jesus, O to love thee (520, chorus)

ROWE, James

b Horrabridge, Devon, 1 January 1865
d Wells, Vermont, 10 November 1933

Son of John Rowe, a copper miner. He emigrated to the United States in about 1890 and settled in Albany, New York. For 10 years he worked for a railway company in New York, and later was superintendent of the Hudson River Humane Society. He wrote songs and edited music for music publishers in Texas and Tennessee, and, after moving to Vermont, he worked with his daughter (who was an artist), writing verses for greetings cards.

Song: I was sinking deep in sin (336)

ROWLEY, Francis Harold

b Hilton, New York, 25 July 1854
d Boston, Massachusetts, 14 February 1952

Educated at the University of Rochester and Rochester Theological Seminary. He served as a baptist minister at Titusville, Pennsylvania, 1879-84; North Adams, Massachusetts, 1884-92; Oak Park, Illinois, 1892-96; Fall River, Massachusetts, 1896-1900; and the First Baptist Church, Boston, 1900-10. He was president of the American Humane Education Society, 1910-45, and became chairman of the board in 1945. His publications included *The Humane Idea* and *The Horses of Homer.*

Song: I will sing the wondrous story (337)

RUNDLE-CHARLES, Elisabeth

See: **CHARLES, Elisabeth (*née* RUNDLE)**

RUSHER, Leslie Charles

b Queenstown, Tasmania, 21 September 1905

After moving to Melbourne with his family in 1916, he was converted at the Brunswick Corps where he became young people's band leader at the age of 18. Later he moved to Kilkenny, South Australia, and was bandmaster there before entering the training college in 1929. He served mainly as a corps officer for about 10 years and joined the editorial department in Melbourne in 1942, and was also a member of Melbourne Staff Band for six years. Subsequently he was editor-in-chief in New Zealand, 1948-57, and then in Australia, 1957-62. He was Territorial Commander in Indonesia, 1962-65, and Korea, 1965-71 and was appointed Travelling Commissioner in 1971, leading campaigns as the General's Representative, particularly in the Far East. He retired in 1973. Several of his songs have appeared in *The Musical Salvationist* and he has contributed poems to Salvation Army anthologies, including *The Merchant of Heaven*, 1944, *Book of Salvationist Verse*, 1963, and *Pilgrims*, 1988. He has also written *Bamboo Notebook*, 1981.

Song: We thank thee, Lord, for answered prayer (642)

RUSSELL, Anna Belle

b Pine Valley, New York, 21 April 1862
d Corning, New York, 29 October 1954

Daughter of Chancey Russell. She lived in Corning, New York, for many years, with her sister, Cora C. Russell, who also wrote hymns. They were members of the First Methodist Church in Corning.

Song: There is never a day so dreary (186)

RYLAND, John

b Warwick, 29 January 1753
d Bristol, 25 May 1825

Son of the Reverend John Collett Ryland, baptist minister at Warwick and later at Northampton, 1759-86. As a child he learnt Hebrew and Greek from his father, and at the age of eight he apparently translated the whole of the New Testament. In 1781, he was ordained as co-pastor of the baptist church at Northampton, with his father, and he continued as pastor there when his father moved to London in 1786. He was one of the founders of the Baptist Missionary Society in 1792 and later served as secretary to the society for about three years. In 1794, he became president of the baptist college in Bristol, and pastor of the baptist church at Broadmead, Bristol. He wrote about 100 hymns, which appeared in the *Gospel Magazine*, 1771-82 and other magazines, and were later reprinted in *Hymns and Verses on Sacred Subjects*, 1862.

Song: O Lord, I will delight in thee (14)

SAKER-LYNNE, Alfred Harmond (or Harmand)

b Chatham, Kent, 30 March 1867
d Ilford, Essex, 23 October 1948

Son of Harmand Lynne, general agent. He became a Salvation Army officer in 1886, serving for a while in the East London District. Subsequently he was bandmaster at Kennington and then at Peckham II Corps, *c*1893. He worked as a clerk and later as an estate manager. He contributed songs to *The War Cry*, 1886-87, and to *The Musical Salvationist*, 1886-93.

Song: You may sing of the joys over Jordan (406)

SAMMIS, John Henry

b Brooklyn, New York, 6 July 1846
d Los Angeles, California, 12 June 1919

He moved to Logansport, Indiana, in 1869. After several years as a YMCA secretary, he studied at Lane and McCormick Theological Seminaries, and was ordained in the Presbyterian Church in 1880. He served as pastor of churches in Iowa, Indiana, Michigan and Minnesota, and then moved to California in 1901. From 1909 until he died, he was on the staff of the Bible Institute of Los Angeles.

Song: When we walk with the Lord (397)

SAMPLES, Iva Lou

b Odessa, Texas, 12 May 1946

She grew up in Odessa, making her first contact with The Salvation Army through the Sunday-school at the age of six. She joined the young people's band six years later, and after graduating from high school, trained at the school for officers' training in Atlanta, Georgia, 1964-66. In 1970 she was appointed field training officer for single women, and later became director of the Salvation Army Girls' Lodge in Atlanta. In 1986 she was apparently living in Tulsa, Oklahoma. She wrote her first songs while she was a cadet, reflecting the 'Joy Strings' style of that period.

Song: I've felt a new and loving touch (215)

SAMPSON, Lily Kells

b Perth, Western Australia, 9 September 1906

She was converted at the age of 15 at Newtown, New South Wales, and then became a corps cadet, before entering the training college from Dulwich Hill Corps in 1926. Her early appointments included service as a corps officer; in a children's home; at territorial headquarters; as a divisional young people's secretary; and on the staff of the training college for two sessions. In 1946 she was appointed to India, where she was territorial young people's secretary, first in Madras and Telegu, and later (after about three years in the Editorial Department at International Headquarters) in the Western India and Southern India Territories. She returned to Australia Eastern Territory in 1956 and for several years served in police court and prison work in New South Wales, and finally as State Social Secretary in Queensland. She retired as a lieut-colonel in 1966. During recent years she has been home league pianist at Burwood Corps, New South Wales, and has also been involved in league of mercy activities.

Song: As the varied way of life we journey (711)

SANDERS, Mark William ('Blind Mark')

b Exeter, Devon, 28 April 1862
d Salt Lake City, Utah, 21 August 1943

He became blind three days after his birth and from the age of 11 was educated at the Institution for the Blind in Exeter. While at school he started to learn the piano. In 1881 he left school and later that year he was converted in a Salvation Army meeting in Exeter during the command of Captain and Mrs Abram Davey. (He later travelled with their family when they went to pioneer Salvation Army work in Jamaica, 1887-88.) For nearly 40 years he travelled around Britain leading meetings as an Army 'special'. He played the organ, piano and concertina, often playing the piano and concertina together (holding one end of the concertina between his knees). In later years he moved to Salt Lake City in the United States, where he served as corps pianist, despite losing the use of his right hand after an illness. He composed his first song in 1886 at the suggestion of Richard Slater, who often wrote down words and melodies from his singing, playing, or dictation. A number of his songs appeared in *The Musical Salvationist*. In 1951 salvationists in the Central America and West Indies Territory provided a marker for his grave with the inscription: 'Singer-Composer, Pioneer-Missionary. Lovingly remembered by West Indian Salvationists.'

Song: I have read of men of faith (686)

SANDERS, William

b England, 1799
d USA, 1882?

He was employed by Hugh Bourne at Bemersley Farm and then became a primitive methodist minister in 1820, beginning in the Tunstall circuit. He subsequently served in the Hull Circuit and in other appointments, and in 1838 was stationed at Pottsville, in America. Apparently, he later lost his sight and retired from the ministry, and lived on a farm near Lawrenceville, Pennsylvania. He wrote a number of poems and hymns, some of which were published jointly with Hugh Bourne in the primitive methodist hymn books.

Songs: Hark! the gospel news is sounding (239)
My soul is now united to Christ, the living vine (361)

SCRIVEN, Joseph (Medlicott)

b near Banbridge, County Down, Ireland, 10 September 1819
d Bewdley, Rice Lake, Ontario, 10 August 1886

Son of Captain John Scriven, of the Royal Marines, and his wife, Jane Medlicott. He was educated at Trinity College,

Dublin, and for two years at Addiscombe Military College, Surrey. A few years after his graduation, his fiancée drowned in the River Bann on the eve of their intended wedding. In about 1850 he emigrated to Canada, settled in Ontario and taught at a school near Port Hope. Later he became a private tutor. He was a member of the brethren assembly in Port Hope. In 1854, he was planning to marry Eliza Roche, and she was baptised in Rice Lake, intending to join the Brethren. Apparently she then became ill, and died three years later. He never fully recovered from the shock and suffered periods of deep depression in later years. One night, during an illness, he left his room and was found to have died in the flume of a dam near Rice Lake. He published *Hymns and Other Verses*, 1869.

Song: What a friend we have in Jesus (645)

SEARS, Edmund Hamilton

b Sandisfield, Massachusetts, 6 April 1810
d Weston, Massachusetts, 16 January 1876

Educated at Union College, Schenectady, New York and at Harvard Divinity School. He became pastor of the First Church (Unitarian) at Wayland, Massachusetts, in 1838, and later served at other churches in Massachusetts: at Lancaster, again at Wayland, and finally at Weston, where he retired. He was joint editor of the *Monthly Religious Magazine*, in which many of his hymns appeared. His publications included: *Regeneration*, 1854; *Pictures of the Olden Time*, 1857; and *Sermons and Songs of the Christian Life*, 1875.

Song: It came upon the midnight clear (83)

SEISS, Joseph Augustus

b Graceham, Maryland, 18 March 1823
d Philadelphia, Pennsylvania, 1904

Son of a miner. He was educated at Gettysburg College and Seminary. He served as a Lutheran minister at churches in

Virginia and Maryland before moving to Philadelphia, where he was pastor of St John's Lutheran Church and then became pastor of the Church of Holy Communion in 1874. His publications included *Lectures on the Gospels* and *Ecclesia Lutherana,* 1860.

Song: Fairest Lord Jesus (177, verse 4?)

SERVOSS, Mary Elizabeth

b Schenectady, New York, 22 August 1849
d ?

Few details of her life are available. Apparently she was the constant companion of her disabled grandmother for 18 years and later nursed her mother at home during an extended illness. She was living in Edeson, Illinois, in about 1906. As a young girl she admired the work of Fanny Crosby, and subsequently wrote a number of hymns and published *The Christmas Sheaf,* *c*1883.

Song: Be glad in the Lord and rejoice (537)

SHAW, Knowles

b Venice, or Butler County, Ohio, 13 October 1834
d near McKinney, Texas, 7 June 1878

His family moved from Ohio to Rush County, Indiana, when he was a few months old. He was converted in 1852, and after teaching for a short time, became an evangelist. In 1874 he was pastor of a church in Chicago, but then returned to his work as a singing evangelist. He lived latterly in Rushville, Indiana, but died in a railway accident while travelling to a revival meeting in McKinney. He published several collections of Sunday-school songs, including *Shining Pearl,* 1868; *The Golden Gate,* 1874; *The Gospel Trumpet;* 1875; and *The Morning Star,* 1877.

Song: Sowing in the morning, sowing seeds of kindness (930)

SHEPHERD, Anne (*née* HOULDITCH)

b Cowes, Isle of Wight, 11 September 1809
d Blackheath, Kent, 7 January 1857

Daughter of the Reverend Edward H. Houlditch. In 1843 she married S. Saville Shepherd. She published two novels, *Ellen Seymour*, 1848, and *Reality*, 1852, and several editions of her *Hymns Adapted to the Comprehension of Young Minds*.

Song: I have heard of a Saviour's love (289)

SHERWIN, William Fiske

b Buckland, Massachusetts, 14 March 1826
d Boston, Massachusetts, 14 April 1888

At the age of 15 he moved to Boston, where he studied music under Lowell Mason and other teachers. Later he was on the staff of the New England Conservatory of Music, in Boston, and held several appointments teaching vocal music in Massachusetts and New York. He conducted amateur choirs and was director of music at the annual meetings of the Chautauqua Literary and Scientific Circle, founded in 1874. He assisted in compiling several Sunday-school hymn books, including *Bright Jewels*, 1869, and *Songs of Grace and Glory*, 1874.

Song: Sound the battle cry (698)

SHIRLEY, William Walter

b Staunton Harrold, Leicestershire, 23 September 1725
d Dublin, 7 April 1786

Son of the Hon. Laurence Shirley, and cousin of Selina, Countess of Huntingdon. He was educated at New College, Oxford, and in 1746 he became rector of Loughrea, County Galway. He was a friend of George Whitefield and the Wesleys, and often preached at revival meetings in England and Ireland.

He contributed to, and helped to compile, some of the hymn books used in the Countess of Huntingdon's chapels.

Songs: Salvation! O the joyful sound (382, verse 3)
Sweet the moments, rich in blessing (634)

SHOWALTER, Anthony Johnson

b Rockingham County, Virginia, 1 May 1858
d Chattanooga, Tennessee, 16 September 1924

He received his early musical training from his father, John A. Showalter, and later studied music under several teachers including H. R. Palmer and George F. Root. (In 1895, he spent a year studying music in England, France and Germany.) He began teaching in 1880, and became widely known in the southern states, as a conductor of singing schools. He moved to Dalton, Georgia, in 1884, to establish a branch of the Ruebush-Kieffer Music Company, but shortly afterwards, he founded his own music company. For more than 20 years, he edited the monthly periodical *The Music Teacher* for his company. He was an elder in the First Presbyterian Church, Dalton, and for some time he served as the music director.

Song: What a fellowship, what a joy divine (768, chorus)

SIMPSON, Albert Benjamin

b Bayview, Prince Edward Island, Canada, 15 December 1843
d Nyack, New York, 29 October 1919

Educated at high school in Chatham, Ontario, and at Knox College, Toronto. After his ordination in 1865, he served as pastor at Knox Presbyterian Church, Hamilton, Ontario; Chestnut Street Church, Louisville, Kentucky, 1874-79; and Thirteenth Street Presbyterian Church, New York, 1879-81. In 1887 he founded the Christian Alliance (later known as the Christian and Missionary Alliance) and served as president of the Alliance and pastor of the Gospel Tabernacle, Eighth Avenue, New York, until he died. He wrote about 170 hymns, which were published in *Hymns of the Christian Life*, 1890, which he compiled with R. Kelso Carter, and in other Alliance hymn books.

Song: Oft our trust has known betrayal (750, chorus)

SLACK, James

b ?
d ?

Little information about the author is available. In 1885, as a captain, he was appointed to South Africa, where he then served until about 1891, latterly with the rank of major.

Song: Salvation is our motto (814)

SLADEN, Hugh Alfred Lambart

b Woolwich, Kent, 9 December 1878
d Esher, Surrey, 6 May 1962

Son of Colonel Joseph Sladen of the Royal Artillery, and Lady Sarah Sladen, daughter of the 8th Earl of Cavan. Before entering the training college in 1897 from New Southgate, where he was a local officer, he worked at the Salvation Army Trade Department in London. His first appointment was in Scotland, but he later served as a divisional young people's secretary, and as Young Men's Counsellor (at National Headquarters). In 1913 he was appointed Territorial Organiser of the new life-saving scouts, and in 1918 became a divisional commander, serving in Newport (South Wales), South Yorkshire, the South-West and North London. Subsequently he was National Young People's Secretary and Staff Secretary at National Headquarters, and then Chief Secretary for the Northern Territory formed in 1936. He was appointed Territorial Commander for Finland in 1939 and, during the latter part of the Second World War, he was responsible for organising the Army's European relief work. He became Secretary of the Public Relations Bureau in 1946, and retired as a commissioner in 1948.

Songs: Sweet the moments, rich in blessing (634, chorus)
Touch me with thy healing hand, Lord (531)

SLATER, Richard

b Clerkenwell, London, 7 June 1854
d Westgate-on-Sea, Kent, 7 December 1939

At the age of seven, he became a member of a drum-and-fife band at the Cromer Street Mission, where he later taught in the Sunday-school. He inherited musical talent from his father, and learnt to play the violin, eventually becoming a music teacher and a member of the Royal Albert Hall Orchestral Society. For several years, he pursued an interest in rationalism, but in 1882 he attended a number of Salvation Army meetings and was converted in a holiness meeting at the Regent Hall in September 1882. A year later he started work in the Army's new Music Department at Clapton, and took charge of the department until he retired as a brigadier in 1913. During his retirement, he resumed his appointment temporarily in 1923, and was promoted to the rank of lieut-colonel. He was known as the 'Father of Salvation Army Music', and wrote more than 500 songs, mostly published in *The Musical Salvationist*, as well as marches, selections and other arrangements for the *Band Journal*. He also prepared a *Dictionary of Music*, c1908, and a booklet, *Salvation Army Song Writers*, 1929.

Songs: Afar from Heaven thy feet have wandered (225)
All I have, by thy blood thou dost claim (473)
All the guilty past is washed away (188)
And is it so? A gift from me (475)
At peace with God! How great the blessing (536)
I have glorious tidings of Jesus to tell (329)
In the fight, say, does your heart grow weary (805)
Jesus is my Saviour, this I know (348)
Jesus, see me at thy feet (292)
None the love of Christ can measure (363)
Oft our trust has known betrayal (750)
Our thankful hearts need joyful songs (926)
Seeds now we are sowing, and fruit they must bear (928)
There is coming on a great day of rejoicing (169)
To save the world the Saviour came (831)
What is the love of Jesus to thee (276)
When wise men came seeking for Jesus from far (92)
Yes, there flows a wondrous river (471)

SLEEPER, William True

b Danbury, New Hampshire, 9 February 1819
d Wellesley, Massachusetts, 24 September 1904

Educated at Phillips-Exeter Academy, the University of Vermont, and Andover Theological Seminary. He was ordained to the congregational ministry and undertook home mission work in Worcester, Massachusetts, and later in Maine. In

Worcester he served as pastor of the Summer Street Congregational Church for more than 30 years. He published a collection of poems: *The Rejected King, and Hymns of Jesus,* 1883.

Song: Out of my bondage, sorrow and night (300)

SMALL, James Grindlay

b Edinburgh, 1817
d Renfrew, 11 February 1888

Son of George Small, a JP in Edinburgh. He was educated at the High School and University of Edinburgh, where he studied divinity under Dr Thomas Chalmers. He joined the Free Church of Scotland when it was founded in 1843 and became minister of the Free Church at Bervie, near Montrose, in 1847. His publications included *Hymns for Youthful Voices,* 1859; *Psalms and Sacred Songs,* 1866; and two books of poetry: *The Highlands and Other Poems,* 1843, and *Songs of the Vineyard in Days of Gloom and Sadness,* 1846.

Song: I've found a friend, O such a friend (345)

SMITH, George Samuel

b St George, Gloucestershire, 12 July 1865
d Downend, near Bristol, 3 June 1944

Son of William Smith, a gardener and nurseryman. When he left school, he started work as a shoemaker. Shortly after The Salvation Army opened in Kingswood, Bristol, in 1879, he was converted. A brass band was formed in 1881 and he served as bandmaster for several years. In 1897 he became a methodist local preacher and for some time was a Sunday-school superintendent and a class leader. He contributed several songs to early volumes of *The Musical Salvationist.*

Songs: Behold him now on yonder tree (108)
Blessèd Lamb of Calvary (538)

SMITH, Walter Chalmers

b Aberdeen, 5 December 1824
d Kinbuck, Dunblane, 19 September 1908

Educated at Aberdeen Grammar School, Aberdeen University and New College, Edinburgh. In 1850 he was ordained as pastor of the Free Church, Chadwell Street, Islington, and subsequently served as minister of other churches, including Orwell Free Church, Milnathort; the Free Tron Church, Glasgow; and the Free High Church, Edinburgh, 1876-94. He was Moderator of the Assembly of the Free Church of Scotland in 1893. His many publications included *Hymns of Christ and the Christian Life*, 1867, and his *Poetical Works*, 1902.

Song: Immortal, invisible, God only wise (8)

SPAFFORD, Horatio Gates

b North Troy, New York, 20 October 1828
d Jerusalem, 16 October 1888

He spent his early years in New York, but in 1856 moved to Chicago, where he had a legal practice and was professor of medical jurisprudence at Lind University (later Chicago Medical College). At various times he was also a Sunday-school teacher, a YMCA worker, and a director and trustee of the Presbyterian Theological Seminary of the Northwest (later McCormick Theological Seminary). He suffered losses in the Chicago fire of 1871, and after the death of four daughters (at sea) in 1873, and a son in 1880, he decided to move to Jerusalem, where he established a missionary rest home, The American Colony.

Song: When peace like a river attendeth my way (771)

SPANGENBERG, August Gottlieb

b Klettenberg, Germany, 15 July 1704
d Berthelsdorf, Saxony, 18 September 1792

Son of Georg Spangenberg, Lutheran pastor of Klettenberg. He was educated at the University of Jena, where he studied law and theology. After a short period in Halle, 1732-33, he joined the Moravian community in Herrnhut, and in 1735 accompanied Moravian settlers to the colony in Georgia. He helped to establish Moravian settlements in Pennsylvania and the West Indies, and in 1742 founded the first Moravian community in England, at Smith House, Yorkshire. He was Moravian bishop for North America, 1744-62, but, after 1762, lived mainly at Herrnhut, Barby and Berthelsdorf, as senior member of the Moravian community, in succession to Nicolaus von Zinzendorf. He wrote a biography of Zinzendorf, 1772-75, as well as his autobiography, 1784, and *An Exposition of Christian Doctrine, as taught in the Protestant Church of the United Brethren,* 1784.

Song: What shall we offer to our Lord (533)

STARK, Malcolm

b ?
d ?

He was a Glasgow architect, often known as 'The Hallelujah Quaker', who had strong links with Bridgeton Corps.

Song: To the war! to the war! loud and long sounds the cry (703)

STEELE, Anne

b Broughton, Hampshire, *c* May 1717
d Broughton, Hampshire, 11 November 1778

Daughter of William Steele, a timber merchant and pastor of Broughton Baptist Church. After her conversion, she became a member of the baptist congregation in Broughton, in 1732. About five years later, her fiancé, Mr Elscourt, was drowned in the River Avon shortly before their intended marriage. In 1760, under the pseudonym 'Theodosia', she published *Poems on Subjects Chiefly Devotional,* two volumes including hymns, poems and psalm paraphrases. A third volume, of miscellaneous poems and prose meditations, was published posthumously, in 1780.

Song: My Maker and my King (616)

STENNETT, Joseph

b Abingdon, Berkshire, 1663
d Knaphill, Buckinghamshire, 11 July 1713

Educated at the Grammar School in Wallingford. At the age of 22 he came to London, where he worked as a tutor for several years. In 1689 the baptist sabbatarian congregation in Devonshire Square, London (which later met in Pinners' Hall) called him to preach and he served as their pastor from 1690 until he died. This congregation worshipped on Saturdays, so on Sundays he preached in other churches, especially the General Baptist Church in the Barbican. He published two collections of hymns, one, in 1697, for the Lord's Supper, and the other, in 1712, for baptism.

Song: O blessèd Saviour, is thy love (515)

STENNETT, Samuel

b Exeter, Devon, 1727
d Muswell Hill, Middlesex, 25 August 1795

Son of Joseph Stennett, a baptist minister, and grandson of Joseph Stennett (1663-1713), the hymn writer. In 1737, at the age of 10, he moved to London with his family when his father became pastor of the baptist church in Little Wild Street, Lincoln's Inn Fields. After 10 years as assistant pastor there he succeeded his father as pastor in 1758. He also preached for 20 years on Saturday mornings at the sabbatarian baptist church where his grandfather had been pastor. He contributed a number of hymns to *A Collection of Hymns for the Use of Christians of all Denominations*, 1782, and *A Selection of Hymns from the Best Authors*, 1787, compiled by John Rippon.

Song: On Jordan's stormy banks I stand (887)

STEPHENS, May Agnew

b Kingston, Ontario, Canada, 1865
d Nyack, New York, 19 March 1935

In 1890. she became a Salvation Army officer from New York 3 Corps, and served on the editorial staff of *The War Cry*, on the training home staff, and in the Candidates' Department. From about 1897 she was associated with the Reverend Albert B. Simpson, as pianist and song leader at the Gospel Tabernacle, New York, and at various conventions. In 1899, she opened the Eighth Avenue Mission, and in about 1902 married the Reverend Harold L. Stephens, who became pastor of Parkdale Alliance Tabernacle, Toronto. They later served for 25 years as evangelists, travelling on campaigns in the United States, Britain and Canada, and then moved to Nyack, New York. She contributed her first songs to *The Musical Salvationist* in 1887 and 1888, and she was one of the editors of *Hymns of the Christian Life, Nos 1, 2, and 3 Combined,* 1908, which included several of her songs.

Song: Is there a heart that is waiting (247, chorus)

STEPHENSON, Thomas Bowman

b Newcastle upon Tyne, 22 December 1839
d Finchley, Middlesex, 16 July 1912

Son of the Reverend John Stephenson, a methodist minister. He was educated at Wesley College, Sheffield, and at the University of London. In 1860 he became a methodist minister and served at churches in Norwich, Manchester, Bolton, Lambeth and Bethnal Green, and later at Ilkley. He was the founder, and for many years the principal, of the National Children's Home, which began in 1869 in a small rented house in London, and later established branches in Bolton, Birmingham and the Isle of Man. He started a scheme to assist young people to emigrate to Canada, and also set up a training course for the Sisters of the Children's Home. He was president of the Wesleyan Methodist Conference in 1891, and in 1903 became warden of the Wesley Deaconess Institute.

Song: The glorious gospel word declares (385)

STEVENSON, Isabel Stephana (or Isabella)

b Cheltenham, Gloucestershire, 31 July 1843
d Cheltenham, Gloucestershire, 28 April 1890

Daughter of Thomas Stevenson, a captain in the army. Little is known about her life, though she is believed to have been a member of the Church of England, and is said to have been an invalid for many years.

Song: Holy Father, in thy mercy (582)

STITES, Edgar Page

b Cape May, New Jersey, 22 March 1836
d Cape May, New Jersey, 7 January 1921

He was a cousin of the hymn writer Eliza E. Hewitt. During the American Civil War he was stationed in Philadelphia, in charge of food for the transient soldiers. Afterwards he was a riverboat pilot on the Delaware River. He was a member of the First Methodist Church in Cape May for more than 60 years, serving as a local preacher and, for a time, as a home missionary in Dakota. His hymns often appeared under the name 'Edgar Page'.

Song: Simply trusting every day (754)

STOCKTON, John Hart

b New Hope, Pennsylvania, 19 April 1813
d Philadelphia, Pennsylvania, 25 March 1877

He came from a presbyterian family, but was converted at a methodist camp-meeting in 1832 and joined the Methodist Episcopal Church in 1838. He was licensed first as an exhorter and then as a preacher, and later served as minister of several churches in the New Jersey Conference area. After retiring from the pastoral ministry in 1874 because of ill health, he was active in evangelistic work and assisted with the Moody and Sankey revival meetings in Philadelphia. He wrote a number of hymns and compiled two collections: *Salvation Melodies*, 1874, and *Precious Songs*, 1875.

Song: Come, every soul by sin oppressed (231)

STOCKTON, Martha Matilda (*née* BRUSTAR)

b 11 June 1821
d 18 October 1885

Nothing is known about the author except that she was the wife of the Reverend W. C. Stockton, of Ocean City, New Jersey.

Song: God loved the world of sinners lost (46)

STODDART, Barbara (*née* WILSON)

b Fair Isle, Shetland, 16 September 1865
d Middlesbrough, 28 January 1915

As a young child she moved with her parents to Kirkwall in the Orkneys. When The Salvation Army opened there she became a salvationist and, in 1886, became an officer. She served in several corps appointments in Scotland and then in Women's Social Work for five years. She married Captain William Stoddart and was stationed with him at corps in Bristol, Devonport and Mousehole, and then in the United States. Returning to Britain they served in other field appointments in Scotland and subsequently in a number of divisional appointments. She was promoted to Glory while Staff-Captain Stoddart was young people's secretary in the Tees Division.

Songs: Blessèd Lamb of Calvary (205)
Bring your tithes into the storehouse (920)

STORM, August Ludvig

b Motala, Sweden, 23 October 1862
d Stockholm, Sweden, 1 July 1914

He was educated at schools in Stockholm and then worked as an office clerk. He was converted in a Salvation Army meeting and became an officer from Stockholm I Corps in 1890. He served at territorial headquarters in Sweden, latterly as a lieut-colonel. He was appointed financial secretary in 1892, and fulfilled his responsibilities despite being seriously disabled in 1899.

Song: Thank you, Lord, for all your goodness (552)

STOWE, Harriet Elizabeth Beecher

b Litchfield, Connecticut, 14 June 1811
d Hartford, Connecticut, 1 July 1896

Daughter of the Reverend Lyman Beecher, a congregational minister, who in 1832 became president of Lane Theological Seminary in Cincinnati, Ohio. In 1836 she married Calvin Ellis Stowe, professor of languages and biblical literature at Lane Seminary. They moved to Brunswick, Maine, in 1850; to Andover, Massachusetts, in 1852; and then to Hartford, in 1864, when her husband retired. She wrote the novel *Uncle Tom's Cabin,* which first appeared in instalments in the anti- slavery newspaper *National Era,* 1851-52, and later wrote other novels, including *Dred,*1856; *Oldtown Folks,* 1869; and *Poganuc People,* 1878. She also published *Religious Poems,* 1867, and contributed three hymns to the *Plymouth Collection,* 1855, compiled by her brother, the Reverend Henry Ward Beecher.

Song: Still, still with thee, when purple morning breaketh (632)

STOWELL, Hugh

b Douglas, Isle of Man, 3 December 1799
d Pendleton, Lancashire, 8 October 1865

Son of the Reverend Hugh Stowell, rector of Ballaugh, near Ramsey, Isle of Man. He was educated at St Edmund Hall, Oxford, and was ordained in 1823. He served for a short while as a curate at Shepscombe, Gloucestershire and Holy Trinity, Huddersfield, before moving to Salford, where he was curate-in-charge of St Stephen's Church and then rector of Christ Church, 1831-65. He wrote a number of hymns for anniversary services of Christ Church Sunday-schools, and included his own hymns in the hymn book he compiled: *A Selection of Psalms and Hymns Suited to the Services of the Church of England,*

1831 (enlarged edition, 1864). His other publications included *The Peaceful Valley*, 1826; *Pleasures of Religion and Other Poems*, 1832; and *Tractarianism Tested*, 1845.

Song: From every stormy wind that blows (573)

STRANG, Christopher

b Glasgow, 6 June 1854
d Partick, Lanarkshire, 14 July 1881

As a young man he was imprisoned several times for theft, and, following his involvement in a burglary in Glasgow in 1879, an aunt at Strathaven invited him to a meeting at a mission church, where he was convicted of sin. Later, he was converted, apparently while he was remanded in prison. After serving a six-week prison sentence in Glasgow, he worked as a painter and attended Salvation Army meetings in the Victoria Music Hall in Anderston. He became a salvationist and in November 1880 came to the training home in London. At times he was unwell, but while he was at the training home he often conducted meetings at Bethnal Green. In May 1881 he was appointed as a captain to Kilsyth, Scotland, but a few weeks later he had to farewell because of severe illness and died shortly afterwards.

Song: A needy sinner at thy feet (282)

STRUTHER, Jan

b Westminster, 6 June 1901
d New York, 20 July 1953

'Jan Struther' was the *nom de plume* of Joyce Anstruther, daughter of Henry Torrens Anstruther and Dame Eva Anstruther. In 1923, she married Anthony Maxtone-Graham. She wrote poems, articles and short stories for several periodicals, including *Punch*, the *Spectator* and the *New Statesman*, and for some time she was a member of the editorial board of *The Times* newspaper. During the Second World War, she lectured in the United States in aid of British War Relief, and in 1948 she married Adolf Kurt Placzek, a member of the library staff at Columbia University. Her books included: *The*

Modern Struwwelpeter, 1936; a novel, *Mrs Miniver*, 1939; and *A Pocketful of Pebbles*, 1945.

Song: Lord of all hopefulness, Lord of all joy (611)

SWIFT, James Frederick

b Manchester, 28 December 1847
d Liscard, Cheshire, 9 January 1931

The son of Joseph Swift, he moved with his parents to Liverpool, where he was educated at the Commercial School of Liverpool College. In 1863 he was appointed organist at the Cranmer Wesleyan Chapel, and later was organist for 10 years at St Andrew's Church, Liverpool, before becoming organist at St Bride's Church, Liverpool, in 1886. He conducted three choral societies in Liverpool for many years and composed songs and instrumental music, often under the pseudonym 'Godfrey Marks'. He published eight of his hymns in *Hymns for Home and Sacred Festivals*, 1875.

Song: And now to thee we render (950)

SWIFT, Susie Forrest

b Amenia, New York, 10 June 1862
d Sinsinawa, Wisconsin, 19 April 1916

Daughter of George Henry Swift, a banker. She was educated at Hillside Seminary and at Vassar College, Poughkeepsie. After teaching for a year in Morristown, New Jersey, she came to Britain in 1884 with her sister Elizabeth (later Mrs Colonel Brengle) and a friend. She attended Salvation Army meetings in Glasgow and then came to the training home in London, where she soon joined the staff and became editor of the magazine *All the World*. During the next 10 years she travelled widely and wrote extensively, as editor of *All the World* and as a correspondent for *The War Cry*. In 1895 she began work among waif and stray children in London and later that year took charge of the Auxiliary Department. She returned to the United States in 1896 and became head of the Auxiliary League in America. In 1897 she joined the Roman Catholic Church and entered the Order of St Dominic, taking the name Sister Imelda Teresa. She directed an orphanage and a Dominican college in Havana, Cuba, and was later associated with convents in Newport, Rhode Island and Albany, New York, before moving to St Clara College, Sinsinawa, in 1913.

Song: Mine to rise when thou dost call me (510)

TALBOT, Nellie

b ?
d ?

Little information about the author is available. She apparently visited London as a delegate from her Sunday-school, c1900.

Song: Jesus wants me for a sunbeam (844)

TATE, Nahum

b Dublin, 1652
d Southwark, Surrey, 12 August 1715

Son of Faithful Teate (or Tate), a clergyman and author. He was educated at Trinity College, Dublin, and wrote extensively for the London stage. He was appointed Poet Laureate in 1690 (or 1692) and Historiographer Royal in 1702. With Nicholas Brady, he prepared *A New Version of the Psalms of David*, 1696, a metrical psalter which was widely used during the 18th century.

Songs: As pants the hart for cooling streams (557)
Through all the changing scenes of life (21)
While shepherds watched their flocks by night (93)

TAYLOR, Gladys May

b Southport, Lancashire, 2 May 1905

The daughter of salvationists at Southport, she became a junior soldier and later a corps cadet there, before becoming an officer in 1927. After a short period as a corps officer in Ryde, Freshwater and Bournemouth, she was appointed to the Editorial Department at International Headquarters in 1928, and served there continuously until her retirement as a brigadier in 1966. She was editor of *The Deliverer*, 1953-66. For many years she was primary sergeant at the New Barnet Corps. She first tried to write a song when she was a corps cadet at Southport, and later wrote verses for various occasions while she was a cadet. Many of her poems for children appeared in *The Young Soldier*.

Song: Jesus, with what gladness I can truly sing (859)

TAYLOR, Gordon Harry

b Liverpool, Lancashire, 28 September 1946

Son of Brigadier Harry W. Taylor, and great-grandson of the song writer, Staff-Captain William Hodgson. Educated at Bancroft's School and the University of London, he was on the staff of the Greater London Council, 1965-86, working on planning, housing and social policy. He was young people's singing company leader, 1964-72, and songster leader, 1966-72, at Woodford (East London) before moving to Croydon in 1972. Since 1973, he has been a member of the Hymn Society of Great Britain and Ireland, and the Hymn Society of America, and contributed articles on songs and singing to *The Musician*, 1973-85. He wrote *A Short Companion to 'Keep Singing!'*, 1976, and is the compiler of this volume.

Song: Have you ever heard the story (96, verse 4)

TAYLOR, Thomas Rawson

b Ossett, Yorkshire, 9 May 1807
d Bradford, Yorkshire, 7 March 1835

Son of the Reverend Thomas Taylor, a congregational minister. He attended schools in Bradford and Manchester and, as a young man, worked for a merchant and then a printer. He studied for the congregational ministry at Airedale Independent College, and was minister of Howard Street

Chapel, Sheffield, 1830-31. For a short while he was classical tutor at Airedale College, but resigned because of ill health. He wrote several hymns and poems, which were published in his *Memoirs and Select Remains*, 1836.

Song: I'm but a stranger here (882)

TAYLOR-HUNT, Leslie

b Cupar, Fife, 27 March 1901
d Frenchay, Bristol, 11 December 1979

Son of Regimental Sergeant-Major Gilbert Hunt. After his father died, he was adopted by his uncle and aunt, Bandmaster and Mrs Taylor, of Weston-super-Mare, where as a child he was introduced to The Salvation Army. During the First World War he was sent in charge of Hastings III Corps, at the age of 16, and then entered the training garrison in the first session after the war. He was a cadet-sergeant and then served in Czechoslovakia, at International Headquarters (in the Overseas, Literary and Secretarial Departments), and at territorial headquarters in Canada. After returning from Canada he relinquished his officership. While he was at International Headquarters he often accompanied General Bramwell Booth on campaigns in Britain and around Europe, as a vocal soloist in meetings led by the General.

Song: Give me a holy life (416)

TERESA of Avila

b Avila, 28 March 1515
d Alba de Tormes, 4 October 1582

Teresa Sanchez de Cepeda y Ahumada entered the Carmelite convent of the Incarnation, near Avila, as a postulant in 1535, and two years later made her profession as a nun. (She was prioress at the Incarnation, 1571-74.) In 1560 she started to plan the reform of the Carmelite Order, returning to the simplicity and austerity of the primitive Rule, and in 1562 she founded St Joseph's, the first reformed Carmelite convent, at Avila. After the General of the Carmelite Order approved the reform, she founded 10 convents, 1567-76, and, following a period of opposition, founded another four convents, 1580-82. At St Joseph's she started to write her *Life*; *The Way of Perfection* and *Meditations on the Song of Songs*, and she later wrote *The Book of the Foundations* and *The Mansions of the Interior Castle*, 1577, a description of her mystical spiritual experiences.

Song: Let nothing disturb thee (956)

TERRY, Darley

b Mirfield, Yorkshire, 19 January 1847
d Rhyl, Flint, 21 January 1933

He was a printer in Dewsbury, Yorkshire, where he was a Sunday-school superintendent for 30 years. For many years he was secretary of the Dewsbury Sunday School Union and represented Yorkshire on the National Sunday School Union council. After his retirement he moved to Prestatyn and was secretary of Trinity Church there for over 20 years. He was a member of the Sunday schools committee of the Methodist New Connexion, 1877-99 and then served as treasurer of the combined Young People's and Temperance Department of the Methodist New Connexion and later the United Methodist Church until 1919. He represented the United Methodist Church on the committee which prepared the *Methodist Hymn Book*, 1933 and published a collection of *Poems and Hymns*, 1904 (second series, 1924).

Song: The Lord is King! I own his power (867)

THOMPSON, Will Lamartine

b East Liverpool, Ohio, 7 November 1847
d New York, 20 September 1909

He was educated at Mount Union College, Alliance, Ohio, and Boston Conservatory of Music, and also studied in Leipzig, Germany. He wrote secular and sacred songs, and was known as the 'Bard of Ohio'. He established a music publishing company in East Liverpool and Chicago and edited and published a large number of song collections.

Song: Softly and tenderly Jesus is calling (264)

THRING, Godfrey

b Alford, Somerset, 25 March 1823
d Shamley Green, Guildford, Surrey, 13 September 1903

Son of the Reverend J. G. D. Thring, rector of Alford. He was educated at Shrewsbury School and Balliol College, Oxford. After his ordination in 1846 he served as curate in several parishes, including Stratfield-Turgis, 1846-50, and Strathfieldsaye, 1850-53, and succeeded his father as rector of Alford, 1858-93. He compiled several hymn books, including *Hymns Congregational and Others*, 1866; *Hymns and Sacred Lyrics*, 1874; and *A Church of England Hymn Book*, 1880 (revised edition, 1882).

Song: Crown him with many crowns (156, verse 2)

THRUPP, Dorothy Ann

b Paddington, Middlesex, 20 or 26 June 1779
d St Marylebone, Middlesex, 14 December 1847

Daughter of Joseph Thrupp, of Paddington Green. She contributed hymns to *Hymns for the Young*, 1930-36, which she edited, and also to Mrs Mayo's *Selection of Hymns and Poetry*, 1838-46, and the Reverend W. Carus Wilson's *Friendly Visitor* and *Children's Friend*. Some appeared anonymously, or with the initials 'D.A.T.', or under the *nom-de-plume* 'Iota'. In 1836 and 1837 she published *Thoughts for the Day*, which included some hymns which had first appeared in the *Friendly Visitor*.

Songs: He walks with God who speaks to God in prayer (580)
Saviour, like a shepherd lead us (845)

TOPLADY, Augustus Montague

b Farnham, Surrey, 4 November 1740
d Kensington, Middlesex, 11 August 1778

Son of Richard Toplady, a lieutenant in a regiment of marines. He was educated at Westminster School and Trinity College, Dublin. While in Ireland, in 1756, he was converted through a sermon by the preacher, James Morris, on the text: 'Now in Christ Jesus ye who sometimes were far off are made nigh by the blood of Christ' (Ephesians 2:13, *AV*). After his ordination, he was curate of Blagdon, Somerset, 1762-64, and of Farleigh Hungerford, 1764-65. He spent a short period in Westminster with his mother, and then became vicar of Harpford and Venn Ottery, Devon, 1766-68, and finally vicar of Broad Hembury, Devon, 1768-78, though he was not resident there after July 1775. In his later years, he preached regularly at Orange Street Chapel in London, 1776-78. He wrote a number of hymns which were published in *The Gospel Magazine*, 1771-76, a magazine which he edited from December 1775 to July 1777, and he compiled *Psalms and Hymns for Public and Private Worship*, 1776, for use at Orange Street Chapel, extensively altering most of the hymns included.

Songs: Compared with Christ, in all beside (565)
Rock of ages, cleft for me (302)

TORREY, Richard T.

b ?
d ?

No information about the author is available. Some sources give his surname as Torry, and he is sometimes described as Richard T. Torrey, Junr. His song seems to have appeared first in the United States in 1863.

Song: O have you not heard of the beautiful stream (252)

TRACY, Ruth Fanny

b Islington, Middlesex, 28 November 1870
d Tunbridge Wells, Kent, 17 September 1960

Her parents were members of the Plymouth Brethren. She first attended Salvation Army meetings in 1888, while visiting a cousin in Dorking, Surrey, and when she returned home she regularly went to meetings at Holloway and Wood Green. Later she began work at International Headquarters, in the Appointments Department of the Home Office, where the head of the department, Staff-Captain (later Commissioner) James Hay, encouraged her to write her first song for *The War Cry*. She became an officer in 1891, and, after training at Walthamstow and Chelsea, was stationed in several corps appointments, including Alcester, Feckenham, and Stony Stratford. She also assisted occasionally at the provincial headquarters in Birmingham. In 1894 she was appointed to the Editorial Department where she worked initially on *The War Cry, The Social Gazette* and *The Young Soldier,* and was later editor of *The Deliverer* for more than 20 years. She retired as a brigadier in 1931. She contributed over 100 songs to *The Musical Salvationist* and other publications.

Songs: At harvest time our eyes behold (923)
I've a friend, of friends the fairest (343)
I've found the secret of success (806)
Lord, I come to thee beseeching (434)
Lord, I pray that I may know thee (435)
Lord, thou art questioning: Lovest thou me (507)
Send out thy light and thy truth, Lord (457)
Where are now those doubts that hindered (399)

TREVELLIAN (or TREVILLIAN), Frederick Alfred

b c1858
d Ealing, Middlesex, 24 October 1925

Little is known about the author, who as band sergeant of Ealing Corps contributed several songs to *The War Cry* and *The Musical Salvationist,* c1890. He was apparently the proprietor of a boarding house.

Song: When you find the cross is heavy (790)

TUCKER, Francis Bland

b Norfolk, Virginia, 6 January 1895
d Savannah, Georgia, 1 January 1984

Educated at the University of Virginia and Virginia Theological Seminary. After his ordination as an episcopal priest in 1920, he was rector of Grammer Parish, Brunswick County,

Virginia, 1920-25; St John's, Georgetown, Washington, DC, 1925-45; and Christ Church, Savannah, 1945-67 (where John Wesley had served briefly, 200 years earlier). He started writing hymns after 1937 when he became a member of the committee which compiled the episcopal *Hymnal 1940*, and he later also served on the committee which prepared the *Hymnal 1982*.

Song: All praise to thee, for thou, O King divine (174)

TURNEY, Edward

b Weston, Connecticut, 6 May 1816
d Washington, DC, 28 September 1872

Educated at Madison University, New York. He served as a baptist pastor at Hartford, and then at Granville, Ohio, 1842-47. He became professor of biblical criticism at Madison University in 1850, and was professor of biblical literature at Fairmount Theological Seminary, Cincinnati, 1853-58. Subsequently, he taught in Washington, DC. He published *Baptismal Hymns*, 1862, and *Memorial Poems and Hymns*, 1864.

Song: I'll go in the strength of the Lord (734)

TURNEY, Frank Samuel

b Westminster, 14 October 1863
d Limpsfield, Surrey, 27 October 1932

Son of a London City Missioner, he was brought up in the Baptist Church, but joined Dawes Road Congregational Church, Fulham, in 1887. Later, he became choir secretary, musical director of the Sunday-school and a deacon there. He was employed for 30 years by the publishers Morgan and Scott, where he was apparently a proof reader and also prepared a tonic sol-fa edition of Sankey's *Sacred Songs and Solos*. Subsequently, he was associated with the Torrey-Alexander revival missions and toured the United States and Australia in connection with Charles M. Alexander's hymn books.

Song: Lord of Heaven and earth and sea (941)

TUTTIETT, Lawrence

b Colyton, Devon, 1825
d St Andrews, Fife, 21 May 1897

Son of John Tuttiett, a surgeon in the Royal Navy. He was educated at Christ's Hospital, and King's College, London. After his ordination in 1848, he served as a curate on the Isle of Wight and then became vicar of Lea Marston, Warwickshire, in 1854. Subsequently, he was incumbent of the episcopal church at St Andrews, Fife, 1870-93, and then retired to Pitlochry. His publications included *Hymns for Churchmen*, 1854; *Hymns for the Children of the Church*, 1862; and *Germs of Thought on the Sunday Services*, 1864.

Song: Father, let me dedicate (916)

TWELLS, Henry

b Ashted, Warwickshire, 23 March 1823
d Bournemouth, Hampshire, 19 January 1900

Educated at King Edward's School, Birmingham, and St Peter's College, Cambridge. He was ordained in 1849, and was successively curate of Great Berkhamsted, 1849-51; sub-vicar of Stratford-on-Avon, 1851-54; master of St Andrew's House School, Wells, Somerset, 1854-56; and headmaster of Godolphin School, Hammersmith, 1856-70. In 1870, he became rector of Baldock, and then served as rector of Waltham-on-the-Wolds, 1871-90, before moving to Bournemouth, where he was priest-in-charge of St Augustine's Church, which he built and partly endowed.

Song: At even, ere the sun was set (558)

VAN DE VENTER, Judson W.

b near Dundee, Michigan, 5 December 1855
d Tampa, Florida, 17 July 1939

Educated at Hillsdale College, Michigan. He studied art and in 1885 toured Europe, visiting art galleries and museums. For several years he taught art in schools and became supervisor of art in the high school at Sharon, Pennsylvania. He was a methodist local preacher, but later became an evangelist, leading revival meetings in the United States, England and Scotland, assisted for many years by the singer Winfield S. Weeden. He spent his later years in Tampa, Florida.

Song: All to Jesus I surrender (474)

VAN DYKE, Henry

b Germantown, Pennsylvania, 10 November 1852
d Princeton, New Jersey, 10 April 1933

Educated at Brooklyn Polytechnic Institute, Princeton University and Princeton Theological Seminary. He was pastor of the United Congregational Church, Newport, Rhode Island, 1879-83 and Brick Presbyterian Church, New York City, 1883-99. In 1899 he was appointed Murray Professor of English Literature, at Princeton University, and later served as United States minister to the Netherlands and Luxemburg, 1913-16. He was chairman of the committee which prepared the presbyterian *Book of Common Worship*, 1905, and also assisted with the revised edition in 1932. His own publications included: *The Reality of Religion*, 1884; *The Story of the Psalms*, 1887; and *The Gospel for an Age of Doubt*, 1896.

Song: Joyful, joyful, we adore thee (10)

VICKERY, Alfred Herbert

b Cardiff, 7 November 1894
d Croydon, Surrey, 19 May 1976

The son of salvationists, he grew up in South Wales and then transferred to South Shields, where, at the age of 18, he was appointed bandmaster. Subsequently he was deputy bandmaster at Leeds West Hunslet. After military service during the First World War, he returned to Leeds in 1918, but shortly afterwards he moved to Thornton Heath, where he served as songster leader for 25 years. He played solo cornet in the Men's Social Work Headquarters Band and was also a vocal soloist. In later years he was a member of the London Crusader Choir. His early song writing was encouraged by Enoch Kent and his first published song, 'Move On', appeared in *The Musical Salvationist* in August 1924. He wrote more than 70 songs for *The War Cry* and *The Musical Salvationist*.

Song: Valiant soldier, marching to the fray (817)

WADE, John Francis

b England(?) *c*1710 or 1711.
d Douay, France, 16 August 1786

He was a Roman catholic layman, who lived for many years in Douay, teaching music and copying manuscripts.

Song: O come, all ye faithful (85)

WAHLSTRÖM, Jarl Holger

b Helsinki, Finland, 9 July 1918

Son of Colonel and Mrs Rafael Wahlström. He came to the International Training College from Helsinki in 1937, and, following his training and a year as a cadet-sergeant, returned to a corps appointment in Finland in 1939. After four years' military service during the Second World War he held various appointments in Finland, including seven years as territorial scout organiser. Later he was divisional commander (Northern Division), 1960-63; Training Principal (and Music Secretary), 1963-68; and Chief Secretary, 1968-72. He became Chief Secretary for Canada and Bermuda in 1972, returning to Finland as Territorial Commander in 1976. In 1981 he was appointed Territorial Commander for Sweden, and later that year was elected General. He retired in 1986. He played the cornet, piano, guitar and mandolin, and composed a number of songs which were published in Finland and Sweden, and in *The Musical Salvationist*.

Song: Greatest joy is found in serving Jesus (857)

WALFORD, W. W.

b ?
d ?

The identity of the author has not yet been established. According to notes in *The New York Observer*, 13 September 1845, he was a blind preacher, while the Reverend Thomas Salmon was an independent minister at Coleshill, Warwickshire, 1838-42. He was described as 'a man of obscure birth and connections, and no education, but of strong mind and most retentive memory'. Some hymn books suggest that he may have been William Walford (1772-1850), the congregational minister at Uxbridge, 1833-48, who wrote a book *The Manner of Prayer*, 1836, but he does not fit the above description.

Song: Sweet hour of prayer, sweet hour of prayer (633)

WALKER, William

b Selkirk, 6 November 1871
d Selkirk, 27 December 1899

After becoming an officer from Selkirk in 1894, he was stationed at several corps in the Birmingham Division, latterly as a captain. He contributed a few songs to *The Musical Salvationist* and *The War Cry*, 1891-95.

Song: Dear Lord, I do surrender (482)

WALLER, Josiah Henry

b Bethnal Green, Middlesex, 15 April 1865
d Auckland, New Zealand, 19 May 1938

Son of Josiah Waller, a lithographic printer. After leaving school he trained as a printer and worked in Fleet Street before joining the staff of the Salvation Army Trade Headquarters. He served for a time as sergeant-major, band sergeant and corps secretary at Edmonton Corps. In 1904 he spent a year in India as manager of the government printing works in Calcutta. He was YMCA secretary in France, 1916-18, and shortly afterwards returned to India as YMCA Press Association Secretary. In 1921 he was appointed superintendent of the London Missionary Society's press in Samoa, and three years later moved to Hamilton, New Zealand, where he started his own press. In 1927 he became YMCA secretary in Suva, Fiji, where he was subsequently manager and proprietor of the Pacific Press. In 1936 he decided to make a final visit to England and India, and returned to New Zealand in 1938, shortly before he died. He contributed several songs to *The War Cry* and *The Musical Salvationist*, 1891-93, and later wrote his autobiography, *Harry: The Unknown Man*, 1934, which he printed in Suva.

Song: Boundless as the mighty ocean (230)

WALTER, Howard Arnold

b New Britain, Connecticut, 19 August 1883
d Lahore, India, 1 November 1918

He was educated at Princeton University, Hartford Theological Seminary, and universities in Edinburgh, Glasgow and Göttingen. For a time, at the age of 23, he taught English at Waseda University in Tokyo, Japan, and after returning to the United States he was assistant minister of Asylum Hill Congregational Church, in Hartford, Connecticut, 1910-13. He joined the staff of the YMCA for India and Ceylon, and went to work at Foreman Christian College, in Lahore, India. He died there a few years later, during an influenza epidemic.

Song: I would be true, for there are those who trust me (491)

WARE, Henry

b Hingham. Massachusetts, 21 April 1794
d Framingham, Massachusetts, 25 September 1843

Son of Dr Henry Ware, a unitarian minister. He was educated at Harvard, and, after his graduation, was an assistant teacher for two years at Exeter Academy, New Hampshire. He was licensed to preach by the Boston Unitarian Association in 1815 and was ordained pastor of the Second Unitarian Church in Boston in 1817. He was professor of pulpit eloquence and pastoral care in the Cambridge Theological School, 1830-42, and for some time was editor of the *Christian Disciple* (later known as the *Christian Examiner*).

Songs: Happy the home when God is there (661)
O God, in whom alone is found (942)

WARING, Anna Laetitia

b Neath, Glamorgan, 19 April 1823
d Clifton, Bristol, 10 May 1910

Daughter of Elijah Waring. She was a member of the Society of Friends (Quakers), but in 1842 joined the Church of England. She visited prisons in Bristol, and was an active supporter of the Discharged Prisoners' Aid Society. She wrote about 40 hymns, which were published in various editions of her *Hymns and Meditations*, 1850-63.

Songs: Father, I know that all my life (485)
In heavenly love abiding (736)

WARNER, Anna Bartlett

b New York, 31 August 1827
d Highland Falls, New York, 22 January 1915

Daughter of Henry Whiting Warner, a lawyer, and younger sister of Susan Bogert Warner. After 1837 the sisters lived for most of their lives on Constitution Island, in the Hudson River, opposite West Point. For many years they conducted weekly Bible classes for cadets from West Point Military Academy, and in 1908 her friend Mrs Sage presented Constitution Island to the United States government on her behalf for the use of the Military Academy. She compiled *Hymns of the Church Militant*, 1858, and also wrote *Wayfaring Hymns*, 1869. Sometimes using the *nom-de-plume* 'Amy Lothrop', she wrote more than 40 books, often in collaboration with her sister. Her publications included the novel *Dollars and Cents*, 1852, and a biography of her sister, *Susan Warner*, 1909.

Song: Jesus loves me! This I know (843)

WARNER, Susan Bogert

b New York, 11 July 1819
d Highland Falls, New York, 17 March 1885

Daughter of Henry Whiting Warner, a lawyer, and sister of Anna Bartlett Warner. Their father bought Constitution Island in 1836 and the family moved there in the following year. She wrote extensively, sometimes using the *nom-de-plume* 'Elizabeth Wetherell'. Her novels included *The Wide, Wide World*, 1851; *Queechy*, 1852; and *Say and Seal*, 1860, which she wrote with her sister, Anna.

Song: Jesus bids us shine with a clear, pure light (841)

WATTS, Isaac

b Southampton, 17 July 1674
d Stoke Newington, Middlesex, 25 November 1748

Son of Isaac Watts, a clothier and schoolmaster. He was educated by his father, and then at the Free School in Southampton, and at the nonconformist academy at Newington Green, 1690-94. He became a member of the independent congregation at Girdlers' Hall, London, in 1693. After about two years in Southampton, he returned to London in 1696 as tutor to the family of Sir John Hartopp in Stoke Newington. He was appointed assistant pastor of the independent congregation in Mark Lane, London, in 1699, and pastor in 1702. Despite periodic illness, he remained pastor when the congregation moved to Pinners' Hall, Old Broad Street, in 1704, and to Bury Street, in 1708. In later years, when unable to preach, he wrote pastoral letters to the congregation in Bury Street. He started to write poetry at the age of six, and apparently wrote his first hymn in about 1694 when he was critical of the psalms used by the congregation in Southampton and his father challenged him to write something better. His hymns, psalms and other poems were mainly published in his *Horae Lyricae*, 1706 (revised 1709); *Hymns and Spiritual Songs*, 1707 (revised and enlarged, 1709); *Divine Songs*, 1715; *The Psalms of David Imitated in the Language of the New Testament*, 1719; and *Reliquiae Juveniles*, 1734.

Songs: Alas! and did my Saviour bleed (105)

Am I a soldier of the cross (678)
Awake, our souls; away, our fears (559)
Before Jehovah's aweful throne (4)
Begin, my tongue, some heavenly theme (26)
Come, let us join our cheerful songs (57)
Come, ye that love the Lord (314)
Give me the wings of faith to rise (879)
I'm not ashamed to own my Lord (735)
Jesus shall reign where'er the sun (160)
Joy to the world! the Lord is come (84)
My God, how endless is thy love (672)
Not all the blood of beasts (120)
O God, our help in ages past (13)
Salvation! O the joyful sound (382)
There is a land of pure delight (898)
When I survey the wondrous cross (136)

WELANDER, David

b Oslo, Norway, 12 March 1896
d Oslo, Norway, 22 September 1967

He became a soldier at Rjukan Corps in 1912, and attended the International Congress in London in 1914, before entering the training college, in Oslo, in the following year. He was a cadet-sergeant and then served in corps appointments, followed by 11 years in the Literary Department. During this time he travelled with the Territorial Commander, Commissioner Mrs Lucy Booth-Hellberg, as a translator. Subsequently he was personal secretary to Commissioner Karl Larsson for four years and then held appointments as young people's secretary, divisional commander (in the Northern and Eastern Divisions), Field Secretary, Chief Secretary and Training Principal. He retired as a colonel in 1960. He wrote a number of songs and played several musical instruments, including the concertina.

Song: Never fades the name of Jesus (63)

WESLEY, Charles

b Epworth, Lincolnshire, 18 December 1707
d St Marylebone, Middlesex, 29 March 1788

Son of the Reverend Samuel Wesley, rector of Epworth. He was educated at Westminster School, 1716-26, and Christ

Church, Oxford. He was a member of the 'Holy Club' at Oxford, and was called a 'Methodist' because he regularly attended the weekly Holy Communion services and observed the method of study prescribed by the University statutes. In 1735, he was ordained, and sailed with his brother John and two friends to Georgia, as secretary to General Oglethorpe, governor of the colony of Georgia. Shortly afterwards, he returned to London, where he met Count Zinzendorf, Peter Böhler, and other Moravians. He found peace with God on Whitsunday 1738, and two days later composed a hymn, probably 'Where shall my wond'ring soul begin'. He travelled extensively, preaching and giving pastoral support to the methodist societies, particularly in Bristol and London. He wrote 9,000 hymns and poems, and although some of his short hymns have only one or two verses, his output represents an average of 10 lines of verse every day for 50 years. Many of his hymns were published jointly with his brother John, but he published some hymns under his own name, including two volumes of *Hymns and Sacred Poems*, 1749, published at the time of his marriage, and *Short Hymns on Select Passages of the Holy Scriptures*, 1762.

Songs: A charge to keep I have (472)
All things are possible to him (407)
And are we yet alive (915)
And can it be that I should gain (283)
Arise, my soul, arise (106)
Blest be the dear uniting love (659)
But can it be that I should prove (714)
Christ the Lord is risen today (143)
Christ, whose glory fills the skies (412)
Come, Holy Ghost, all-quickening fire (207)
Come, Holy Ghost, our hearts inspire (651)
Come, let us use the grace divine (784)
Come, sinners, to the gospel feast (234)
Come, thou all-inspiring Spirit (210)
Come, thou everlasting Spirit (191)
Come, thou long-expected Jesus (79)
Depth of mercy! Can there be (286)
Equip me for the war (568)
Forth in thy name, O Lord, I go (667)
Gentle Jesus, meek and mild (793)
Give me the faith which can remove (720)
Hark! the herald angels sing (82)
He wills that I should holy be (419)
Help us to help each other, Lord (662)
How happy every child of grace (880)
I want a principle within (425)

I want the gift of power within (214)
If so poor a soul as I (492)
Jesus, all-atoning Lamb (497)
Jesus, I fain would find (594)
Jesus is glorified (195)
Jesus, lover of my soul (737)
Jesus, my strength, my hope (596)
Jesus, my truth, my way (597)
Jesus, the gift divine I know (601)
Jesus, the name high over all (60)
Jesus, we look to thee (603)
Let earth and Heaven agree (62)
Lo! He comes with clouds descending (161)
Lord, in the strength of grace (505)
Lord, we believe to us and ours (216)
Love divine, all loves excelling (438)
Master, I own thy lawful claim (509)
My God, I am thine (355)
O come and dwell in me (441)
O for a heart to praise my God (444)
O for a thousand tongues to sing (64)
O how happy are they who the Saviour obey (367)
O thou who camest from above (199)
O what shall I do my Saviour to praise (372)
Rejoice, the Lord is King (164)
Saviour, we know thou art (629)
See how great a flame aspires (165)
Soldiers of Christ, arise (695)
Spirit of faith, come down (756)
Talk with me, Lord, thyself reveal (636)
Thou Shepherd of Israel, and mine (639)
Weary of wandering from my God (305)
What shall I do my God to love (55)
What shall I render to my God (23)
When shall thy love constrain (307)
Who are these arrayed in white (909)
Would Jesus have the sinner die (140)
Ye servants of God, your Master proclaim (24)

WESLEY, John

b Epworth, Lincolnshire, 17 June 1703
d St Luke upon Old Street, Middlesex, 2 March 1791

Son of the Reverend Samuel Wesley, rector of Epworth. He was educated at Charterhouse School, London, 1714-20, and Christ Church, Oxford. After his ordination, he served for a short while as curate to his father, but having been elected a Fellow of Lincoln College, Oxford, he became a tutor at the college in 1729. In Oxford, he joined his brother, Charles, and other friends in a society known as the 'Holy Club', or 'Methodists', which met for Bible study and prayer and also visited prisons and workhouses. In 1735, he sailed as an SPCK chaplain to Savannah, Georgia, and on board met a group of Moravians from Herrnhut, also bound for Georgia. He started to learn German, and translated some of their hymns into English. In America, he published his first hymn book, *A Collection of Psalms and Hymns*, 1737. After returning to England, further contacts with Moravians, including Peter Böhler, convinced him of the need for personal faith in Christ, and in May 1738 he wrote: 'I felt I did trust in Christ, Christ alone for salvation.' During his subsequent itinerant ministry, he travelled 250,000 miles and preached 40,000 sermons in churches, in the open-air, and in the methodist societies which he established and encouraged for more than 50 years. He compiled a large number of hymn books, the most significant being *A Collection of Hymns for the Use of the People called Methodists*, 1780.

Songs: Before Jehovah's aweful throne (4)
Come, Saviour Jesus, from above (480)
Commit thou all thy griefs (715)
Give to the winds thy fears (721)
I thirst, thou wounded Lamb of God (424)
Jesus, thy blood and righteousness (116)
Now I have found the ground wherein (746)
O God, what offering shall I give (516)
O thou to whose all-searching sight (453)
The love of Christ doth me constrain (526)
What shall we offer to our Lord (533)

WHITFIELD, Frederick

b Threapwood, Shropshire, 7 January 1829
d Lower Norwood, Croydon, Surrey, 13 September 1904

Educated at Trinity College, Dublin. After his ordination he served successively as curate of Otley; vicar of Kirby-Ravensworth; senior curate of Greenwich; and vicar of St John's, Bexley. In 1875 he became incumbent of St Mary's, Hastings. He published several books of poetry and prose, including *Sacred Poems and Prose*, 1861 (2nd series, 1864); *The Casket* and *Quiet Hours in the Sanctuary*.

Song: There is a name I love to hear (69)

WHITING, William

b Kensington, Middlesex, 1 November 1825
d Winchester, Hampshire, 3 May 1878

Son of a grocer, he was educated at school in Clapham and at King Alfred's College, Winchester. In 1842 he was appointed master of the choristers at Winchester College Choristers' School, and served there for 36 years. He wrote a number of hymns and also some poems, which were published in his *Rural Thoughts and Scenes*, 1851, and *Edgar Thorpe, or the Warfare of Life*, 1867.

Song: Eternal Father, strong to save (569)

WHITTIER, John Greenleaf

b Haverhill, Massachusetts, 17 December 1807
d Hampton Falls, New Hampshire, 7 September 1892

He was a Quaker and spent his early years working on the family farm. After studying briefly at Haverhill Academy, he was editor of *The American Manufacturer* for a few months during 1829, and then edited the *New England Weekly Review*, 1830-32. He became secretary of the American Anti-Slavery Society in 1836; edited the *Pennsylvania Freeman*, 1838-40; and later was corresponding editor of the *National Era*, 1847-60. His first poems appeared in the Newburyport *Free Press* in 1826, and his first book, *Legends of New England in Prose and Verse* was published in 1831. The complete edition of his *Poetical Works*, 1898, included more than 500 poems, but he did not claim to be a hymn writer, and said that very few of his poems were written for singing.

Songs: Dear Lord and Father of mankind (567)
Immortal love, for ever full (496)

WHITTLE, Daniel Webster

b Chicopee Falls, Massachusetts, 22 November 1840
d Northfield, Massachusetts, 4 March 1901

As a young man he worked as a cashier in the Wells Fargo Bank, Chicago. During the Civil War he served with Company B of the 72nd Illinois Infantry, and he was apparently converted while he was a prisoner after the Battle of Vicksburg, through reading a New Testament given to him by his mother. At the end of the war he was promoted to the rank of major and returning to Chicago he was treasurer of the Elgin Watch Company until 1873. He was then encouraged by Dwight L. Moody to become an evangelist, and was assisted in his revival meetings at various times by the singers Philip P. Bliss, James McGranahan and George C. Stebbins. He wrote many of his hymns under the pseudonym 'El Nathan'.

Songs: Have you any room for Jesus (241)
I know not why God's wondrous grace (730)
Not my own, but saved by Jesus (514)
There shall be showers of blessing (637)

WIGGINS, Archibald Raymond

b Kensal Green, Middlesex, 14 April 1893
d Christchurch, Dorset, 20 November 1976

He attended a Church of England Sunday-school, but was converted in the Methodist Church, and later became a salvationist at Harlesden, where he was a member of the songster brigade formed in 1911. He started work when he was almost 14, and, before entering the training college at Clapton in 1914, he was assistant secretary at the Connaught Club in London. After corps and divisional appointments he was appointed to the editorial department in 1922, subsequently serving as editor of *The Life-Saving Scout and Guard, The International Demonstrator, The Bandsman and Songster* and *The Musician.* He was for a time a member of the International Staff Band. In 1947 he moved to Australia as editor-in-chief, returning to London in 1951 as assistant editor-in-chief and editor of *The War Cry.* He became editor-in-chief in the following year, and in 1957 he was appointed Personal Literary Secretary to the General. He retired as a lieut- commissioner in 1959. He wrote over 250 songs and, for more than 50 years, contributed at least one song each year to *The Musical Salvationist*. He was the author of volumes 4 and 5 of *The History of The Salvation Army*, 1964 and 1968 and also wrote biographies of Richard Slater, *Father of Salvation Army Music*, 1945; of Theodore H. Kitching, *T.H.K.*, 1956; and of Bandmaster George Marshall, *Triumph of Faith*, 1958.

Songs: Blessèd are the poor in spirit (95)
　　　　I dwell within the secret place (728)
　　　　The flag is yours, the flag is mine (779)
　　　　Thine is the Kingdom, Lord (171)
　　　　Thou art the way, none other dare I follow (529)
　　　　Though in declaring Christ to the sinner (530)
　　　　Who shall dare to separate us (554)

WILLIAMS, Peter

b Llansadyrnin, Carmarthenshire, 15 January 1722
d Llandyfeilog, Carmarthenshire, 8 August 1796

Educated at Carmarthen College. He was converted through the preaching of George Whitefield, and after his ordination in 1744 he became curate of Eglwys Cymmyn. In 1746 he joined the Welsh Calvinistic Methodist Association and was an itinerant preacher, but he later built a chapel in Water Street, Carmarthen, and became minister there. He published a Welsh hymn book in 1759; a Welsh Bible with annotations, 1767-70; *Hymns on Various Subjects*, 1771; and a biblical concordance in 1773.

Song: Guide me, O thou great Jehovah (578, verse 1)

WILLIAMS, W. A.

b ?
d ?

No definite information about the author is available. He was apparently a minister in the United States, *c*1884-1914.

Song: I bring to thee my heart to fill (489, chorus)

WILLIAMS, William

b Cefn-y-Coed, near Llandovery, 11 February 1717
d Pantecelyn, near Llandovery, 11 January 1791

He studied medicine at Llwynllwyd Academy, but, after hearing the Welsh evangelist Howell Harris preach in Talgarth churchyard, he decided to enter the ministry. He was ordained in 1740 and served as a curate in Llanwrtyd and Llanddewi-Abergwesyn for about three years. He then joined the Calvinistic Methodist Association and became an itinerant minister in 1744, preaching throughout Wales for more than 45 years. He was known as 'The Sweet Singer of Wales' and wrote almost 1,000 hymns in Welsh and more than 100 in English, published in his various collections, including *Alleluia*, 1745-47; *The Sea of Glass*, 1752; *Hosannah to the Son of David*, 1759; and *Gloria in Excelsis*, 1771.

Song: Guide me, O thou great Jehovah (578)

WILLIS, Ellen H.

b ?
d ?

Little information about the author is available. She published an anthology of her verse, *I left it all with Jesus, and other poems*, dated 'Hampstead, October 1875'.

Song: I left it all with Jesus long ago (333)

WILLIS, Love Maria (*née* WHITCOMB)

b Hancock, New Hampshire, 9 June 1824
d 1908

In 1858 she married Dr Frederick L. H. Willis, and for many years lived in Rochester, New York, and later at Glenora, on Seneca Lake, New York. She was a unitarian.

Song: Father, hear the prayer we offer (570)

WILSON, Lucy Sarah (*née* ATKINS)

b Chipping Norton, Oxfordshire, 28 December 1802
d Islington, Middlesex, 25 January 1863

In 1829, she married the Reverend Daniel Wilson, rector of Upper Worton, Oxfordshire. He became vicar of St Mary's, Islington, in 1832, and served there for more than 50 years. She wrote *Memoirs of John Frederic Oberlin,* 1829.

Song: O Lord, thy heavenly grace impart (517)

WINCKLER, Johann Joseph

b Lucka, 23 December 1670
d Magdeburg, 11 August 1722

Son of Gottfried Winckler, town clerk of Lucka, Sachse-Altenburg. He was educated at the University of Leipzig and was then appointed as preacher at St George's Hospital and St Peter's Church, at Magdeburg, in 1692. He became chaplain to the regiment of Prince Christian Ludwig, in 1695, but after the Peace of Ryswijk, in 1697, he went on a tour in Holland and England. Returning to Magdeburg, he was appointed deacon of the Cathedral, in 1698, and later became chief preacher there in 1714. He wrote about 25 hymns, which appeared in Porst's *Gesang Buch,* 1708; Freylinghausen's *Neues geistreiches Gesang Buch,* 1714; and other collections.

Songs: Strive, when thou art called of God (816)
       The love of Christ doth me constrain (526)

WINDYBANK, Walter Henry

b Stroud, near Petersfield, Hampshire, 25 January 1872
d Leicester, 27 January 1952

He left school at the age of 12 and was apprenticed to saddlery and harness making. He was converted in 1886 and became young people's sergeant-major at Petersfield before becoming a cadet in 1891. He trained in Chelsea and subsequently served as an officer for almost 40 years, including six years in Scotland and two years in Ireland. His corps appointments included Aberdeen Citadel, Exeter Temple, Wood Green, Norwich Citadel, Hull Icehouse and Leicester Central. He retired in 1931 as a major, and for some time afterwards was an official visitor at Leicester Prison. He wrote many songs and poems, contributing to Salvation Army publications, including *The War Cry* and *The Musical Salvationist*.

Songs: Be strong in the grace of the Lord (679)
Just outside the land of promise (433)
We praise thee, heavenly Father (870)

WINKWORTH, Catherine

b Saffron Hill Liberty, Middlesex, 13 September 1827
d Monnetier, France, 1 July 1878

Daughter of Henry Winkworth, a silk merchant. In 1829 her parents moved to Manchester, and later she lived with an aunt in Dresden, 1845-46, where she studied German. After 12 years at Alderley Edge, Cheshire, she moved to Clifton in 1862. She became secretary of the Clifton Association for the Higher Education of Women, in 1870, and was one of the promoters of Clifton High School for Girls. From 1875 she was a member of the council of Cheltenham Ladies' College. Her translations of German hymns were published in *Lyra Germanica*, 1855 and 1858, and *The Chorale Book for England*, 1863, and she also wrote *Christian Singers of Germany*, 1869 (short biographies of German hymn writers).

Songs: All my heart this night rejoices (73)
Leave God to order all thy ways (738)
Now thank we all our God (12)
Praise to the Lord, the Almighty, the King of creation (19)
Strive, when thou art called of God (816)

WINSLOW, John Copley (Jack)

b Hanworth, Middlesex, 18 August 1882
d Godalming, Surrey, 1 April 1974

Educated at Eton, and Balliol College, Oxford. He was ordained in 1907, and served as a curate in Wimbledon, 1907-11; as a lecturer at St Augustine's College, Canterbury, 1911-14; and then, for 20 years, as a missionary in India, at

Dapoli, Ahmadnegar, Kolhar and Poona. After returning to England he was successively curate of Milton, 1936-37; vicar of Beckley, 1937-38; curate of Hanworth, 1939-42; chaplain of Bryanston School, 1942-48; and chaplain of the Lee Abbey Community, Devon, 1948-62. He wrote many poems and hymns, and published several books, including *The Church in Action*, 1936; *The Lee Abbey Story*, 1956; *When I Awake*, 1957; and *A Testament of Thanksgiving*, 1974.

Song: Lord of creation, to you be all praise (506)

WITTENMYER, Sarah Ann (*née* TURNER)

b Sandy Springs, Ohio, 26 August 1827
d Sanatoga, Pennsylvania, 2 February 1900

The daughter of John G. Turner, she was named Sarah Ann, but was usually known as Annie. In 1847 she married William Wittenmyer and three years later moved to Keokuk, Iowa, where she helped establish a methodist church and founded a free school for children and, later, a Sunday-school. During the Civil War, she was secretary of the Soldiers' Aid Society in Keokuk, and organised relief work, recruiting nurses and appealing for medical supplies. In about 1871 she moved to Philadelphia, where for 11 years she published the *Christian Woman* magazine. She was the first president of the National Woman's Christian Temperance Union, 1874-79, and was president of the Woman's Relief Corps, 1889-90. She wrote a number of hymns and several books, including *Women's Work for Jesus*, 1871; a *History of the Woman's Temperance Crusade*, 1878; and *Under the Guns*, 1895.

Song: All glory to Jesus be given (535)

WOLCOTT, Samuel

b South Windsor, Connecticut, 2 July 1813
d Longmeadow, Massachusetts, 24 February 1886

Educated at Yale College and Andover Theological Seminary. He was a missionary in Syria, 1840-42, and after returning to America, served as a congregational pastor in Belchestown,

Massachusetts; Providence, Rhode Island; Chicago, Illinois; and Cleveland, Ohio. For some time, he was secretary of the Ohio Home Missionary Society. He wrote more than 200 hymns.

Song: Christ for the world, we sing (825)

WOODWARD, George Ratcliffe

b Birkenhead, Cheshire, 27 December 1848
d Highgate, London, 3 March 1934

Educated at Harrow, and at Gonville and Caius College, Cambridge. He was ordained in 1874 and was curate of St Barnabas, Pimlico, 1874-82 and again, 1894-99, having been vicar of Little Walsingham, Norfolk, 1882-88, and rector of Chelmondiston, Suffolk, 1888-94. He was curate of St Mark's Marylebone, 1903-06, and then retired, moving first to Bloomsbury and in 1916 to Highgate, where he assisted at St Augustine's Church. He produced a new edition of the 1582 hymn and song collection *Piae Cantiones* in 1910, and, with Charles Wood, compiled several editions of *The Cowley Carol Book,* 1901-19, and *Songs of Syon,* 1904-10.

Song: This joyful Eastertide (153)

WORDSWORTH, Christopher

b Lambeth, Surrey, 30 October 1807
d Harewood, Yorkshire, 21 March 1885

Son of the Reverend Christopher Wordsworth, rector of Lambeth, and nephew of the poet William Wordsworth. He was educated at Winchester School and Trinity College, Cambridge. After his ordination, he was headmaster of Harrow School, 1836-44, and was appointed canon of Westminster in 1844. Subsequently he was vicar of Stanford-in-the-Vale, cum Goosey, Berkshire, 1850-69, and then Bishop of Lincoln, 1869-84. He published sermons, pamphlets, letters and other books, including *A Commentary on the whole Bible,* 1856-70. He wrote almost 130 hymns which were included in *The Holy*

Year, or Hymns for Sundays and Holy Days and Other Occasions, 1862 (2nd edition, 1863), which he compiled.

Song: O Lord of Heaven and earth and sea (15)

WOULDS, William Henry

b Ruskington, Lincolnshire, 23 February 1874
d Southend-on-Sea, Essex, 5 September 1940

Son of Daniel Woulds, a wheelwright. He was first attracted to The Salvation Army by a village open-air meeting in 1890, and later, when he came to London, followed a march to Holloway I Corps, where he was converted. He entered the Woolwich Garrison in 1892 and after five months' training served for 42 years as a corps officer in Scotland, Ireland and England. He was last stationed at the Hadleigh Farm Colony Corps, and retired as a major, in 1934.

Song: Lord, here today my great need I am feeling (610)

WREN, Brian Arthur

b Romford, Essex, 3 June 1936

Educated at Royal Liberty Grammar School, Romford, and at New College and Mansfield College, Oxford. He was minister of Hockley and Hawkwell Congregational Church, Essex, 1965-70, and then consultant for adult education, Churches' Committee on World Development, 1970-75, and staff member of Third World First, 1976-83. Since 1983 he has been a freelance writer, speaker and educator on world development, worship and peace, and also editor of Oxfam's youth magazine *Bother*. His publications have included *Education for Justice*, 1977 (2nd edition, 1986), as well as study packs and other adult education materials. He contributed to *Contemporary Prayers for Public Worship*, 1967, and was a member of the committee that compiled *New Church Praise*, 1975, for the United Reformed Church. His hymns have been published in *Mainly Hymns*, 1980; *Faith looking Forward*, 1983; and *Praising a Mystery*, 1986.

Songs: Christ is alive! Let Christians sing (142)
Life is great! So sing about it (544)

YOUNG, Andrew

b Edinburgh, 23 April 1807
d Edinburgh, 30 November 1889

Educated at the University of Edinburgh. He was appointed headmaster of Niddry Street School, Edinburgh, in 1830, and then became head English master at Madras College, St Andrews, in 1840. He retired from St Andrews in 1853 and returned to Edinburgh, where he was for some time superintendent of Greenside Parish Sabbath School. He contributed hymns and poems to various periodicals and published a collected edition of his poetry, *The Scottish Highlands and other Poems*, 1876.

Song: There is a happy land (897)

ZINZENDORF, Nicolaus Ludwig, Count von

b Dresden, Germany, 26 May 1700
d Herrnhut, Saxony, 9 May 1760

He was educated at the Adelspädagogium at Halle, and at the University of Wittenberg, where he studied law. After travelling in Holland and France, he was chief councillor to the Elector of Saxony at Dresden, 1721-27. In 1722, he allowed a group of Moravian refugees to settle on his estate at Berthelsdorf, in a community called 'Herrnhut' ('the protection of the Lord'), and in 1727 he returned from Dresden to live at Berthelsdorf and later became bishop of the Moravian community in 1737. Subsequently, during a period of exile from Saxony, he founded a Moravian settlement at Herrnhaag, in Wetteravia, and established Moravian communities in England, Holland, North America and the West Indies. He spent his later years at Herrnhut, 1756-60. He wrote over 2,000 hymns and compiled several hymn books, including *Sammlung geistlicher und lieblicher Lieder*, 1725 (with supplements and appendices, 1728-31).

Songs: I thirst, thou wounded Lamb of God (424, verses 1 and 2)
Jesus, thy blood and righteousness (116)
O thou to whose all-searching sight (453)

PART THREE

Notes on songs and authors
North American supplement

compiled by
Lt. Colonel Houston Ellis (R)

963 Faith of our fathers!

FABER, Frederick William (see page 298)

This popular hymn is widely used by protestant churches. The last stanza is especially fine and Christian in spirit.

In the preface to the 1849 edition of his *Hymns* Dr. Faber wrote: It seemed in every way desirable that Catholics should have a hymn book for *reading*, which should contain the mysteries of the faith in easy verse or different states of heart and conscience depicted with unadorned simplicity. He succeeded in large measure in his undertaking to give Roman Catholics good modern hymns, but he wrote many, such as *Faith of our fathers*, which have a wide circulation among all protestant churches.

964 O God, beneath thy guiding hand

BACON, Leonard

b Detroit, Michigan, 19 Feb., 1802
d New Haven, Connecticut, 23, Dec., 1881

Leonard Bacon's father, a congregational missionary, had settled in Detroit, where he hoped to convert the Indians. After attending Yale, Leonard went to Andover Theological Seminary. His *Hymns and Sacred Songs for the Monthly Concert* (Andover, Mass. 1823), the first American collection of missionary hymns, appeared while he was a student there. *"O God, beneath thy guiding hand"* was written in 1833 while he was a professor at the Yale School of Divinity for the bicentennial of the founding of New Haven.

965 The Star-spangled Banner

KEY, Frances Scott

b 1779
d 1843

"The Star-spangled Banner" by Act of Congress, March 3, 1931, became the national anthem of the United States of America. This great song was born in the mind of Frances Scott Key during the bombardment of Fort McHenry in Baltimore. Key wrote the famous words on September 15, 1814, that were later to become this

National Anthem on March 3, 1931, after witnessing an all-day and all-night gunfire on the fort by the British.

He conceived his poem during this vigil, noting his impressions and emotions on the back of an envelope, completing the work immediately on arriving at his hotel in Baltimore after being released from being held on the British ship.

Frances Scott Key was born in Frederick County (now Carroll), Maryland, at the Key homestead *"Terra Rubra"*. The original home is no longer standing, but has since been restored with another on the same site. He began his career as a lawyer in Frederick County, and is buried in Frederick's beautiful Mt. Olivet Cemetery, where the Key monument honors his grave.

966 God of our fathers

ROBERTS, Daniel C.

b Bridge Hampton, L.I., New York, 5 Nov., 1841
d Concord, N.H., 31 Oct., 1907

Roberts' hymn, *"God of our fathers"* (National Hymn), was written in 1876 for a "Centennial" Fourth of July Celebration of the United States at Brandon, Vermont. In 1892 it was included in the Protestant Episcopal Hymnal, and later this patriotic hymn was included in many other American hymnals.

Dr. Roberts graduated from Gambier College in 1857. After serving as a private for a time in the Civil War, he later was ordained as a minister in the Protestant Episcopal Church.

967 O beautiful for spacious skies

BATES, Katherine Lee

b 1859
d 1929

This great patriotic song of the United States was written in 1893 by Miss Bates, Professor of English at Wellesley College, to the hymn tune *Materna*. Some time before writing it she had made a trip to Colorado, and from the summit of Pike's Peak had envisioned the spacious skies above the fruited plains.

Commenting on this hymn Miss Bates said, "All through the years requests have come to use the song in one way or another. . . . I am only too glad to give it free as my own slight gift to my country."

Orbiting the earth in the summer of 1960, Echo I, the United States communications balloon satellite, served as the dramatic relay for this, the first song, indeed the first music, ever to be projected to and returned from outer space.

968 My country 'tis of thee

SMITH, Samuel F.

b Newton Centre, Mass., 21 Oct., 1808
d Newton Centre, Mass., 16 Nov., 1895

Samuel F. Smith, while a Boston minister, wrote this song for a service at the Park Street Church on July 4, 1831. Until *"The Star-Spangled Banner"* was selected in 1931 this song was a prime candidate for the national anthem of the United States, with many Americans still standing when singing it.

In selecting the tune, Smith was unaware that it was also the tune of the British national anthem. However, when he first heard the tune, Smith later recalled, "I instantly felt the impulse to write a patriotic song of my own adapted to the tune. Picking up a scrap of waste paper which lay near me, I wrote at once, probably within half an hour, the hymn as it is now sung everywhere."

969 I love to tell the story

HANKEY, Katherine (see page 314)

b Claphan, Surrey, England, 1834
d Westminster, England, 9 May, 1911

This song was part of a long poem about the life of Jesus, by Miss Katherine Hankey, a successful writer on religious subjects and a member of the Clapham sect, an evangelistic order. The tune by William Fischer was a favorite in the Moody and Sankey revival meetings.

"Tell Me the Old, Old Story" is also a part of this extended poem.

970 We gather together
Netherlands Folk Hymn (trs. BAKER, Theodore)

Unknown Dutch Patriot, 16th. century - 1626

BAKER, Theodore

b 1851
d 1934

This hymn celebrated the freedom of the Netherlands from Spanish domination. The English translation by Theodore Baker was originally printed in 1917.

Archibald T. Davison wrote that "If frequency of request, and spirit in performance, are criteria, the most popular of all was . . . the Netherlands folk hymn, the *'Prayer of Thanksgiving.'*"

971 I come to the garden alone

MILES, C. Austin (see song 974)

b Lakehurst, N.J., 1868
d Philadelphia, Pa., 10 Mar., 1946

The author stated he was working in his photographic dark-room when the Bible fell open at John 20, the portion containing the account of Mary's meeting with Jesus. His senses prepared by the dim light, he saw the entire scene before him, as in a vision. He writes: "Under the inspiration of this vision I wrote as quickly as the words could be formed the poem exactly as it has since appeared. That same evening I also wrote the music."

C. Austin Miles also wrote nearly 3,000 other hymns including *"Dwelling in Beulah Land,"* "Win them one by one," and *"If Jesus goes with me."*

972 The way of the Cross leads home

POUNDS, Jessie Brown

b Hiram, Ohio, 31 Aug., 1861
d 1921

At the age of fifteen, she began to write regularly for religious publications. Among her published works are more than four hundred gospel song texts. Mrs. Pounds also wrote *"Any where with Jesus," "The Touch of His Hand on Mine," "Beautiful Isle of Somewhere,"* and *"I know that my Redeemer liveth."*

973 Near to the heart of God

McAFEE, Cleland Boyd

b Ashley, Mo., 25 Sept., 1866
d Jeffrey, N.H., 4 Feb., 1944

A graduate of Park College, Parkville, Mo., he also studied at Union Theological Seminary. After presbyterian pastoral work McAfee served as professor of systematic theology at McCormick Theological Seminary in Chicago.

974 Dwelling in Beulah Land

MILES, C. Austin (see song 971)

At thirty, C. Austin Miles became editor and manager of a music publishing firm in Philadelphia, later with the Rodeheaver Company in Winona Lake, Indiana. He also served as a music director in churches, camp meetings, and conventions. He wrote, among his many songs, *"In the Garden."*

975 Spirit of God, descend

CROLY, George

b Dublin, Ireland, 17 Aug., 1780
d Holborn, England, 24 Nov., 1860

In 1804 Croly took the degree of Master of Arts at Dublin University; in 1831 the degree of LLd. After receiving holy orders he labored in Ireland until 1810; then moving to London where he devoted himself largely to literature. Dr. Croly's hymns were published in his *Psalms and Hymns for Public Worship*, 1854. The scriptural subject of this hymn is from the text, *"If we live in the Spirit, let us also walk in the Spirit."*

976 How firm a foundation

"K" in Rippon's Selections, 1787

In 1886 Rev. H. L. Hastings, of Boston, while in London looked up the *Tune Book* used in Rippon's *Selections* and found that this hymn was commonly sung to the tune *"Geard,"* which was composed by R. Keene, at one time a leader in the singing in Dr. Rippon's church.

It had long been a custom for composers who write both words and music to put their names to the music only or to put the name to the music and their initials, sometimes reversed or otherwise disguised, to the words.

Mr. Hastings comes to the conclusion: "In view of all the facts, we think we may consider the question settled and definitely assign the authorship of this hymn to R. Keene, a precenter in Dr. Rippon's church and the author of the tune 'Geard,' to which it was sung.

The last line of the hymn is based upon Hebrews 13:5, "*I will never leave thee, nor forsake thee*," which in the Greek is much more emphatic. A footnote to the last line of the hymn in *Rippon's Selections* refers to Dr. Doddridge's translation of this verse: "*I will not, I will not leave thee. I will never, never, never forsake thee.*" Other scripture connected with this famous and confident hymn is 2 Peter 1:4 "*Exceeding great and precious promises.*"

977 Lead on, O King eternal

SHURTLEFF, Ernest W.

b Boston, Mass., 4 Apr., 1862
d Paris, France, 29 Aug., 1917

This hymn on the Christian warfare was written by the author in 1887 as a parting hymn for his class and fellow-students at Andover Theological Seminary, from which he graduated in 1887. It was published that same year in the author's *Hymns of the Faith*. This, like some of our other fine hymns such as "*My country, 'tis of thee*" and "*My faith looks up to thee*", is a tribute to the writing of theological students, while still young.

This lyric has the poetic flow and fervor of a true hymn with the second verse being considered especially fine.

Shurtleff served as a pastor in Buenaventura, California; Plymouth, Massachusetts; Minneapolis, Minnesota; also organized the American Church in Frankfurt-am-Main, Germany.

978 Take up thy cross

ACKLEY, Alfred Henry (see page 233)

Alfred Henry Ackley was educated at Pennsylvania State University, Union Theological Seminary, and at the Royal Academy of Music in London. Ordained a presbyterian minister, he served in the District of Columbia, Pittsburgh, and Escondido, Calif.

Among others, his sacred songs include: *Only Shadows*, *He*

Lives, I never Walk Alone, It is Morning in My Heart, God's Tomorrow, When God is Near, In the Service of the King, and *Somebody Knows.* The song, *"Take up thy Cross"*, has been used by God over the years in bringing many to Christ and many into full-time service.

979 Are ye able?

MARLATT, Earl

b Columbus, Indiana, 24 May, 1892
d Winchester, Indiana, 13 June, 1976

Earl B. Marlatt, Methodist educator and administrator, received degrees from DePauw University, Boston University, the University of Berlin and Oxford University. After a period as associate editor of the *Kenosha* (Wis.) *News*, he entered the U.S. Army, serving during World War I as a lieutenant in the field artillery.

After serving as dean of the School of Theology at Boston University, he later became professor of religion, Perkins School of Theology at Southern Methodist University, Dallas, Texas.

Among other hymns written by Dr. Marlatt are: *"Spirit of Life, in This New Dawn"*, and *"Through the Dark the Dreamers Came."*

980 Truehearted, wholehearted

HAVERGAL, Frances Ridley (see page 316)

This inspiring hymn on faithfulness to the Savior was first published in the author's *Loyal Responses*, 1878. This poetic call to courage and to fidelity to Christ which abides in the head and heart of those who sing the words quickly became one of her most popular and effective hymns.

Few poets have consecrated their gifts of head and heart and pen more fully to Christ than she did, and few lives ending at forty three years have left behind more pleasing and precious literary treasures than are found in her poems of Christian faith and love and service.

981 We've a story to tell to the nations

NICHOL, H. Ernest

b Hull, England, 10 Dec., 1862
d Hull, 1928

This song, composed in 1896 to promote world missions, appeared in the *Sunday School Hymnary* in 1905. Most of Nichol's songs appeared under the anagram of Colin Sterne, after he took the degree of MUS. BAC. at Oxford in 1888.

He abandoned his intended career as a civil engineer to study music, writing a large number of tunes, mainly for Sunday school anniversary services.

982 Rejoice, ye pure in heart

PLUMPTRE, Edward H. (Pronounced Plum-tee)

b London, England, 6 Aug., 1821
d 1 Feb., 1891

This *Processional at Choral Festival*, based on Psalm 20:4 and Philippians 4:4, was written in May 1865 for the Peterborough Choral Festival of that year, and was used extensively in Peterborough Cathedral. It is now more widely used than any other of the author's hymns. The rhythm of his verses has a special attraction for musicians, its poetry for the cultured, and its stately simplicity for the earnest-minded follower of Christ. All of his hymns are considered elegant in style, fervent in spirit, and broad in treatment.

Edward H. Plumptre was educated at King's College, London, and University College, Oxford, graduating as a double first in 1811. After taking Holy Orders in 1846 he rapidly advanced as a theologian and preacher, serving in many important academic and Anglican Church posts.

983 Great is thy faithfulness (see page 53)

CHISHOLM, Thomas O. (see page 274)

984 In my heart there rings a melody (see page 69)

ROTH, Elton M. (see page 402)

985 Lead me to Calvary (see page 100, King of my life)

HUSSEY, Jennie Evelyn (see page 334)

986 Christ is alive! (see page 22)

WREN, Brian (see page 452)

987 Life is great! (see page 103)

WREN, Brian (see page 452)

988 O for a thousand tongues (see page 128)

WESLEY, Charles (see page 440)

989 Beneath the cross of Jesus (see page 16)

CLEPHANE, Elizabeth C. (see page 276)

990 Victory in Jesus

BARTLETT, Eugene M.

b Waynesville, Mo., 1885
d 1941

E. N. Bartlett, gospel singer, composer, teacher, editor and publisher, left us *"Victory in Jesus," "Just a Little While,"* and *"Everybody Will Be Happy Over There."* For a number of years, Bartlett conducted singing schools throughout the South.

"Victory in Jesus" was written in 1939, two years before his death. Bartlett speaks of the joy of salvation in personal testimony: *"then I repented of my sins and won the victory."* The song has become very popular in evangelical churches.

991 Tis' so sweet to trust in Jesus

STEAD, Louisa M. R.

b Dover, England, 1850
d Penkridge, Southern Rhodesia, 18 Jan., 1907

Born of Christian parents, Louisa was converted at the age of nine and called as a missionary as a teen-ager, working in the Cape Colony of South Africa.

She wrote: In connection with this mission there are glorious possibilities. One cannot in the face of peculiar difficulties help saying, "Who is sufficient for these things?" but with simple confidence and trust we may and do say, "One sufficiency is of God."

992 The Saviour is waiting

CARMICHAEL, Ralph

b 1927

Ralph Carmichael's compositions, produced in the late twentieth century, include the use of folk musicals in Christian communications "to guide youth in discovering a meaningful life in Christ." His more than two hundred songs, with his recordings, and film scores add up to an incredible musical output from this ingenious and creative Christian.

Soon after *"The Saviour is waiting"* was written, Carmichael went with Dr. Bob Pierce to Japan for some evangelistic crusades at which this song was extensively and effectively used for Christ. The popularity of the hymn spread like wildfire, taking its place as a well-known invitation hymn around the world.

993 How great thou art (see page 135)

HINE, Stuart K. (see page 325)

994 O Canada

LAVALLEE, Calixa (music), 1842–1891
WEIR, Robert Stanley (English), 1858–1926
ROUTHIER, Adolphe-Basile (French), 1839–1920

"O Canada!" was approved as the country's national anthem by the Canadian Parliament in 1967 and officially adopted on June 27, 1980. The music was written by composer Calixa Lavallee in 1880 and the words, in the French language, by Judge Adolphe-Basile Routhier, in May of the same year. The song was not heard in English Canada until 20 years later. It was sung in Toronto in 1901 for a

visit by the future King George V, but the literal translation was not well received. The English translation was written in 1908 by Robert Stanley Weir, a Montreal lawyer, with the words being somewhat altered in 1967, Canada's centenary.

Bibliography

Ah Kow, Adelaide, *Arthur S. Arnott*, SP & S, Ltd: London, 1944.
Antliff, William, *The Life of the Venerable Hugh Bourne*, George Lamb: London, 1872.
Andrews, J. S., *A Study of German Hymns in Current English Hymnals*, Peter Lang Ltd: Berne, 1981.
Avery, Gordon, *Companion to the Song Book of The Salvation Army*, SP & S, Ltd: London, 1961.
Bacon, Ernest W., *Pilgrim and Dreamer: John Bunyan—His Life and Work*, Paternoster Press: Exeter, 1983.
Bainton, Roland, *Here I Stand: Martin Luther*, Lion Publishing: Tring, 1987.
Baird, Catherine, *Reflections*, SP & S, Ltd: London, 1975.
Baker, Frank, *Charles Wesley's Verse: An Introduction*, Epworth Press: London, Second edition, 1988.
Baker, Frank (editor), *Representative Verse of Charles Wesley*, Epworth Press: London, 1962.
Barkley, John M. (editor), *Handbook to the Church Hymnary, Third Edition*, Oxford University Press: London, 1979.
Barrows, Cliff (editor), *Crusader Hymns and Hymn Stories*, Hope Publishing Company: Chicago, 1967.
Bishop, Selma L., *Isaac Watts: Hymns and Spiritual Songs, 1707-1748*, Faith Press: London, 1962.
Booth, Catherine Bramwell, *Bramwell Booth*, Rich and Cowan: London, 1933.
Booth-Tucker, Frederick, *The Consul: A Memoir of Emma Moss Booth-Tucker*, SP & S, Ltd: London, 1927.
Braley, Bernard, *Hymnwriters 1*, Stainer and Bell: London, 1987. (Chapters on Thomas Ken, William Cowper, Reginald Heber, William Walsham How and John Ellerton.)
Brand, Will J., *With Sword and Song*, SP & S, Ltd: London, 1975.
Brown, Arnold, *The Gate and the Light*, Bookwright Publications: Toronto, 1984.
Brown, John (revised Harrison, Frank M.), *John Bunyan (1628-1688): His Life, Times and Work*, Hulbert Publishing Co: London, 1928.

Brown, Theron and Butterworth, Hezekiah, *The Story of the Hymns and Tunes*, American Tract Society: New York, 1906.
Carpenter, Minnie L., *Commissioner John Lawley*, SP & S, Ltd: London, 1924.
Claghorn, Gene, *Women Composers and Hymnists: A Concise Biographical Dictionary*, Scarecrow Press: Metuchen, New Jersey, 1984.
Clissold, Stephen, *St Teresa of Avila*, Sheldon Press: London, 1979.
Colquhoun, Frank, *A Hymn Companion*, Hodder and Stoughton: London, 1985.
Collier, Richard, *The General Next to God*, Collins: London, 1965. (The Life and Influence of William Booth.)
Coslet, Dorothy G., *Madame Jeanne Guyon: Child of Another World*, Christian Literature Crusade: Fort Washington, Pennsylvania, 1984.
Coyne, J. J., *Cardinal Newman*, Catholic Truth Society: Birmingham, 1957.
Cutts, Peter, *New Church Praise Commentary*, Church Life Department, United Reformed Church: London, 1981.
Dallimore, Arnold, *A Heart Set Free: The Life of Charles Wesley*, Evangelical Press: Welwyn, 1988.
Dearmer, Percy, *Songs of Praise Discussed*, Oxford University Press: London, 1933.
Edwards, Brian H., *Through many dangers*, Eurobooks: Welwyn, 1980. (Biography of John Newton.)
Ellinwood, Leonard (editor), *The Hymnal 1940 Companion*, The Church Pension Fund: New York, Third revised edition, 1956.
Escott, Harry, *Isaac Watts: Hymnographer*, Independent Press: London, 1962.
Fossey, Leslie, *This Man Leidzén*, SP & S, Ltd: London, 1966.
Fountain, David G., *Isaac Watts Remembered*, Henry E. Walter: Worthing, 1974.
Frost, Maurice, *Historical Companion to Hymns Ancient and Modern*, William Clowes Ltd: London, 1961.
Furlong, Monica, *Puritan's Progress*, Hodder and Stoughton: London, 1975. (Study of the life of John Bunyan.)
Garland, Henry J., *The Life and Hymns of Dr Philip Doddridge*, Stirling Tract Enterprise, 1951.
Gealy, Fred D., Lovelace, Austin C. and Young, Carlton R., *Companion to the Hymnal*, Abingdon Press: Nashville and New York, 1970.
Gill, Frederick C., *Charles Wesley: The First Methodist*, Lutterworth Press: London, 1964.

Green, Julien (translated by Heinegg, Peter), *God's Fool: The Life and Times of Francis of Assisi*, Hodder and Stoughton: London, 1986.

Green, V. H. H., *John Wesley*, Thomas Nelson & Sons Ltd: London, 1964.

Grierson, Janet, *Frances Ridley Havergal: Worcestershire Hymnwriter*, Havergal Society, 1979.

Gunn, Judith, *Bunyan of Elstow*, Hodder and Stoughton: London, 1985.

Hall, Jacob H., *Biography of Gospel Song and Hymn Writers*, Fleming H. Revell: New York, 1914, reprinted 1971.

Hart, Joseph, *Hart's Hymns: Including the Supplement and Appendix, and the Author's Experience*, W. H. & L. Collingridge: London, 1882.

Hayden, Andrew J. and Newton, Robert F., *British Hymn Writers and Composers: a Checklist*, Hymn Society of Great Britain and Ireland, 1977, amended 1979.

Hildebrandt, Franz and Beckerlegge, Oliver A. (editors), *The Works of John Wesley, Volume 7: A Collection of Hymns for the Use of the People called Methodists*, Oxford University Press: London, 1983.

Hine, Stuart K., *Not you, but God*, The author: Burnham-on-Sea, Somerset, 1982.

Hine, Stuart K., *The Story of How Great Thou Art*, The author: Burnham-on-Sea, Somerset, 1958, enlarged edition, 1983.

Houghton, Elsie, *Christian Hymn-Writers*, Evangelical Press of Wales: Bridgend, 1982.

Hughes, Derrick, *Bishop Sahib: A Life of Reginald Heber*, Churchman Publishing Ltd: Worthing, 1986.

Hughes, Glyn Tegai, *William Pantycelyn*, University of Wales Press: Cardiff, 1983. (Life and work of William Williams.)

Hustad, Donald P., *Dictionary-Handbook to Hymns of the Living Church*, Hope Publishing Company: Carol Stream, Illinois, 1978.

Hustad, Donald P. (editor), *Fanny Crosby Speaks Again*, Hope Publishing Company: Carol Stream, Illinois, 1977.

Ingram, Tom and Newton, Douglas, *Hymns as Poetry*, Constable: London, 1956.

Julian, John (editor), *A Dictionary of Hymnology*, John Murray: London, Second edition, with a new supplement, 1907.

Kelynack, William S., *Companion to the School Hymn Book of the Methodist Church*, Epworth Press: London, 1950.

Kerr, Phil, *Music in Evangelism and Stories of Famous Christian Songs*, Gospel Music Publishers: Glendale,

California, Third edition. 1950.

Lawson, John, *A Thousand Tongues: The Wesley Hymns as a guide to Scriptural Teaching*, Paternoster Press: Exeter, 1987.

Lawton, George, *Within the Rock of Ages*, James Clarke & Co: Cambridge, 1983. (Study of the life of Augustus Toplady.)

McCutchan, Robert G., *Our Hymnody*, Abingdon-Cokesbury Press: New York and Nashville, Second edition, 1942.

Martin, Brian, *John Henry Newman: His Life and Work*, Chatto & Windus: London, 1982.

Martin, Hugh and Thomson, R. W., *The Baptist Hymn Book Companion*, Psalms and Hymns Trust: London, 1962, revised edition, 1967.

Milgate, Wesley, *Songs of the People of God*, Collins Liturgical Publications: London, 1982.

Mockler, Anthony, *Francis of Assisi: The wandering years*, Phaidon: Oxford, 1976.

Moffatt, James and Patrick, Millar, *Handbook to the Church Hymnary: Revised edition, with supplement*, Oxford University Press: London, 1927, supplement 1935.

Nuelsen, John L. (translated by Parry, T., Moore, Sydney H., and Holbrook, A.), *John Wesley and the German Hymn*, A. S. Holbrook: Calverley, Yorkshire, 1972.

Orsborn, Albert, *The Beauty of Jesus*, SP & S, Ltd: London, 1947.

Orsborn, Albert, *The House of My Pilgrimage*, SP & S, Ltd: London, 1958.

Osborn, G., *The Poetical Works of John and Charles Wesley*, 13 volumes, Wesleyan-Methodist Conference Office: London, 1868-72.

Parry, K. L. (editor), *Companion to Congregational Praise*, Independent Press Ltd: London, 1953.

Pollock, John, *Amazing Grace: John Newton's Story*, Hodder and Stoughton: London, 1981.

Raeper, William, *George MacDonald*, Lion Publishing: Tring, 1987.

Reynolds, William J., *Companion to Baptist Hymnal*, Broadman Press: Nashville, Tennessee, 1976.

Reynolds, William J., *Hymns of our Faith: A Handbook for the Baptist Hymnal*, Broadman Press: Nashville, Tennessee, 1964.

Rodeheaver, Homer A., *Hymnal Handbook for Standard Hymns and Gospel Songs*, AMS Press Inc: New York, 1975, reprinted from 1931 edition.

Routley, Erik, *An English-Speaking Hymnal Guide*, Liturgical Press: Minnesota, 1979.

Ruffin, Bernard, *Fanny Crosby*, Barbour and Company, Inc: Westwood, New Jersey, 1976.

Ryland, John, *Hymns and Verses on Sacred Subjects, by the late Rev John Ryland, with a biographical sketch*, Daniel Sedgwick: London, 1862.

Sabatier, Paul (translated by Houghton, L. S.), *Life of St Francis of Assisi*, Hodder and Stoughton: London, 1894.

Sale, D. M., *The Hymn Writers of Hampshire*, Winton Publications Ltd: Winchester, 1975.

Sankey, Ira D., *My Life and Sacred Songs*, Hodder and Stoughton, and Morgan and Scott: London, 1906.

Scott, Carolyn, *The Heavenly Witch: The Story of the Maréchale*, Hamish Hamilton: London, 1981. (Biography of Catherine Booth-Clibborn.)

Slater, Richard, *Salvation Army Song Writers: Biographical and Historical Notes of Seventy Writers and on over 500 of their Songs*, SP & S, Ltd: London, 1929.

Slater, Richard, *The Salvation Army Dictionary of Music*, The Salvation Army Book Department: London, 1908.

Smith, H. Augustine, *Lyric Religion: The Romance of Immortal Hymns*, Fleming H. Revell Company: New York, 1931.

Taylor, Cyril V., *Hymns for Today Discussed*, The Canterbury Press, Norwich and the Royal School of Church Music, 1984.

Taylor, Gordon, *A Short Companion to 'Keep Singing!'*, The author: Croydon, Surrey, 1976.

Telford, John, *The Methodist Hymn-Book Illustrated in History and Experience*, Epworth Press: London, Seventh edition, 1959.

Thompson, Phyllis, *Madame Guyon: Martyr of the Holy Spirit*, Hodder and Stoughton: London, 1986.

Triggs, Kathy, *George MacDonald: The Seeking Heart*, Pickering and Inglis: Basingstoke, 1984.

Triggs, Kathy, *The Stars and the Stillness: A portrait of George MacDonald*, Lutterworth: Cambridge, 1986.

Tyler-Whittle, Michael, *Solid Joys and Lasting Treasure*, Ross Anderson Publications: Bolton, 1985.

Unsworth, Madge, *Mildred Duff*, SP & S, Ltd: London, 1956

Upham, Thomas C., *Life, Religious Opinions and Experience of Madame De La Mothe Guyon*, Sampson Low, Son & Co: London, 1854.

Watson, Bernard, *Soldier Saint*, Hodder and Stoughton: London, 1970. (Biography of George Scott Railton.)

Whittle, Major and Guest, William, *P. P. Bliss: His Life and Life-Work*, Morgan and Scott: London, nd.

Wiggins, Arch R., *Father of Salvation Army Music: Richard Slater*, SP & S, Ltd: London, 1945.

Wiggins, Arch R. 'The Songs of the Salvationist' in *The Bandsman and Songster*, January 1935-December 1937 and *The Musician*, January-July 1938.

Wiggins, Arch R., *THK—Theodore Hopkins Kitching: A Biography*, SP & S, Ltd: London, 1956.

Williams, Harry, *Booth-Tucker: William Booth's First Gentleman*, Hodder and Stoughton: London, 1980.

Wilson, John, *A Short Companion to 'Hymns and Songs'*, Methodist Church Music Society, 1969.

Also Available Through Your Trade From the Same Publisher:

1989 American Brass Ensemble Series

James E. Curnow, Editor

GRADE I (Very Easy)
FAIREST LORD JESUS, *James Curnow*
JESUS LOVES THE LITTLE CHILDREN, *Stephen Bulla*
JESUS LOVES ME, *Paul Curnow*
JUST A CLOSER WALK (Solo for Bb T.C., B.C. or C Instrument), *William Broughton*

GRADE II (Easy)
WHAT A FRIEND, *William Broughton*
RESCUE THE PERISHING, *Stephen Bulla*
ANGELS WATCHING OVER ME (Solo for Eb or F Instrument), *Paul Curnow*
ALLELUIA, *James Curnow*

GRADE III (Intermediate)
MAY JESUS CHRIST BE PRAISED, *James Curnow*
ONWARD, CHRISTIAN SOLDIERS, *Ray Steadman-Allen*
THE JOYFUL SOUND (We Have Heard the Joyful Sound) (Solo for Bb T.C., B.C. or C Instrument), *Stephen Bulla*
BREATHE ON ME, BREATH OF GOD, *William Himes*

GRADE IV (Intermediate/Advanced)
GO, TELL IT ON THE MOUNTAIN, *Barrie Gott*
SPIRITUAL MEDLEY (Sing-A-Long Medley), *William Himes*
GLORY TO HIS NAME (Solo for Eb or F Instrument), *James Curnow*
MY FAITH LOOKS UP TO THEE, *Stephen Bulla*

1989 American Brass Solo Series

GRADE I   JUST A CLOSER WALK (Solo for Bb T.C., B.C., or C Instrument), *William Broughton*
GRADE II ANGELS WATCHING OVER ME (Solo for Eb or F Instrument), *Paul Curnow*
GRADE III THE JOYFUL SOUND (Solo for Bb, T.C., B.C., or C Instrument), *Stephen Bulla*
GRADE IV GLORY TO HIS NAME (Solo for Eb or F Instrument), *James Curnow*

1990 American Brass Ensemble Series

James E. Curnow, Editor

GRADE I (Very Easy)
FAITH OF OUR FATHERS, *Stephen Bulla*
WERE YOU THERE? (When They Crucified My Lord), *Paul Curnow*
TAKE TIME TO BE HOLY (Solo for Eb or F Instrument) *William Broughton*
AND CAN IT BE. (Sagina), *James Curnow*

GRADE II (Easy)
IN CHRIST THERE IS NO EAST OR WEST (St. Peter), *James Curnow*
HOLY, HOLY, HOLY (Nicaea), *Stephen Bulla*
JACOB'S LADDER (Solo for Bb T.C., B.C., or C Instrument) *Ray Steadman-Allen*
ALL HAIL THE POWER OF JESUS' NAME (Coronation), *William Himes*

GRADE III (Intermediate)
STAND UP AND SHOUT IT , *William Broughton*
ANGELS WE HAVE HEARD ON HIGH, *Paul Curnow*
LORD, I WANT TO A CHRISTIAN (Solo for Eb or F Instrument) *James Curnow*
WAY BEYOND THE BLUE (Do Lord), *Stephen Bulla*

GRADE IV (Intermediate/Advanced)
MORE ABOUT JESUS, *Ray Steadman-Allen*
SCRIPTURE SING ALONG, *William Himes*
LOVE LIFTED ME (Solo for Bb T.C., B.C., or C Instrument) *Stephen Bulla*
THIS LITTLE LIGHT OF MINE, *Barrie Gott*

1990 American Brass Solo Series with Piano Accompaniment

GRADE I   TAKE TIME TO BE HOLY (Solo for Eb or F Instrument), *William Broughton*
GRADE II JACOB'S LADDER (Solo for Bb T.C., B.C., or C Instrument), *Ray Steadman-Allen*
GRADE III LORD, I WANT TO BE A CHRISTIAN (Solo for Eb or F Instrument), *James Curnow*
GRADE IV LOVE LIFTED ME (Solo for Bb T.C. or C Instrument), *Stephen Bulla*

1991 American Brass Ensemble Series

James E. Curnow, Editor

GRADE I (Very Easy)
O GOD, OUR HELP IN AGES PAST, *Stephen Bulla*
SEARCH ME, O GOD (Solo for Bb T.C., B.C., or C Instrument), *James Curnow*
ARE YE ABLE?, *William Himes*
O MASTER, LET ME WALK WITH THEE (Maryton), *Paul Curnow*

GRADE II (Easy)
GOOD KING WENCESLAS, *James Curnow*
OPEN MY EYES (Solo for Eb or F Instrument), *William Broughton*
VARIATIONS ON "AZMON", *Stephen Bulla*
STAND UP, STAND UP FOR JESUS (Geibel), *Paul Curnow*

GRADE III (Intermediate)
CLEANSING FOUNTAIN (Covenant), *William Broughton*
BALM IN GILEAD (Solo for Bb T.C., B.C., or C Instrument), *William Himes*
BLESSED ASSURANCE, *Stephen Bulla*
COME THOU FOUNT OF EVERY BLESSING, *James Curnow*

GRADE IV (Intermediate/Advanced)
SING-ALONG, *William Himes*
FAITH IS THE VICTORY (Solo for Eb or F Instrument), *Stephen Bulla*
COME, THOU LONG EXPECTED JESUS (Hyfrydol), *Ray Steadman-Allen*
JUST AS I AM, *James Curnow*

1991 American Brass Solo Series

GRADE I   SEARCH ME, O GOD (Solo for Bb T.C., B.C., or C Instrument), *James Curnow*
GRADE II OPEN MY EYES (Solo for Eb or F Instrument), *William Broughton*
GRADE III BALM IN GILEAD (Solo for Bb T.C., B.C., or C Instrument), *William Himes*
GRADE IV FAITH IS THE VICTORY (Solo for Eb or F Instrument), *Stephen Bulla*

Pricing and Ordering Information

American Brass Ensemble Series

American Brass Solo Series

For further information, contact your Territorial Music Secretary or the publisher:

The Salvation Army
Music Department
1424 Northeast Expressway
Atlanta, Georgia 30329   (404) 728-1300